International Studies in Sociology and Social Anthropology

VOLUME 116

Adversarial Case-Making

An Ethnography of English Crown Court Procedure

By

Thomas Scheffer

BRILL

LEIDEN • BOSTON
2010

On the cover: Trial by jury. © fotolia

This book is printed on acid-free paper.

Detailed Library of Congress Cataloging-in-Publication Data:

Detailed Library of Congress Cataloging-in-Publication data are available on the Internet at http://catalog.loc.gov

Scheffer, Thomas.
Adversarial case-making : an ethnography of English Crown Court procedure / by Thomas Scheffer.
p. cm. -- (International studies in sociology and social anthropology)
Includes bibliographical references and index.
ISBN 978-90-04-18726-9 (hardback : alk. paper) 1. Great Britain. Crown Court--Sociological aspects. 2. Criminal courts--Social aspects--England. 3. Criminal procedure--Social aspects--England. I. Title. II. Series.

KD8286.S34 2010
347.42'05--dc22

2010021648

ISBN 978 9004 18726 9
ISSN 0074-8684

PRINTED BY DRUKKERIJ WILCO B.V. - AMERSFOORT, THE NETHERLANDS

CONTENTS

LIST OF FIGURES

FOREWORD

Is this monograph a case? A case of what: of academic writing, of an institutional ethnography, of a law-in-action study? No matter the many possible answers, the reader may consider this book as having its own history of (case-)making. The book's history is not a linear accumulation from start till ending. It involves many ideas, numerous pretests in talks and drafts, various social case-making investments, and a whole series of versions. A lot of ideas and work never made it into the book – and got lost on the way of making it. The same applies to interviews, observations, criminal cases, and my field experience: most of what I kept in my memory, notebooks, case folders, etc. remained in drawers and binders outside this book case. But who knows how all these mattered nonetheless?

The same applies to the organisational conditions of case making: research funding was granted by the *Deutschen Forschungsgemeinschaft* (DFG); basic equipment such as offices, computers, copy machines, etc. were provided by my hosting universities, the *Freie Universität Berlin* (FU Berlin) and, for the final production stages, the *Humboldt Universität zu Berlin* (HU Berlin). All this is easily taken for granted and its contribution too often neglected. Without the research aid (just like legal aid in criminal cases) this case of a book would not exist. All this material and organisational support is necessary but largely invisible part of the book, not unlike the firm or the chambers for the solicitors' and barristers' criminal case-work.

The case-making of this book involves various career stages and versions, not unlike legal statements in criminal procedure. My case-studies and conceptual deliberations had to pass various pre-tests and assessments such as my own efforts for improvement, ethnographers' feed back in colloquia, socio-legal discussions in local workshops, general acknowledgement on international conferences, valuable comments by 'next door' readers, often contradictory blind peer reviews, the editor's final commentary, or my own final corrections. Looking back, all these ideas, concepts, formulations, paragraphs, or chapters gathered in this book seem to have passed a long and winding career. Looking back, authoring something as a social scientist means to a large degree to expose it to these arrays of listeners, readers, reviewers, etc. – and fitting it into these relevant others' positions and knowledges.

The case-making history of this so called monograph involves even more indirect as well as direct contributors. There are, for instance, the author's sociology and methods teachers such as Karin Knorr Cetina, Stefan Hirschauer, and Klaus Amann. I enjoyed their ethnography and ethnomethodology classes at my home university in Bielefeld Germany. There was, what is more, another rather debated figure from the Bielefeld years, Niklas Luhmann, who died in 1998, and who turned from a distant adversary into an influential force that had an impact on nearly all chapters of this book. There are, for instance, socio-legal scholars, such as Max Travers, Reza Banakar, Bettina Lange, and Martha Komter who helped me position my early 'English' work in the wider law-in-action community. Another community of scholars – namely Lucy Suchman, Estrid Sørensen, John Law, and Tiago Moreira – was influential because they lured me to link courtroom studies with Science and Technology Studies. Until today, the Ethnomethodologist Michael Lynch serves as a point of reference for my endeavours somewhere in-between legal discourse and ways of knowing.

Some co-producers were even closer involved in actually making this case. There was – and somehow still is – the research group "Comparative Micro-Sociology on Criminal Procedure", namely my colleagues Kati Hannken-Illjes and Alexander Kozin, who involved me in challenging debates on the integration of various types of data or on the nature of ethnographic experience. There was, moreover, a group of committed assistants, namely Jan Schank, Matthias Michaeler, Steffen Albrecht, and Rixta Wundrak who challenged me in terms of the procedure frame and the trans-sequential method. Our discourse studies on political, mass-mediated inquiries left some traces in this book.

This book appreciates contributions that are even more direct. Helping hands and thoughtful brains of others turned the book-project into something doable and achievable. Sonja Lehmann supported me during the tricky final stage of the writing process. Hyo-Eun Shin brushed up and streamlined my English throughout. She worked through several versions and became my indispensable translator from English to English (sic!). At the end, she co-authored the final chapter on the case in the common law case-system. It is not a total monograph after all.

One group of people served as *the* case-makers. They became so without fully grasping what all my case-work was about (I did not either). They had to imagine what my research was motivated by and leading towards. They could not be sure, whether I fully understood the implications of their activities (Here, they resemble their clients and witnesses that often do not know much about the relevance of certain motions and formulations). In the field 'out there', I had the chance to build up trusting relationships: with basically two solicitors and 'their' barristers. I came into the position to learn and write about adversarial case-making only with their consent, tolerance, expertise, and communicativeness. I thank them for their explanations and stories, their humour and patience.

Once this book is completed, it can enter various signifying processes, just like the criminal cases as complex signs in/of the adversarial case-system. Numerous signifying processes come into mind: debates on the "socio in socio-legal studies," efforts to link discourse analysis and ethnography, studies on text and talk relations, or theories on adversarialism as a legal-political mode of governance. I hope that this case finds more recipients than "twelve jurors" and receives a more articulate response than the binary "guilty" or "not guilty."

INTRODUCTION

This book is concerned with the temporalities of legal practice, or more precisely, with the ways both past and future are overly present in legal case-making. It perceives case-makers as people – whether co-authors, ghostwriters, representatives, or spokespersons – that are concerned with *the* case's past and that anticipate its future, and by doing so perform the identity of it in the light of competing cases. This is not to say that case-making is a one-dimensional and linear accumulation. This is to say, however, that cases derive from activities in time and that these activities leave and apply traces that render case-making observable, both to members and sociologists.

The sociological appreciation of activities in time and the members' temporal orientations goes back to scholars such as Pierre Bourdieu, Anthony Giddens, Max Weber, or – even further back – to Karl Marx. They all consider time as a crucial marker for the current social or historical situation and its members or contemporaries. Urgencies, proximities, the right moments, waiting times, all these are properties of social time that an action theory or a theory of praxis need to take into account. In his classic version of the temporalities of (political, collective) praxis, Marx claims that "(M)en make their own history, but they do not make it just as they please; they do not make it under circumstances chosen by themselves, but under circumstances directly encountered, given and transmitted from the past."[1]

Marx's famous dictum, applied to adversarial case-making, could be rephrased like this: 'Parties make their cases, but they do not make them just as they please; they do not make their cases under circumstances chosen by themselves […].' Legal case-making is situated and interested in Marx's existential sense: it is not an academic meditation; it is not a routine application of universal rules; it is not a detached report on what has happened. Case-making is situated and interested because it contributes to loosing or winning, to punishment or release,

[1] Dutt provided this translation of *The 18th Brumaire of Louis Bonaparte* in 1963. This is Marx' German phrase from 1852: "Die Menschen machen ihre eigene Geschichte, aber sie machen sie nicht aus freien Stücken unter selbst gewählten, sondern unter unmittelbar vorhandenen, gegebenen und überlieferten Umständen." ([1852]1963:115).

to urgencies and right moments. This book is concerned with adversarial case-making "under circumstances directly encountered, given and transmitted from the past", forasmuch as these circumstances range from *still valid* police protocols documenting the first responses of the accused, the facts as gathered and assembled by the case-making team *up to now*, to the spatial and symbolic position from which all witnesses address the jury *in the near future*.

Marx's phrase was, at his time, a plea for political activism safeguarded by historical consciousness. Not acting upon the 'given circumstances' would be doomed to failure. Ignoring the – multiply layered – circumstances would pervert even well-intentioned acts and the highest ethical goals. Something similar holds true for case-making. The 'current situation' is "transmitted from the past" to various degrees and in diverse specifications. 'Making' in the present always rests on something already given; there are facts, rules and regulations already in place; there are resources available that derive from earlier and elsewhere; there are restrictions dictated by previous claims. Ambitious case-making tries to manipulate the circumstances, to act upon the past, to link up with prior events, and by doing so it creates history for events to come. The "directly encountered circumstances" unfold in the adversarial procedure, that is in the regulated and spatiotemporal formation of 'what counts as given (the case)' in a current situation. Procedure as an abstract standard welcomes whatever case will come, while procedure as a concrete meaning-production frame operates on a single-case-basis. Both aspects of procedure interrelate on various levels.

Adversarial case-making adds a systematic designation to this. The political and legal scholar Robert A. Kagan defines adversarialism as a system of governance driven by three major forces: (1) formal legal contestation, (2) litigant activism including fact-finding and (3) decentred decision-making.[2] All three forces together characterise the English

---

[2] Adversarial legalism seems to differ largely between the UK and the USA. Regarding the latter, Kagan lamented the omnipresence of adversarialism as a "mode of governance" (2001:5). It expanded from the legal sphere to other societal arenas such as politics or industrial relations. Some legal and political scholars claim that adversarialism expands regionally as well, for example when undercutting the European Union or International Courts (Kelemen 2006). In the UK, in comparison, adversarialism seems less forceful and rather restricted. This is reflected in lower legal costs figures and in smaller percentages of lawyers compared to the USA, in recurrent state reforms of judiciary and procedure, or, overall, in a relatively higher scale of political centralism. More than twenty years ago, Hughes referred to the UK context as "muted adversariness" (1971) and explained this characterisation with less distrustful

Crown Court procedure. Similarly, Taslitz, who is concerned with the costs and limitations of adversarialism, identifies "three primary features: (1) [adversarial fact-finding] glorifies jury deliberation, (2) informed by the competition of equally matched lawyer-representatives, (3) in service of a preference for the fragmentation of power" (2006:1591). The criminal legal process in English Crown Courts combines these adversarial features: a weak centre (the state authorities) receives partisan versions of a legal matter (by prosecution and defence) and delegates the decision to a deliberative body (the jury). How are cases made in such an adversarial setting?

The definitions mentioned above and their recurrent references to legal contestation and decentred decision-making provide us with first provisional guesses: cases are made by putting facts to a test in a legal contestation. Facts lose or gain weight because they are challenged by the opponent. Moreover, facts acquire relevance only insofar as they are exposed to the counter-forces in the legal arena. This mechanism fits the public (or popular) understanding of adversarial law: the 'high noon' moment in court, when the opponents confront their versions in front of the jurors.[3] Movies, documentaries, theatre plays, newspaper articles, etc. depict the witness examination, especially cross-examination as moments of contingency and as events of truthfulness.

The following definition of adversarialism highlights other features of case-making and legal meaning-production:

> Broadly speaking, adversarial procedure leaves most critical pre-trial and trial decisions such as discovery, the framing of issues, the choice of witnesses, the questions directed to witnesses, and the order of proof in the hands of lawyers. The central percept of the adversary system is that the sharp clash of proofs presented by opposing lawyers, both zealously representing the interests of their clients, generates the information upon which a neutral and passive decision maker can most justly resolve a dispute. (Asimow 2007:653)

norms concerning the rights of suspects, the particularities of jury selection and admissibility of evidence. The more radical form of US-American adversarialism, on the other hand, is explained by the legal culture, the weak central government, and the influence of the legal profession. The rules of the game are constantly reassessed by partisan lawyers and, therefore, become increasingly technical.

[3] Van Koppen and Penrod use the same semantics when relating to "John Wayne" (2003:347) as an icon of adversarialism compared to "Judge Dee" (Ibid.) epitomising the inquisitorial concept of justice.

Adversarial case-making is 'in the hands of lawyers': lawyers carefully develop the case from 'raw' materials. Lawyers make cases by anticipating the adversary's case, the counterpart's tactics, and the circumstances of the contest in court. These calculations enter what one could call the mobilisation of the case, its meticulous preparation. The case is designed by legal professionals accustomed to the technical and historical circumstances – the performative restrictions and possibilities – of the Crown Court. The Crown Court fits the previous definitions. It cultivates adversarialism:

> The striking peculiarity of the Anglo-American trial is that we remit to the lawyer-partisans the responsibility for gathering, selecting, presenting, and probing the evidence. Our trial court, traditionally a jury sitting under the supervision of the judge conducts no investigation of its own. The court renders a verdict of guilt or innocence by picking between or among the evidence that the contesting lawyers have presented to it. (Langbein 2003:1)

The legal historian Langbein (Ibid.) showed, by asking for the origins of lawyer-centeredness in the English Crown Court, how the criminal legal process elevated professional lawyers into the core positions. According to him, the legal system did not only develop certain rights and rules of fairness; it also silenced the accused in the name of an increasingly technical procedure. Case-making became lawyer-controlled.

Following Kagan in his chapter on "Deciding Criminal Cases" (2001) as well as legal scholars debating the "vanishing trial,"[4] case-processing on the procedural backstages supersedes the argumentative staging of cases, especially in the American context. By way of informal plea bargaining sessions lawyers decide their competing cases or case projects outside court. Judicial reforms in England point in the same direction: plea bargaining on the basis of the lawyers' cases is preferred to a full blown jury trial. The "sacred time" (Taslitz 2006) of jury deliberation is replaced by the administration of designed cases. The defendant who agrees to this early closure – who, from a judicial system's perspective, saves time by waiving his or her rights – receives a reward, a so called sentence discount, for his or her early guilty plea.

---

[4] For the recent, rather critical debate on the phenomenon, see the special issue of the *Journal of Dispute Resolution*, 2006 (1). It contains contributions on the situation in the USA, England, and Europe.

A third dimension of case-making seems largely overlooked in the literature on adversarialism: the case's becoming in time or, more precisely, in the procedural course. The case is the upshot of some programmed accumulation. Here, case-making proceeds by persistently inquiring into the same matters, by collecting 'more versions of the same', and by keeping them available due to an advanced procedural apparatus and memory. The accumulation of versions depends on reliable dossiers, on close transcriptions and on their availability for all procedural purposes. The accumulation of versions reminds of file-keeping inquisitors who turn mundane utterances – and even silence – into decisive clues and definite reasons. In the same manner, Damaska (1986), in her critique of populist and unsystematic jury- and lawyer-centred adversarialism, links this archival mechanism to the state and its non-partisan, 'more reliable' bureaucracy. In the Crown Court procedure, case-administration and the file-keeping activities are carried out by the Crown Prosecution Service (CPS), the instructed Police, and the defence solicitor. This (distributed) procedural archive alters the way testimonies are received and tested. It alters the ways by which what is said or written turns relevant in due course.

The micro-studies presented in this book elaborate on three mechanisms – staging, mobilisation, and replication – in order to account for the complex dynamics of adversarial case-making. All three are productive forces in the Crown Court procedure. All three demand a close analysis of their interplay on a case-by-case basis. The mechanisms of case-making serve various purposes in this law-in-action study: their interplay links ethnography and discourse analysis, it links the everyday of casework and the effects on a case-to-case basis. Their interplay points out what it takes to master this and why amateurs are at risk to fail. The mechanisms of case-making move the mainstream dualism of law-of-the-books and law-in-action[5] into a dynamic field of forces.

Each mechanism employs legal rules, professional techniques, social resources, and various knowledges in order to render something legally relevant. What is more, the focus on mechanisms of case-making illustrates adversarialism close to its actual working. Adversarialism is no

[5] Amongst many others, see the transcript-based courtroom studies by Atkinson and Drew (1979), Drew (1992), Matoesian (1993), Lynch and Bogen (1996), or Harris (2001). For an overview of "law-in-action" research from a wider ethnomethodological perspective, see Travers and Manzo (1997). For a rather critical-structuralist perspective, see amongst others Conley and O'Barr (1998).

longer an all encompassing form as implied by Kagan. It does not 'capture' an entire legal culture like, for example, the 'American way of law'. This does not mean that micro-ethnographic analytics are less political or that they ignore power relations and the overall legal culture. However, instead of generalizing the adversarial condition, I rather respecify the ways in which adversarialism manifests itself and works on the level of individual cases.

What is more, attentiveness to the mechanisms of case-making organises "thick comparison" (Scheffer and Niewöhner 2010). It emphasises differences in degree rather than differences in kind. It allows for overlaps and heterogeneity. It bridges the otherwise hermetic divide between adversarial and inquisitorial systems in order to understand procedure as a field of meaning-production in its own right. Procedure, from the perspective advocated in this legal ethnography, is the frame in/by which law operates. Much of the law is related to procedure. It is dedicated to whether a legal procedure applies at all (e.g. defining offences or exceptions), to what procedure applies (lower or higher court, trial by jury or Magistrates), to procedural rights of individuals (right to legal representation), to the parties' procedural status (burden of proof, rules of disclosure). If law operates by procedure, then law has to be studied in the light of regulated and case-related procedure, not the other way round.

Unlike mainstream legal studies and legal philosophy, this ethnography of legal procedure does not aim at a master narrative on legal systems or legal cultures. It rather offers a micro-foundation of the latter, specifically adversarialism. For an exploration of adversarialism-in-action I have chosen the English Crown Court procedure – not the entire English legal system – as *the* perfect example. The Crown Court procedure shows all relevant features that Kagan used in his broad definition: two competing fact-finding parties, decentred decision-making by jury and judge, and a weak centre throughout. In this setting, I studied case-making mostly from the point of view of the defence. The defence comprises the client who instructs his or her solicitor, the instructed solicitor who would then instruct a barrister, while the latter represents the case in open court. This winding team-building parallels winding case-making.

Crown Court cases, different to cases heard in inquisitorial settings, derive from a relatively long pre-trial phase and a relatively short trial. The extended pre-trial allows and relies on self-organised fact-finding, on exchanges in form of debates and agreements over versions, and on scripts for the examinations in court. It culminates in demonstrations of two competing cases in front of judge, jury, and the public. The tendency towards two fully fledged cases makes the Crown Court procedure a costly, time-consuming, and contingent contest. Recurrent attempts by the English government to further diminish the role of the Crown Court in favour of the Magistrates' Court are countered by arguments praising the democratic and deliberative qualities of trial by jury. The Crown Court counts as *the* last resort of adversarialism proper.

This ethnography deals with specific criminal cases in the English legal system: only those 'few' that are dealt with by the (higher) Crown Court. Criminal cases arrive at the Crown Court because of three formal reasons: (1) the offence is triable only on indictment (such as murder, manslaughter, rape or wounding with intent); (2) the defendant charged with an 'offence triable either way' chooses trial by jury;[6] (3) the Magistrates decide that the maximum adequate penalty would exceed their powers.[7] Due to these formal conditions, it is the lower Magistrates' Courts which deal with the vast majority of cases. In 2002, one of the years during my periods of fieldwork, Magistrates' Courts decided nearly a million cases (944,929), Crown Courts dealt with less than a tenth of that caseload (81,766). The majority of these cases are "either way"-cases based on charges such as grievous bodily harm or robbery (85.2% of Crown Court cases). More serious charges are rare: treason or murder (class 1, only 1.5% of all committals), manslaughter, rape, etc. (class 2, 3.4%), or other offences triable on indictment only such as aggravated battery, causing death by dangerous driving, etc. (class 3, 9.9%).[8] The defendants' choice of trial by jury is commonly explained by a "prosecution bias" of the Magistrates, resulting in a speedy inquisitorial handling. Ashworth, in his assessment of the "Criminal Process" (1998) adds two further, interrelated reasons: the public's bigger trust in the Crown Court and the broader

[6] This category includes offences of intermediate seriousness, such as theft, handling stolen goods, obtaining by deception, or burglary. The client faces a tricky decision: while the jury is more likely to acquit, the Crown Court judge may hand down a higher sentence in case of a guilty verdict.

[7] According to the Magistrates' Courts Act 1980 the maximum imprisonment in summary offences is up to 6 months. The maximum aggregate term is up to 12 months.

[8] See Judicial Statistics 2002, Chapter 6 (www.dca.gov.uk/judicial/jsar02/judicial_stats6.pdf).

representation of minorities. The defendants' choice of the Magistrates' Court is, reversely, explained by statistics: lower sentences, shorter waiting times for trial, and shorter trial hearings. On the other hand, once on the Crown Court track, defendants have a bigger chance to walk free. The Crown Court is, according to figures, not the most relevant, or the most efficient criminal court in the English legal system. However, it provides for highly visible, fully fledged case-making. It provides a perfect environment to grasp adversarial case-making.

This ethnography investigates case-making from two profoundly different perspectives that reflect the double-nature of procedure. Procedure is shaped on a case-by-case basis. Here, each procedural history, each formation of statements, each balance of powers, etc. is different. By the same token, procedure provides us with standards, measures, and rules that apply to all Crown Court cases. In other words, procedure helps us identify cases as Crown Court cases by ways of certain legitimate expectations or certainties, e.g. that a trial takes place before judge and jury or that certain rules of disclosure apply. It is because of the double nature of procedure as a frame of action and meaning-production that this ethnography approaches adversarial case-making in light of four case-studies and in light of four general properties or activities, such as file-work or legal precedence. Case-studies and cross-case studies inform each other. Each of the four case-studies highlights practical challenges of concerted case-work, such as designing a counter-version in a case of assault, scripting a case for/during the trial hearing in a case of "wounding with intent", introducing expert knowledge against a defence of "automatism", or engaging the moral self of a client who appears incapable of uttering signs of regret in a case of "murder" or "manslaughter". The four cross-case studies introduce general properties of adversarial case-making such as related temporal frames of procedure, divergent styles of file-work, procedural resources for conducting the trial hearing, and the completed case as a complex sign.

On field access

Reflexive ethnography teaches us that field access is already part of the ethnographic study. This is true not just in practical terms of conducting an ethnographic study, but also in a diagnostic sense, because the individual conditions of field access teach something about the field under study. In the second chapter, I will reflect on field as a problematic analytical entity. In this introduction, I will recount core methods that rendered certain sites and phases available to my ethnographic endeavour.

Accessing case-making – instead of a workplace, trial hearings, or a legal profession – requires specific adjustments and movements by the field researcher. He or she needs to get inside the rhythms and flows of casework. In other words, she needs to be there when it takes place and access the media by which casework is rendered available to others and in time. How then can the ethnographer tell that she is 'in'? In a lecture on fieldwork, Erving Goffman named "true tests of penetrating a group":

> People sometimes assume that if they're told strategic secrets, that's a sign that they're 'in'. I don't think that's too good a sign. One thing is, you should feel you could settle down and forget about being a sociologist. The members of the opposite sex should become attractive to you. You should be able to engage in the same body rhythms, rate of movement, tapping of the feet, that sort of thing, as the people around you. (1989:129)

Goffman's criteria for being 'in' explicate ideals of humanist empathy: The fieldworker shares the group members' habits, their communality, their social situation. This allows the researcher to comprehend what *they* are doing, why *they* do things this way, what *they* currently respond to, how *they* avoid doing other things, etc. Obviously, accessing case-making is about people and their habits, about personal relations and trust.

Legal ethnography is typically not about "penetrating a group" (Ibid.) only. It is also about accessing a number of discursive artefacts such as files, documents, arenas, meetings, archives, etc. These various sites complicate the task of access, since there is no single test to pass. There are additional "true tests" to pass (Ibid.). As a result, the socio-legal ethnographer should be able to answer questions like these: Do you grasp what she is doing when making this file note? Could you complete the phrase by which 'your' barrister addresses his colleague in a plea bargaining session? Do you get to the 'heart of the case' from reading the file? In the following, I retell my way 'in'. It is not a linear success story. It is a journey not just to offices, courts or prisons and their people, but also to the archives of the law. My fieldwork started in 2002 and proceeded in successive phases. I alternated fieldwork and analytical breaks as suggested by Spradley (1980).[9] My breaks between the eight, six and three months of fieldwork allowed me to file, review and index the manifold case material, and to re-organise it primarily in terms of possible chains or sequences of meaning-production. But where did I start some years ago?

1st phase of gaining access: in the criminal court

In terms of access, the court seems an unproblematic site since 'open court' is considered a basic condition of fair trial.[10] Correspondingly, I visited the Crown Court just as any other member of the public. There is no need, I thought, to identify myself as a researcher while speculating about the various backgrounds of the other onlookers in the public gallery. While some nervously followed the proceedings, others waited outside the courtroom to be called in. Although I was just a 'member of the public', I had to realise that I did make myself noticeable as having a different agenda. No other 'citizen' turned up for various hearings in a row. No other 'citizen' came, stayed and left just on his own.

The open court appeared as an observation-friendly site compared to other relevant sites, such as the solicitor-client-conferences or the jury sitting. This was at least my initial impression fostered by first visits. The only restrictions became apparent in form of security checks banning 'private' means of documentation.[11] Once in the public gallery, I chose the higher ranks to have a good view on the scenery. Later on, I moved down to the front benches in order to watch closely and listen to the protagonists. What a performance! From the gallery, the court hearing resembled a theatre play: trapping the audience's gaze in the 'here and now'.

---

[9] There is a lot of Goffman's advice on fieldwork (1989:129) that I did not and would not follow: I became (too) "friendly with people"; I took "seriously what people say"; I ended up in "two-person situations" rather often. But: I stayed in the field for "one or two years".

[10] See the "statement of principle made by Garoutte J in the Californian case of *People* v *Hartmann* [1894:37 P 153]. The trial should be 'public' in the ordinary common-sense acceptation of that term. The doors of the court-room are expected to be kept open, the public are entitled to be admitted, and the trial is to be public in all respects" (Blackstone's Criminal Justice 1998:1050).

[11] In a Practice Direction issued in 1981, the use of tape-recorders is classified as "contempt of court" unless they are used "for purposes of official transcripts or proceedings" (Archbold 2000:2341).

Profiting from the hearing's recipient-design
Up there, I enjoyed a 'perfect position'. I was an undisturbed and not disturbing observer. I could overlook the scenery. Conceptually, as well, my position made much sense. Everything relevant had to pass through this needle-eye and to be expressed right here, in front of the jury. More surprisingly, I could even follow the dealings. Everything seemed nicely explicated. Did I profit from the involvement of all the other laypeople in court: the public and the jurors as the ambassadors of common sense? I reached this kind of optimism when I started taking notes of these nicely summarized stories, simplified arguments, repeated definitions, plain narratives, etc. This was the point when things started to get somehow complicated.

Taking notes in court
The notepad has to be blamed for the complication. I was about to leave after a couple of brief sentencing hearings, when the usher came over. She was the first human being in this setting to address me. "You cannot take notes just like that", she protested as if everybody knew this, except me. Being exposed like this, I was struggling for words. "You could at least ask the clerk for permission", she went on. Shaking her head in disbelief she walked out of the courtroom and apparently expected me to follow. "Yes, the clerk." I rushed to add an apology: "I am a German researcher, sociologist." She just walked ahead and directed me to the clerk in charge of today's hearings – a young civil servant, rather elegant and talkative. Eventually, he gave me qualified permission to take notes: "No problem, but not up there…"

Gaining a status, taking a position
He offered the 'press bench' as the perfect position for a researcher. I sat on the right-hand side of the sound recordist[12], opposite the witness-box and right in front and below the jury. This placement became the standard solution for my extra-role: here I could take notes in line with the court's casting. Guests took me for a journalist, while

[12] The recordist operated the only authorised tape-recorder: a double deck cassette recorder with one tape or the other being changed at intervals. A transcript of the tape may be used if a case later goes to appeal. The recordist switched the tape-recorder on when the judge entered the courtroom, and off when the judge left. Additionally, he scribbled the case-number on the tape case.

the court staff soon referred to me as the "researcher from Germany".[13] From the press bench, matters looked different. People were not just talking heads from a distance: they were whispering and sweating; they exchanged notes or browsed magazines, etc. Then there were others, carrying files, delivering messages and distributing copies. Down here, the inner circle looked like it was constantly moving. With time the staff got used to me. They included me in/by their small talk during the breaks when the legal machinery stood still.[14]

A failed attempt to change positions

My position was renegotiated when I asked to move to a different place in the courtroom. I could not see the jury from the press bench which seemed unfortunate regarding my 'research field' at the time. The clerk claimed, "The jurors don't do anything special. They are simply sitting there watching." "Like puppets", I was teasing, which provoked the recordist's friendly protest: "Do not insult our highest legal institute!" My request failed. There would be no other bench available for me. All seats were reserved either for the defence or prosecution representatives. At least, that is what the clerk told me. There was nothing I could do to get a view on the whole interplay but move back to the public gallery again.

Following paper trails

It is hard to say what exactly triggered my dissatisfaction with the press bench in court. It was probably the amount of paper that entered the hearing and was used throughout complex chains of instruction or the frequent reference to "what the file says." Another more general impression made me rethink my position: the mode of talk in court, the 'artificial' questioning of witnesses, the 'learnt by heart answers', the permissions to 'refresh' one's memory, etc. Things seemed preconfigured in various respects. I hoped that the procedural backstage, such as

[13] As to the first, my outfit quite likely resembled the typical journalist. One judge asked – launching a chain of command – his clerk to ask the usher to ask the recorder to address politely the issue of appropriate dress in court. He was concerned about me not wearing a jacket. The old shorthand writer did not know how to phrase it: "The judge would appreciate if you could leave your jacket on during the hearing." "Or shall I better come in a suit?" "Well, yes, that would be excellent." The same day I got myself a dark-blue suit.

[14] Here are some common openers: "How can you study this without any knowledge of the law?" "Which system is better: the German or ours?" "What do you think: guilty or not guilty?"

client-lawyer meetings, file entries, instructions, etc. could somehow show how trials are prepared and rendered possible. What I became interested in was the configuration of procedural events and the anticipation of these events in preceding casework.

2nd phase: accessing preparation

At this point, I cannot draw on all the repositioning that occurred during my field trip. I only refer to two major shifts: me accessing a small law firm and, later, a barristers' chamber.[15] I moved on, generally speaking, to the work-benches of the intertextual, durable, and multi-local projects of representation, to the offices and encounters in which cases are composed and mobilised.

Finding a law firm

I found my law firm less through methodical search than by coincidence. It was a colleague at the local sociology department who brought me together with her husband who happened to be a 'partner' in a local law firm. It took some animated conversation on 'this and that' only to make him invite me to stay. To him, he assured, I was "no problem whatsoever." He seemed to have an itch to support this German guest. We drew up a contract regulating the "dress code" and "confidentiality." Moreover, I became liable to report any "results" to the firm first. What can be learnt from this with respect to field access? I suppose the fact that I was conceived as an outsider and harmless academic helped a lot to disperse doubts and fears at the onset of our 'cooperation'.

Getting my personal scout

The 'partner' then formally invited me to come over and use his firm for my "sociological inquiries." Once in the firm, I was introduced to two criminal lawyers: *Jack* working on Crown Court cases and *Jane* in

[15] The English particularity of the two professions feed into an ongoing discussion: at times, 'solicitors' demand the right to speak for the case in Crown Court as well. At other times, 'barristers' demand the right to take clients directly. Their cooperation and division of labour also provide grounds for mutual complaints: the 'process lawyers' complain about uninformed, incomplete and badly researched instructions; the 'street lawyers' complain about badly prepared, little engaged, and not very fierce barristers. In their everyday working life, both sides harmonize very well vis-à-vis their clients: whilst one side is reassuring and motivating (solicitor), the other (barrister) does appeal to law and experience.

charge of Magistrates' Court cases. I repeated my assurance: "I don't wish to evaluate your work. I am simply interested in how you prepare cases here in England." In the beginning, I shared an office with Jack. I happened to spend entire hot summer days just sitting there with him. Our office sessions were only interrupted by coffee-cigarette-breaks. During these breaks we never talked about the cases (but on football, the town, Germany). We became some kind of team-mates: he explained to me what a 'good solicitor' does; I explained to him what it means to conduct ethnographic fieldwork.

Negotiating data access and data collection

After we had spent two weeks next to each other, I felt ready to ask Jack if photocopying – instead of writing off – filed documents (such as police protocols, defence statements, written correspondence, etc.) would be a problem. He asked me to blacken names and addresses. This change in data-recording was a huge step in terms of field access. It opened up a whole 'representational economy' that would have remained covered otherwise. The justification for my request was straightforward: casework is in large part paperwork and must be recorded and studied in its course. During the next half a year I was busy filling both my notebook and my research case files.

New staff in the second fieldwork phase

One year later I went back to the firm for a second phase of fieldwork. In the meantime, a lot had changed. Jack was gone; his cases were taken over by Jane, the Magistrates' Court solicitor. These personal discontinuities forced me to renegotiate field access and to explain once more my data needs and research purposes. I referred back to the old agreement and could add the first results of the research process. Jane, a novice in the Crown Court setting, turned out to be careful and protective when it came to file access or her meetings with clients.

Restricted access to special meetings

Special occasions reintroduced the question of access. The solicitors would frequently deny access, especially when it came to lawyer-client meetings or to the conferences with a barrister. The reasons given for this occasional closure were, of course, 'external': the client did not agree or it would be too much to ask for in his or her difficult situation. Jane was particularly hesitant, perhaps due to her 'intense' and 'personal' style of working with the client (see chapter IV). Later on, her hesitation vanished. She included me more and more often and she did so without even asking her clients. She would then introduce me as her German researcher from the university: "He is not interested in you, he is interested in me." She would smile and add: "Well, in my work."

Following the course of casework

It was one of these special occasions when I met the next informant: a young barrister (36) with a good deal of work experience (12 years). I asked him to have me for a short while, so that I could see what actually happens to the solicitor's preparation work. The week that I had initially asked for turned into a whole month, and the months into four months of extra fieldwork. Through the barrister I was introduced to new sites of the legal process: the plea bargaining, the pre-hearing conferences, the library work at the Chambers, etc. The new access imposed novel restrictions: the barrister vetoed when I asked him whether I could make a copy of the work-hours-list in a murder case. He preferred making the copies himself. Through him I got to know a certain 'high' culture of hospitality. We went out for meals to discuss the matters and/or to celebrate triumphs. I experienced the same with his colleague who would later take over his role. 'Having me' turned into a compound adviser-advised relationship extended by gestures of sociability.

Retrospectively, field access appears as fragmented including different sites, different activities, different professional cultures, and knowledges. As a consequence, field access turned into an ongoing task that was never fully completed. Starting at the Crown Court, the field quickly expanded in time and space. In retrospection, I kept track of this expansion by applying a number of fieldwork rules: (a) Understand case-making through the members' point of view and methods! (b) Accompany practitioners over a longer period of time in order to grasp full circles of case-making! (c) Include the co-productive resources related to the members' efforts and methods of casework! (d) Explore the developmental stages of the case-in-becoming in tune with the programmed procedural course!

These rules turned field access into an ongoing business of changing intensity. Accessing buildings, settings, events, relations, documents, archives, etc. was at no point negotiated once and for all. By renegotiating access, I encountered 'unknown' boundaries to cross, back regions to explore, unofficial material to include. Access itself turned into an activity of field-construction. As a challenge, it exceeded the tasks – for example, creating trust and maintaining good relationships with the *natives* – that are usually ascribed to 'gaining access'.

Rendering case-making observable

> Inside the offices, paperworkers produce and combine documents. Their desks are covered with paper: with files, bundles, and briefs. And the production goes on. Solicitors dictate notes, secretaries key in letters, and the legal clerks organise the facts of the case. It is through paper-trails that things are set into motion for the day in court. In other words: statements, arguments, narratives, and their human carriers are assembled to make a case. The mounting dossier indicates what needs to be drafted, collected, and posted *next*. It gives the 'full picture' as well as the missing links. At this site of the legal machinery, the socio-legal ethnographer faces, however fascinated by courtroom dramas, a writing culture.
>
> Legal mobilisation, however, includes face-to-face work: people need to stand up and speak out in court. They need to articulate the written, to stage it, to convey it to an overhearing audience. The day in court requires an ensemble set to co-enact the matter 'here and now'. The case, therefore, involves a whole bond of players, props, and material. However infected by 'archive fever', the socio-legal ethnographer deals with an impressive performative culture.
>
> And there is more: the interplay, the competition, the terror of failure. At least two social projects and individual ambitions are at odds here, putting the respective other under pressure and tension. The cases unfold and are elaborated in the contest between defence and prosecution. They are both prepared to challenge, weaken, and undermine the adversary's case in front of the jury. The socio-legal ethnographer faces, however fascinated by the means, formats, and methods of case-construction, a contingent and risky power game: Competitive mobilisation.

Writing culture, performative culture, or competitive mobilisation – there are a number of perspectives that touch on the craft and on the dynamics of case-making. The three shed light on the temporal and sequential features of legal casework. They link what is commonly held apart: pre-trial and trial,[16] preparation and performance, text and talk,

[16] An early socio-legal study on the pre-trial was presented by McBarnet (1977). She noted that "interactionist detail cannot provide a total explanation of the processes of conviction. In the first place, it understates the structural influences of the legal system's rules, checks, and definitions on the construction of reality. In the second place, it underplays how much the events and information observed in court have been shaped long before the stage of public trial is reached" (175). For studies of legal preparation see also Sarat and Felstiner (1995), Konradi (1997) and Travers (1997).

matter and rule.[17] But how do these perspectives nest in the social situations that ethnographers share with their informants?

De-centring social situations

Goffman's question of 'what is going on?' is at the heart of micro-sociological research. Socio-legal scholars started with a similar curiosity: What goes on in court? What happens in client-barrister conferences? How does plea-bargaining proceed? Symbolic Interactionists argue that 'what goes on' depends largely on the meaning negotiated and ascribed by the participants (Denzin and Keller 1981). Structuralist scholars argue that 'what goes on' and 'what can be done' are patterned by cultural frames and scripts (Gonos 1977). Focussing on case-making provides additional answers on 'what goes on'. It weighs occurrences as preceding and succeeding moments in the course of procedure. Through this extra framing, the ethnographer accesses discourse practices and legal relevancies that would otherwise remain undetected.

The nature of interaction analysis changes fundamentally when one addresses the procedural dimension. It moves closer to what participants are confronted with and to what they still achieve. The participants of Crown Court hearings, for instance, are confronted with statements and interviews they have given at earlier stages of the case. They had better relate to these prior statements during their court-performance. In this way, counsels and witnesses in court resemble Michel de Certeau's "consumers" (1984): they pick up, mix, and modify various pre-products. In the procedural frame, they repeat, copy and paste, and avoid "fresh talk" (Goffman 1981:172) as overly risky.

In the legal setting, face-to-face interaction is one frame of meaning production amongst others. Similarly, Niklas Luhmann approaches talk next to other communicative media:

> Writing and printing make it possible to withdraw from interaction systems and nevertheless to communicate with far-reaching societal consequences. By deciding to use the communicative form of writing, one can reach more addressees over longer periods of time, but this decision suggests that one withdraw from interaction, if it does not force one to do so.

[17] There is a large amount of research on the relationship between text and talk. For an overview, see Mulkay (1986) or Smith (1985). See also the author's study on the entanglements of text and talk in the German asylum procedure (Scheffer 1999).

> The differentiation of this mode of communication [writing] from interactional nexuses has more than quantitative significance: it enables a mode of working that could not be attained within interaction and thereby an augmentation of the difference between society and interaction to which the societal system and interactional systems can orient themselves. (Luhmann [1984]1995:427-8)[18]

Multi-modality is pertinent to our study of case-making. Through face-to-face interaction alone, members could not attain spatiotemporal expansions such as rendering available the procedural past, linking procedural sites, or performing "identity constancy and identity transformation" (Garfinkel 2006:151 sqq.). We better not reduce case-making to a series of talks or meetings.

Complexities

Detecting case-making creates several methodological problems. To give one example: it is impossible to record legal casework in its entirety. Casework is, to a large extent, momentary and passing. Detecting case-making has to cope with "multi-sitedness" (Marcus 1998). Casework takes place at the client's home, in the law firm's offices[19], and right outside the courtroom. It takes place in barristers' chambers and in the interview rooms at court too. Caseworkers operate via correspondence, telephone conversation, or infrequent meetings. As a result, adversarial case-making is diachronic and synchronic. Already by tracing single statements on their way to court, the fieldworker can get lost in the intertextuality of legal discourse. Given the multi-modality and multi-sitedness of case-making, the ethnographer often gets in touch with a selection of the overall investments and inputs only. What is more, adversarial case-making appropriates a

---

[18] Luhmann argues that nowadays "the gap between interaction and society has become unbridgeably wide and deep. [...] At no other time has it been less possible to view the societal system as composed of interactions and to consider adequate theories that conceive society as 'commerce', exchange, dance, contract, chain, theatre, or discourse" (1995:430).

[19] The law firm's office shows some similarities with the laboratory as described by Latour and Woolgar: "A laboratory is constantly performing operations on statements; adding modalities, citing, enhancing, diminishing, borrowing, and proposing new combinations. Each of these operations can result in a statement, which is either different or merely qualified. Each statement, in turn, provides the focus for similar operations in other laboratories. Thus, members of our laboratory regularly noticed how their own assertions were rejected, borrowed, quoted, ignored, confirmed, or dissolved by others." (1979:86 sqq.)

whole range of (inter-)acts that are not appropriately grasped as homogenous writing and talking. They are better captured as hybrid forms: as written speech and spoken texts.

Fortunately, it is not just researchers who are confronted with such problems. Lawyers have to deal with the complexity of case-making as part of their everyday work. Despite the enormous number of incoming calls, letters or documents, they need to ensure that no important detail, no official deadline is missed. They try to keep track of the circulating statements through checklists, sketches or diagrams (see Suchman 2000). Solicitors try to control their careers, their distribution inside and outside their fraction. The lawyers' management of complexity is object and means to our study of case-making.

Tracing case-making

How can one investigate extended and multi-sited projects? One way is to focus on its products 'in the making': the statements, pieces of evidence, and lines of defence. From this perspective, I propose to approach *becomings* as historical singularities: the career of an alibi (chapter I) or the positioning of experts (chapter IV). These analyses track down single features that travel through situations and that are marked by their various involvements. In the course of case-making, *becomings* gain weight – and configure future events. The focus on *becomings* sharpens our understanding of how "law-in-action" (Travers and Manzo 1997) proceeds at a local level and within a socio-material infrastructure.[20] At this point, I recount some techniques and methods that I used to study adversarial case-making.

The lawyer's presentation of the case

The solicitor's introduction of single cases – initiated by my "What are you working on right now?" – was a useful starting point. My informants provided brief and pointed stories of "what this case is about." These accounts often named a key incident over which there would be some disagreement between prosecution and defence. The solicitor's

[20] A rich line of references to approach *becomings* is provided by the laboratory studies in Science and Technology Studies (STS) examining research processes. By opening the black boxes of scientific practice, ethnographers face an assembly of things and people, human-machine-interaction, local politics of demonstrating results and so forth.

presentation usually combined a factual and a legal section. He or she described "what happened" and "technicalities" that were relevant to the casework at that point in time. It is important to note when exactly this description occurs in the legal process.

Selecting single issues

These presentations convey what my solicitors call the "heart of the case" or the "crucial point." From the solicitor's point of view, this is what one uses to determine 'now' whether this case is to be won or lost, or whether it should or should not go to court. The "heart of the case" may well be a medical attestation, the eye-witness' identification of the perpetrator, or a psychological report on the "mental state" of the accused. It may be something seemingly minor, and the researcher may fail to notice it when studying the file solely. The "heart of the case" may attract the attention of prosecution and defence to different extents. This, again, depends on the actual phase of case-making: in the final stages, circumstances are presented as having dictated the case right from the beginning; preliminary investigations, in contrast, select foci with great optimism that may be disappointed as the case unfolds.

Tracing issues through paper trails

It is important here to identify at what point in time an issue enters the file for the first time, how this entry is composed, and in what medium. Is it an official letter, a file note dictated by the solicitor, or one of her secretary's meticulously composed to-do-lists?

> In a burglary case, I found the first entry of the "self-harmer"-hypothesis in a file note on a telephone conversation that the solicitor conducted with the co-accused partner of the client. During this telephone conversation, the young woman mentioned a talk with a neighbour. The neighbour made allegations about the complainant: The reported/photographed injuries (deep cuts under her left eye) may have been self-inflicted. The co-accused was advised to inform her solicitor right away and to instruct him to take a statement from this neighbour. This piece of information, the solicitor added in the note, seems "really important."

From this point, the topic ("self-harm") can be followed through the file. Does it occur again? Where is it mentioned again and how? How is the issue promoted from one entry to the next? Every single file-entry is to be noted!

The schedule of procedure

I gained a better overview of an issue's "social career"[21] by placing it in the procedural course. The date of the charge, of the indictment, of the Plea and Direction Hearing, of the deadlines for disclosure or the trial hearing provide vital contextual information, e.g. on urgencies, relevancies, and initiatives. When, in relation to these dates, does the issue arise? How does it affect or alter the projected schedule? This background helped me to get an idea of how solicitors channel, adjust, and enforce facts and arguments.

> Time for preparation: The "Direction Hearing"[22] took place two weeks ago. Today the matter is listed for an application by the defence asking for full disclosure of the medical notes reporting the complainant's medical history. The prosecuting barrister applies for another adjournment: "The medical report can be served within a month's time, my Lord." The counsel for the defence complains about the further delay and then accepts. In fact, nobody seems really upset about postponing the trial hearing for another three weeks – apart, perhaps, from the defendant who is awaiting the trial in custody. Still, the defence has got plenty to do until the day in court.

Reconstructive interviews

How something becomes a key issue is not just a matter of file-analysis. The researcher tries to participate in 'most' instances of casework before they somehow translate into filed documents. Sometimes it is just an idea that was brought up in a kind of brainstorming session during the solicitor-client meeting or in a conference with a barrister. Histories of case-making are accessible as well through interviews with caseworkers. One could call these interviews biographical, although they simply deal with the 'biography' of statements or cases. The researcher can ask the caseworker how a point came up and how it translated into different media. The interview might be combined with a presentation of the case-file.

---

[21] The career metaphor has been used for persons and things. See, for example, Cambrosio, Limoges and Pronovost (1990), Doering and Hirschauer (1997), and Koptytoff (1986).

[22] Direction Hearings allow the parties to plan the jury trial. The parties can estimate the time needed to hear all the witnesses; they can agree on certain facts which helps reducing the time necessary; they can indicate the debated issues and their respective positions.

Data-sheets

In order to trace the career of a statement through the procedural course, I assembled the following information. In the aforementioned case of burglary, a log entry took the following shape:

Date	Participants	Incident	Content	Function for case
(12.6^{+2})*	Solicitor – co-accused	Telephone conversation	Neighbour claims that 'victim' is self-harmer	New line of argument; evidence for the defence-case

Fig. 1: Data-sheet for "self-harmer"

The statement's career starts with the client-solicitor meeting, where the co-accused mentions what her neighbour (a potential witness) has once claimed about the alleged victim ("self-harmer"). According to this 'idea', the alleged victim may have injured herself as she, allegedly, did several times before. It takes much more casework (and many more entries) until the neighbour is enrolled as a witness and until his statement is available as an official element of the defence. What was initially just an anecdote needs to be documented in order to get other people involved. At a later point, the potential statement needs to be authorised – meaning connected to an actor and his/her social credibility. In court, the statement requires a human voice: somebody speaking up right in front of the jury. I traced the career of this statement through the case-file and related encounters. Every reference triggered new entries in the data-sheet. The sheet, in this sense, gathered all traces left by casework. The traces represent, as well as perform, the statement's "becoming."

Towards the systematics of case-making

Tracing case-making does not lead to singularised stories. As in the example above, the "recruitment of witnesses" in one case can generate hypotheses for other case studies. The perspective across cases highlights the procedural frame and its systematic effects. Here are some explorations into the systematics of case-making.

* What does this date mean? The two numbers separated by the dot resemble an imagined date that signifies the real duration of the casework. The +1 or +2 etc. signifies the first, second etc. year of my fieldwork from which the piece of data originates. The reader can use this number system to place the case-making and the ethnographic analyses in a relational time frame, without depriving the participants of their right to anonymity.

- Involvement and circulation: Who gets involved in case-making? How, for instance, is a statement distributed within the defence ensemble before it is disclosed to the prosecution? Who is excluded from the exchange? By following the log entries, one encounters a sequence of different circles: from one-to-one consultation to complex divisions of labour.
- Rhythm and frequencies: How quickly do statements circulate? With what frequency do exchanges occur in relation to the procedural phases? Do they accelerate? These queries led the researcher to examine urgencies and routines of casework. They hint at lawyers' allocation and priorities of their efforts. They reveal what participants experience as the 'hot' and 'cold' phases of procedure.
- Social careers: The statement-in-becoming has a social career in terms of rise (or fall) and of growing (or diminishing) weight and impact. Applying this insight, the researcher can identify several stages of acknowledgement and status attribution: from when it was just an item of gossip, to when it became a hopeful line of enquiry, up to a vital component of the case in court. Most careers, however, are brief: many statements stay on the level of 'just ideas'. They are neither fixed nor disputed.
- The transformations of statements: Statements are not just written and spoken, but whispered, drafted or read out. This variety of representation keeps them flexible and adjustable to local purposes. They also trigger the multiplication of versions. Early statements are risky since it is hard to account for all their future applications. Representational projects come under threat especially by 'impulsive' statements. Lawyers insist on drafting statements before they are delivered to the procedural public.
- The unsaid: The analyst might become aware of 'rather successful' careers: statements that were once carefully chosen to represent the case in court, but, in the end, did not make it to the witness-box. This calls for supplementary ethnographic interviews about the concrete circumstances of selection with those who decided not to use this idea or that piece of information any longer. Now we can observe even the words that remain unspoken, the claims that are suppressed.
- Micro-functionalism: Each entry in the datasheet can be re-specified as a solution for certain problems at this very procedural moment. A completed log, read in this way, implies resourceful queries for related projects of case-making: within one case or across cases.

Is the intervention in case A utilised in the cases B and C as well? Does the translation of claim I repeat for claim II?

The data-logs suggested above are just a starting point on the way to analyse rather common patterns of adversarial case-making. The book switches between the two faces of procedure: a single case and a cross-case perspective.

The specificity of the database

These methodical instructions are not representative for all criminal legal procedure. Documented casework varies considerably according to the level of criminal courts. There are huge differences between cases heard in the Magistrates' Courts and cases heard in the Crown Court. The scope of data varies also according to the case-making party. In this book, I focus almost entirely on the defence side,[23] while the prosecution side comes into view only indirectly – through the documents disclosed to the defence – or concerning a very specific aspect with a focus on expert witnesses (chapter III). What is more, a rather inquisitorial regime would provide another set of modalities and natural data: a single dossier, the judge's dictation, and a preference of his oral casework. Cases are inseparable from the media that render them available to others and in time.

Case-making is rooted in an inscription apparatus that provides the ethnography with loads of highly specific data. Why is it, as Latour puts it for another judicial apparatus that, "texts are omnipresent" (Latour 2010:129)? It is worth asking why the English defence-file constituted such a rich source for the purpose of tracing case-making. How did the researcher's purpose liaise with the lawyers' determination to organise, order, document, and report their ongoing casework? How was the research enabled by what was locally available? Are there, to modify Garfinkel's study of record-keeping in hospitals, any "good reasons for *good legal records*" (1967:186)? Here are some:

- Accounting: In the defence file, the solicitor in charge of the case employs a standardized system of book-keeping to account the law firm's expenses and to facilitate the granting and calculation of legal

[23] It is this partial view that, at times, makes me refer to the main informant as *my* barrister and the defendant as *our* client.

aid. According to this system, solicitors are asked to document all casework that takes longer than six minutes. These units – specified "as telephoning about X", "writing letters to Y", "perusing file," or "drafting statement" – are recorded and later quantified for billing purposes. For this reason, the fieldworker also finds work documented that did not lead anywhere.

- Time management: The lawyer in charge uses the file to reconstruct *what* has been done so far and *what* needs to be done in the near future. Outstanding work is prompted by solicitors' diary notes, printed out and delivered by the secretary at the beginning of each office day. The order and transparency of the file are supposed to guarantee that the lawyer meets the many appointments, deadlines and duties that come along with defending a Crown Court case.
- Accumulation: The file is the object and source of casework. It secures, organises and effects profits from earlier investments. Day-to-day casework is principally about 'keeping the file in order' and 'doing what the file requires'. Before the trial, defence work largely takes place as interaction between file and solicitor, the latter indicating further transactions to be made (with the client, witnesses, barrister, the CPS, etc.). From this, strings of correspondence and representational projects come together in the solicitor's office, the defence party's "centre of calculation" (Latour 1987).
- Division of labour: Crown Court cases are handed over by the solicitor to a barrister, hired and instructed by the law firm to represent the defence in court. The barrister receives the main information for the trial through the "brief to counsel." The division of labour (between solicitor and barrister) requires more paperwork and filing. The legal file is assembled and kept for a whole (defence) team shielded form the adversary (prosecution) team.
- Urge for completeness: Lawyers frequently complained about "incomplete" files, although to me they seemed amazingly comprehensive. They read the files as being in need of something: "Where is the response to our letter from the Crown Prosecution Service?" "Why is the statement still not signed?" "When do I need to finish this brief?" A file's 'incompleteness' stimulates further file- and casework.

The specificities of the database raise a more general methodological as well as political problem that has been described by Star and Strauss as "hidden work" (Star and Strauss 1999). There is a lot of work done by clients, witnesses or their peers that, due to the files' system of accountability, never finds its way into the legal files. This 'work' may entail his or her (illegal) 'threatening and intimidating' of the others' witnesses, him/her managing worries and fears, or his/her learning a story's details by heart. The researcher may get a glimpse of this hidden work in the problems raised by the client during the confidential talks with his lawyer. From just the files, one can only speculate on what it means for the client to *have* and to *be* a case:

> Shortly before trials one can witness the tension rising even amongst the professionals: a tighter schedule, an increasing assiduity, an escalating busyness, a higher rate of correspondence, of meetings and telephone consultations. Work becomes breathless before the 'day of reckoning'. The same might apply to defendants. Some report that they were unable to sleep "the night before." They have been told by their lawyers: "Make sure you remember all of it! Do not confuse the dates!" In this way, clients are increasingly captured by the contingencies of the case.[24]

Performances in court run the risk not only of being badly prepared in legal and technical terms, but of being thwarted by, the 'human factor'. Thus, what takes place is at times mysterious and surprising even for the insiders: why did these witnesses not appear in court; why did their best witness suddenly suffered amnesia?

Outlook

This ethnography explores ways of case-making, or more precisely, the complex movements that drive adversarial case-making. Adversarial case-making, I argue, combines specific mechanisms that are indicative of the idea of adversarialism (such as staging vis-à-vis the jury) with other mechanisms that introduce elements that appear rather foreign to adversarialism (such as bureaucratic replication by way of filing). Adversarial case-making in the Crown Court procedure displays an assemblage of mechanisms that come to a halt only with the final judgment. The settled case, the way it is reported, prolongs the overall common law case-system. As a complex sign, it enters signifying processes in terms of analogous matter, rule, and decision.

[24] This resembles Luhmann's micro-sociological observations ([1969]1989) on the increasing entanglement of the parties in the legal procedure. They buy, one might say, into the 'open' game and feed into the procedural history with self-made decisions, which they will be held accountable for.

The eight chapters of this book explore methods and effects of professional case-making in two different formats: case-study and topical study. The two formats alternate, which provides the reader with different perspectives on case-making. (I) The first case study follows a story on its way to court. The "alibi" is employed at various sites and requires investments of varying kind. The career shows how defendant and caseworker are pushed towards risky moves and, eventually, into the shared and contested areas of case-making. Right after (II), the procedure is conceptualised as a multi-temporal event-process-relation. The chapter offers methodical rudiments to account for the procedure's trans-sequentiality. This conceptual view provides orientation to (III) a study of the barrister's casework on the day of the trial hearing in a case of "wounding with intent." Here, ephemeral objects such as marks or jottings gain systematic relevance as self-made and local devices for case-making. After this trans-sequential analysis, the book offers a more general study on different styles of file-work (IV): the instrumentalist and the humanist style. While the latter emphasises face-to-face interaction, the instrumentalist style relies rather on close human-file interactions. The differences are explained by regular procedural demands that translate into diverging professional habits and habitual ethics. The third case-study (V) views adversarial case-making from an epistemic perspective. It asks how expertise is introduced into the procedural arena. Expert knowledge, in order to suit the adversarial framework, requires some modest moves that fit it into the existing division of knowledges. The sleep walking expertise borrows from and invokes the common sense, the instructed case, and the agreed upon facts. With a view on the preceding chapters (VI), I ask about the procedural infrastructure that furnishes court hearings. Courtroom, case file, and the replicated story provide indispensable resources for the current dealings. The three resources explain: the provision of complex institutional interaction, the hearing's embedding in the procedural course, and the situated interplay of the mechanisms of adversarial case-making. The last case study (VII) moves on to the final stages of case-making. It examines the Crown Court's dealing with guilt and regret. The procedure cultivates an anti-inquisitorial form of (indirect) moralising. The defendant is not forced to explain him- or herself vis-à-vis the jury and the public. The defendant is protected from moral exposure, while, at the same time, he or she is invited to engage in 'semi-private' character work. The procedure repeatedly confronts the offender with the moral implications of what she or he has done. The last topical chapter (VIII) deals with what may or may not follow case-making. The decided and reported case is tuned in to signifying processes. As a case-sign, it may gain relevance in the overall case-system in terms of legal matter, procedural rule, or binding decision. The case-system renders the case available for future case-making by analogy and precedence. Case-making, however, is more than the triangulation of matter, rule, and decision; case-making constantly produces side-effect: an excess and diffusion of truth versions, effective rulings, and decisive selections.

In the conclusion, I recount and review the mechanisms of adversarial case-making and how they work in combination. The distinct mechanisms only come into view due to the ethnographic framing of procedure as relations of event and process: events and *their* process, process and *its* events. In this view, each case-making mechanism – staging, replication, and mobilisation – surfaces as a distinct event-process relation. Case-making and 'doing procedure' turn out to be intimately entangled. In the procedural frame, the participants and parties have to contribute to and employ various case-making mechanisms simultaneously. This is why adversarial case-making constitutes precarious positions and involvements.

I. A CASE OF ASSAULT: THE RISE AND FALL OF AN ALIBI

Meaningful case-properties, such as stories on what 'really happened' derive from contingent activities and vicissitudinous projects. They are ridden with prerequisites and demand much from the case-makers. In order to show how parties invest into their cases, I trace the rise and fall of an alibi-story in an assault case. I followed the alibi's career from its first appearance to its demise.

The first case-study introduces case-making by accounting for a story-in-process and how its turns into something of legal relevance. We encounter the case-in-becoming on various levels: on the level of the individual case by not knowing yet what it will be all about; on the level of the individual idea or claim by not knowing yet whether it will turn into a fact; or on the level of the cast by not knowing yet who will serve as a witness. The case-study will show the absence of law on the surface level and the procedural prevalence of the story-form. Stories appear as core items of case-making: as something to design and arrange. Lawyers, accordingly, work as professional story-(re)tellers - as specialists who know where, when, and how to present stories in the procedural course.

The first case study, what is more, introduces the manifold textual data provided by the defence file plus related communications. I utilised all I could find in the records about Linda Queen's ("our client" and later defendant) alibi-story and its procedural life in order to understand how it gained (and ultimately lost) relevance for 'its' Crown Court case. The data and its dating allowed me to follow the lawyers' investments into the story and their professional calculations attached to them. However, a story is not just a passive object. The alibi-story bound together many details: places, episodes, the cast, reasons, etc. It arranged these details (or indices) in a temporal and social order. Both properties, the story's detailedness and the ordering of details, offer some criteria to assess its validity. Because of these intrinsic qualities, stories allow legal amateurs as well as professionals, informed insiders as well as unacquainted outsiders to assess it. Stories seem to be the perfect interfaces to link law and common sense, judiciary and the people.

I chose the alibi because it allows me to highlight two aspects: its mobilisation, which are the investments necessary to turn it into a case-story, and the risks to be taken in the process of mobilisation. As a result, the case study shows the becoming and fading of Linda's alibi on its way to the Crown Court: from its first appearance for the defence to its various manifestations. The alibi demands attention and investments in formal, literary, and strategic ways. It requires internal properties (temporal and spatial indices) and external properties (deadlines and formats of delivery). The reconstruction places the casework conducted at a certain point in time into an extended sequence of a procedural past and future. The reconstruction of the story's career gives way to an understanding of procedure as a dynamic sense-making frame.

The ontological versions of the alibi-story and its analysability

The alibi-story passes through a career that transcends single manifestations as text or talk. The career transgresses local employments, but also trans-local circulations.[1] By 'career', I refer to the story's changing status within the case-in-becoming. I infer the story's status by determining whether and how the defence ensemble is willing to invest into it (for example to rewrite or 'thicken' it) at that time, and whether and how lawyer and client make use of the story (for example as a "defence statement" or in case summaries) to represent the defence. The analysis of the story's career relates to "natural data," meaning data that emerges by way of the participants' casework and doing procedure.

The natural data provides us with three ontological versions of 'what a story is' in this legal setting: story as process, as event and as object. (1) *Story-as-process* marks out stages of production, a gradual completion from one version to the next.[2] One finds arrays of versions in the file that my informants described as necessary to advancement and completion. In contrast, when it came to brief descriptions of the state

[1] See for a similar perspective, Limoges et al. (1990) and Cambrosio et al. (1991) who traced a policy dossier on its way through a ministry. Meehan (1993, 2000) reconstructed the making of police statistics or, as he calls it, their "organisational career" from the citizen's call to the police response. Latour (1999a) followed samples of soil from the rain forest to the scientist's desk.

[2] Cicourel analysed accounts given in interviews, protocols, and reports in light of the practitioners' interpretations and background assumptions. Similarly to the analysis suggested here, his ethnography on "juvenile justice" focuses on the ways "objects

of the art, the informants would highlight risks and deficits of the story-at-hand. (2) *Story-as-event* highlights the moments of articulation. In protocols and reports the story appears as the upshot of local conditions: as story-telling. Story-telling reflects the audience and the expected reception. The story-as-event comprises local conditions: the interaction order, the performed rituals, or the (missing) support by various story-tellers and story-listeners. (3) *Story-as-unit* reminds of the fact that the participants' casework presumes a relatively stable object in order to organize its procedural life. The story, from this angle, is seen as an "actant" (Latour 1987) capable of causing various effects in a network of relations. The story-as-unit allows participants to follow up on each other across procedural stages.

The three perspectives on the story provide the empirical grounds for a trans-sequential analysis. Such an analysis would, completely undertaken (see chapter V), join Goffman's "moment-by-moment analysis" (1981) of the story-as-event with a stage-by-stage analysis of the story-as-process. Both perspectives hinge on the story-as-unit. Without its stability, the analysis would not be capable of integrating the story's eventfulness and processuality. The study of the alibi-story puts an emphasis on the story-as-process: its career in the course of case-making.

Where to start and how to follow

An alibi is the strongest possible account against an allegation. The alibi does not explain an offence, unlike accounts of self-defence, jealousy, or sleep-walking (see chapter III). It does not deny particulars of the offence such as accounts that simply lower the degree of responsibility (see chapter VII). It shares no grounds with the accusing account, except the time of the alleged crime. This complete denial leaves open whether the (alleged) incident took place at all.

The allegation derives from the (alleged) victim's account of what happened. The 'victim' is, at least at this point, the only prosecution witness. Similar to the alibi, the allegation-story travels the whole way to the Crown Court. It appears in the case summaries before the pre-trial and trial hearings or in the "instructions to counsel."

---

of interest (the juvenile and the descriptive accounts) are transformed … in order to prepare the object for definite evaluation and disposition" (Cicourel 1968:16).

See, for instance, the following version in the instructions for the defence barrister[3] before the first Plea and Directions Hearing on the 29th of March 2001 in the Crown Court:

> Mr Vic alleged that a female who he didn't recognize went to his sister's house where he was staying at the time on the 10th of November 2000[4] about 1.10pm, this female was asking for his sister and the female then walked off. The female then returned, and the female made a threat towards his sister, and the female then approached him and allegedly head-butted him and then struck him above his left eye. The female allegedly then started picking stones up from the garden and throwing them at him. He states that a female he knows as Kim S. also stood in the garden at the time.
>
> He then alleges that he saw the female was holding a knife in her right hand, and she brought the knife down towards him, and it struck his chest. He alleges he got the knife off the female and threw it away, and then the female and Kim S. walked off and picked up the knife and then walked off towards Prince Alley, X-Town. He then went back inside, and he alleges he then saw the female return to the front garden and pick up a toy and throw it at the window.

At its very first articulation, the alibi-story was a counter-story. It was a response by the one alleged to an allegation which remained, just like the alibi, not invariable throughout the procedure. From the defence's point of view, I started to log every contribution to it in a data-sheet. The table consisted of rows for short messages and of columns for date and format plus addressee of the message. The resulting worksheet for the alibi showed more than 50 entries. Here is a small extract:

Tasks	16.1^{+2}	25.1^{+2}	26.1^{+2}	23.3^{+2}	25.4^{+2}
"Perusing Claire's report on client's statement at police"	File note				
"Fix an appointment with client to amend statement"		Diary note			
"… it would be helpful if we could meet soon …"			Letter to client		

Fig. 2: Data-sheet for Statement-Becomings

[3] The solicitor instructs the barrister on the grounds of the client's instructions. See Boon and Flood (1999) on the politically embattled division of labour between the organised professions of solicitor and barrister.

[4] I assign such fictitious dates in order to warrant those involved sufficient anonymity, while providing temporal orientation in terms of time spans and rhythms within the procedural course.

The data-sheet performed various functions: it served as a transcript of how the solicitor contributed to the alibi project; it recorded the rhythm in which the solicitor attended to this matter; it related the contributions to procedural dates and stages; it gave an overview of the various media and formats of attendance; it sketched the relations and networks set up by this casework. On the side, the log documented when and how the "alibi" became topical in the procedural course.

When did the alibi-story first enter the case-making? How did the story reach the court? The answers to these questions are less straightforward than one might wish. The story was in use at different sites at the same time. It was hyperactive. The threefold perspective on the alibi-story – as process, event, and unit – generates another *second order* story on the risks, the contingencies, and the tensions that evolve with its mobilisation.

In the following, I analyse how the story actually entered the defence-case. In an intermezzo, I integrate the investments in a provisional model of mobilisation. What is more, I complement the model by retracing the history of its decline. The story lost its central position for the defence case-in-becoming due to certain points of attack. As a conclusion to this chapter, I sketch what one could call the 'duality of mobilisation'. Every participating party, in order to deliver what would be a powerful contribution, needs to take certain risks, and is subjected to certain failures.

The rise of the alibi

First, the career of the alibi resembled a success story. The alibi, as soon as it entered the procedural stage, appeared as the rising star of the contest. It promised to overcome all allegations and all fears of punishment. Rather quickly, it became the trump card of the defence team. As such the lawyers furnished and expanded the alibi. They re-specified it, thickened it, gathered support, and made it 'fit for trial'. As an effect, the story became increasingly elaborated.

Entering the career path

In general, lawyers consider the defendant's first responses to police questioning as risky and potentially damaging. Some clients damage their case beyond repair because they are overwhelmed by the situation, because they want to rid themselves of allegations instantly (like Linda Queen), or because they do not take the case sufficiently seriously (see also chapters V and VII). Some first defence stories turn out to be (too) ambitious, as (perhaps) in the case of Linda Queen, or too lenient or casual. From my own field experience, the majority of cases are based on self-allegation only, or based on the suspect's answers during the police interview. Either way, the first response has a huge impact on what needs to be done next and what cannot be done for the client anymore. Let us briefly consider various types of first responses:

- In cases without a first defence, the solicitor starts collecting ideas on how to undermine the allegation. During conferences, the solicitor would involve the client in this destructive casework. The solicitor would suggest typical counter-arguments from pragmatic case-types, such as signs of provocation in a case of battery. The solicitor turns the client into a source of counter-facts and into an assistant to develop them.
- In cases where the accused countered the accusation, the solicitor would check the first defence for weak points, for points that the counterpart would use to challenge it. The focus of casework lies on thickening the account as well as organizing support for it. Everybody or everything that could demonstrate that the defendant's claims are feasible is welcome: eye witnesses, expert witnesses, or artefacts as silent witnesses.
- The majority of cases fall somehow in-between an extensive first defence and a blank. Here, the suspect provided some kind of defence together with some de facto admissions. This mix of positive and negative starting points complicates casework. It requires constructive *and* destructive casework. The lawyer would try to expand the counter–facts; she would try to degrade the damaging parts.

The alibi-story is coherent with the second type of first responses. Linda Queen offered in her second police interview – her first interview as the accused – a complete rebuttal of the alleged victim's account: she was not there at the time of the incidence; she was somewhere else; she was not involved in any of this. The alibi's career, thus, started before the solicitor's casework. It became available to the (later) procedure already during the police interrogation – although at that point it was just this, a reply to police questioning. This means, once the suspicion was processed as an official indictment by the CPS, her responses during the police interview became part of the procedural memory.

On the 21st of January, more than two months after the alleged incident, a police officer confronted Linda Queen with an accusation of having assaulted a young man in front of his sister's house. As we learnt before, the man called Andy Vic claimed that she punched him, head-butted him, threw stones at him, and even stabbed him. As a response to this allegation, Linda presented a minimal, but complete alibi. The co-present solicitor, Jane, considered her account as the heart of the defence-case at the time. The story entered the defence file in form of Jane's written notes. There was no reason for the solicitor to prevent Linda Queen from making such far-reaching claims. There was no reason for the solicitor not to take the alibi as her client's basic instruction: 'Represent me in this manner!'

According to the solicitor's recollection, the interviewing police officer started the questioning by confronting Linda with *the* reason for regarding her as suspect, the identification parade: "Is there anything that you would now like to tell us following that identification parade and following that identification?" Just before, the complainant had selected Linda out of nine people. It was *her* who was seen at the crime scene, and it was her that was identified later on. From now on, her answers would be framed as defence, as attempts to find a way out. In principal, there were not too many options to counter the strong accusation. (a) She could confess. (b) She could admit that she was there, but that, in fact, nothing as such had happened. (c) Additionally, she could defend herself by explaining why the 'victim' identified her. (d) Linda could bypass the damaging evidence and counter it by a separate account: an alibi.

The solicitor noted her first defence in detail. The notes turned the story into a succession of points, numbered from one to thirteen. The alibi-story started with point 6 of her statement as suspect:

6. I think it was Kim's sister who wanted some cigarettes, and so we went to get some. I remember that we went back across the wooden gate; it was on our way back to her mum's home that we passed a woman and a lad. Kim told me that the woman was called Lucy, and that she was having problems with her.
7. I thought that the lad with Lucy was her boyfriend. He was carrying some shopping.

8. Next to the wooden gate, I remember that there is a sort of stony road. I don't know where it leads, as I didn't go up it.
9. Kim, me, and the other girl, who was about 8, stood at the end of the stony road whilst Lucy and the lad were a bit further up it.
10. Kim and Lucy started to argue. The lad, who I heard was called Andy, dropped his shopping. He seemed to be aggressive. I did not join in the argument, but stood close to Kim.
11. noticed that whilst the argument was going on, a police van was stopped at the end of the lane…
12. I can't really recall how long the argument lasted. I did not join in, and I did not in anyway threaten Andy or Lucy or use any form of violence against them.
13. Following the argument, we went straight back to Kim's mother's home… (21.1^{+1})

The solicitor's draft reworked Linda Queen's answers into a narrative succession advancing from one point to the next (see chapter V).[5] The story provided characters, a course of events, and even explanations for why the main prosecution witness may have identified her. Linda's account introduced four characters: **Kim,** a friend of the accused and a probable defence witness to confirm the alibi; **Andy**, who is the complainant and the most important prosecution witness; **Lucy**, who is Andy's friend and who apparently started the argument; and **Linda** (herself), the by-standing observer and story-teller who finds herself wrongly accused. The account was peppered with seemingly unrelated details, such as the police van (point 11), the age of her friend's sister (point 9), or the gate and the stony path (point 8). Forensic psychologists would consider these as authenticity devices or as attempts to create authenticity.

The alibi works in the here and now, and it carries vast implications for the procedural course. In this double perspective we can ask first of all: What did the alibi do in the police interview? For the interviewee, the alibi provided a helpful counter-position against the accusation by the police officer. The alibi helped the accused, Linda, to save

[5] Harvey Sacks calls this "the canonical form of stories" (1978).

face, to fend off the aggressive questions, to get out of this unpleasant situation altogether. For the moment, the alibi was a helpful and effective device. More than just denying the accusation, her alibi-story offered an explanation why Andy Vic, the complainant, might have picked her out of nine. The police released her within only twenty minutes time.

The story was also productive in other ways. It involved a number of (absent) agencies and (future) activities. The alibi-story entered the casework of prosecution and defence. The police got to know how the accused will try to overturn their findings. The police decided on whether further inquiries were necessary before the case was handed over to the CPS. (They decided to interview the friend, Kim, first.) Furthermore, the defence received first material for its case and first instructions how to represent it. The solicitor communicated the story as a source of different possible strategies and further inquiries. (One of Jane's suggestions: "I pointed out to client that she needs to be able to have other witnesses in her defence…")

This productivity on both procedural sides would not have been achievable (for the professional bodies) or accessible (for this research) in the initial (spoken) form. In order to enter the defence-case, the alibi-claim had to be put into writing. Initially, this writing was not manifested in an interview protocol by the police, but in a noted and later type-written report by the solicitor. The latter replaced the question-answer play at the police station by a monologue ascribed to her client. (Of course, the ethnographer would have documented the police interview differently.) It resulted in a narrative – as if Linda told this story in one go, never interrupted, or pressurized by a police officer.[6] We will see later that turning dialogues into monologues is a core technique of producing accountable and stable case material.

As a stabilized unit, the alibi-story operated on both sides of the legal competition. It became a hard-fought "value object" (Latour 2010:140) for the adversarial contest. Two months later, the CPS turned

[6] I observed a similar transformation in German asylum hearings. In a first phase (gathering information), the executive dictated the applicant's answers as if they had come about in a fluent, uninterrupted speech. In a second phase (testing answers), the executive highlighted his questions and comments in order to indicate how to interpret the asylum seeker's answers (Scheffer 1998b).

the allegations into an official indictment. There were three counts put to Linda Queen, now defendant of a Crown Court matter:

> *Count 1*: Affray contrary to Section 3 (1) of the Public Order Act 1986, the particulars being that on the 10th day of November 2010 Linda Queen used or threatened unlawful violence towards another and her conduct was such as would cause a person a reasonable firmness present at the scene to fear for his personal safety. *Count 2*: Having an offensive weapon contrary to Section 1 (1) of the Prevention of Crime Act 1953, the particulars being that on the [...], without lawful authority of reasonable excuse, she had with her in a public place namely Prince Alley, X-town, an offensive weapon, namely a 6inch lock knife. *Count 3*: An assault occasioning actual bodily harm. The particulars of the offence are that on the [...] Linda Queen assaulted Andy Vic, thereby occasioning him actual bodily harm.

Jane, in charge of the Magistrates' Court cases, transmitted the matter to her colleague, Jack, in charge of Crown Court cases. On the 21st of February 2001, Jane wrote this note to Jack (and to the file). Jack sat just one door and office away from her: "Also note that I have put together a draft statement from what I recall she said at the police interview in her defence." Later on, Jack contacted Linda, "our client," on the basis of this draft statement, presenting it as "our" knowledge from which "we" proceed. Jack tried to involve Linda in her own case. He wrote to her on a weekly basis:

> 5.3^{+1} solicitor>client: It isn't clear from the instructions we have from you at the moment, at roughly what time you say that argument took place. I need to know whether or not you believe that argument near the iron bridge took place at around 1.10pm or whether at that time you were somewhere else completely different, and if that is the case, then we need to prepare an Alibi Notice and serve that on the Prosecution.
>
> 12.3^{+1} solicitor>client: That Alibi Notice has to be served by no later than Friday 13th April, so I need you to arrange an appointment to see me at the office as quickly as possible so we can discuss this. [...] If we do not provide the Alibi Notice then we will not be able to refer to this at the trial and that could severely harm your defence, if of course the alibi is potentially relevant.

Jack, in his letters to client, links 'her' alibi-story to formal requirements, here a procedural rule of admissibility. He links it as well to the legal matter ("your defence") that will be placed in front of the deciding body in the Crown Court.

Aiming for one (single) Notice of Alibi

For the defence solicitors, the alibi constituted the "heart of the case", the centre of their representation project. The solicitor in charge of Crown Court cases seemed, however, puzzled by the client's unreadiness to cooperate. His reminder is both, a warning ("harm your defence") and a possible explanation for her disengagement ("if of course …"). At the same time, he knew: this story could win the trial for the defence. The client would be cleared of all allegations: no charge, no prison. But all these effects were, at that time, no more than potentials of the story. The solicitor's letter to client indicated how they could be and needed to be developed. The story required, firstly, more details ("what time") and, secondly, the client's authorization ("arrange an appointment").

In order to introduce a valid alibi, the procedure demands an official 'notice' to be disclosed by the defence to the CPS three weeks before trial. This requirement follows a procedural rationale: the "rule of disclosure" prevents 'surprise attacks' in court. The defence must not surprise the adversary with fundamental counter-claims that have not been introduced before and that could not be tested in advance. Without this rule, Linda could – as a witness in court – advance her alibi claim in unexpected directions or come up with another defence. The adversary, unable to counter this claim immediately, would ask for an adjournment. The notice requirement thus allows both parties to orient themselves towards and prepare for 'likely cases.'

The approaching deadline together with the client's non-attendance caused considerable business in the solicitor's office. Not that the solicitor got nervous himself or concerned, but the lawyers, at this point in time, shared the feeling that this teenager just 'messed it up' by sheer carelessness. The deadline was present by way of diary notes that the solicitor produced as a reminder for himself to remind the client of this open task. In this sense, her failing to attend a meeting left representational sub-projects open-ended. The file stayed open; the tasks remained uncompleted. At this time, the solicitor wanted to enter a stage of text-work. If the client just allowed him to, the solicitor would phrase and rephrase the alibi-story in order to impress and discourage the opponent. Or he would explore another line of defence, if the alibi turned out to be error-prone. Instead of engaging in these activities of case-construction, the solicitor was forced to just issue letter after letter of motivation.

His letters did not make her come, not even contact the law firm. It was the Plea and Direction Hearing that made the client turn up, eventually. Shortly before the hearing, a law firm's representative and the barrister who was hired in the meantime met for a twenty minutes conference. The paralegal reported:

> 2.4^{+1} paralegal>solicitor: Complete P.D.H. form. Client inform re guilty plea at this stage. Go through evidence of .... Kim with her on iron bridge in X-town when she had confrontation with Andy. Denies ever going to his house. We need to trace Kim as alibi witness. Jack to arrange conference.

The trial hearing was adjourned to the 27th May. The defence gained time. The file reports of the solicitor's efforts to arrange a conference with Linda and the barrister. On 5th April he wrote to client: "We need to prepare a Notice of Alibi and serve that on the Crown Prosecution Service." On the very day of the deadline, the client finally turned up in the law firm. About five months after the story's first appearance at the police station, the client instructed the defence to represent her accordingly. The solicitor prepared a draft version of the "Notice of Alibi":

> 13.4^{+1}: ... At about 11.00am, Kim approached the Defendant and then they returned to the house where Kim had come from, which was 10 Oxford Street, X-town. It was approximately a 5 or 10 minute walk to the house, and so they would have got to the house at about 11.05am/11.10am. The Defendant then spent one hour at the house until just after 12.00pm. At the house at that time was Kim, the slightly younger sister Kristy (aged about 11), Kim's elder sister, her boyfriend whose name the Defendant does not know, Kristy's father who, at the time, was the boyfriend of Kim's mother (Julia). ... The Defendant stayed at the house for about one hour until about 12.05pm/12.10pm. At that point the Defendant, Kim and Kristy left the house because Kristy wished to buy some cigarettes. After purchasing the cigarettes the three of them ...
>
> Dated ...
>
> Signed
>
> [plus Law Firm/Address]
>
> To: The Court
>
> To: The Crown Prosecution Service

Compared to the first version written by the duty solicitor, this draft version of the alibi-story shows a number of transformations. (1) It is rendered 'official' and 'formal' by a title: "Notice of Alibi." This frame demands special attention and reading. It promises certain relevance and accepts certain duties. It is complemented by the formalities at the end: date, signature, firm, etc. The story is turned into a formal declaration. (2) Apart from being simply much longer – its length doubled compared to the first version — it now offers a multitude of details. It includes time propositions, more characters, places, artefacts, activities, etc. This version seems less like a story told here and now, but rather like a report that is carefully put together in order to anchor the alibi claim in the 'world out there' (Potter 1996:chapter 6). Some of these details are obviously added up. They do not derive from detached memory work, but from engaged calculations. Some passages read like solutions to a math word problem or like a completed cloze text. They resemble inferences from initial hypotheses.

Despite all the details, or because of the necessity to arrive at a detailed account, the solicitor complained that the alibi lacked exactly this: facts, precision, substantiation. The lack of temporal specification even made him prepare two versions of the "Notice of Alibi." Each version completed the alibi-story from a temporal starting point: 10.50am or 11.50am:

> 13.4[+1] Solicitor>paralegal: I enclose a copy of the two alibi statements which I had to draft at the moment because Linda is a little vague as to the time that she first went to X-town on the day concerned. It was either 10.50am or 11.50am. She cannot be more specific, unfortunately. I have not yet provided the details of the alibi to the prosecution and I intend to speak to Counsel first before I do so. I know that I was supposed to do it by 13 April but if need be I will send it on 16 April, and I do not think the CPS will have any great objections to that.

In a file note, the solicitor explicated the problems caused by each version and their respective temporal specifications. He entered two alternative time-series: the one given in the version above and the other moving the course of events by exactly one hour. The facts, it becomes clear, are inferred, not remembered. They are constructed in order to fit a wider network of anchors, such as bus timetables or substantiated claims by the adversary party. Each of the two versions carried different implications for the allegations:

> 13.4[+1] file note: Therefore, any Alibi Notice will be a little complicated because we are unsure of the timing where Linda was. If we take it on the earlier time version then at 1.10pm when Linda is supposed to have been on Queens Drive, X-town according to the statement of Andy Vic, she would probably have been back at Oxford Street after they had got the

> cigarettes and had the argument with Mr. Vic and his sister. If we take the later time version, again bearing in mind the prosecution allegation that we were on Queens Drive at 1.10pm, the alibi will have to be provided by probably Kim and her little sister because at that time we would probably have been walking to get the cigarettes and then shortly thereafter coming across Vic and his sister on the iron bridge.

For the time being, the solicitor could not settle for one version. He delegated this forensic dimension to the law enforcement agencies. He reported in a letter to his client that he served "two Notices of Alibi upon the Crown Court and the CPS". In the same letter, he expressed hope that the 'exact time'-issue will be resolved in due course:

> 16.4+1 solicitor>client: The police now have to duty interview any prospective alibi witnesses and therefore they will, I think, first be speaking to Kim and also her mother. Hopefully Kim will at least confirm what she has said to our representative and what you say in your statement.

The solicitor managed to fulfil the formal requirements of the Alibi Notice, announcing it on time – and he did so under conditions of uncertainty. He issued two versions without being able to choose one. He left it to the other side to find out. By doing so, the alibi-story caused further police inquiries. The official notice turned the alibi-story into a probable resolution of the matter. The police was supposed to inquire into the story's details as if it were just as probable as the victim's version.

The story in the "Instructions to Counsel"

The alibi's career towards official disclosure was full of twists and turns. The story was constantly in need for re-specification and additional support. The solicitor, from his bureau, had to align more agencies in the course of the story's composition/employment for the coming trial. He had to bring the minimal defence ensemble for English Crown Courts – consisting of solicitor, client and defence barrister – into being. The latter is hired for the Crown Court trial as the official voice of the case, as its certified representative.

To capture this phase of casework, we have to zoom out. My account resumes the story's career three weeks before the not-yet-adjourned trial. The solicitor was hastily lining up client and barrister. Again, the alibi-story played a focal role here. It somehow forced the three to agree on a central issue: what is the case. The deadline for disclosure ahead, the solicitor intensified the information flow with the barrister's office (and the Counsel's clerk). He handed over *a* bundle of papers comprising the printed and drafted alibi-story along with a copy of the official indictment and Jane's initial summaries of the police interview. The solicitor informed the barrister in a way that did not simply transmit the story but promoted it as *the* key element of "our case". Would the barrister consent to this high ranking? Two weeks before the two Notices of Alibi were issued to court and CPS, the solicitor presented another version in his "instructions."

> 28.3[+1] solicitor>barrister: She was interviewed at X-town Police Station in the presence of X from instructing Solicitors. She confirmed that she had been in X-town and met her friend Kim, and that they had been to Kim's house, and they then went out with her little sister to buy some cigarettes. She stated that they came across a male and female, and an argument ensued between that male and female and Kim and her sister. She stated that the male involved took an aggressive stance. She denied that there had been any violence whatsoever between her and the male. She believed the male to be called Andy, and Counsel will have noted the aggrieved in this allegation is Andy Vic who on the 10th November was staying with his sister who lives at 13 Queens Drive, X-town. That is on the main Council housing estate in X-town, and our client has indicated she would not go onto that estate willingly because she has an ex-boyfriend who lives on the estate and would not wish to bump into him.

The instructions did not just aim at delivering necessary information. They, moreover, opened up the opportunity to test the story in a protected and friendly environment. In this way, some points were highlighted that benefited the story's usability. For instance, it was mentioned that the "aggressive guy" was in fact identical with the aggrieved.

What is worth emphasizing is that, by transporting the alibi-story via 'the instructions', solicitor and barrister managed to synchronize their views on the case. Here again, the story showed its productivity: it allowed the lawyers to refer to and work on a shared object. Solicitor and barrister could, on this basis, deliberate *strategic* (the positioning of the story in the case) as well as *tactical* questions (the steps to strengthen the story). The story, however, was demanding as well. Once chosen as being at the core of the case, the story imposed some practical steps to take:

> 28.3[+1] solicitor>barrister: We have asked our client whether she can provide us with any information that might assist *us* in tracing Kim to see if she was prepared to give a statement. We appreciate her assistance is

> perhaps unlikely, but in any event client has not provided any information which could lead to tracing her.

From now on, *the case* was somehow established as a shared concern between the two professionals. This does not mean, however, that the defence ensemble was fully integrated. Or, to put it differently: the ensemble's integration was apparently not completed yet. At least, this was a complaint made by the solicitor to the barrister (perhaps to excuse some delays in his casework). In any case, there was, from the solicitor's point of view, a lack of assistance by the client. Without Linda it seemed difficult to find Kim, the only and vital alibi witness.

And just to remember, there was not much time left: within two weeks time the Alibi Notice had to be disclosed. Should the defence announce an alibi without an alibi witness? Would such a case be strong enough to withstand the allegations and to convince the jurors? Because of the strong claims to be mobilized, the story seemed in need of social support. At least, this was the view taken by the two lawyers continually assessing 'the score' in the light of the coming hearing.

The story in the "draft statement" of the alibi witness

The file gives an idea about the difficulties and efforts to meet the potential alibi witness. These solicitor's notes were produced prior to and after the disclosure of the "Notice of Alibi":

> 29.3^{+1} Attendance note: Enquiries into the present whereabouts of Kim and to endeavour to obtain an Alibi Statement from her will charge max. of £100
>
> 13.4^{+1} file note: Tracing agent to locate possible alibi witness after receiving LSC authority [legal aid permission]
>
> 16.6^{+1} file note: Agent found Kim and could talk to her

Because of the deadline, solicitor and barrister took the risk of publishing the Notice of Alibi without getting hold of a statement by the alibi witness. (The deadline, an effect of *the procedural rules*, interfered quite severely with the casework. It determined the value of 'trumps', meaning their usability in trial.[7]) Solicitor and barrister took a chance at

[7] Such interferences set the conditions for mobilisation and might provide concrete angles to compare different legal systems. One could ask, for instance, how such interferences matter, how they contribute to the mobilisation in question, how they co-produce narratives, and how they inflict silence. Such a view on the use of legal rules as 'active' standards for performances seems useful to compare criminal trials.

introducing the unsupported alibi in order to keep the alibi defence in the game. Moreover, they were quite certain that the alibi witness would enter a statement before the court hearing. After all, they just followed the client's instructions – and the alibi-story was just this: Linda's instruction to her legal representatives.

After some failed appointments with and searches by the police, it was the law firm's paralegal who eventually got hold of Kim. She made a statement to him (not to the police). Her account entered the defence file and circulated in the defence team.

> 7.8^{+1} paralegal>solicitor: There is a wooden gate on x-road, which has a footpath on it. When on this footpath we met a girl called Lucy and her boyfriend, whose name I do not know. I had trouble with Lucy on previous occasions and we ended up arguing… But at no time, did I or Linda assault anybody…

The alibi gained persuasive power by this version. Kim re-narrated the alibi-story and used its main indices: names, sites, sequence. One can call this multiplication 'proof', or better 'confirmation'. The account seems to confirm the alibi because it resembles it (without being a copy) and because it is supportive (without being a friendly turn). It seems even better than the original alibi:

> 13.8^{+1} solicitor>barrister's clerk: Counsel will recall that two alibi notices were filed in respect of our client, the first one on the assumption that she had arrived in X-town on the day concerned at about 10.50 am and the second on the basis of her arriving in X-town at about 11.50. She could not recall the precise time of her arrival but it was either of those two times. Counsel will see from Kim's statement that this is consistent with the later alibi. Kim confirms that she met our client at 12.00 pm in X-town and then walked her to 10 Oxford Street.

The solicitor appreciated Kim's contribution as helpful evidence on behalf of the defence. Despite this supportive evidence and according to the "burden of proof", it was not on the defence to prove its case anyway. The following file entries reflect the lawyers' positive assessment of the alibi and their willingness to invest in it:

> 13.8^{+1} solicitor>client: Kim's statement pretty much confirms the alibi statement prepared on your behalf last year. She has indicated that you arrived in X-town on the day concerned at around 12 pm …
>
> 13.8^{+1} solicitor>Clerk to Barrister: I enclose a copy of the statement that she has given to representative. Our client's alibi statement is fairly consistent with Kim's statement.

> 27.9^{+1} solicitor>Clerk to Barrister: I do think we should send this to the CPS but perhaps Counsel will telephone me and confirm he agrees.
>
> 5.10^{+1} solicitor>Kim: I would be grateful to receive a response from you as a matter of urgency as to whether you can confirm you will attend Court for hearing of the above matter.
>
> 1.11^{+1} solicitor>CPS: Enclose a copy of a statement we have taken from Kim, you will recall that in the past Police has been attempting to obtain a statement from this witness but without success.

The solicitor, Jack, was convinced that Kim's statement would make a good ally for the upcoming debate in court. He was confident that with such support the prosecution-case looked rather feeble. By disclosing this statement to the CPS, he did not only announce additional evidence to be presented in court, but also exercised the strength of the defence-case. There was, a few weeks before trial, a scent of triumph in the air: Will the prosecution give in? Will they surrender? In any case, up to this point the story granted the defence a promising position for the upcoming trial.

Intermezzo

In the law firm's office, the alibi-story underwent several transformations which are worth recalling at this point of our linear reconstruction. The story was rendered relevant in legal terms, by adding more details and by ascribing authorship. Similar to Latour's semiotic approach on "science in action" (1987), "circulating reference" (1999a) and in his legal ethnography on the "Conseil d'Etat" (2010), one can continue re-specifying the operations necessary to accomplish relevance. The story's co-authors expanded its spatiotemporal reach. They used fundamental operations that, at the same time, marked career stages of the alibi:

- Turning talk into text: Oral responses were turned into text. As (copied) text, the story became available at different sites simultaneously. Participants referred to the story on paper – as authentic representation – in various encounters and for several local purposes.
- Reframing dialogical turns: Linda's responses at the police station were converted into a linear monologue, separated from its earlier discursive neighbours. The original statement was polished towards fact. It was purified and freed from contextual ballast.
- Addressing various others: The solicitor could forward the monological text in various directions. The solicitor used versions of

the written story to address, first of all, the various members of the defence team and to keep them updated. Later versions were reserved for the hostile environment, here the adversary party and the legal authority.

- Organising support: The story gained weight through "allies" or "friends" (Latour 1987:31) brought in by the instructing solicitor. The end of its social isolation (Ibid., 33) made it harder for opponents to reject the alibi. The opponent had to invest more in order to reject claims.

A diagram displays these operations as stages of mobilisation. They are necessary to turn a local account into a lasting story. Mobilisation appears as an orderly sequence of prescriptions and provisionally reached properties:

Demands of a story's mobilisation	***Investments into***
(1) Obliterate its design: "*This is how the story was told all along!*"	***Authorship***
(2) Give details: "The story is about the world out there!"	***Factuality***
(3) Integrate all details: "*It makes sense!*"	***Coherence***
(4) Relate it to the debate: "*This and this is important!*"	***Relevancy***
(5) Guarantee it personally: "*I pledge, it is the truth!*"	***Accountability***
(6) Hold it: "*The same is true tomorrow!*"	***Duration***
(7) Back it up: "*I have witnesses!*"	***Support***
(8) Involve expert witnesses: "*This is possible!*"	***Evaluation***
(9) Make it circulate outside the ensemble: "*That's our case!*"	***Publication***
(10) Stick to your account: "*All along I said that ...*"	***Repetition***

Fig. 3. Mobilisation as Accumulation

Following the defence's point of view, we recounted a series of investments into the story's properties such as authorship, coherence, out-there-ness, concreteness, etc. The investments were made on the procedural backstage: at the solicitor's desk, in the law firm's conference room, in a Crown Court's interview room, or, perhaps, out there 'round the blocks'. Mobilisation is a sequential production in which interim states provide the grounds for further investments:

> (1/2) Before creating modules, the account is presented as a monologue (Authorship). (2/3) Before thickening the account (Factuality), a story-line is construed (Coherence). (1-4) This background is used to emphasize what seems relevant for the trial (Relevancy). (5/6/9) Before anything is fixed (Duration) and disclosed (Publication), the account

seeks authorization (Accountability). (7/9) The team tried hard to organize support for the story before its publication. In our case, the defence did succeed only after the disclosure of two Notices of Alibi. (8/9) Before disclosure (Publication), the story is presented to the barrister. Here the defence position receives a kind of evaluation, rehearsal, or review. (9/10) Once published, the account should be used as a draft for all coming applications (Repetition). In that way, the published version is binding.

The story's weight built up stepwise. It was nurtured by methodical investments. Core investments – into authorship, coherence, factuality and so forth – were considered, tried and implemented before the story was allowed to circulate outside the defence ensemble. Only after being assessed as sufficiently strong and solid, the story was allowed to represent the case 'outside'. Case-making, thus, involves and avoids certain social circles[8]:

(1) A narrow 'confidential' circle includes the defence ensemble: the solicitor in charge, the represented client, and the hired barrister. In our case, the three met several times before the trial hearing. The narrow circle can be selectively expanded by satellites such as eye witnesses or expert witnesses, etc.
(2) A wider 'affiliated' circle comprises the law firm's staff including secretary, paralegal, and the researcher. The members of this circle would, in a broader sense, contribute to and, at least, show general interest in the current state of the case.
(3) An even wider 'hostile' circle comprises the solicitor and the barrister representing the CPS. They are expected to examine the story critically. Before the hearing, this circle is reached by means of disclosure, by preliminary conferences, and by plea bargaining sessions.
(4) The widest 'public' circle is reached once the case enters the court stage. Here, the open court including the jury and the audience get to know the case-stories plus the arguments for certain rule application and decision-making.

Case-making is not simply about expanding and extending the story's impact; it is at the same time about disciplined "impression management" (Goffman 1959), about restricting information flows and about "information control" (Goffman 1963).

[8] Paul Rock portrayed the various social circles of a Crown Court (1993) as an organisation in great detail. I refer to the social circles of the Crown Court *procedure*, including pre-trial and trial.

Why are lawyers so cautious? Do they aim for some extra 'legal aid'-money? Do they apply some kind of professional overcare? Or are there procedural mechanisms that lie at the heart of this? In order to grasp the *duality of mobilisation*, we need to move on from the success story to the story's decline. The decline leads us to the threats, to worst case scenarios, to the risks of mobilisation. For the practitioners, this 'dark side' of mobilisation is more than just thought-provoking. It is real and it is demanding. It shapes the story to the same extent as does the prospect of sheer triumph.

The story's decline

At this junction of the story's career, the alibi became the "heart of the case" for the defence. It was individualised and officially introduced. It was fixed and broadly available. It was supported (by a witness), acknowledged (by the client) and promising (to the defence ensemble). The story, this was the shared expectation, would play well its assigned role on the decisive procedural stage: as *the* legal argument that outweighs the allegations. The defence had, in light of the recent developments, good reasons to count on the alibi. However, the story's career was not yet completed. The story got involved in more contingent encounters. Or put more precisely, the story was forced into the limelight of procedure. It had to be staged in open court.

The ultimate stages of mobilisation put the story and those who counted on it under enormous pressure. In the subsequent steps, the story was exposed to hostility, critique and risks – all implicated in what I will conceptualize later as the duality of mobilisation. Latour's "science in action" (1987) points in the right direction. For Bruno Latour, counter-forces and undermining manoeuvres are integral features of scientific reasoning. In an analogous manner, solicitor and barrister estimated potency and weakness of their case 'so far' in the light of expectable counter-attacks. The lawyers knew pretty well what to expect from the competing colleagues as representatives of the adversary party.

Seeking and missing support

The investments into the alibi were proportionate to its promise. The alibi-story was considered the strongest weapon in the hands of the defence. It offered the strongest conclusions in favour of the defendant: 'She was not there!'; 'She could not have done it!' Facing an effective alibi, the prosecution would be forced to give in: "We rest our case!" The court would withdraw the charges. But Linda's alibi did not lead to anything like this. Rather the opposite happened: the alibi disappeared, faded away, or rather it withered. What went wrong?

At first, the alibi's decline was not more than professional scepticism. The solicitor came across a suspicious point in the "list of unused items" during one of his file sessions. The CPS had disclosed the list according to the "rules of disclosure." Put simply, the caseworker for the prosecution published a list of all materials obtained for the detailed alibi claim. The solicitor checked the served list and found "item 6: tape of police interview with Kim S." He ordered it, while being unsure about its effects on the matter. It could be relevant. He considered it his duty to ask for it:

> 7.9^{+1} file note: perusing item 6 from unused material schedule received from CPS and seeing that it relates to Kim's taped interview regarding this matter but unsure whether the notes were prepared by the Police Officer. We will need to get the tape of that and get it transcribed before the trial because it may contain things that help us but it may contain things that harm us. Need to write to CPS urgently about that.

The solicitor did not know what to expect. He did not know whether the item would bring boon or bane. He feared it but he considered it of potential. In his file note, he justified his demand note to the prosecution in general terms. He needed to know what the prosecution already knew. He needed to close the information gap. How did Jack obtain "item 6?" Disclosure, while being a basic procedural right, turned out as tricky. The solicitor had to try hard, over a relatively long period of time.[9] It took persistence to obtain the item:

> 24.8^{+1} CPS>solicitor: (disclosing) the list of unused items
>
> 7.9^{+1} file note: perusing item 6 … seeing that it relates to Kim's taped interview regarding this matter
>
> 27.9^{+1} solicitor>barrister: alibi witness interviewed by police shortly after the incident

[9] In one of the governmental reports on the Criminal Justice System the following sample could easily serve as an illustration of the often-criticized 'time-consuming and inefficient legal economy'. However, economy might provide such evaluations based on a misleading paradigm. There might be some strategic moves involved that decide upon the speed and direction of responses.

28.9[+1] solicitor>CPS: Could you please let us know whether you are to serve any further documentation in light of the content of that statement

6.10[+1] Diary note: Has CPS responded to recent correspondence? *No* [hand written]

12.10[+1] CPS>solicitor: I am satisfied that to the best of my knowledge and belief there is no further prosecution material requiring disclosure to you at this stage.

8.1[+2] solicitor>CPS: We do not appear to have received a response from you to the second paragraph of our letter…

10.2[+2] CPS>solicitor: Please find enclosed a copy of item 6 of the Unused Schedule as requested by yourself.

7.3[+2] File note: Perusing item 6 from unused material schedule received from CPS and seeing that it relates to Kim's taped interview. […] It may contain things that help us, but it may contain things that harm us.

8.3[+2] solicitor>CPS: Item 6 are hand written notes regarding the Police interview of Kim, but it is unclear whether the notes have been prepared by one of the interviewing Officers or by Kim's solicitor, who was present. We would be grateful if you could supply us with a copy of the taped interview, as there clearly may be evidence within that evidence that assists our case.

3.5[+2] Diary note: Perusing transcript of taped interview between Kim and Police to see how different her comments are in that interview compared to the alibi statement she has given us and seeing that her comments confirm that our client is guilty of these offences.

It took the defence more than 7 months (from 28.9[+1] to 3.5[+2]) to get hold of the mysterious "item 6." Shortly before trial, the solicitor received the transcript of the police interview dating back to the 17.11[+1] (which was only one week after the alleged incident and 1½ years before the trial hearing). The solicitor found himself confronted not just with another version of Linda's alibi-story – about "the gate," the walk back home, or the incidental argument with this aggressive guy later known as Andy –, but with an independent account. A new story, so to speak. Kim entered that account as a response to her being interrogated as a suspect "of conspiring to commit an assault:"

PC Cast your mind back to the 10th…
Kim Linda started begging to my mum and what she'd done and that, saying that she'd head-butted him, scratched him with the knife, stuff like that, and then she put the knife on the table and police knocked in the door, then they come in, they got the knife and

> that, Linda was hiding behind the door, the kitchen door, then I had to tell the police it was my knife… (17.11^{+1} [received 3.5^{+2}])

No gate, no argument, no alibi – and a disaster for the defence. The solicitor had to face a kind of "surprise attack" by his own (imagined) defence ensemble. His (former) 'alibi witness' did not just miss out some details. She squarely contradicted her friend's version: she reported that actually Linda committed the assault and how Linda started hiding and manipulating incriminating evidence. According to Kim, relevant 'irregular case-making' took place before the police entered the scenery. "Item 6" turned out to be disastrous: the alibi-story lost its backing; the defence lost its best witness; the defence was confronted with new evidence against the defendant.

> 4.5^{+2} solicitor>paralegal: … this is not very helpful and in effect points the finger straight at Linda as being responsible for this offence. Kim of course is our alibi witness, and therefore I have grave concerns as to her ability to help us even if she does turn up at court next Tuesday. I have not told Linda about it as I did not want her heading straight to Kim's house and doing something she might regret.

The same day and despite this devastating evaluation, the solicitor went on seeking supportive evidence for Linda's version.

> 4.5^{+2} solicitor>barrister: With reference to our client's alibi defence, I enclose a copy of the relevant bus timetable confirming times of buses from X to Y and back.

Why did Jack still invest in the alibi after the devastating "item 6?" Why did he not give in and recommend a guilty plea? The reason was given in the same letter. It concerned the open status of Kim's statement and the question of how it could become relevant for the trial. At this point, relevance resembled an increasingly technical question. See as well the solicitor's comment in a letter to the barrister about the police interview with Kim:

> 4.5^{+2} solicitor>barrister: I do not know if the prosecution are aware of the content of this interview, although I suspect the police must have listened to it and presumably disregarded the evidence, given Kim's apparent lack of credibility. Obviously, we have not sent a copy of the transcript to the Crown.

Jack concludes:

> 4.5^{+2} solicitor>clerk to barrister: Linda assures me that Kim will be at Court because she will want to help out her friend and therefore I have

> not issued a witness statement. But having read this transcript I am wondering now whether it will do more harm than good in getting Kim to Court. [...] Obviously, if she did give evidence and support Linda's alibi and then was cross-examined regarding the comment she made to the police in interview, then her credibility would be destroyed.

The adversaries seem to play hide-and-seek. 'Who does know what' becomes a matter of professional speculation.

The loss of the alibi in open court

So far, we collected versions of the story and investments into it. The resulting career appeared as a linear developmental process: a success story. Only now, when entering the court stage, are we reminded of another aspect that was only referred to in passing: the account's eventfulness; its local contingency; its situated nature. The defence, in order to attach full procedural value to the alibi, had to stage it vis-à-vis judge and jury. The alibi would fully count only as a witness testimony standing cross-examination.

The new quality of the court stage, one might assume, lies in this: from the stepwise preparation-process of the alibi, we move over to a single moment of oral examination. However, the shift from producing an account to consuming it as a script is not abrupt and total. The alibi was received as a representation already before: at the police, in the Notice of Alibi, or on the way to court when the barristers exchanged positions in order to evaluate the shared grounds for a plea bargaining. At all these instances, the users developed the account *and* consumed it; they invested in it *and* utilized it. The extra quality of staging lies, I argue, in the altered weight of the account: it was no longer a promise that can be withdrawn. The alibi, once being articulated from the witness-stand, passed a point of no return. There was no way to render it irrelevant or non-existent; once staged, it was out there in the court's open.

> Does this explain why Linda seemed hesitant to attend court at all? She told the paralegal on the morning of trial that "she has fractured her wrist over the weekend and cannot be at Court." Ten minutes later the paralegal phoned the solicitor to learn that "she has now arrived at Court." (8.5^{+2})

Which role did the alibi-story finally play in court? How did the defence relate to it after it was so seriously contradicted by the only available alibi witness? Did the defence use it at all? And if so, how did the defence team deliver it in front of judge, jury, and opponent? The allegation-story made its first appearance in the trial hearing during the "friendly examination" of the 'victim'. The prosecuting barrister had called and examined his (only) witness, Andy Vic, who was subsequently cross-examined by the defence barrister. The witness found himself positioned in the witness stand vis-à-vis judge and jury:

Fig. 4: The Crown Court from the Witness Stand. Photograph from http://lcjb.cjsonline.gov.uk/area4/images/court_room_ijw.JPG. © Crown

Now the (only) defence witness, the defendant, was called into the witness stand. The defence barrister's questions followed the story as instructed:

Q And did your route take you across a gate?
A Yeah, there's a big wooden gate.
Q Was there any incident on your way to the shop?
A No, not on the way there.
Q Did anything happen as you came back?
A Kim bumped into some woman she knew and started an argument with her, they were just having a big argument.
Q Right, just pause there a moment. (8.5^{+2})

The defence barrister and the defendant, Linda, unrolled the account in synchronized roles. The barrister directed the re-narration. His questions provided orientation to both, details and episodes: the gate, the walk, the incident – and what happened at these spots. The questions led Linda to right answers ("And did your route take you across a gate?"), while her answers ("No, not on the way there.") establish grounds for the next question. This technique of collaborative narration minimised the risk of 'bad' surprises, whether deriving from forgetfulness, confusion, or second thoughts. The written and instructed story in the hand of the barrister guided his directions. As a script, the story contributed to the fine-tuned and well-integrated defence ensemble.

After Linda had 'recalled' the quarrel by the wooden gate successfully, the barrister moved on by asking for certain details of this incident:

> Q All right, and can you remember any of the people who were with that lady?
> A I remember there was a lad there, he wasn't pretty … he was pretty young, he was about our age so … [After her going about her glasses that she didn't wear that day.]
> Q All right. Well, tell us about the person who was with the lady Kim was arguing with; the lad. Did he have anything in his hands for example?
> A He had shopping bags in his hands. He'd been … it looked like they'd all been shopping and he was quite big, about our height, about our age and he just .. he went to come forward towards Kim.
> Q Yes.
> A But he got grabbed hold of by the other woman and went 'No just leave it', and they just carried on arguing and they left and we left. (8.5^{+2})

The alibi reached the court but lacked the support of any other witness. This lack caused some severe adjustments. The account did not, as it had done earlier, provide multiple links to the characters (the name "Andy" remained unmentioned), the location and the time of the incident. The delivered alibi did not launch any of its implicated and proposed counter-attacks, for instance, regarding the complainant's involvement. Shortly after Linda briefly assured that she never went to the scenery of the crime ("I don't even know where it is!"), the barrister concluded: "Your honour, that's all the evidence called on behalf of the defendant."

What impression did the alibi-story make in court? It looked rather feeble, more like a timid suggestion than a self-confident and founded alibi. Because the story was deprived of its strong claims, there was no need for the adversary to challenge it. Instead of asking tricky questions or trapping the witness in inconsistencies, the prosecutor used the cross-examination to introduce another version of 'what really happened'. The barrister consolidated the contradictions between the versions of defence witness and prosecution witness. He evoked a single version, of course in favour of the prosecution-case:

> Q Well, let me suggest this to you; what happened when you got to X-town was that you found out, didn't you, about this argument between Andy's sister Lucy and Kim?
> A No.
> Q You weren't the witness to any argument between them, you were told of an argument?
> A I was?
> Q You were told.
> A I am—.
> Q Of a dispute between them, weren't you? And you decided that you'd lend a hand in that, didn't you? (8.5^{+2})

The defendant denied the hypotheses, but her denial dwindled. Once in cross-examination, Linda seemed incapable of finding a way back to her original account. The barrister's imputations exploited the unfounded state of her claims. He offered a counter-narrative without founding it himself. Interestingly enough, the prosecuting barrister kept the alibi-story in play. While neglecting the overall scenario, he picked up on selected elements: on names, actions, places. He undermined the story's integrity by way of deconstruction and by singling out and reinterpreting single features, such as the encounter by the gate. But the prosecuting barrister did not stop there. Moving on, he confronted Linda with statements from her first police interrogation one day after the alleged incident (and one day after Kim's first interview). Now, the barrister was attacking Linda's personal integrity directly. See the following series of "yes/no interrogatives" (Raymond 2003):

> Q And when the police came to see you the next day and arrested you, you lied to them.
> Q And you followed that up with a number of lies, haven't you?
> Q Contents of both those interviews, in fact, are lies, aren't they? (8.5^{+2})

The barrister stated that the defendant was lying throughout the investigation. He did so three times in a row. What appeared formally as a series of questions, came across as a staccato of allegations. The prosecuting barrister made vast use of the rhetorical device of repetition.

He rubbed it in, so to speak. His repetitive use of "lie" and "lying" was meant to leave a lasting impression on the jurors. He used repetition along with emphatic speech and simple wording, all designed for the Crown Court jury as the "overhearing audience" (Atkinson and Drew 1979) in this highly specific "persuasion situation" (Frederick 1987).

Weakened as it was, the story was not elevated to the final rounds of the trial hearing. It did not enter the defence barrister's final address to the jury. Instead, he simply reminded of the limitations of the prosecution-case in light of "the burden of proof:"

> It's not the defence's job to prove that their version is right, still less is it the defence's job to say what actually did happen outside that house no. 11 Queens Drive. If anything did happen, it's not for us to say what it was or who is involved in it. It's for the Crown to prove it and that's absolutely fundamental.
>
> In my respectful submission, after you've looked at all the evidence in this case you're going to be concerned to put it at its lowest, at the quality of the evidence that they have been able to produce from the one witness they have put before you. (8.5^{+2})

Towards the duality of mobilisation

The story appeared for the last time[10] in the judge's summary that he gave just before the jury retired to the jury's room to consider the verdict. How did the story appear? The judge did not specify the story's status or weight for the debate at hand. He did not use the word "alibi:"

> They went to the local shop to get some cigarettes. This involved going through a gate. On the way back, there was this confrontation, and she says that there was a lad there who was about our age. She did not know him, she didn't say that she'd ever seen him before. She gave a description but that's all. And there was a confrontation. They appeared to all have shopping bags, she said, and a bit of shouting going on. She stood behind Kim and didn't become involved at all. It lasted, the incident lasted about 5 minutes apparently, and then they went back to Kim's house. Then she got the bus to go home, and she was in X-town altogether for about one hour, that is what she says. (8.11^{+2})

[10] That is, for the "last time" *in* the procedure. I do not know much about the time after and the arenas outside the procedural sites: the local community, the media, the homes and (former) friendships of those involved.

At this point, the story had lost its force. Once the "heart of the case" and *the* great white hope of the defence ensemble, the alibi-story ended up as a marginal note. No longer did it attract attention. Former supporters, current users, and future decision-makers lost interest. Now it was Linda who found herself unsupported. The paralegal reported the same day: "Linda was found guilty by the jury as they obviously did not believe her evidence." In the later sentencing hearing (8.12^{+2}) she was sentenced to 12 months youth custody for the assault. Under normal conditions she would serve 6 months.

What can the story's rise and fall teach us about adversarial case-making? The story is far from being innocent, which is what its recipients knew all along. The story is far from being uncomplicated or natural, which is what their designers knew all along. The story is far from being chosen at will, which is what its users increasingly realise in the procedural course. Therefore, the rise and fall of the alibi demonstrates the duality of mobilisation. In order to specify this duality, I refer to the diagram that I introduced in the intermezzo.

Figure no. 3 displayed stages of mobilisation aiming at certain properties. The investments are ordered sequentially: later ones require properties that are provided by former investments. In this way, figure 3 illustrated an accumulation. Only the story's fall irritated this developmental vision. The story-production seemed no longer mastered and under control. The following diagram, therefore, highlights that the investments are under threat. Claims are only temporarily stabilized. They are at risk of being undermined by the adversary. Each stage of mobilisation exposes itself to certain attacks:

Compared to figure no. 3, the left and the middle column remain identical. The left column still shows the progression of story-production. The middle column still shows the properties that caseworkers invest in. I add the right column in order to identify the immanent risks of undermining. The central point is: adversarial case-making pushes the parties to take risks and to anticipate these risks before the publication of the account.

The columns can be read as a confrontation of arguments and counter-arguments. Such reading, however, would ignore the temporal dimension: the situated moves of protecting or exposing claims in relation to the adversary. The columns and arrows point at the eventfulness and process-character of the account, to the stop-and-go-traffic of legal procedure. What is more, the investments on each side happen in reverse order. This is why the *long arrows* on each flank point in

How to mobilise an account?	***Conditions of impact***	**How to undermine the given account?**
Blackbox the account's production: "*That is the story as it was told!*"	***Authorship***	Identify intentions (centring authorship) or collaboration (de-centring authorship)
Isolate modules and make them fit: *"It makes sense!"*	***Coherence***	Show that phrase A does not fit to phrase B or C
Give details: *"The story is about the world out there!"*	***Factuality***	Prove that the *when, where, who and what* do not fit to a 'given reality'
Relate it to the debate: "*This and this is important!*"	***Relevancy***	Show that claims do not matter
Guarantee it personally: "*I swear, it is the truth!*"	***Accountability***	Question the character of 'the author'
Hold it: "*The same is true tomorrow!*"	***Duration***	Use later findings against the 'old' account
Back it up: *"I have witnesses!"*	***Support***	Repeat all points and contrast all versions
Make it circulate within the ensemble; test and improve the claims	***Rehearsal***	Unmask the construction of evidence and seek the weak link
Make it circulate outside the ensemble: "*That's our case!*"	***Publication***	**Start challenging the inherent claims: Look for the weak links!**
Stick to your account: *"I always said that …"*	***Replication***	Contrast all versions and produce discrepancy

Fig. 5: Duality of Mobilisation

different directions: the mobilisation heads forward to establish a solid case while the adversary forces start challenging already attained qualities. The *short arrows* on the left stress the inner rehearsals/pre-tests conducted *before* the account is allowed to leave the secure environment of the defence team. Here, self-critique checks the account for flaws, weaknesses, contradictions, and so forth – before it is 'too late'. The *short arrows on the right* follow the undermining forces that are fully activated (only) after disclosure. As soon as the story is fully revealed, the CPS can do now what the defence did previously with the initial accusation: they can look for weak links. From now on until trial, the adversary's undermining forces are at work.

The alibi-story shows the duality of mobilisation, not because of its decline in the second part of the chapter, but because of the lawyers' prospective risk-assessment and risk-management already in the first half. There is apparently much awareness for the vulnerabilities of procedural accounts and for the needs to protect them. Practitioners share a sensitivity for the fact that claims integrated in a story tend to stabilize each other – and, if undermined, destabilize each other similar to a chain reaction. The alibi is mobilised *and* at risk, which links procedure closely to contingency, both conceptually and empirically.

The adversarial procedure demands risk-taking. The duality of mobilization provides us with answers for questions such as these: Why did the defence take the risk of entering the alibi without any supportive witness? Why did they enter details in the Notice of Alibi without knowing for sure? In order to count (at all), Linda's alibi had to go down the entire procedural course: it was documented, drafted, signed, distributed, disclosed, publicly narrated, etc. With these demands, the procedure multiplies the costs for making claims and multiplies the points of attack, which are the opportunities for challenging them. This duality is a strong procedural push-factor. It is the price to pay for receiving a verdict 'once and for all' – a lawful and legitimate decision that will be fully acknowledged by the community.

At this point, we can leave our extensive case-study with a first impression of case-making and its entanglements. The reader is introduced to the rich natural data that adversarial case-making produces. The reader is, moreover, introduced to our temporal take on this data. The utterances and inscriptions are not interpreted as a jigsaw or as a multi-text scattered to a two-dimensional space. It is rather analysed as "moves in a game" (Sacks et al. 1974:696). Case-making is even trickier than that, because as an exchange system it involves more than just one mode of contributing to it, more than just one mediality to render these contributions available. Case-makers contribute by talking privately, by writing official letters, by perusing the file for new ideas, by checking the adversaries' arguments, etc. There is, it seems, no routine practice, no custom, no method that would capture its overall regularity. There is, moreover, no single space to it, no laboratory or workplace that would host and structure it all. There is not even a sole, linear progression that would inhabit all the efforts and investments. The alibi-case suggests a diversion from a plain analytical framing. We face an ongoing see-saw between talk and text, tests and facts, utterances and statements, production and consumption. This see-saw, the following chapter suggests, places legal case-making in a multi-temporal field of event *and* process.

II. FRAMING LAW-IN-ACTION

This chapter is a plea for a novel kind of framing: one that allows us to observe law-in-action across various mediations; one that allows us to grasp the complexities of cases in becoming; one that reflects on its limitations and that accounts for its partiality. This multifaceted framing results in a trans-sequential method: a method that follows case-making over a longer period of time and that participates in a series of more or less contingent events. As a result, we obtain an eventful process and processed events of case-making.[1]

Observing lawyers doing their casework is not new. We find studies in sociology of law, in legal anthropology, in discourse analysis, and in organization studies that deal in one way or another with what lawyers do and why they do it. The most radical microscopy of how they do it is provided by ethnomethodological studies of law-in-action. Scholars like Harvey Sacks, Harold Garfinkel, or Paul Drew, amongst many others, ask for "the methods by which legal settings and situations such as a call to the police, police interrogations and courts and trials are socially organised" (Hester and Eglin 1992:17). They conduct so called "studies of work" (Garfinkel 1967) and attempt to render observable the very details of this work. As Ethnomethodologist, Lynch argued that "when they investigate activities in the legal professions, sociologists tend to describe various 'social' influences on the growth and development of legal institutions while taking for granted that lawyers write briefs, present cases, interrogate witnesses, and engage in legal reasoning." (Lynch 1993:114) In this chapter, I focus on a key point of this book's methodology: that in order to understand case-making down to its very details, the ethnography needs to frame these details according to the case-makers' practical orientations and involvements.

Originally, the law-in-action approach developed in opposition to the law-of-the-books orientation towards doctrines (Pound 1910). Pound did not aim at denying the force of written law, but at turning it into an empirical question. Law-in-action was supposed to evaluate law in light of its implementation and application to real cases: its

[1] An earlier version of this chapter was published in *Human Studies* (Scheffer 2007a).

imperfect reality, the limited impact of legislation, and the ideologically coloured interpretations of it all. Until now, law-in-action scholars have studied with enthusiasm the official sites at which law is applied: the police office, the courtroom, the law firm, the public administration, etc. My own perspective on case-making originates in these studies of law-in-action, but it adds new complications and new perspectives to it. Law-in-action, I argue, is not identical with what goes on in court, what is said by lawyers or clients, or how disputes are carried out. Rather, criminal law-in-action operates in a complex field of discourse practices. The critical task for law-in-action research is to demarcate this field and to capture the practical status of those practices in terms of real cases.

What was the practical status, for instance, of Linda's alibi? In the first case study, I gathered file material and related communications and put them in a chronological order, a succession, a series of events. By following the alibi through its various appearances, I did not just account for various sites and moments; I also explored a process of mobilization that turned the alibi into a discursive, legally relevant object. Case-making, thus, draws on various settings, participants, objects, and media. It takes place in and responds to a dynamic (legal) discourse formation, a heterogeneous field of signification.

Where and when is the field?

"Where is the field?" is a question hardly ever asked by ethnographers who 'just' approach institutions, cultures or regions.[2] Often, ethnography is carried out without problematising where and when one should conduct participant observation; it is carried out as if it was self-evident that the ethnographer was already in the field. I argue that such presuppositions are shaken once the ethnographer allows for alternative versions of where/what the field is, in which, for instance, law-in-action operates. Those basic concerns with framing 'what is done and what this doing does' (Dreyfus/Rabinow 1987:219) turn ethnography into a "theory-oriented research practice" (Hirschauer 2005), an analytic project.

[2] The "where"-question is asked by Gupta and Ferguson (1997), Fog and Hastrup (1997), Amit (1999), Abu-Lughod (2000), Behar (2003), etc.

Social theorists are not surprised that ethnography does not engage in theorizing the field per se. Ethnography – due to its dominant naturalism – is reproached as being descriptive and uninterested in raising theoretical problems. Martyn Hammersley, for instance, criticizes that ethnographies simply "portray the phenomenon of interest 'in its own terms.' [...] Ethnographers' commitment to the reproduction model obscures, from readers and perhaps even from ethnographers themselves, the [theoretical] relevancies that structure their accounts" (Hammersley 1990:609).[3] Recent comments repeat this basic critique: David A. Snow and his colleagues observe a "tendency of ethnographers to neglect the theoretical relevance and potential of research" (Snow et al. 2003:182). Similarly, qualitative research is frequently categorized as being unaware of or ignorant towards theoretical implications. Additional critique of the qualitative theory-method relation comes from within. Ethnographers, in particular, criticize the process of specialization that qualitative research underwent over the last fifty years. Qualitative researchers became specialists in a single method such as biographical interviews, conversation analysis, objective hermeneutics, etc.,[4] with each method involving largely unreflected theoretical assumptions on the activities studied.

In this line, ethnography has been acclaimed for overcoming methodical specialization and for challenging respective technical/reductionist standards of interpretation. Accordingly, sociologists such as Pierre Bourdieu or Karin Knorr-Cetina present ethnography not as a method amongst others, but as a strategy to choose and fit a sensitive set of methods to a distinctive field. Ethnography, in this understanding, does not follow a pre-set programme. There is no predetermined recipe for the collection and interpretation of ethnographic data. Rather, ethnography proper explores the spatiotemporal extensions, the reproductive operations, or the data available.

---

[3] There are, however, many ethnographers who do not fit Hammersley's critique. One may think of Rabinow (1977), Comaroff and Comaroff (1992), Hirschauer (1991), Bourdieu and Wacquant (1992), Eriksen (2001), or Bourdieu (2003); all scholars who would engage in theorising and theoretical critique. Theorizing means (at least) two different things to these scholars: using ethnographic data from the field to discuss disciplinary problems; using disciplinary concepts to theorize on the field.

[4] See the increasing amount of methods presented in the handbooks of qualitative research – and their several editions – by Patton (2002), Flick et al. (2004), or Denzin and Lincoln (2005).

Asking "where the field is" stipulates theorizing. In other words, ethnography engages theory as long as it remains open for various versions of what/where exactly the field might be, how it can be rendered observable, and how observed instances relate to it (Scheffer 2002). This de-naturalisation of ethnographic research lies at the heart of what it means to conduct "analytical ethnography," which is an ongoing dialogue of empirical and theoretical perspectives (Lofland 1984; Hirschauer and Amann 1997).[5]

Our concern finds precedence in what Michael Lynch and David Bogen (1996) called "postanalytical ethnomethodology." Their conversation and discourse analytical explorations of the Iran-Contra Hearings turn "postanalytical" because observed members attend to various meaning-producing frames. Lynch and Bogen reject "conversation" as *the* predominant frame. They reject a master theory of communication, practice, discourse, or institutions. No theory is privileged to explicate 'what goes on'; no concept serves as an unquestioned foundation:

> Our descriptions are assailable, defeasible accounts, uncommitted to any single analytical model of conversational pragmatics or communicative ethics. Our Ethnomethodological approach therefore is postanalytical in the sense that we presume that, and selectively describe how, the sources of intelligible action and defensible judgment are not contained within even the most elaborate system of prescriptions and specifications. (Lynch and Bogen 1996:287)

Lynch and Bogen exhibit a potpourri of widespread theories: Derrida's deconstruction, Garfinkel's documentary method of interpretation, Turner's ritual theory, and Habermas' discourse ethics. The role of these theories is twofold: for the committee members 'in-action', they provide valuable means to deal with their practical tasks; for the researcher, they offer valuable means to tackle the complex practical implications of what goes on. Analytical ethnography, as well as postanalytical ethnomethodology, recognises the productive role of theories and concepts for explorative studies. Theories and concepts are not

---

[5] Hirschauer merges ethnographic description and theorizing: "This local transposition [of the observer] is inspired by a scepticism that one could easily understand the natives without taking the risk of giving up a safe sociological 'standpoint'. Therefore, the second transposition is one of concepts: putting sociological concepts and ways of looking into surgery, and vice versa." (1994:344) Hirschauer's transpositions move beyond the common "ethnographically relevant strategies for theoretical development," namely "discovery, extension, and refinement" (Snow et al. 2003:194).

used as prescriptions or templates; rather, they enter the ongoing interchange of empirical and theoretical perspectives. The interchange re-specifies both perspectives.

In the following, I do not want to define analytic ethnography[6] or contrast it with other ethnographic programmes.[7] Instead, I carry out a rather playful exercise: I confront my ethnographic observations from Northern English Crown Courts, law firms and barristers' chambers with two temporal frames: event and process. The confrontation of event and process elicits scenarios, reflections, additions, sketches, etc. The question "where and what is the field?" is rephrased not only in spatial terms, but in terms of time. In other words, I combine the spatial concern ("Where is the field?") with a temporal one ("When is the field?").[8] This move renders local phenomena more general (and complicated) and general concepts more specific (and down to earth) than commonly considered. It narrows down both theory and empirical research. Put short, it animates an empiric-analytical dialogue.

This framing question is hardly ever asked by ethnographers: When is the field? When does it take place? These explorations put an emphasis on "the temporal dynamic of social formation" and they articulate aspects, such as "continuity, rupture, emergence" (Spurk 2004:41). The following dialogue between my ethnographic data and concepts of time/timing imply that both may alter due to it. The concepts of time matter for the articulation of data, while the data may well particularise the temporal concepts. Accordingly, this chapter relates practical features of casework in English criminal law to temporal conceptions originating from social theory, history or organisation studies. The arranged field notes demonstrate, firstly, the need for revision of the temporal conceptions. Secondly, they demonstrate the empirical resonance of these concepts and their revisions, here of the

---

[6] There are various attempts: Lofland (1995) promotes a cognitive turn in contrast to an interpretative style; Hirschauer and Amann (1997) advocate a dialogue between empirical work and sociological theorizing; Snow et al. (2003) link "analytic ethnography" to grounded theory. Traditional anthropological studies distinguish between "descriptive and analytical ethnography" (Chaudhury and Das 1973).

[7] Amongst the variously proposed programmes are "collaborative ethnography" (Lassiter 2005), "praxeography" (Mol 2002), "technography" (Anderson 1997), "focussed ethnography" (Knoblauch 2001), or "processual ethnography" (Moore 1987). Problematic here is the implicit othering: '*other* ethnographies do not care for technology, praxis, theory, etc.'

[8] Additionally, this move may counter the widespread and often criticized "timelessness" of social theory (Rosa 2005:461; Hassard 1990; Adam 1994; Bash 2000).

relation of event and process.[9] Both may contribute to new "ethnographic research strategically designed to reveal both the 'there and then' and the 'here and now'" (Katz 2004:301) of a field of practice.

The necessity for an empiric-analytical dialogue is apparent in my ethnographic descriptions of occurrences in the field. What is going on?

> Two barristers, complete with robes and wigs, are going into a huddle. They are brooding over a document: the protocol of the prosecution's main witness being interviewed by the police. They are sitting at a table in the Barristers' Lounge at a northern English Crown Court. Each of them has a copy of the defendant's earlier statement in front of him, which is a copy of the protocol of the police interview in an "indecent assault" matter.
>
> I am sitting quietly – and somehow staggered — at the table with them. I shadow 'my barrister' like an assistant or a trainee. My field uniform: a dark suit, white shirt, and tie. I am following the conversation, busily taking notes and smiling about occasional jokes and digressions. I am looking over 'my barrister's' shoulder to see what is actually happening between the two and with the copy of the interview protocol.
>
> Only later, when I hold a copy of the "jointly revised" protocol in my hands, will I be able to understand what has actually been going on. The barristers have slashed entire passages. They agreed that they would not address those in court. Defence and prosecution will not attend to the slashed passages, neither in friendly nor in cross-examination. The passages are effectively deleted from their competing cases and from the trial agenda.

In conceptual terms, I ask how their brief meeting is linked to case-making. Or, more precisely: How is the interactive revision of the protocol predisposed or preconfigured in the former case-work? How do the barristers' compromises and protocol notes matter in the further course? These questions are, I suggest, questions about the relation of events and process in/as English Crown Court procedure. They are about what enters and what does not enter case-making, e.g., in this meeting and from that time on.

[9] The idea to focus on event and process relations shows some striking similarities to Moore's "processual ethnography" together with her call to pay "ethnographic attention to events" (1987). However, her idea of process connotes big societal change that is often only illustrated by events rather than achieved by it. In comparison, I propose to analyse event and process in close interrelation, or, to use Georg Simmel's concept, in "Wechselwirkung" (1989).

Event and process in Social Theory

Ethnography can profit from sociological concepts that seem rather devious at first sight. The 'event and process'-pair is commonly employed in historical sociology. Scholars like Sewell ask how episodes or occurrences relate to the course of history.[10] They offer conceptualizations such as: "... what has happened at an earlier point in time will affect the possible outcomes of a sequence of events occurring at a later point in time." (Sewell Jr. 1996b:262 sq.) They mobilise elaborated concepts such as "path dependency", "chains of reactive sequences," or "self-reinforcing sequences." They arrive at models, such as the one suggested by James Mahoney (2000:514) to define "path dependency":

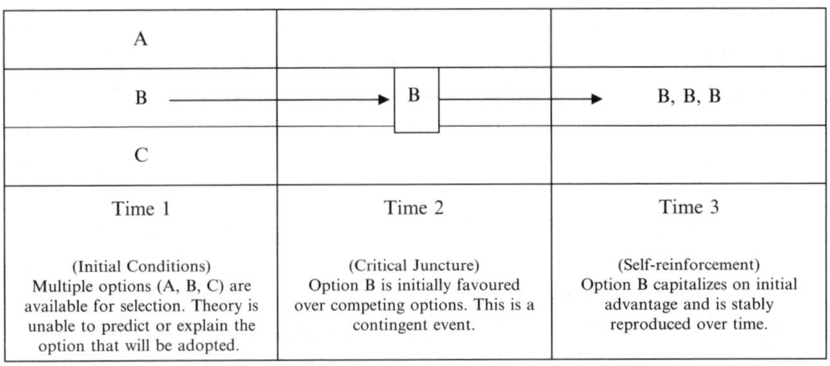

Fig. 6: Model of Path-Dependency taken from Mahoney (2000:514)

Mahoney's model in historical sociology[11] centres on causal chains, on beginnings, on the question what actually constitutes an event, on

[10] According to Sewell (1996b), historical sociology uses "three temporalities": chains of events (history occurs from one event to the next), teleological processes (history moves through events towards a final state), and path-dependent developments (a steadily moving history is only occasionally 'derailed' by revolutions, disasters, etc.). The latter variant is performed by Max Weber when he relates processes of rationalisation to charismatic situations (cf. 1980: 654–687).

[11] Mahoney provides the following explication: "Figure 1 offers a schematic illustration of the place of contingency in path-dependent, self-reinforcing sequences. In this example, three potential options [...] are available for adoption at Time 1. On the basis of the initial conditions present at this time, as identified by one or more explanatory theories, the eventual adoption of a particular option [...] cannot be predicted or explained. In this sense, given the initial conditions and certain theoretical understandings of causal processes, one could hypothetically 'rerun' history many times, and there would be no reason for believing option B would be adopted with any more

the construction of linearity, and on synchronic and diachronic events. Aside from the methodical problems in applying the model to historical cases, Mahoney's conceptualization reminds us of the necessity to place observed events in time and to define their relevance (for subsequent events) as well as their eventfulness (their contingency). In this regard, Mahoney's model links up to theories of history, such as Nietzsche's "wirkliche Historie," Foucault's "genealogy" or Braudel's "longue durée."[12]

It is not contested that a historic event, such as "The French Revolution" – the (modern) "present par excellence" (Luhmann 1998:1006) – differs in relevance and weight from, to return to our field of study, a trial hearing or a plea bargaining session between barristers. However, in order to adopt a conceptual angle on the event-process pair in historical sociology, I suggest preliminarily bracketing its dimensions.[13] I am interested in the relations of event and process rather than in material definitions of the two concepts in separation. I spell out variant relations of event and process for the empirical case under study. I ask: which aspects of adversarial case-making can be observed by choosing one relation or the other?

In the following, I introduce relations of event and process as heuristics and delimit them from more common dualisms, for example, action and context or structure and agency. The variants of event/process provide the background for my actual objective: sketching out an ethnographic vision on adversarial case-making that operates two

---

frequency than the alternative options. The initial adoption of option B during the critical juncture period (Time 2) is therefore a contingent event. As the figure suggests, once option B is contingently selected, it is stably reproduced across time in future." (2000:513 sq.)

[12] Foucault explains the Nietzschean genealogy as a specific event-process relation: "The *wirkliche Historie* transposes the relationship ordinarily established between the eruption of an event and necessary continuity. An entire historical tradition (theological or rationalistic) aims at dissolving the singular event into an ideal continuity – as a teleological movement or a natural process. 'Effective' history, however, deals with events in terms of their most unique characteristics, their most acute manifestations. An event, consequently, is not a decision, a treaty, a reign, or a battle, but the reversal of a relationship of forces, the usurpation of power, the appropriation of a vocabulary turned against those who have once used it." (1977:154)

[13] The same argument is used by Elias and Scotson (1993) in order to demonstrate the applicability of the relation between establishment and outsiders on configurations "big and small alike". It remains an identical figuration, no matter the scale.

temporal dimensions simultaneously. Event/process, I hope, will allow for a "movement back and forth between the 'inside and the outside' of events" (Clifford 1993:126), here for an analytics that enters and traces their "before and after."

A heuristic pair of concepts

I begin with a provisional paraphrasing of event and process, which is sufficiently open for empirical variants and which, at the same time, gives a first idea of what actually is related – and defines each other. The event is commonly identified as (relatively) compact and local: for instance, a trial hearing, the client-lawyer conference, etc. According to this language, a last meeting with a witness, for example, would not appear as a continuation of another event, but rather as a new one. Calling these meetings 'events' does not determine their qualities. In other words: their eventfulness may vary next to their shape, features, etc. Events are distinguishable according to weight, meaning and contingency. A glance at common synonyms for 'event' may provide an idea:

> SYN.—occurrence is the general word for anything that happens or takes place [an unforeseen occurrence]; an event is an occurrence of relative significance, especially one growing out of earlier happenings or conditions [the events that followed the surrender]; an incident is an occurrence of relatively minor significance, often one connected with a more important event [the award was just another incident in his career]; an episode is a distinct event that is complete in itself but forms part of a larger event or is one of a series of events [an episode of his childhood]; a circumstance is an event that is either incidental to, or a determining factor of, another event [the circumstances surrounding my decision]. (Webster's Dictionary 2005)

We will see that "anything that happens" or "takes place" indicates change for something else; it indicates a relational vision and a retrospection. The notion of process, on the other hand, emphasizes a temporal stretch that can include several moments or sequences. Process is not necessarily bound to a single place or constellation: for example, the plea bargaining comprising ongoing negotiations inside and outside court; the defence party's casework being performed in a complex social and temporal division of labour; or the barristers' ongoing appropriation of the case by help of successive inscriptions. Again, consulting the common meanings of 'process' may give some orientation:

> A series of actions, changes, or functions bringing about a result: the process of digestion; the process of obtaining a driver's license. A series of operations performed in the making or treatment of a product: a manufacturing process; leather dyed during the tanning process. Progress; passage: the process of time; events now in process. Law: the entire course of a judicial proceeding. (Webster's Dictionary 2005)

We will see that "a series of actions …" implies experience of the latter: an episode, a step towards, a developmental stage. On this level of provisionally paraphrasing the concepts, we can already see how the two temporal dimensions include each other. Each concept seems to implicate its opposite number: a process acquires a progression from one 'event' to the next; an event acquires change that is fully realised from the 'processual' perspective. Separated definitions – here the punctiform, local event; there the extended, translocal process – lack the critical reference that turns each into a workable concept. Event and process seem complementary.

Here, I do not aim at providing fixed definitions. Instead, heuristic indeterminacy allows me to keep concepts open, hoping that they will become clear by and in their mutual relationship. This way, the concept of 'event' can be reconsidered against the background of various event-process relations. Seen from a process-perspective, events can vary in their eventfulness. The same is true for the concept of 'process'. Seen from an event-perspective, the process can be more or less integrated, determined, or ordered; that means its processuality is not defined *a priori*. Both concepts – in spite of and due to their fuzziness – are well suited to serve relational heuristics. They respecify each other from case to case.

The common alternative: action and context

Before elaborating on the event/process heuristics, let me turn to another, more prominent pair of concepts: action and context. Interpretive sociology regards context as the necessary condition for ascribing meaning to a given act and thus for interpreting it. Rational choice scholars, on the other hand, have emphasized the causal links between context and action. According to the latter perspective, the (relevant) context enforces certain selections and choices. In the spirit of these rather dualist and conventional approaches on action/context, I provide some background for the (above introduced) barristers' meeting that took place shortly before trial:

> Both barristers are male, middle-aged, and white, like the majority of their professional colleagues (see chapter IV). They maintain polite, distinguished manners.[14] They invite me to stay and show much interest in my research. I feel like being hosted by a special *class*. (Indeed, my informant seemed a barrister from head to toe. His father had also worked as a barrister.) It is often said that the northern English barrister is – his 'distinction' notwithstanding – more accessible to the 'social question' than his southern, more detached counterpart.
>
> The two barristers meet at Crown Court right before the jury trial. The Crown Court building in North End is about thirty years old. It does not possess the symbolic and overwhelming weight of old courthouses. Rather, it resembles a town hall or a jobcentre. A court employee sells sandwiches and drinks, a service which makes many barristers remain in the courthouse, even during the sometimes lengthy intervals between sessions. Quite often, meetings take place in the Barristers' Lounge rather than in a nearby café or restaurant as is common elsewhere, especially in the old, often very dark and baroque courthouses.
>
> Crown Court statistics show an average length of trial of 6.5 hours in 2001 (as compared to 13 hours in London Circuit). Is this 'speediness' attributable to a different mix of offences, or also to better cooperation between parties before trial? Are trial times shorter here because barristers are more selective about what is still to be debated? Do they maintain more case-spanning contact-systems that help them compromise? Local variation contradicts the promise of equality before the law.

These cursory notes refer, albeit unsystematically, to legal and cultural conditions: the venerable profession of the barrister, the building complex, the average speed of 'case completion,' etc. All these are candidates for relevant context information. Similarly, the ethnographer could deliver accounts on the role of the Barristers' Chambers (are there any friendly ties between the adversaries?), on the judge's personality and style (how tightly does he hold the reins?), on the legal rules on "indecent assault" (what parameters are to be proven?), or on recent decisions on admissibility (did the barristers act accordingly?). How do these contextual features acquire significance in the formation of cases? Do they all matter and, if so, how?

---

[14] It seems as if the "public man" (Sennett 1992) *did* survive in the habitus of the barrister. Politeness, cultivated small talk, and discreet affectation all are manners that are expected of the barrister as a public figure. This may explain why there are biographies, monographs, cartoons, and criminal stories dealing with the figure of the barrister (cf. Morison and Leith 1992). In comparison, other legal professions lead a rather shadowy existence, for instance, the clerk (cf. Flood 1983), or the solicitor.

The concept of context is contested as being either too wide or too tight. Ethnomethodological Conversation Analysis (CA) emphasizes the self-referential character of (inter-)activities. Under conditions of co-presence, interactivities unfold a powerful dynamic of their own. The wider context plays a role only where context components inscribe themselves into the mode and the course of the interaction (Schegloff 1987). Rather, any contribution co-constitutes its relevant (narrow) context or frame. Context is reduced to a most narrowly conceived context, adjacent contribution, while the wider context remains passive or 'in waiting.'

Critical Discourse Analysis (CDA), on the other hand, operates with a wide understanding of context. Context here refers to social conditions inscribed in the actors' bodies and orientations. In this view, a social contradiction, hegemony, or dispositiv configures even the most casual events. Discourse as ideology or script appears to be 'at work' everywhere all the time. It is always already in place and does its work powerfully behind the actors' backs. Can we translate these – admittedly caricatured - concepts of context into versions of what happened during the barristers' meeting and why? I describe the barristers' meeting in terms of narrow and wide context:

> Narrow context: The barristers meet, each equipped with their own checklists of what he would consider as irrelevant or inadmissible (in favour of their cases). The barristers can only be sure that a certain piece of evidence is deleted if they reach an agreement on this. How do they get their points through? How do they convince the respective other that something should not be part of the trial hearing? They work through the protocols, page after page. "Do you have anything on page 5?" They make sure that nothing is left out and that only checked protocols serve as the script or a contrast for the witness examination in front of judge and jury.
>
> Wide context: The barristers present this exercise differently to me. They emphasize the routine and the self-explanatory aspects of their 'slashing show'. The barristers explain that they only apply rules of admissibility of evidence to the protocols. In this version, the barristers are implementing law. No more. They present themselves, additionally, as being bound by their instructions. Thus, I understand, they are able to finish thinning out the 80 pages of interview protocol with the according speed. In view of the law and the case at hand, this is how they must act. The barristers simply followed the law. Their meeting was just an appendix to legal conventions. If they did not do it, the judge would remind them to.

Is context 'external' to activities 'inside'? Is context a more or less forceful, more or less mediated influence on what actors do or decide?

Before I return to the event/process relations, I outline more alternatives to the widespread context/action dualism.

Beyond action and context

There are a number of approaches that escape the dualism of (intentional) action and (structural) context. For instance, systems theory takes the difference of 'system' and 'environment' as the starting point for sociological analysis of communication – not action. The various operatively closed, meaning-generating systems of interaction – or procedure (Luhmann [1969]1989) – are only loosely and selectively tied to an environment. Human beings, for example, in their entirety are relegated to the environment of the interaction system. They appear 'here and now' only in so far as they are addressed or referred to. Meaning-production is closely connected to selections which divide the present from both an irretrievable past (previous selections no longer available) and a contingent future (future selections still available). Sociality proceeds by points of no return. For George Herbert Mead, it is from here (and now) that the dimensions of past and future come into perspective; they are mere effects – not causes or horizons – of the very present (Flaherty and Fine 2001). They co-emerge with the event. Context is a moving horizon.

Integrative approaches, such as actor-network theory (ANT), on the other hand, emphasize the dependence and 'clamped' character of events in relation to a complex division of labour. In this view, what appears as a 'heroic', intentional and subjective action of a judge or a barrister is only possible due to manifold alliances and connections. It is embedded in a material infrastructure (Latour 2010) that directs, empowers, and enables the action. ANT emphasizes the performance of socio-material assemblages. As distributed agency they expand the temporal and spatial reach beyond human capability. "Acting at a distance" (Latour 1987:223) also affects a restructuring of what passes for an event. There is no definite way to ascertain when something is set in motion and how far it expands. The same seems true for the barristers' meeting. Let me provide another translation of theory into field notes.

> There are a number of conditions that do not lie outside the event, but surpass it: for instance, the two barristers are already acquainted; they meet without their instructing solicitors or the clients concerned; judge and jury are excluded from the negotiations in the barristers' lounge

> (they only receive its results); the meeting is happening shortly before trial (under time pressure); there is business-like and routine cooperation (rather than arguing, debating, convincing, etc.). In the course of the 'slashing show', the barristers enact a whole range of investments. Both barristers have underscored and slashed certain paragraphs of their instructions prior to the meeting. (Barristers calculate some of their fees by the number of pages they are expected to work over.) They have done so in the protocol version that had already been served on paper by their instructing solicitors two weeks in advance.

The duality of structure and action forces a division of dynamics and durability, of running time and circumscribing space. Systems theory emphasizes – in line with CA – that 'context' itself represents an effect of systemic operations. ANT emphasizes how an 'inside' is only made possible by previous/external achievement and embeddedness. In the following, I attempt to operate two dynamic levels of analysis side-by-side and in relation to each other: event *and* process. I also elaborate on the question how, in contrast, approaches limit themselves to look at *either* event *or* process.

Eventful process, processed events

There is a broad spectrum of possible event and process combinations. In order to capture this analytical variety, I start with those approaches that form the ends of the scale.[15] At both end points the event/process relation is dissolved in favour of one side: either in terms of a process-bias or event-bias. By way of these extremes, I realise the variety of possible relations in between. I suggest the following spectrum:

	Event/Process Relations			
Pure Event	Strong Eventfulness	Strong Interplay	Strong Processuality	*Pure Process*

Fig. 7: Spectrum of Event/Process Relations

[15] This scale reminds of the differentiation of discourses as provided by Foucault: "In short, I suspect one could find a kind of gradation between different types of discourse within most societies: discourse 'uttered' in the course of the day and in casual meetings, and which disappears with the very act which gave rise to it; and those forms of discourse that lie at the origins of a certain number of verbal acts, which are reiterated, transformed or discussed." (1972:220)

In the following, I outline both ends of the event/process spectrum. The descriptions of the 'pure event'-approach and the 'pure process'-approach will remain fragmentary and sketchy. Their main purpose is to gauge the many possibilities in between. On this basis, I am going to discuss relations of event and process in the third part of this chapter, in particular with a view to different degrees of eventfulness and relevance. My exercise will be successful if it becomes clear that and how the relation of event and process can generate a fruitful discriminatory ability for ethnographic studies. It will be successful, moreover, if it leads to relations of event *and* process that transcend both the "reification of process" (Vayda et al. 1991:320) and the "presentist bias" (Katz 2004:299). Only then does the event/process relation offer a framing device that is consistent with the ethnographic aspiration of cultural or practical comprehension.

Event and process coincide

The variant on the left of the spectrum concerns 'events in process'. Here events unfold internally in a sequential fashion. "Why now?", ethnomethodological Conversation Analysis (CA) asks, referring to the position of an utterance in the course of spoken interaction, conceptualized as an exchange of turns. In CA, an utterance is qualified as a turn in the immediate course of the event. The utterance is part of producing an event, and it is embedded in the process of unfolding the same event. This gives rise to aesthetics of proximity, to a primacy of immediacy.[16] Something acquires relevance only when it surpasses the moment-by-moment unfolding of meaning.

The conflation of event with process in the concept of 'conversation' is highly productive. It allows interpreting all spoken contributions, provided they occur here and now (meaning they can be registered by all participants), as turns and commentaries in their immediate relationship. The conflation further allows locating meaning between participants (rather than 'in their heads'), and thus renders meaning an observable phenomenon. Due to the dominance of local accomplishment, the analysis does not need to look at future or past events. "Everything's here!" – at least enough to answer the question of how an

[16] On the primacy of immediacy in Foucault's early writings, see Michon (2002:188 seq.).

event (such as an emergency call or an interview) is produced locally and interactively.

Event and process can only coincide if everything that matters or that takes place is interactively established right here, right now. Meaning is public and fully available to the members. Utterances that are unavailable to the conversational counterpart, that address absent others, or reach out to events yet to come are only included in their proximate significance for the co-present participants (Scheffer 1998a). In this sense, participants do not appear as strategizing, memorising and habitual subjects. They do not serve multiple tasks, ongoing projects, or synchronic frames. They are mere "turn-takers", attachments to this very situation and its interactive order (Goffman 1971:9). The sequential analysis of conversation is reduced to the "Now" of the face-to-face interaction.

> I can provide only hypothetical[17]answers on how the barristers' meeting is produced interactively. The barristers' "doing collaboration" would be characterized by the alternating, ordered and successive invocation of the protocol text. Following CA, I would ask how the protocol text is used in producing the session, rather than where the protocol text and the respective suggestions for deletion emerge from. I would limit the function of the protocol to that of a medium for communicative collaboration. What, then, are the rules to be followed in order to ascertain success of the common enterprise?
>
> I imagine the protocol as the structuring device, next to the gestures, pauses, and turns. I notice that the round proceeds page by page[18] of the copied interview protocol: "Where are we now?" — "On page 9!" Turning the pages is a helpful device: it allows for shared orientation; it organises those sections in which suggestions are expected and made; it visualizes results; and it suggests what will follow next. The barristers' notes are relevant to the situation in so far as they display the end of a theme and an opening or readiness for a subsequent one. After they have dealt with all the evidence, the barristers switch back to the casual style they displayed in the beginning. They address me again: "Any questions?"

---

[17] Nobody was allowed to carry recording devices inside the courthouse. Thus, my material is limited to fieldnotes, documents, defence counsel's notes, and official court protocols.

[18] To Schütz, intersubjectivity is experienced exactly like this: through the common direction towards an object, cf. Knorr-Cetina and Bruegger (2002). Shared objects such as medical records or computer screens play a central role in "activity theory" (Engeström 1995) and in "workplace studies" (Knoblauch and Heath 1999). A "boundary object" (Bowker and Griesemer 1989), in comparison, denotes the shared but divergent use by various communities of practice, e.g. visitors to the museum and its natural scientists.

CA as well as workplace studies, reconstruct the interactional work that renders the conversational and institutional event (e.g., an emergency call or a patient-doctor consultation) possible. The meeting comes into focus as the participants' 'interactive accomplishment'. For this "Radical Interactionism" (Athens 2009), event and process do not only coincide; the analysis also discovers a series of sub-events in the (internal) processual course. CA emphasizes the process-in-event, its sequential unfolding. The event-process, with its defined beginning and end, includes a series of internal incidents that successively open and close a space of possibilities. This perspective sharpens the view for the minutiae of the verbal collaboration and for the mode of selection that operates here and now.

> In this sense, the barristers' verbal exchange impressed me. During the initial plea bargaining exchange, they addressed each other as if they were the conflict parties themselves: "Are you sure you did not set up this thing ..." "No, I did not! I already told you that ..." This 'as if' jargon creates an atmosphere of directness. The barristers performed, I understood, a serious game that put them right into adversary positions. The second personal pronoun (Did you ...?) provokes strong reactions (No, I did not ..!). Their exchange 'as if' playfully introduces an eagerness to identify themselves with the represented case and to act out the conflict 'in his or her name'. Overall, the two barristers distinctively marked their positions. This is not what I expected from professional lawyers' talk.

How well does the model of process-in-event fare in its empirical scope? How can we identify its most suitable empirical application? Michael Lynch and David Bogen, in their call for a postanalytical ethnomethodology, criticized formal CA exactly for the lack of such concerns and for its all-purpose use of *conversation* as the "generic domain" (1996).[19] Our framing exercise carries opposite implications: Are there any events, for instance social encounters that are not oriented in their

[19] They explain: "The generic domain of conversation is not the only relevant backdrop against which singular events take on their specificity and sensibility." (Lynch and Bogen 1996:286) And by referring to their own empirical case: "While a spectacular case, when construed as an occasion of talk at work, may recall general properties identified by conversation analysts, such properties may be irrelevant to a consideration of the spectacle as such. Recognizable constituents of the event, such as a speaker's presence on television, his wearing of a uniform, his being surrounded by cameras, and his speaking on behalf of the government, do not become materially irrelevant simply because the talk largely is composed of generic procedures that can be found elsewhere." (Ibid.)

courses towards previous and subsequent encounters? Are there social encounters that are conducted without any (completed) build up and (anticipated) follow up? Or, put differently: What is the empirical case best fitted to the premise of lacking memory and anticipation?

> Regularly, people exchange friendly greetings in the courthouse lobby. Some know each other from former trials, others do not know whether the addressed person may be relevant or not, many are strangers to each other. Most of these exchanges are in no way relevant to any proceeding inside the courtrooms. They do not enter the legal discourse. The exchange remains a singular event, identical with itself – but irrelevant from the point of view of the process. I do not need any additional information pertaining to the time before or after in order to understand this moment for all it is and can be: a greeting in the lobby (not much different from greetings elsewhere).[20]
>
> However, the exchange of greetings may be situated differently. I learned that the situation changes radically once the barrister identifies probable witnesses amongst the 'visitors'. In this way, the barrister's stroll in the lobby may be a strategy to acquire some orientation prior to the plea bargaining session or the trial. The barrister may grasp the strength of the adversary's case by passing through the waiting zone: "Let's see who they got to testify!" It happened once: 'my' barrister came back from such a trip, and he was still impressed not only by the fact that all "their witnesses" had actually showed up, but also by their neat and respectable appearances: "All in suits and ties!" Our client was wearing his Manchester United shirt.

The model of process-in-event is attractive because it teaches us basic lessons on what Emanuel Schegloff called "conditions of possibility" (1987). The conditions of possibility refer to the conversation's structural capacity to foreclose certain expressions, modes of speech, participants or reactions. In the question-answer-exchange of the cross-examination, for instance, the witness is denied a position to affirm, correct or dismiss the barrister's use of his or her answer. Similar constraints appear in other pre-structured speech-exchange systems: in asylum hearings (Scheffer 2001), in news interviews (Heritage and Greatbatch 1991), in the White House press conference (Schegloff 1987). The event and process relation, however, may show that an entire range of local conditions of possibility is pre-distributed, and that it can shape more than the actual speech-exchange: for

[20] The ethnographer needs to acquire some literacy concerning the "cultural icon" (Goffman 1971), here of greetings, e.g., how they are exchanged and when they are rather inappropriate.

example, the availability of knowledge, the circulation of documents, the opportunity to prepare (and use) a script, or the accessibility of various publics.

Process without events

The opposite alternative in the event/process spectrum is provided by *ex post* analyses that reconstruct complex productive processes. This perspective necessitates defining a product from the start. What is produced here and there, now and then? Criminals, outsiders, inmates, but also scientific texts, airplanes, or nations might be products of social processes. The concept of process is widely and loosely used to "counter the persisting view of society as an enduring entity with definite and permanent boundaries" (Vayda et al. 1991:319). With hindsight, events appear only in their contributions to the productive process. Processual analysis reconstructs the sequence of these contributions and passes over their locality and historicity. The events are swallowed up.[21] In legal discourse, we could ask about the production of a protocol, a witness statement, of "reasons" (Hannken-Illjes 2006) or a case. The latter is done by legal anthropologists under the heading of "law as process." Scholars like Gulliver, Moore, Griffith, etc. (see Collier 1975) followed disputes through their informal and formal developmental stages. They arrived at developmental schemes, at culturally specific tendencies, and at directions of these processes. However, they did not provide an understanding of how legal or dispute processes are integrated — how feasible they are in the first place – and how they make themselves available to any process analysis.

[21] Similarly, it has been attempted to conceptualize phenomena such as delinquency or deviation as processes characterised by a series of developmental stages. "The conception of social problems as social process recognizes their essential constructive function in the adaption of a society and its culture to social change. The emergence of social problems is natural and inevitable" (Burgess 1961:383). Burgess summarized: "The concept of social process transcends while it includes the concepts of social disorganization and conflict of values" (Ibid.). Events do not mediate contingency or tension with the overarching process; rather, they report on the achievements that process is capable of – time and again. Correspondingly, 'cases' run through typified phases: "The term 'societal process' is used here to denote the organization, disorganization, and reorganization of a society, community, or social group" (Ibid.:385).

> My ethnographic field changed drastically once I followed solicitors around. Instead of visiting court hearings, I was confronted with the solicitors' formulation of letters, their file-work, or their use of the archive. The files were placed before the solicitor according to the rhythm of the case, meaning before certain deadlines, hearings or dates. The solicitor would speed up this rhythm by dictating "diary notes" with explicit and dated work instructions. The drafting of statements was a crucial activity in this regard. The solicitor would go through the client's story over and over again. He would place changes in the first, second or third draft in order to make the document/account more robust. This internal phase of drafting was followed by a phase of external circulation. The document, once signed by the client, would be disclosed to the prosecution and the court. The account turns binding for later accounts.

In this regard, the barristers' meeting is just one step in a longer chain to produce the legally valid and available statement. The phases of production are accumulated in the document: from early, to later, to definite versions. The protocol-production process takes place in, among others, the barristers' meeting, but the meeting itself appears only indirectly: through the traces or inscriptions it leaves on the document. When studying the various versions, as we did in the first case study on the alibi-story, I organised these traces as selection, reduction, amplification, etc. Thus, written statements emerge from a series of transformations of once local utterances. The transformations matter in so far as some versions become "binding" (Scheffer et al. 2009) at one point in the procedural course.

There are fascinating constructivist studies on this kind of production or creation.[22] The reality (of the case, the crime, the dispute) is not given, but derives from a process of world-making. Bruno Latour, in this context, makes a plea for analyses that explain the continuous extension of practice across space and time – mediated by technology and artefacts. He focuses on the circulations and connections that link a series of moments in a process. 'Process without event'-approaches

[22] A key figure for this line of thought is supposedly Braudel and his concept of "longue durée" (1969). This is not to say that Braudel conceptualizes history as continual process. Rather, he follows structural ruptures: "One was born within one particular state of society (that is to say, simultaneously, a mentality, some frames, a civilization, and especially an economic civilization), which several generations have known before us, but everything can collapse before our life ends" (quoted in Michon 2002:187). Process opposes event.

testify to expanding, accumulating, linear and final developments. Here, events are reduced to minimal ontological status: they are space-times that are traversed by processes.[23]

> I imagine the development of a witness statement 'heading' for court as an increasing detachment from the first appearance and an anticipation of the final procedural stage. The procedure allows this kind of placement in time: a procedural past that is available to this party only or to the adversary; a procedural future that is sketched out in form of prescribed positions inside and outside court. In any case, the procedural passage turns the witness statement into a scripted document, open to all parties and utilized by the one "lending it his or her voice" as a binding script or a requisite resource. These achievements relegate events – such as the barristers' meeting – to mere displays, in which process shows itself at work and proves its productivity. The barristers just carry out another 'necessary' step in the formation of the single case. In this perspective, the ethnographer can focus on the various versions of the witness statements. By organising them in a line, I discovered rules of selection and arrangement transforming the original statement from one version to the next.

'Process without events' creates homogenous accumulation, a steady and linear course without abrupt change of direction. *Ex post*, all these moments appear as inevitable steps or phases towards a goal, "as if processes had lives of their own [...] and were regulated by some larger dynamic in history" (Vayda 1991:329). Is there anything that could disturb this progression, this solidified movement? The only option imaginable seems to be a complete breakdown of the social circuits, an accident leading to the collapse of established functions: a revolution. The counter-point to event-bias is thus constituted by a reduced process of production or construction that is completed in standardized, functional events, but that is not challenged by these events. Functions are fulfilled, no matter what happens in a single moment. In other words: theorizing in this line relies on various tolerances and indifferences in order to ignore 'compelling' and 'irritating' variations.

[23] Ritual chains of events also seem to be orientated towards a goal. The task of analysing ritual chains of events demands a retrospective understanding: which sequence of events does – time and again – achieve this particular community and its emotional effects. The emphasis lies not on eventfulness, but rather on the regular achievement of collectivisation, cf. Collins (2004).

Processual events

After these considerations, how can I conceptualize an alternative to event-bias and process-bias? To approach the variants between 'pure events' and 'pure process', I suggest focusing on the interplay of event and process. Processual events add to the process by means of an organised memory and legitimate expectations. They direct the process or an "interval" towards later "critical dates" (Hubert 1999).[24] Let me introduce another variation of the barristers' meeting:

> The barristers are enabled to cooperate in a particular and reliable way. I took a note of the materials that were imported into the meeting, that the meeting took for granted, and that the meeting did not provide itself: the written statements, the forms requested by the court management, the instructions and the brief, the client's latest comments before the meeting, the notes and checklists made on the way to court. Other materials are in reach: the instructing solicitor brings the complete case-files to court; the casebooks and statutes are kept in the court's library; each barrister keeps his or her personal copy of Blackstone's Criminal Practice nearby. The materials are not just symbols of 'history' or 'importance'; they are communications that can be easily activated by referring to them. They are, what is more, conditions for what is talked about. The written (procedural) history creates inconsistency and problems when it is ignored; it creates limitations and passivity when being simply acknowledged as legally binding. I understand the art of advocacy as some kind of 'creative respect' towards the sources.

From the point of view of the legal proceeding, the barristers' meeting is one chance next to others to get rid of unnecessary ballast, unsolvable problems, agreed-upon facts, etc., in order to reduce the thematic scope of the jury trial to its minimum. The procedure provides incentives to reach agreements out of court, based on previously textualized and exchanged material. These agreements can be far-reaching, such as bargaining the truth. They can also be less important (and hardly visible) like the 'slashing show' mentioned above. The barristers' meeting is an expression of procedural management or process design. The procedure grants decision-making authority to the barristers who

---

[24] Hubert describes the relation of process and event by help of different categories: intervals and critical dates. The "critical dates interrupt the continuity of time" (1999:51); "intervals [are, TS] bounded by two associated critical dates" (Ibid.:53); "the critical dates are equivalent to the intervals they limit" (Ibid.:56), etc. Hubert uses these concepts in order to understand the "representation of time in religion and magic" (Ibid.:51).

represent their teams or parties and who act on the basis of instructions. There are chains of delegation, next to series of preliminary meetings and successions of negotiations.

Claiming that an event is processed does not render the event irrelevant. The opposite is often the case. The process may empower the event. The process may multiply its effects and consequences. In return, the process can never fully determine the event's course. It remains contingent to some degree.[25] The process allocates a certain competence to decide, to direct its course, to reassess its past, or to declare its termination. This contingency is precisely the 'junction' that is inherent in legal procedure.[26] The most prominent example of the procedural appreciation of the event's eventfulness is the court trial as such:

> Initially, I was convinced that this is "where the action is:" the trial hearing. My multi-sited ethnography did not entirely dispose of this widespread belief. I am convinced now that a trial gives room to a dramatic finale of a complex process. The trial in court is meant to represent a rupture and (also) to bracket what has been recorded and archived on the pre-trial stages. It is supposed to bracket the hearsay, the previous convictions, the early failures, the unlawful evidence, the speculations and guesswork, etc. It is supposed to highlight the eye-witness accounts, the details, the contradictions, the inconsistencies, etc. It is framed and performed as an event, but not without referring back to legitimate parts of its history.
>
> The trial is not meant to just repeat, just re-enact, or just stage the accumulated facts. Rather, the procedural mill is once again exposed to this event. It is put to a test. In this respect, the jury plays a key role. The jurors are meant to take a fresh look at what is laid out in front of them. Nothing but the performed case should enter their 'common sense'. Nothing but the spoken words of witnesses should impress their 'good judgment'. In this fashion, media reports, neighbours' opinions, or the parties' extrajudicial persuasion – all these 'manipulations' are banned from the jury's decision-making process. The procedural rules do not

---

[25] Or as Mead put it, "the emergent event, that is, […] the occurrence of something which is more than the processes that have led up to it" (1932:1).

[26] This point links up with Foucault's "archaeology" (1972). Here, discourse includes both event and process, and subsumes both under a third element, the discursive machinery. The discursive formation – being the element producing discourse(s) – utilizes both aspects. Foucault uses the central role of the event as envelope and contingency to oppose a historiography that is oriented towards linearity and progress, or a structuralism that solidifies into patterns of order. According to Valverde, Foucauldian discourse analysis tries "to find ways of analyzing events and processes that would not begin by presupposing a dichotomy between the surface and the depths …, between 'appearances' and 'reality'" (2003:12).

even permit the parties to hand out written documents to the jurors. The rationale behind this regulation: such inscriptions imply more truthfulness compared to the 'subjective' testimonies performed before the jurors' eyes and ears. The trial event shall not be subjugated to the pre-trial process.

The trial hearing appears as an event not in contradiction, but in correspondence with the process. Its eventfulness is not just permitted, but configured by the legal process and its legal-cultural 'traffic rules'. In the same perspective, how can the initially sketched, rather inconspicuous meeting between the barristers be conceptualized as an event in process? One possible answer: it is the process that restricts and furnishes the barristers' deal. Their negotiation of reality – what counts as case and what does not (any longer) – is simultaneously situative and processed. In this line, I understand events as situated in ongoing processes. This does not imply strict determination; however, it does imply that 'free' speech, external to any formation, cannot be rendered meaningful. The 'autonomous' negotiator or the 'free' speaker is a possibility conditioned by a more or less thought-out procedural design.

The process, as a whole, appears partially and stepwise, in light of its sequentiality. By way of its sequential unfolding, the process sets its own teleology (for now); it forestalls its own likely future(s); it points towards its possible routes and directions. This is where "sequence points" are spun on.[27] Sequence points include a before and after – and thus create the process for themselves. Events do not mark stages on the way to a given goal – as in functional approaches; rather, they assign spaces of contingency to be analysed accordingly as they progress – as an array of routinely 'healed' crises. Events, in this perspective, are processing instances. They generate the process from moment to moment. "After all," Sally Falk Moore stresses, "events are to processes what categories are to structures" (Moore 1987:736).

Events in process gauge contingency and predictability. They initiate intervals which in turn make a difference for the interval to follow. In this line, Karl E. Weick differentiates between phases of design,

[27] So called "objective hermeneutics" (Oevermann 1979) operate a reconstructive type of sequential analysis. Events confront a speaker with an obligation to decide. In order to go on, he/she must choose between options. The analysis unfolds the space of possibilities at any given point of decision-making by way of mental experiments. Sequential analysis is then charged with the task of reconstructing methods of choice in terms of general laws of their operation.

selection, and retention in the "Process of Organizing" (Weick 1985). Each of these phases provides a contingent space of decisions, albeit framed by an organised structure of opportunities. The 'recurrent' process is, at the same time, subjected to change. This way, processes can retrieve phases of selection or even of design by way of feedback. Weick (1985:68) provides this illustration:

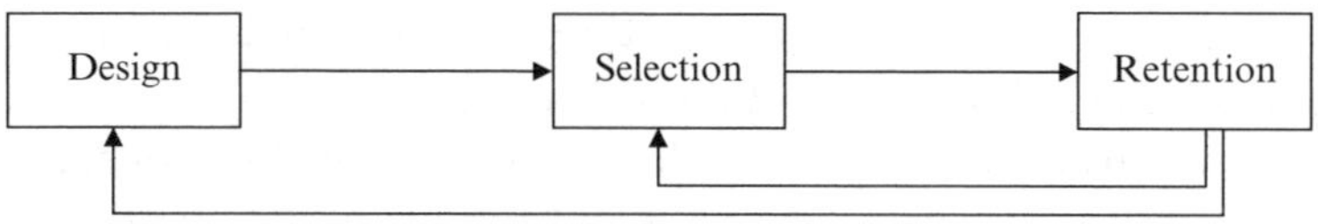

Fig. 8: Feedback-Model by Weick (1985:68)

Process is directed but not mechanical. Events are processed but not predictable. The processual phases[28] correspond to events or chains of events, although they do complete some preconceived operation for the process. The all-too-emphatic concept of events seems overcome, and so is the mechanistic concept of process.

Weighing event and process

As soon as we assume close connections between events and process, the question arises how these connections are characterized in terms of sequence and relevance. The relational view leads to questions such as the one asked by Sally Falk Moore: "How was the present produced? But the fieldworker must also ask, 'What is the present producing? What part of the activity being observed will be durable and what will disappear?' " (Moore 1987:727) There is no lack of variations on where to place events in processes: the history of events, for example, takes the incident as the initial spark for various processes.[29] The 'Storming of the Bastille' appears as consequential or revolutionary *ex post*

[28] Weick's three phases remind of the first, second and third turn as it is conceptualized in CA (cf. Sacks et al. 1974). The first turn is followed by a reception which is then corrected or (often tacitly) confirmed in the third instance. On this shared basis, the next turn-taking is performed.

[29] On this, Weberian historical sociology provides an interesting point: "Not Julius Caesar, but Caesarism; not Calvin, but Calvinism is Weber's concern" (Gerth and Mills 1957:55). Weber is concerned with the routinization of charismatic shocks, a charismatic person's continuing effects rather than their actions; however, charisma can only be analysed as an event against the background of a *longue durée*.

(cf. Sewell Jr. 1996a). In this fashion, events lay the foundation for a 'new era': for instance, the time after the Versailles peace treaty, or the era after the Japanese attack on 'Pearl Harbour'. Secondly, in micro-sociology – particularly in Goffman's and related dramaturgic studies – the opposite tendency can be found. The process is seen as the run-up to the actual event. The former prepares, adjusts, coordinates, etc. Without training, exercises, rehearsals, pre-trials, etc. the actual performances would be unimaginable. Here, the process serves as a back-stage from the point of view of the staging.

A third variant displays a tendency to dissolve the process into a chain of contingent events. Jack A. Goldstone differentiates this singular chaining – "...it just happened that this happened first, then this, then that, and is not to happen that way again" (1998:833) – from repeatable processes.[30] History as succession results in an "and then, and then, and then"-type of sequentiality. Events are always embedded in a chain of other events. Each event (also) counts for previous and subsequent events. In this way – seen as a linear progression – events appear as preparation *and* follow-up, as vanguard and rearguard in light of the surrounding events. This embedding does not relieve ethnographic reconstruction from the problem of how the chaining of events is accomplished.

These three differing placements of events in process carry implications for the weight and the relevance of the present. They hint at the presence of the (processed) past and at the future of the (eventful) present.

Early and late events

On this basis, we can re-examine the initially cited considerations from historical sociology, stating that events are systematically different according to their position in the process. In this line, the respective weight of events can be differentiated. While some events are 'ground-breaking', others remain 'marginal'. This fits the insight from

[30] Mahoney cites the 'speculative' study by Isaac et al. (1994) as an example: "To simplify their sophisticated event-structure argument, they show how [Martin Luther] King's death (Event A) caused the failure of the Poor People's Campaign (B), which in turn led to massive summer riots (C), which ..." (2000:526) Also see Vayda et al.: "Those with a more restricted concept in mind sometimes use the term 'process' to refer to a set of connected events occurring according to specifiable rules and within specifiable parameters of time." (1991:319).

historical sociology, or from sequential analysis more generally, that "earlier parts of a sequence matter much more than later parts, an event that happens 'too late' may have no effect, although it might have been of great consequence if the timing had been different" (Pierson 2000a:263).[31]

Incidents change their faces, according to where in the process an event is localized. Early events easily gain a formative and binding force with regard to later events (cf. Scheffer et al. 2009). This is rather conspicuous in my initial example from the field: the meeting serves to prepare the trial. The event gains its relevance, orientation and direction from what is to follow. Correspondingly, some studies focus on final or conclusive events and their preparation (for instance, tribunals, exams or elections). Here, processes of writing, aimed at developing a speech or preparing a decision, are studied (cf. Cambrosio et al. 1990). Other studies centre on preparatory practices, which serve to position, adjust and combine the various bodies (cf. Hirschauer 1991). The anticipated event serves as the horizon for a whole set of activities.

Past events demand attention as well. They do so not as totalities (this would be unfeasible), but as remembered and binding entities. Once processed, such entities require attention and may serve as threats or traps throughout the following events. The opposite may be true as well: only by help of past events – and the semi-products deriving from them – one may be able to reach a certain conclusion at the final stages. This temporally distributed agency appears in writing processes as well as in decision-making processes. A manuscript for a speech, for example, degrades the speaker to an 'animator' *and* assures the accident-free delivery of a highly complex matter. A good portion of speech-production is re-located to previous stages.[32]

> Preparation is an issue within the parties to the process. Are we well prepared? Do we have all the necessary information? Do we know how our witnesses are going to testify? Can we rely on their appearance in court? How can we assure that the witnesses 'deliver' in line with our

---

[31] Abbott (1983) points out that the sequence of events makes a fundamental difference – or rather, that the sequence is inscribed in the events themselves. Cf. Pierson (2000b) on political processes.

[32] Such a perspective seems apt to analyse different cultural techniques, such as PowerPoint presentations, playback, or memorising. See, for a good example, Goffman's chapter on the "lecture" (1981).

> case? Would they stand cross-examination? Scripting, rehearsal and critique are common stabilizing techniques in legal casework.
>
> Preparation is not just a matter for each party (or ensemble) independently. It is also a shared task: together, the parties work out the case in formal series of sessions with a judge (pre-trial hearings) or without her/him (e.g. in plea bargaining). The two barristers attempted to focus the upcoming trial by giving it a workable agenda. They minimise witnesses' enunciations and their probing in cross-examination.
>
> Judicial reform programs and court management reforms refer to precisely this cooperative preparation when they aim to increase system efficiency. The parties should be clear about what is disputed and what is not.[33] The same programs mean partial preparation when it aims at increasing fairness in the system. Both sides must be on equal terms: they must dispose of sufficient time and information to assemble their case and to scrutinize the other case.

However, in these directed processes, not only preparation plays a role. There are other qualities, emerging from the event to come. For example, participants have to wait, pass time, and endure tension and anticipation. This 'route to the event' itself can be made the object of research. Thus, in my example, one major point of reference for government programs is to reduce long waiting periods in order to relieve all participants – 'victims' as well as 'perpetrators'. The idea is that the pre-trial should not lead to a 'pre-conviction' by way of long times in custody or extended obligations.[34]

The opposite variation is less often considered in research. What happens *after* an event has taken place? What follows from an early event? One example here is provided by political scientific research on implementation. It takes its point of departure in a passed law or an executive order which results from an event (Act of Parliament) and is then fed into an attached process. How, if at all, is the legal text broken down to social practice? Other research on "events and after" can be found in new institutionalism. Greenwood et al. (2002) present

[33] This demand is explicated by the Office for Criminal Justice Reform: "Until recently, there has been no clear accountability or system for ensuring that cases turn up at court ready to proceed. The Effective Trial Management Programme (ETMP) has produced a framework which sets out the roles and responsibilities of all parties to progress criminal cases; and a process which ensures that cases are properly prepared and ready to go ahead on the day they are listed to be heard" (2004:12).

[34] During the period of my field research, defendants had to wait an average of 14.8 weeks before their trials. For clients in custody, this waiting time was two weeks shorter. Defendants on bail had to wait an average of 15.8 weeks before trial. The figures are collected and published by the Home Office.

a model of "institutional change" that focuses on so-called "jolts," which destabilize established practices. As Munir explains, they "take the form of social upheaval, technological disruptions, competitive discontinuities or regulatory change" (2005:94). Starting from destabilization, institutional change is initiated by new players, by innovation and by the diffusion of a new practice. The emergence of jolts bears on the question of individual capabilities for (sudden) adjustment and improvisation.[35]

> The barrister, albeit seemingly the decisive figure in the defence team, can only work with the material provided to him by the solicitor's casework and research. His work is about extending, improving, and – first and foremost – aptly engaging the instructed case on the court stage. Confronted with (flawed) early statements, barristers complain, in particular, about their limited capabilities for action. "Too late" is a typical commentary when faced with the "facts."
>
> Barristers complain when they are confronted with "surprises:" about the bad performance of their witness, about their stupidity, bad memory or lack of preparation. A client may change her or his testimony drastically. Suddenly and unexpectedly, the witness may fall silent in fear or burst out in panic. The balance of the respective cases shifts without the barrister being able to intervene accordingly. Barristers are impressed and agitated by such turns, simply because they happen rarely. They do not fit the habitual alternation of preparation and enactment.[36] Besides, these moments changed my own understanding of the court hearing: not as the performance of scripts, but as conditioned by a nexus of texts. The witness seems confronted with a discursive mine field composed of all the accumulated statements.

The sequence or temporal positioning – early or late – of an event does not in itself determine its relevance. However, both positions in process can explain impact. Put simply: early events can induce a certain tendency or problem to the following process; late events can impress the final decisions due to them being fully available or memorable. In addition: midpoint events may serve as decisive turning points.

---

[35] Mahoney provides one example: "The contingency of conjunctures is precisely why some historical sociologists argue that 'agency' can be especially efficacious during these periods" (2000:546). "Conjuncture" refers to the intersection of two separate processes.

[36] In light of this and while being positioned in ongoing processes, participants may retrospectively construct events as ruptures or jolts in order to justify errors, poor performance or changes in the practical course (cf. Munir 2005). They may ask for more time, more resources or for novel privileges to deal with the "unexpected situation."

Halfway through the process, the (memorised) past and the (anticipated) future come into reach.

Relevant and irrelevant events

The event in process seems a valuable model to decide on the relevance of events. Is an event important? "Event-philosophers" such as Nietzsche, Foucault, Deleuze, or Stengers define events as being relevant per se (Fraser 2006). An event would not be called an event, if there was no rupture, turning point, or emergence attached to it. Another way of ascribing relevance to events is to treat an occurrence as representational. The event, then, deserves appreciation because it stands for an entire culture or everyday life. Another strategy does exactly the opposite. It purposefully presents a rare and unusual occasion in order to implicate the relevancy of both, study and data.[37]

The concept of event-in-process does not ascribe relevancy per se, nor does it deduce relevance from the process-in-the-event alone. It distinguishes relevant from irrelevant events by relating them to the process and to other events in (this) process. It asks what an event takes up and what it contributes. An event, for example, can display such radiant force that it overshadows everything before and after. Only the event is not yet overshadowed by the archive, by deals, or rigid obligations. In these eventful cases, the process seems to impose hardly binding, fixing or structuring standards. Nobody knows what is going to happen. "Hang in there!" is the practitioner's promise in the face of "irrelevant preliminaries": "Nothing has happened yet, really."[38] A pending matter is anticipated here, because, so far, not much is set.

> This is also the case with references to edited protocols: depending on the witness, the barrister assigns more or less weight to the protocol text: "The evidence is overpowering!" or "Let's wait and see if she testifies!"

[37] Geertz's (1973) ethnography of "deep play" in Balinese culture mixes the two strategies. Firstly, the ethnographer arrives at a secret place. He witnesses an extraordinary occurrence. Secondly, the ethnographer implies that cock fights are customary on Bali. They are performed in the described fashion time and again. This double strategy reflects the relation of home and field from the ethnographer's point of view.

[38] A good example is provided by sports: players and coaches alike tend to emphasize, following a series of promising tests, that only the actual competition counts and that achievements in training or friendly games do not account for "The Big Day." Likewise, in juridical practice there are irrelevant exhibition matches and relevant championship matches.

> Assessments of this sort are based on secondary information about witnesses: that a witness is unwilling to appear in court; that she or he might change her or his mind; that some allegations were merely raised as a threat. The high number of admissions of guilt on the day of trial demonstrates this weighing – and the fact that, even in the face of overwhelming evidence, this evidence must yet be realised in the witness-stand on trial day.[39]

Here, the process of producing statements is probed in light of the event. The process encounters 'events that matter'. This impending disappearance of process can be grasped in conceptual terms: process degenerates into a prelude or mere chains. It merely serves to link the decisive events. It emerges from local events, not the other way around. This relation resembles what Moore calls "diagnostic events" (1987:730), which are events that are diagnostic for answering questions "on the extent to which the manufacture and control of particular cultural and social constructions is or is not in local hands" (1987:736).

A gradual disappearance of eventfulness in process can be found where the 'course of things' is already fixed. Correspondingly, one merely endures or sits through a session (as opposed to fighting battles). This kind of tendency to disappear can also be explained by approaches emphasizing a "temporal division of labour" (Zerubavel 1979): from the outset, an event is populated by various pre-products which restrict the options and delimit uncertainties. Under circumstances of divided labour, not everything is accomplished immediately, but some things earlier and others later. This concept is closely linked to what Hägerstrand called "the colonization of the future" (1985). Room for invention and creativity shrinks due to inscriptions, plans, standards, formats, etc. that stem from the past. Similarly, we could concede for our criminal procedure:

> The court trial is pre-designed in content and course. The participants know where to sit, when to speak, whom to address. The court serves as a discourse automat. Additionally, the procedural rules organise a communicative epistemic process. The parties disclose and receive the recorded statements. The barristers assess, condense, and translate the evidence into judicial moves. The in-court lawyers know about the other party's evidence weeks before they sit next to each other in the courtroom. The written statements allow forecasts on what to expect. They

---

[39] In 2003, this occurred in 63.4 % (12,444) of "cracked trials." Out of a total of 81,766 cases dealt with in the UK, the appreciable number of almost 20,000 falls into this category of scheduled hearings that did not take place.

> allow strategies to decide on what to aim at and how. Strong and weak points are nicely set up, even before judge and jury step in.
>
> The statements serve as measures of the relative strengths of the cases. Only in this way we can explain the relevance of the above described deletions by the barristers: they testify to the document's relevance vis-à-vis the following trial. The document is binding. It can even lead to the event being 'cancelled': the several-day-long jury trial is turned into the fixed assessment of a penalty. This, at least, can happen if the two parties decided to enter a deal on account of the written evidence in light of the court's interaction order. Once again, the past would triumph over the present.

With these inputs, eventfulness is diminished – meaning here, the 'opportunity' to put up something new and unexpected to the world. The prepared event is debauched to a pure formality. Local performance does not seem to matter.[40] The court hearing merely extends the "circulation of references" (Latour 1999a), without bringing new ones into the game. The matter is settled. The dice seem to have been cast.

> Confronted with the files, defendants plead guilty – even on the day of trial. This plea activates compromises – honoured by the government – to abbreviate the trial: the prosecution agrees to reduce the offence(s) in return for the 'guilty plea.' A related – inconspicuous, but nonetheless effective – way to reduce the hearing's eventfulness has been mentioned already. Portions of the witnesses' statements are slashed from the record. That means, those passages are erased that should no longer appear in the legal process and its events. The space of possibilities is reduced outside court, while the decision-makers (the jury) have no opportunity to observe these erasures.

Systematic preparation can reduce eventfulness to a point where the event loses its relevance. The event is dominated by the process preceding it. Its past and future are disposed of. In this case, the event does not launch new products. Rather, the event is merely crossed by advanced products, without leaving traces on these products. To put it more generally, eventfulness turns into a variable of 'its process.' But why then is an emptied out event – an almost 'non-event'[41] – still performed and communicated?

---

[40] Many ethnographies or workplace studies gain their appeal from the opposite movement: they show how work steps that seem 'irrelevant' and routine ("That's just the way it's done!") are indeed contingent and that there is something to be gained from a more intense look. This also includes studies which focus on the reception of media products (Keppler 1994) and mark this reception itself as contingent events.

[41] This abstraction refers to the notion of "non-place" by Augé (1995).

Some events, I suggest, have a largely ritualized meaning for the process at hand. They serve to provide for the proper performance of something already laid out. With reference to the court trial, for instance, the cases made are rendered decidable. Thus, the following decision is binding due to conventional speech acts, due to a sequence of communicative formats, due to the court's standardised positioning, due to the co-presence of all mandatory participants, etc. Everything that the parties sorted out before only gains validity through the correctly staged court hearing. In this sense, some hearings come down to downright rituals; the pure performance of form regardless of content. Although not more than just a formality, the prefabricated case cannot acquire the force of law without it being presented right here, right now, and in the right way.

Outlook: the adversarial procedure as eventful process

The framing question of "When is the field" turned out to be a valuable irritation. It triggered analytical puzzles that I worked on by discussing (implicit and explicit) concepts of event and/or process on the one hand, and by reframing ethnographic experiences in light of variant event/process relations. This postanalytical exercise involved reformulations of theoretical and empirical works, because each performs its own variant of event and process, mostly without making it explicit. The heuristics of event/process could demonstrate a more basic point. Theoretical works lean towards certain empirical cases, while empirical studies favour a particular analytics.

The relation of event and process probed accounts and approaches in places that usually go 'unharmed'. It worked as an antidote for both radical localism ('here and now') and radical determinism ('path-dependency'). It opened up a full range of event/process relations, in order to 'tare' social time-spaces according to the empirical case at hand. More so, the relation of event and process is helpful in reviewing one's own "tales from the field" (Van Maanen 1988). It is sufficiently flexible enough to address the socio-logic of the individual field. Unsuspicious presumptions as well as conclusions are rendered problematic insofar as they are marked as particular versions against possible others.

Further stimuli emanating from the pair can be shown in the analysis of events. Events are emphatically 'celebrated' in performance research. The poststructuralist tradition emphasizes the potentiality for resistance, renunciation, or reversal. Alternatively, events are analysed in isolation, merely as an intimate dialogue amongst strangers: without before or after and without any idea of their relevancy for what follows or cannot follow any longer. The plea for researching constellations of event/process – e.g., in legal procedure, political negotiation, research projects – also aims at this: to understand the event in its relevancy, and thus to make micro-sociological analytics macro-sociologically available. All these considerations render event-process relations a valuable conceptual tool for institutional ethnography as well as for postanalytical ethnomethodology.

The foregoing use of concepts can be called postanalytical because it avoids giving preference to any theory of either 'the event' or 'the process'. Accordingly, the two temporalizations were conceptualized broadly and captured a spectrum of relations: on one end, a firm process makes the events disappear; on the other end, decisive events dispose of the process. On this basis, various relations of dominance or asymmetries were imagined. Events dominate processes that precede and/or follow it. A process may dominate events, especially in cases when the latter are placed at the very end of the former. In light of the variants, what version rather fits the Crown Court procedure? Can event and process be observed in equilibrium? The adversarial procedure provides strong incentives for conceptualizations of this sort, precisely because here strong (read: solidified) processes and strong (read: contingent) events are conducted side-by-side. In this regard, it is no surprise that our multi-sited field – with its client-lawyer conferences, plea bargaining sessions, or public court hearings – instructed the discussion of event-process relations.

In the Crown Court procedure, events can be characterized according to their contribution to the formation of cases. Events are more or less consuming or producing; importing or exporting; peripheral or central; commenting or participating. In other words, many – but not all – procedural objects (such as the alibi-story in chapter I) are variously used: in pre-trial hearings, in trial hearings, in the exchange of files, in archival work, etc. The procedural events are thus only one time-space among others. Around and through them, we find not just one but many (intertwined) processes of case-making: knowledge processes, communication processes, decision-making processes. Each operates on the dual basis of events and process.

Legal procedure creates processes with *their* events and events with *their* processes. All these mark legal procedure as a fascinating frame of meaning-production and a tricky research unit. In the next chapter, we will focus on the process of knowing from the point of view of *the* Crown Court event: the jury trial. In epistemic terms, this event demands certain concessions by those who should know (and not know). The expert witness performs his expertise by fitting it into a composite division of knowing.

III. A CASE OF INDECENT ASSAULT: FITTING SLEEP-WALKING EXPERTISE IN

The interplay of events and process allow the parties to stage highly complex case-demonstrations. In the following case, each party produced an expert in order to assess the defendant's claim that he was "sleep-walking" when 'automatically' touching Mrs Vic's sleeping body[1]. The case-study is concerned with the precise ways the two experts are placed in the midst of the Crown Court division of knowledges. The 'immodest' division demands recognition by the 'modest' experts, meaning situated articulations of knowing and not-knowing.

The last case-study dealt with the mobilization of an alibi-statement. It emphasised process over event and showed how case-making involves a whole series of versions of one story and various encounters and dimensions to weigh it against the adversary's allegation-story. The following case-study[2] puts an emphasis on the (processed) event. It asks how a statement is staged in court, or to be more precise, how it is meticulously placed in the midst of the procedural event called trial. In the case under study, two psychological experts assess the sleep-walking account of the defendant who is charged with indecent assault. The expert testimonies get entangled with other forms of knowing in the jury trial. Their knowledge claims get restricted by various neighbouring knowledges: the certified facts, the instructed case, the opposing expert, and the common sense. Knowing is delegated and distributed. This division of knowing corresponds, if we apply Robert Kagan's (2001) definition of "adversarialism", with the decentred decision-making and with the various authorities involved in this.

It is Wednesday morning. I take the train and arrive comfortably early for another day in court. The ten jurors had to wait longer though. With two days delay, the Court is ready to listen to the opening statement by the prosecuting barrister. I cannot wait to see how he, my current informant, deals with this case (so far, I only saw him as defence barrister). The defendant faces a serious accusation, one of indecent assault. The complainant testified to the police that he, I call

---

[1] In this case, the ascription of the (prejudgemental) category of victim is not debated by the parties. This is why I abstain from adding inverted commas.

[2] An earlier version of this case-study was published in Science, Technology and Human Values (Scheffer 2009).

him Mr. Grab, touched intimate zones of the victim's body while she was asleep. Mr. Grab denied a wilful act. He delivered, as the prosecuting barrister phrases it soon after, "a slightly unusual case, of course, with sleep-walking." Technically speaking, the court deals with a defence of "automatism."[3] The sleep-walking defence, if successful, results in a denial of Actus Reus, a denial of the criminal act itself.[4] In his introductory note, the prosecuting barrister presents the dispute to the jury as follows:

> Mr. Calm and Miss Vic went to bed, and during the night Miss Vic was woken by somebody touching her between her legs, around the area of her vagina, the top of her thighs and on her bottom. At first she thought it was Mr. Calm who she was sharing the bed with but then looked up to see somebody else, name unknown, but recognized him as one of Mr. Calm's friends, and there is *no doubt about it*, it was this defendant, sat on the side of the bed and realised that it was him who was touching her, Mr. Calm being asleep still in the other side of the bed, Miss Vic effectively between the two. *As you can imagine*, this startled Miss Vic, and she shouted out. [...] What the defendant in fact is saying is that he was sleep-walking, not in control of himself, not making an intentional assault in any way whatsoever. If that is the case, then he may not be guilty. The Crown case is *of course* that this was an intentional assault, an intentional touching; and, to assist you with that, as his honour indicated to you yesterday, you are likely to hear expert evidence in this case from two psychiatrists who have some understanding of the area of sleep-walking in general. (3.11[+2])

There are a number of interesting details in this official protocol excerpt. There are, for instance, examples of how this account tells apart facts from accusations ("no doubt about it" and "as you can imagine"). One may notice, moreover, the "of course" uttered by the prosecuting barrister. The phrase "of course" sharpens the contrast between the cases of prosecution and defence. It introduces a first impression (disbelief and laughter) and a second impression (scepticism and assessment) of the matter. What interests me is how the court and the parties cast the two psychiatrists. They are meant to "assist you"

[3] Automatism is "broadly defined as state in which an individual's mind does not accompany his or her physical bodily actions" (Wells and Wilson 2004:5). See also Williams (2000).

[4] From the judge's summary: "If, because of the sleepwalking, the defendant's state of mind was such that at the time of the act in question, his ability to exercise voluntary control was totally destroyed, he is not guilty of the offence" (4.11[+2]). See for some background into the "sleep walking disorder" and the defence of automatism, Thomas (1997).

(the jury/the jurors) rather than, for instance, tell the jurors how to decide. The "of course" (simplicity) and the "assistance" (complexity) constitute a sharp disparity. This disparity and the contribution of experts is the concern of this chapter.

By this focus on knowing and the court's division of knowledges I give only a partial view on the case. The case carries other perhaps even more interesting implications. For instance, sleep-walking defences excite debates within English judicial politics and feminist criminology. What is more, critical socio-legal scholars as well as political reformers would be concerned with the 'problematic treatment' of "the Victim and other witnesses" (Matoesian 1997:55). In other debates, the case could serve as a strong example of how 'the legal system' in regard to certain offences creates absurd results, how it is 'in poor shape', how it is 'a farce'. For the Home Office, the Ministry of Justice, or the Attorney General's Office, it may read as an exemplary case for the "justice gap" that is diagnosed frequently, particularly with regard to "sex crimes"[5] and in comparison with European jurisdictions.[6]

Interrogating a single case

In the following, "case" coincides with two usages. Case is, firstly, a specific "indecent assault case" that occurred in my ethnographic field. Each facet of the case is relevant to convey the case in legal-practical terms, meaning here, the role and effects of a "sleep-walking defence."[7]

[5] Sexual crimes, ranging from sexual assault to rape, are strongly debated. Critiques examine how lawyers use "dirty tricks" or "lack interest" (Temkin 2000) when it comes to these cases. Konradi studied "sex crimes" from the point of view of the prosecution and found that "too little" preparation is invested "too late" (1997).

[6] By contrasting official allegations and actual convictions, governmental criminologists observe that only a minimum of complaints are actually prosecuted, a small share of which, eventually, end in convictions. See Mooney (2000) and Walby and Allen (2004).

[7] There is a long and winded career of the so called "sleep-walking defence." Thirty years ago, the object ("sleep sex") was presented as highly dubious (Bonkalo 1974). It was common for defendants to receive counsel from his attorney to "forget about this business of sleepwalking because a jury will never believe you!'" (Rosenfeld and Elhajjar 1998:272). Only later it became exceptional (Rosenfeld and Elhajjar 1998), then somehow frequent (Shapiro et al. 2003), and properly defined (Cramer Bornemann et al. 2006). Sleep-walking became recognized by way of legal and scientific authorities. Recently, guidelines for assessing such cases (named criteria: the individual history, the sudden arousal, the family history, etc.) solidify the object for the court (see Mahowald 2003).

Case is here, secondly, an analytical category. It is an answer to the eminent question: "What is it a case of" (Ragin 1992a:1)? I offer the following answer: it is a case in which both parties request and mobilise expert evidence for a jury trial. How, I ask, do they place the expert evidence in the legal arena? What are the ways of knowing (in) this case? How does the Crown Court procedure allow other knowledges to enter?[8] The answers turn the past legal case into a precedent case of Socio-Legal studies and Science Studies.

The answer to "What is it a case of?" emphasizes the "instrumental" (Stake 2000:437) character of the study, namely that the case is examined "to provide insight into an issue or to redraw a generalization" (Ibid). This instrumentalism does not exclude ethnographic details, but demands them: "The case is still looked at in depth, its contexts scrutinized, its ordinary activities detailed, but all because this helps the researcher to pursue the external interest" (Ibid.). I reconstructed this 'case within the case' by help of field notes, especially on the days in court, the defence file (containing, inter alia, the correspondence, the solicitor's notes, and the final expert reports), and the official court transcript.

I argue that in order to place an expert successfully in the court's division of knowing[9], this very expert needs to engage some modest acts of sharing and borrowing knowledge. As a start, I choose "the phenomena to be explained as they exist for the people living them" (Katz 2002:255), meaning here, the admittance of 'not knowing' in the application of other knowledges. Here, not knowing does not undermine, but substantiate credibility.[10] Borrowing other knowledges is common amongst laypeople who try to argue on 'scientific objects' or 'specialists' issues' such as climate change or genetics. These modest acts are little discussed when it comes to experts. According to the literature, experts receive credibility due to their high status, their established

---

[8] On the relation of law and knowledge production, see amongst other authors, Jasanoff (1995; 2005), Nelken (2006) or Valverde (2003). The latter takes "interest in the workings of law not in order to move it closer to justice or to make it more rational or both but, less normatively, in order to study the mechanisms by which law, rather than simply using facts in the form of 'evidence', also produces knowledge" (2003:5).

[9] Akera represents the division of knowing as one layer amongst others in a hierarchical "ecology of knowledge" (2007). The layers include "actors, artefacts, knowledge/skills, organizations, occupations and disciplines, institutions, macroscopic institutions, and historical events" (Ibid.:419).

[10] The distribution of knowledges is closely linked to the "distribution of credibility" (Shapin 1995:260). It is at the core of "credibility-managing schemes" (Ibid.).

methods, and their convincing performances. The sleep-walking case reminds us of another equally relevant factor: the expertise fits into the overall authoritative division of knowing because they *do not know* themselves.

Science Studies literature on experts shows a preference for knowing over not knowing. The critical literature emphasizes how legal knowledge is insufficient, half-baked, or biased. Critiques refer to asymmetrical and hegemonic knowing: the mismatched competition of legal and extralegal knowledges (Collins 1999), the displacement of alternative sources of authority (Jasanoff 1995), or the appropriation of peripheral knowledges by law (Tomlins 2000). In the case of psychological expertise, commentators warn that psychologists "are taking over the courtroom" (Coles and Veiel 2001). I argue that experts, contrary to the adversarial competition of the "hired guns," limit their own claims and take in knowledges of others. They intervene in the legal course by borrowing from other knowing bodies represented in the procedural arena. In this line, the expert witnesses in the sleep-walking case rest their conflicting advices on top or, rather, in the midst of certified facts, partial cases, scientific consensus, and the common sense.

The experts' compatibility reminds us of Robert Boyle's idea of the indifferent "modest witness." Boyle's role model laid moral and political foundations to experimental sciences (see Shapin and Schaffer 1985; Shapin 1994). The "moral witness" knows by fitting into a system of knowledge-production comprising a technical apparatus (e.g. measuring devices, manipulating machines, etc.) and ethical rules of austereness. The modest witness is an "almost invisible figure" (Olesen and Markussen 2001:15). The expert's compatibility reminds us, moreover, of Haraway's critique of Boyle's postulate of neutrality and instrumentality. In alliance with the experimental apparatus, the indifferent scientist may contribute to an overall immodest project. The latter may well overrule our ethical consensus. It may cause cruelty and brutality. Haraway's "modest witness@second millennium" (1997) takes a political stance; she reintroduces morality into the project of science. Her call for modesty proper derives from reflections on the scientist's partial position. Partiality is unavoidable due to the situated character of scientific practice. At this point, one may think of two frames of modesty/immodesty: one frame refers to the interactional or dramaturgical level (decorum, recipient design, impression management, etc.); the other shows on the level of explicitly calculated or tacitly approved effects (decision, intervention, interference, etc.).

Next to practicalities and politics, the modest witness may contribute to an overly societal and cultural state. The performance of modesty may show as a prerequisite vis-à-vis complex distributions of knowledges that some authors identify as an attribute of "knowledge societies" (Albrow and King 1981; Stehr 1994; Stichweh 2004). Is modesty necessary in order to perform credible expertise? Is it a means to overcome what Social Studies of Science identify as disruptions – due to specialization, commodification and concealment – by ways of modest 'not knowing'?[11] The modest expert, I suggest, becomes part of the court's "epistemic culture" (Knorr 2003:1 sq.) and its "moral economy" (Shapin 1994:383 sqq.). The modest expert may contribute to the court's overall 'immodest' fabrication of decidability (Magnus 2007).

Expert evidence in criminal proceedings

Law and Society Studies, Social Studies of Science, and Discourse Analysis provide a substantial amount of research on the role of expert witnesses in legal decision-making processes in various legal cultures. In this section, I point out the spectrum of the experts' legal impact, meaning their relevance for the shaping and the outcome of criminal cases. This spectrum ranges from minor to fundamental, from unrecognised to authoritative. While some expert witnesses provide foundations and judgments to the legal process, others fail to do so. I chose four examples from criminal legal processes. They are neither ideal types nor representative. Rather, they are points in the continuum of relevance. Together they remind us of the contingent nature of expertise. The four selected studies display triumph, routine, or plight of expert testimonies in relation to relevant other knowledges:

- Michel Foucault's lectures on "abnormality and normalisation" deal with the role of mental health experts in the "medico-legal discourse" (Foucault 2004). The rather immodest experts assess the defendant's psychological state and nature and by doing so, they attach both reality and morality to the matter on trial. Foucault shows how law and science join as a novel and forceful dispositiv. For Foucault,

[11] Accordingly, studies on experts observe both: the drive towards "democratizing expertise" (Blok 2007) and "interactional expertise" (Collins 2002) on the one hand, and the growing "management of knowledge" (Fuller 2001), including its economic exploitation, on the other hand.

these two regimes build a perfect couple because they share the will to knowledge. They unite to one normalising force. In this duet, the psychological or psychiatric experts create what Foucault calls "a double" to the deed and the defendant. The defendant is no longer simply somebody who carried out an illegal act, but somebody of a different nature who exists outside the moral collective. Expertise shows why the 'abnormal' individual was able to commit the crime and why there is an enduring risk of reoffending. In Foucault's version, there is no strangeness between law and psychology:

> They function as discourses of truth because they are discourses with a scientific status, or discourses expressed exclusively by qualified people within a scientific institution. Discourses that can kill, discourses of truth, and, the third property, discourses – you yourselves are the proof and witnesses of this – that make one laugh. (2004:6)

Legal facts and scientific expertise work hand-in-hand – and would not be able to maintain their weight without the respective other. How do the sleep-walking experts balance legal evidence and psychiatric diagnosis?

- Gail Stygall compares the expert witness to other witnesses in adversarial settings. She is interest in the ways expert witnesses are cross-examined and the range of responses available to them. Ordinary witnesses lack a number of rights that are granted to the "privileged experts" (Stygall 2001). The former are regularly interrupted (rather than invited to talk), confronted with closed questions (rather than open ones), and treated as incompetent (in remembering or explicating). Stygall distinguishes three major "privileges" (2001:329): the right to "amplify" (Ibid.:335), the right to contradict by using a "contrastive well" (Ibid.:337), and the right to draw conclusions with the "professional so" (Ibid.). She explains these privileges by the recognised status of expert witnesses as professionals. Judge, lawyer and expert share a symbolic, moral and social status outside *and* inside the court. Each represents an entire institution: law, science or the state. Their implicitly universal stance provokes critique: expert witnesses, when siding with one party, may betray the idea of science. How do our experts combine scientific universalism and adversarial partisanship?

- Roger Shuy reflects on the sacrifice he made for his legal service. He emphasizes the differences of science and law. Shuy served as a forensic linguist in many civil and criminal cases in US-American courts. He experienced assets and drawbacks as an 'insider' (Shuy

1993; 2000). He identifies advantages, for instance, that "the data is gathered for us by the legal system" or that "we don't need to worry about whether or not the issue is one that will grab our audience" (Shuy 2000:68). The list of inconveniences, on the other hand, is long:

> Short time limits imposed by a law case, as opposed to the more familiar time limits enjoyed in everyday academic pursuits; an audience almost totally unfamiliar with our field; restrictions on what we can say and when we can say it; restrictions on what we can write; restrictions on how to write; the need to represent complex technical knowledge in ways that can be understood by people who know nothing of our field while maintaining our role as experts who have deep knowledge of these complex technical ideas; constant changes or jurisdictional differences in the field of law itself; and maintaining an objective, nonadvocacy stance in a field in which advocacy is the major form of presentation. (Shuy 2000:68–69)

Shuy marks the differences of legal and academic knowledge-production and knowledge-performance. The two cultures make him, comparable to ethnographers in their fields, an insider (as consultant or expert) *and* an outsider (as an academic linguist). The necessary assimilation comprises time discipline, the use of an unscientific language, the appreciation of procedural rules, and the need for oversimplification. Are our sleep-walking experts geared towards popularization and simplification as well?

- Michael Lynch and Simon Cole discuss how an expert witness, Cole himself, failed. The expert was rejected as a "meta expert" (Lynch and Cole 2005) on fingerprint identification[12] in a preliminary hearing. The judge weighed his contribution as invalid ('junk science') and unhelpful on various grounds: no scientific validation, no positive discrimination, and no concept of adequate truth claims. Lynch and Cole discuss whether the judge's rebuff reflects the expert's lack of a positivist framework or his unfamiliarity with the "language games of the courts" (Lynch and Cole 2005:297). They conclude: "Credibility for the field would arise less from any abstract theoretical apparatus and more from the contingent set of associations, press clippings, and precedents that accrue as the field becomes entrenched and normalized" (Ibid.). On the side, the authors discuss other reasons: the relevancy of the

---

[12] *People v. Hyatt*, No. 885212000, 2001 WL 1750613 (N.Y. Sup Ct., 10 October 2001).

scientific consensus[13], or the expertise's legal usability, meaning its potential to take a stand and to tell right from wrong. Cole, in a separate comment on their reflections, explains the plight of his 'immodest' expertise by his lack of experience (2006:857). In a later case he apparently "applied the lessons learned in *Hyatt*. I did not attack fingerprint evidence; I just emphasized my credentials as a scholar" (2006:858). How do our sleepwalking experts relate to one another? Are they adversaries through and through?

The four versions show expert witnesses as boundary-crossing figures. The four journeys from science to law turn out to be rather triumphal or rather disastrous. The analysed experts differ in their impact on judicial decision-making. They sketch out a spectrum of practical relevancies: from a restructuring force, to a privileged player, to an insider/outsider status, to an irrelevant contestant. This spectrum calls for attention to the contingent nature of expertise. Whether an expert witness does or does not gain impact is an empirical question.[14] Another lesson can be drawn from the range of corresponding knowledges. The four studies place the expert vis-à-vis different knowledges. Witnesses as well as Counsels need to perform what one could call 'multiple boundary work'. This chapter picks up on both lessons.

Sleep-walking expertise and its relevant other knowledges

The expert, in order to legally matter, takes up and borrows from other knowledges. He does so by stating that 'something is not known by me but by X', that 'we all know', that 'the literature says', that 'something is known by Y as well', etc. These moral, interactional and epistemic transactions concern the give and take of knowledge ('I know something that assists your diagnosis.'), the mutual acknowledgement ('You know X, while I know Y.'), the assembly of knowledges ('Altogether we know.'), and the credibility granted by the recipients ('We believe

---

[13] See the following remark: "We would do well to remind the reader that the defense was, after all, seeking to have Cole testify about the limitations of fingerprint evidence, perhaps the most widely trusted form of forensic evidence used in criminal trial, at least until the advent of DNA typing" (Lynch and Cole 2005:295).

[14] Thus, I agree with Shapin that "there should be no such thing as a theory of how credibility is achieved, at least in the sense of one of those grand theories that would offer an adequate formula for how it is done regardless of the setting and the nature of the case at hand" (1995:261).

that X knows.'). By all these transactions, the expert demarcates 'his knowledge' vis-à-vis certain other knowledges. But what are the other knowledges? We provisionally answer this question on the basis of a longer excerpt originating from the friendly examination of the prosecution expert, in the following called Prof Con. The examination took place on the 3rd day of the jury trial. In the excerpt, some moments are consecutively numbered:

Q So the *confusion on waking*, is that inevitable?
A I would place much more emphasis on that or on the two factors. The difficulty in rousing somebody from sleep-walking in the first place and the confusion that's present afterwards, [1] and Dr. Pro would. Certainly, much of the literature [2] says that the expectation is that there would be this confusional state on wakening and difficulty in arousing, and I guess that's where I think in this particular case I have most concern and why my view is that this was not a sleep-walking episode.
Q Because that is [3] a feature we have a description of where on the evidence – and it will be for the jury of course at the end of the day – the evidence [4] appears to be that Mr. Grab responded to a comment made, for instance.
A It wasn't so much that. [5] I take Dr. Pro's point that I'm not sure that that was a considered response that took a lot of thought, but I was listening to [6] Mr. Grab's own evidence. I mean, what he said was that he realised he was in Mike's bedroom. I think what he said was he realised that his presence was making Miss Vic agitated, which is fairly lucid thought. I think he said he decided [7] not to apologise at that point because he thought he was making the situation worse and it was better for him to go off to his own bedroom. That [8] doesn't sound like somebody who's confused about where they were, particularly someone who hasn't sleep-walked before or has sleep-walked only 10 years before. I guess one would have expected [9] complete puzzlement and bafflement and take some time to realise where he was, what was going on, and [10] I'm not sure that lucid thought, 'Well, I'm making the situation worse, I'd better leave and I'll apologise in the morning' is consistent with somebody coming out of a sleep-walking state.
Q [11] So having a rational thought process like that rather than complete befuddlement, you say, suggests not sleep-walking.
A [12] That's right. He doesn't really give much description at all of being confused. I think he himself said it took him a few seconds to get his bearings, which is much quicker than one would expect. [13] Also I thought it was quite interesting, her account that, I think she said Mike was very difficult to wake up or he took some waking, I think, is what she said. He was probably in deep sleep and the same

level of sleep as you would expect somebody who is sleep-walking. He certainly wasn't drunk from the evidence that I've heard. She said he had hardly been drinking at all. [14] You would have expected Mr. Grab to be as difficult to rouse as Mike was rather than coming round so easily.

Q So you see a comparison between Mike and Mr. Grab.

A That's right. [15] One is very difficult to rouse; the other is fairly easy to rouse. I think it's [16] much more consistent with him, if one is saying that he was in some sort of sleep state, is for him to have been in this partially awake state [17] that Dr. Pro described where one is [18] easily roused and one isn't disoriented and confused. One does come to one's senses relatively quickly. (4.11^{+2})

The Crown Court trial hearing follows a standardized and ritualized sequence (Scheffer et al. 2009). Expert witnesses are examined after the eye-witnesses. Prosecution witnesses are heard before the witnesses for the defence. The sequence of appearances performs the "burden of proof" that typically lies with the prosecution. However, the two experts on sleep-walking were heard in the opposite order: the defence claims the possibility of sleep-walking first; the prosecution claims the impossibility of such a claim right after.

On the conversational plane, the protocol reveals some patterns: Firstly, the expert does not give a talk or speech. Instead, he is guided through the testimony by a series of closed questions asked by the barrister. The barrister initiates the expert's responses. Questions *and* answers place the expertise in the midst of a division of knowing, while reserving some space for the expert's unique contribution. A few examples from the excerpt may clarify this: the expertise states the common scholarly comprehension of sleep-walking ("much of the literature") [2, 10]; the expertise shares the perspective with the other expert ("and Dr. Pro would") [1, 5]; the expertise picks up on the certified facts ("I was listening to Mr. Grab's own evidence") [3, 4, 6, 7, 11]; the expertise utilizes demonstrations for the jury's common sense ("That doesn't sound like somebody…") [8, 9, 10]; the expertise develops and applies a diagnostic criterion ("one is … one is not") [12–17]. The latter establishes a litmus test on *this* sleep-walking. It includes all relevant other knowledges, meaning the certified facts, the instructed case, the other expert, and the common sense.

In the following, I analyse the enactment of expert knowledge in the jury hearing according to four relevant other knowledges. The experts 'modestly' adopt features of the certified facts (1), the case instructions

(2), the competing expertise (3), and the common sense (4). How is this done in detail?

Expert evidence and the certified facts

In his lectures on normalisation, Foucault described the extension of legal evidence by psychiatric experts. The facts were surpassed in order to lay bare the abnormal. The modern criminal procedure accumulates "certified facts"[15] throughout the pre-trial and the trial. In the sleep-walking case, the experts borrow facts from both procedural phases: from the police interviews with the victim, the eye witnesses, and the accused, and from the witness testimonies in court just completed prior to the expert testimonies. They perform these sources as facts in order to create stable reference points for their diagnosis. They perform them as facts by treating them as symptoms of the defendant's psycho-physical condition at the time of the reported event. Here, knowing is distributed because the experts do not provide independent or competing facts.

The expert for the defence received certified facts already months prior to the hearing. Dr. Pro studied police statements that were given by the alleged victim, her partner and the suspect. In his *written* expertise, Dr. Pro treats these texts as if they were 'historical documents' to be interpreted. Additionally, Dr. Pro utilized accounts that he received "during my interviews with him." From these sources, he deduced relevant factors such as the defendant's "personal history of sleep-walking" or "the amount of alcohol consumed before the alleged incident."[16]

The expert for the prosecution, Prof Con, did not file a report. He was hired only shortly before the jury trial. An earlier trial hearing was adjourned because the prosecution could not counterbalance the defence expert. The new hearing was rescheduled to provide the expert

[15] The notion is developed by Luhmann: "Legal facts are made fit the legal framework; they have to facilitate as much as possible the deductive use of legal norms. They have to support the presentation of legal validity by conveying the impression that, given the rules, the decision follows from the facts of the case. They have to be certified facts" (1992:1430).

[16] There is an emphasis on the empirical grounds of the expert's judgement: "Q. In order to prepare the reports for court you obviously need to go into some of the background and the like. Would you take a history and various things from a patient? A. Yes. We take a full history, a family history, a personal history, occupational history, and so forth."

with the full witness testimonies. This allowed him to witness the witness examinations 'live on stage'. This, then, was Prof Con's task: commenting on the facts and their use by the defence expert. The prosecuting barrister mentions the limited empirical grounds of Prof. Con's expertise in passing:

Q Thank you. I think in this case, although you have not had the opportunity to assess or examine Mr. Grab yourself, you have seen all the case papers and the reports prepared by Dr. Pro who we have just heard from. Is that right?
A That's correct. I was initially asked to comment on Dr. Pro's findings." (4.11^{+2})

In the course of the following examination, the prosecuting barrister selects claims from the witness statements, asking 'his expert' for an opinion. Does the reported arousal fit the scientific criteria for sleep-walking? Does it exclude sleep-walking? There are only few 'facts' that actually allow such speculation. Prof Con's conclusion [7] shows how facts and expertise are linked up, how the latter turns facts into indicators, and how this fusion arrives at strong conclusions [8]: "I guess one would have expected complete puzzlement …" The expert does not just adopt and interpret the facts. He transforms them. He turns them into supportive or confutative signs of sleep-walking. He does so by selecting indicators that fit the facts and by choosing facts that fit these very indicators. This "documentary method of interpretation" (Garfinkel 1972) is not just about interpretation; it is at the same time about fact-production. It renders the 'touching', the 'arousal', or the 'leaving' real for all practical purposes.

The connection of local facts and general diagnostics is not just a method or an exercise. It is also a norm for the public demonstration. Expert knowledge, without being applied to the facts, is rendered deficient by the court. In this line, the expert testimony and the questions put to the expert witness are at times received as unrelated. In this extract, the judge intervenes in order to direct the scientific knowing back to the "actual detail of this case:"

Q And from what you say then would it be possible for someone to be difficult to wake up but quickly come to orientation or *vice versa*?
A I think you're starting to split hairs a bit. I'm not going to give answers which I'm not too sure on.
JUDGE: Shall we get to the actual detail of this case and ask the doctor to comment on that rather than generalizations? (4.11^{+2})

The judge demands the application of scientific knowledge to the legal matter at hand. His "Shall we get to the actual detail?" presumes that the expert knows this detail, that he accepts the details as factual grounds for his judgement, and that his expert judgement is applicable to the matter. The expert's basic operation to account for these demands is to consult and assess only facts that are available to judge and jury as well.

Expert evidence and the instructed case

In the Crown Court procedure, experts are not experts called by the court, but experts called by a party.[17] This adversarial foundation thwarts the "myth of epistemological innocence" (Jasanoff 2005:54). It makes experts "see themselves as members of a prosecution or defence 'team' rather than as impartial witnesses answerable to the court" (Wells and Wilson 2004:8). In our case, the defence expert was hired and instructed first. Only afterwards, the prosecution engaged Prof Con to counter the defence expert's inferences. In the initial correspondence, he would insist that he gives expert evidence "not for the Crown but for the court." Later, the prosecuting counsel would reveal to me that "it was difficult for us" to find an expert who would reject the sleep-walking claim.

Briefly before the trial, the prosecution team gathers for the first time. Barrister and expert go through core indicators and select the evidence that supports the assertions. The expert provides the counsel with 'good questions' for the trial hearing. The counsel, in reverse, makes sure that the answers will be in line with the overall prosecution-case. The conference lasts no longer than twenty minutes. The barrister-expert exchange continues — by way of written notes — during the friendly examination of the defence expert: Prof Con points out some critical aspects of use for the prosecuting counsel in his subsequent cross-examination. Prof Con rapidly took his role as a member of the prosecution team.

---

[17] Lynch cautions S&TS scholars to appear as experts in the adversarial court: "An appearance as an expert witness in a trial or pre-trial hearing in an adversary system exacerbates those difficulties [keeping symmetry, impartiality], because of the common expectation that such a witness should put forward testimony supporting one side or the other in a dispute" (2006:2).

In the course of his casework, the prosecuting counsel develops specific ideas of how to use and involve 'his expert'. He highlights passages that are good for a rebuttal of the sleep-walking defence. From the police statements, he selects indicative passages that will be used by the expert later on. Two days after the trial, my barrister-informant recalled this in an ethnographic interview based on the brief and his notes[18]:

> I've underlined "his friend was still sitting on the bed" – that's the defendant – and she was talking to him, and he said "No, I didn't." Now, that's particular in the lights of his being sleep-walking, and even without getting to the expert's evidence, him responding and saying, "No, I didn't," was something I thought might be important. [...] Again, highlighted things he seems to recall on waking up that one wonders whether he would if he was sleep-walking, knowing that that was an issue in the case. So, the fact he felt embarrassed, and the fact that he thought he was trying to get into bed. Those are the kind of things. And then, when it comes to being asked about his history of sleep-walking, he's asked "Have you sleep-walked before?", and he says "not that I'm aware of," and that it was only ten years ago. And so I underlined those bits perhaps being relevant to how much sleep-walking history he has. (Interview, 6.11[+2])

The barrister prepares the examination in court by referring the evidence to the general diagnostics. He arrives at first conclusions already before his meeting with Prof Con. His partial conclusions, however, require a different voice in order to fit the court's division of knowing. They require an expert. In the course of the pre-trial, the barrister puts his hypotheses to test his expert's support. Prof Con, in return, suggests questions to be asked in court.[19] This way, the expert witness – compared to an ordinary witness – seems even more privileged than Stygall imagined. The privileges range from the right to answer questions to the preparation of some of the questions.[20]

---

[18] More qualitative researchers use file based interviews, but they do so in isolation. Stegmaier, in his qualitative research on judge's casework (2008), added direct observations of the workplace, plus direct observations of the judge's handling of the file during the interview. The common focus on the information-processing mind in the study of judges' work is criticised by Latour: "[...] we should provisionally leave the specific mental dimension to one side in order to focus on the subject matter of their [judges] activity, on the basis that their particular way of being right is not explained by the form of their thinking but by its content" (2010:128).

[19] Just as Saks assumes: "In a well-prepared case, lawyers and experts learn much from each other during consultations prior to trial" (1990:303).

[20] See Konradi's critical evaluation of prosecutors' preparation of their witnesses (1997). She identifies a systematic lack of preparation due to staff shortage in the Crown Prosecution Service.

The lawyer-expert alignment develops differently for the defence. Dr. Pro is asked for a written report, which in return requires some assurances that it will be, by and large, in line with the sleep-walking defence. This assurance is necessary because the report will represent the case for the defence. In fact, Dr. Pro's report adds new directions and new promises. It valorises the first account that Mr. Grab gave already in his police interview. The defendant is encouraged to stick to his version. The "skeleton argument"[21] explicates the report's significance for the defence:

> 1. […] the principal defence relied upon by the defendant is that if any such touching did occur, that he was in a state of sleep-walking at the time. If made out, this would mean that at the material time the defendant was acting as an automaton. 2. In order to support this defence, the defendant has the benefit of expert evidence from consultant forensic scientist … 3. Without reciting the detail of the report from Dr. Pro…, it appears that it is a properly arguable position that an act such as the one alleged against the defendant may be committed by an individual whilst sleep-walking. (1.11^{+2})

Dr. Pro classifies the sleep-walking defence as something that 'cannot be excluded': The act "may be committed […] whilst sleep-walking." The defence-case, in return, concentrates on this core: "Our claim is possible, while their accusation leaves room for reasonable doubts." To sum up, both experts reach the court as integral parts of the respective party.

Expert evidence and its opposite number

Prof Con is meant to offer a competing version and, by doing so, to reject Dr. Pro's 'vague possibilities'. One would expect this constellation to be divisive. In this line, socio-legal scholars discuss and dramatize the "battle of experts" (Weihofen 1935; 1950; Slovenko 1999). By doing

[21] The counsels discuss their skeleton arguments in order to choreograph the hearing. The prosecuting counsel: "So it's by reference to the law, having read that, the facts of this case and the psychiatrists' reports, I have indicated what course I think the court should take. And as it happened, we got through it. There wasn't really much legal argument because we decided he was either not sleep-walking and then he was guilty, or he wasn't, and it was. Well, firstly, if it was an assault or not; secondly, if he was sleep-walking, he was certainly not guilty. That's how we gonna put it to the jury." (Interview, 6.11^{+2})

so, they downplay the shared grounds on which such a 'battle' may arise. Prof Con and Dr. Pro, in this line, introduce the respective other as a "colleague." They praise each others' reputation and credibility. What are the practical conditions of this courtesy?

The court ensures that the two experts are brought in line. It ensures, moreover, that the experts are provided with the same case-material and scientific background. The following excerpt stems from the phase of the hearing before the jury is sworn in:

> Defence Counsel: Your honour, from the defence point of view there are two reports from Dr. Pro. In addition, I wonder if I can enquire whether your honour has had in effect a research paper.
> JUDGE: This is…?
> Defence Counsel: It has got a heading, "Original research".
> JUDGE: On what is described as sexsomnia.
> Defence Counsel: Yes.
> JUDGE: I got that this morning, yes.
> Defence Counsel: Your honour, I am not sure how far, if at all, that will feature but, your honour, it is one that certainly Dr. Pro has considered and, your honour, no doubt he can discuss with Professor Con.
> JUDGE: I think a copy of it should be sent to the professor today. We do not want to be wasting time tomorrow if he has not had a chance to see it.
> Defence Counsel: Your honour, certainly. I asked my instructing solicitors last week to do whatever they could to make sure that the professor had a copy of it. (2.11^{+2})

The adversary experts are expected to exchange "original research" before the hearing. They are expected to do so with mutual respect and with the perspective to reach some consensus. The expert knowledges are tuned by ways of material supply: Prof Con is provided with Dr. Pro's reports. Additionally, he is invited to take into account some new scientific literature that apparently lies at the heart of Dr. Pro's expertise. All this can still set the conditions for the often criticized "battle of experts" (Weihofen 1935; 1950). The following statement, however, gives a different impression. Instead of a battle, we find support of the other's categories and criteria:

> Q Perhaps the easiest way to deal with this for the jury is to, if we can, go through the criteria in the manner we have just done with Dr. Pro and start by looking at the five options he gave to the court … (4.11^{+2})

And later on:

Q In assessing sleep-walking, the criteria by Dr. Pro, I think, are factors that help us decide, would you agree with that they are the correct kind of criteria?
A Yes, I think that Dr. Pro's review and summary of sleep-walking is accurate. One thing I would add, I suppose, is the only conclusive way to know whether somebody is sleep-walking or not is actually to have an EEG, which is electrical measurements of the brain while the action is happening. That would happen, for example, in a sleep lab with somebody who had recurrent complaints of sleep-walking. You would usually videotape them, have an EEG, and you could then demonstrate that it was sleep-walking. Without that you're very reliant on the characteristics of the behaviour, what witnesses might say about it, what the individual himself says about it and, as Dr. Pro was doing, try to put together the various components to say, 'Is this likely to have been sleep-walking or not?' (4.11^{+2})

Question and answer compliment Dr. Pro's work. His assessment is 'state of the art'. It derives from the scientific literature. It marks out Dr. Pro as a full member of the scientific community.[22] On these grounds, Prof Con announces shared epistemic limitations:

> I should say neither Dr. Pro nor I is a sleep-walking specialist. We're forensic psychiatrists, and certainly much of my knowledge of sleep-walking, although I have dealt with cases before, comes from what I've read in the literature from academic studies of sleep-walking… (4.11^{+2})

These limitations, however, would not hamper their capability to discriminate sleep-walking from other phenomena. They still master the epistemic object.[23] This solidarity diverges from the inquisitorial prejudice. It diverges from the 'meta-expert' case presented by Cole and Lynch[24], as well. In our case, there are no attacks on professional integrity, scientific status, or on the disciplinary standard.

---

[22] In the UK, a rather bureaucratic alternative is offered through the accreditation by the Council for the Registration of Forensic Practitioners (CRFP). The standard for registration is "safe, competent practice" (1999:107). In order to renew the registration, practitioners have to "demonstrate that they have stayed up to date and maintained their competence" (Ibid.). For a general discussion, see a report by the House of Commons (2005).

[23] Wells and Wilson (2004) criticize the strategies that expert witnesses use in order to escape the scarcity of their knowledge. (a) The experts try to read from the biographical past whether the claimed psychological malfunction is probable at all. (b) The experts reconstruct the occurrence in order to find hints that do speak for or against the possibility.

[24] Cole summarizes his position vis-à-vis the other experts the way it was interpreted by the judge: it "concerned a case in which my science studies expertise was

This does not mean, however, that the experts fully agree. There are decisive differences when it comes to their judgements. The prosecuting expert differs from his colleague in the actual application of the shared criteria. Prof Con uses the criteria in an additive manner. He adds up clues against the sleep-walking claim. Dr. Pro, in contrast, uses the criteria in a consecutive manner. No single criterion can rule out sleep-walking. Each criterion is, he argues, insufficient to eliminate "reasonable doubts" (Heffer 2007). This basic difference in applying the shared criteria for sleepwalking is not debated in front of the jury.

Expert evidence and the common sense

The expert is not meant to go all the way down to the verdict. Prof Con would not resolve the matter. Dr. Pro would not advise the jury on how to decide. The experts address the jurors' common sense in rather modest ways. Shuy mentioned some appropriate ways to actually address the jury's common sense, while at the same time acknowledging its powers: providing the jurors with background knowledge, simplifying the research results,[25] and giving choices. Michael Lynch and Ruth McNally raise awareness for the court's "boundary work" (Lynch and McNally 2003) that distinguishes *and* constitutes common sense and scientific expertise. The court delimits the impact of experts in order to preserve the jury's autonomy as the "judges of the facts."

The sleep-walking expert addresses the jury's common sense in three ways. (1) He gives examples ("of children sleep-walking") that are knowledgeable not only to scientific experts or researchers. The example allows for some rule of thumb on "how long it can take … to become aware again." (2) The expert provides the court with a simple

---

'put on trial', the issue being whether I would be permitted to testify as a 'meta-expert' at a criminal trial about the limitations of fingerprint evidence. The judge memorably accused me of practicing 'junk science' for suggesting that latent print examiners were inappropriately donning the mantle of science" (2006:857).

[25] The instructing barrister explained for our sleep-walking case: "You might use soundtracks or catchphrases that sum something up. That happened, say, in this case when the experts are trying to explain to the jury something that they may not readily understand, or understand the relative importance of various criteria. Our expert said confusion on waking up in the sleep-walking case was very important, and he said 'Top of the Truth', that's how important he viewed it, and that's the thing that said it wasn't sleep-walking most of all. And when he says 'Top of the Truth', that's perhaps simple, it sticks in their mind more, that's something you'd underline and take a note of, especially so to use it to address the jury later on." (Interview, 6.11[+2])

demonstration. His reasoning ('the speed of arousing') derives from his 'scientific' reading of the facts:

> I think he himself said it took him a few seconds to get his bearings, which is much quicker than one would expect. Also I thought it was quite interesting, her account that, I think she said Mr. Calm was very difficult to wake up or he took some waking, I think, is what she said. He was probably in deep sleep and the same level of sleep as you would expect somebody who is sleep-walking. (4.11[+2])

The evidence, it seems, is full of 'hidden clues' that are revealed thanks to the expert knowledge. Prof Con invites the jurors to follow his demonstration and to draw their conclusions. The expert turns the jurors from mere believers into analysts who (should) have learnt how to diagnose the facts themselves.[26] Additionally, his "I think" and "I believe" limit the competences down to the details of the case, meaning, he abstains from taking a full decision himself. (3) The expert evidence offers condensation. It draws inferences from the aggregate evidence for the case at hand. It codes the details and enters these pros/cons into two columns in a decision memo: points are either proven beyond reasonable doubt or they are not.

> Q So you would put it in the negative column (a) because it happens 10 years ago.
> A And it's just the one off.
> Q And secondly, because there is only one incident of it.
> A Yes, and ... (4.11[+2])

The question-answer culminates in a clear opposition that resembles the bipolar decision that is required by the jury. In this way, the expertise is coupled with the jury's task. The expert concludes:

> Q And so taking all those cumulatively, in your opinion, does this point to an episode of sleep-walking or not?
> A My view is that all the evidence is against sleep-walking, and I think it's very difficult and it would be very difficult to come to the conclusion that he was sleep-walking.
> Q Thank you, Professor. (4.11[+2])

It is a fine line between assisting the jury and taking over its function. The expert evidence retains the line by ways of modesty and

[26] Stygall argues "that when juries shifted rapidly from speaking and investigating witnesses to silent receivers of evidence, a new economy of discourse practices emerged, one that privileged expertise" (2001:329).

caution: "in your opinion" and "My view is" or "I think." What is more, Prof Con uses a ramified negative phrase: "…it would be very difficult to come to the conclusion …" The latter serves as the utmost position under conditions of distributed knowing. Replacing "very difficult" by "impossible," for instance, would disrespect the jury's sovereignty. Assisting the common sense denotes that the expert turns something undecidable into something decidable – and into something that still requires a decision. The division of knowing simplifies *and* mystifies areas of knowledge. Something unknown is turned into something known, while something known is turned into something that requires a decision still.

The expert for the defence, while being confronted with the same diagnostic criteria, paints a different, rather "confusing picture"[27] of the matter. On first sight, his opinion seems to leave more room to the jury. Again, the common sense is assisted and invoked at the same time:

> Q Amnesia Tis always the case with a sleep-walker, is it not?
> A Amnesia for the period of sleep-walking is just about always the case but, again, there are instances when people have been sleep-walking and they may have some minor degree of recollection for what happened, but as a generalization you would say that it certainly is expected to be a complete amnesia. (4.11[+2])

Dr. Pro performs a similar understanding of the court's distributed authority to resolve 'whatever case'. He understands that it is for the jury to decide. However, he presents the decision that is left to the jury differently. While Prof Con presented it as being facile, Dr. Pro seems to complicate it. While Prof Con made the final decision 'nearly' disappear, Dr. Pro makes it 'nearly' impossible:

[27] Dr. Pro renders the decision complicated by adding more interpretations and versions to the certified facts: "Q. Just to take one example, we know that Mr. Calm appeared to be as close to Miss Vic when she screamed and was upset – and the evidence suggests that he did not come round as quickly as Mr. Grab. A. Yes, but I'd also point out, perhaps confusing the whole picture a bit more, that in all this Miss Vic wakes up, so of course there is the issue, you know, how clear her recollection and how accurate her recollection is. So we've not only got Mr. Grab's account which may or may not be accurate, we've got Miss Vic's account which I could say may also or may not be accurate, because she's waking up in an apparently very confusing, very frightening situation with a strange man, apparently, sat on the bed and, in her own words, goes into hysterics. So, I mean, this whole area is just not clear cut." (4.11[+2])

Q [...] I think often you said well, you might expect this, you generally may expect that. Would I be right? It does not necessarily mean that an absence or the presence of a particular factor has an overwhelming determinative view as to whether someone might have been sleep-walking or not?
A None of the factors that I have given, in my opinion, determines whether Mr. Grab was sleep-walking or not. If I can just expand a little further to state the obvious. Mr. Grab may well be telling the truth, could well be telling the truth. On the other hand, he could be telling a lie to cover up some other scenario, and that is obviously a matter for the jury at the end of the day to determine. (4.11^{+2})

The experts suggest different decision programmes. Prof Con suggests a kind of questionnaire to be filled in by the jury. His questionnaire resembles what recent legal reforms demand in order to assist the jurors' memory and to discipline the jury's assessment. It is this 'urge to simplicity' that Shuy complains of in light of his own experience as forensic-linguistic expert. Complex matters are reduced to their most simplistic forms. But the opposite is possible as well: Dr. Pro complicated the matter in order to suggest a way out. He suggests a kind of general scepticism towards certainties. He applies the highest standards of the burden of proof.

Common sense gains a certain role in the division of knowing: it is all-embracing *and* limited, knowledgeable *and* ignorant, apparent *and* conceded, present *and* absent. The experts perform these tensions by *just* assisting, informing or suggesting. This means first of all: the modest expert does not — and should not — take over.[28] The common sense, moreover, reminds us of different availabilities of knowledges in the criminal court. While the written expertise or police statements are available to all professionals, the common sense appears rather as an abstract expectation. The common sense cannot be known. It cannot be accounted for. It can only be invoked. Its indefinite spirit serves as a guarantee that the decision remains open until the very end.

---

[28] This is stated by the court of appeal in a case of "provocation to murder:" "We adjudge Lowery v. R. to have been decided on its special facts. We do not consider that it is an authority for the proposition that in all cases psychologists and psychiatrists can be called to prove the probability of the accused veracity. If any such rule was applied to our courts, trial by psychiatrists would be likely to take the place of trial by jury and magistrates. We do not find that prospect attractive and the law does not at present provide for it" (*Turner* [1975] Q.B. 834).

Discussion: distributed knowing and judicial decision-making

Earlier in this chapter, I presented a range of versions on how experts gain or lose relevance in the legal process. I briefly discussed four studies that did not just open up contingencies, but hinted towards relevant other knowledges for expert testimonies: the certified facts (Foucault's powerful psychological expert), the instructed case (Stygall's advantaged expert witness), the adversarial expert (Lynch and Cole's manqué expert), and the common sense (Shuy's adapted forensic expert). By referring to court transcripts, interviews, my field notes and to the case-file, I identified all four references in a single case. The sleepwalking experts take up the certified facts, while avoiding self-made assumptions; they form an alliance with their counsel, while avoiding contradicting judgements; they quote from the other expertise and avoid critiquing it directly; they hand over supportive conclusions to common sense, without competing with its 'wisdom'. Expertise is a diplomatic achievement.

The expert evidence enters the division of knowing by showing respect, by adopting other knowledges, by restricting its own claims, and by admitting not knowing. The normative character of this "interactional expertise"[29] is accentuated when we, like Stygall did, compare it with ordinary (eye) witness testimonies in the light of the four other knowledges. (1/facts) The ordinary witness serves as an isolated epistemic subject. His or her truthfulness should emerge without example. (2/case) She must not be coached in order to avoid the voice-over of the original and true experience. (3/expert) She is not supposed to meet, observe, or evaluate other witnesses in order to avoid collusion or replication. And lastly, (4/common sense) the ordinary witness must not give her opinion. She is formally committed to her direct experience. How is it that experts are allowed to divert from this epistemic decorum, or more so, that they are expected to adopt other knowledges in these respects? The answer touches again on the Crown Court's division of knowing and its procedural function. The division bears the court's authority to pass a judgement:

[29] The experts perform what Collins and Evans call "interactional expertise," meaning "enough expertise to interact interestingly with participants" (2002:254) and enough expertise "for a combination of contributory expertises to take place" (Ibid.:256).

- The division does not just ease the decision; it distributes the responsibilities for the verdict as well. A jury, in this regard, is not left alone, but is instructed, advised, equipped, excused and so forth. The absence of accountability for a (wrongful) decision supports this 'helpful' dispersion of responsibility. Overall, the case is turned into a decidable matter, both by transforming the matter and by forming a deciding body.
- The division of knowing performs the trial hearing as a contingent event. It marks out 'issues' that are not decided yet: a bounded zone of uncertainty.[30] The ways the experts relate to the facts and to the common sense are crucial here. The experts introduce the facts as enigmatic: one should not just review them without advice; one should by no means "laugh about" (Foucault 2004) them. The jurors must wait and listen carefully. They must not decide before all the evidence is presented. The cases, however 'crazy' or 'startling', are turned into serious claims that require thorough assessment.[31]
- As the exit point, the court derives at a decision proper, which means, a decision that could neither be avoided nor predicted. Contingency is performed even *ex post*. Nobody knows why and how the jury arrived at its verdict. The black-boxing of jury deliberation performs the trial once again as the all decisive event.

The Crown Court's authority to decide whatever case derives from a division of knowing. The division includes modest experts. The division in total, however, is rather immodest. The court claims to know what lies in the past, and what made itself available only through highly selective and ambiguous traces. What is more, the court employs a knowing body, the jury, which knows everything and nothing at the same time. The jury is not identical with the common sense (out there); the jury's common sense is domesticated for the court's division of knowing. This becomes obvious once 'we' invite people to judge the

[30] Geertz identifies the "skeletonization of fact so as to narrow moral issues to the point where determinate rules can be employed to decide them" as the "defining feature of legal process" (1983:170).

[31] "But forensic expertise consists precisely in integrating the initially peculiar and unusual into usual, thus renormalized, routine procedure" (Seibert 2004:229; my translation). Interestingly enough, the seriousness, once fully performed until the end of the trial, turns once again into a rather joking and disrespectful posture of those involved in the legal process. The former representatives as well as the former epistemic subjects, once exempt from their procedural discipline, turn into commentators of the 'ridiculous' stories.

case outside court.[32] Quite likely, 'we' would treat the matter as clear-cut as the prosecuting barrister implied in his introductory speech. The verdict would be "of course" one of "guilty beyond reasonable doubts." The jury, in contrast, passed a "not guilty" verdict.

Mr. Grab was acquitted – and *we* do not know whether the jurors accepted the sleep-walking defence or whether they rejected Miss Vic's story in the first place. Public opinion hinges on the first version. This is reflected by reactions in the press on 'similar' acquittals. Everyone seems to know what the decision was all about:

> News 24, 19th March 2005 - Sleepwalker acquitted: Police warned later that the publicity surrounding the case might tempt genuine criminals same defence.
>
> Toronto Sun, 30th November 2005 - It's ruled sleep sex: A Toronto man has been acquitted of sexual assault charges as medical officials said he was asleep at the time, with a disorder known as "sexsomnia". The judgment outraged women's groups.

As an outlook, I suggest a number of reasons why the sleep-walking defence is opportune under existing conditions: an adversarial expert can hardly achieve falsification on grounds of probabilities; the prosecution does not dispose of sufficiently high-profile experts; case-independent diagnostics are under-developed[33]; established indicators do not fit the vague eye witness accounts well. More factors work in favour of the sleep-walking defence: the small number of precedence cases; the common sense is unfamiliar with this kind of defence; a cautious jury may opt for pure chance, no matter how small this chance in fact is. This implies that with pure increase of such defences, the situation may change. In other words: the procedural diagnostics are subjected to learning processes at the various sites of the division of knowing: the experts, the judges, the counsels, the witnesses, and common sense[34]. The favourable conditions imply, moreover, that an

---

32 So far, I did not obtain any serious review of the defendant's story in various rounds of friends and colleagues. People were rather laughing or, even, being outraged by the defence. This is, of course, not representative knowledge.

33 Various commentators made this point: "To date, no ultimate biochemical, psychometric, radiologic, neurophysiologic, or other diagnostic markers have ever been conclusively defined nor required for the diagnosis of 'somnambulism'" (Rosenfeld and Elhajjar 1998:276). For "psychological blow automatism cases [...] opinion amongst experts is diverse and based on relatively few empirical studies of human behaviour" (Wells and Wilson 2004:8).

34 And more so the perpetrators, critiques added. Scholars remind of the "opportunity for individuals to feign the defence of psychological blow automatism in order to

acquittal is rather unlikely in inquisitorial settings, where "the report of the official expert is usually conclusive" (Ploscowe 1935:508), meaning it is rather definite and immodest.

In the following chapter, I put the emphasis on processuality in an event/process relation again (see chapter I). More specifically, I examine the role of the file and of filing activities for legal care and advocacy, for client centeredness and casework. File-work, similar to delivering expert knowledge, hinges on practical demands of the Crown Court procedure. When imagining legal file-work or record-keeping, one would generally expect, if at all, just minor differences amongst solicitors. The opposite is true. There coexisted profoundly different styles of file-work even in my small law firm.

---

receive a complete acquittal" (Wells and Wilson 2004:6). Or, as McSherry cites from a Canadian case: "Automatism is easily feigned and all knowledge of its occurrence rests with the accused" (2000:280).

IV. FILE-WORK AND PROCEDURAL CARE

Case-making and procedure are intimately linked. This is shown by ways of comparing the file-work of two solicitors working next door to each other. Jack and Jane explain their filing habits by applying diverse versions of legal care and diverse ideas of client-centeredness. The different styles of file-work may as well point to the different procedural regimes (Magistrates Court or Crown Court) served by the two solicitors. Their styles are fostered by practical procedural demands.

So far, I referred to files and filing on an individual case level. In this chapter[1] I analyse files and filing from a cross-case perspective as a matter of cultural techniques that the legal professionals learn and inhabit. File-work, while being considered as indispensable when it comes to case-making and case-management, is generally received with reservation or even criticism. It is conceived as overly bureaucratic and technical. Files symbolize an anti-humanist momentum of legal discourse as regimented by a technocratic, rule-bound, formalist hegemony. Files are ascribed a tendency to distort and exclude the actors' emotions and beliefs. They distract the busy lawyers from the real problems, the real causes and the real fears and wishes. Solicitors themselves utter concerns about the rising hegemony of formal odds and ends.

Once we move closer to the actual file-work in the law firm, the role and image of the file looks less uniform and threatening. This is how we can explore the diverse practical meanings of filing. This is how I found exemplary styles of file-work: one can be called the instrumentalist style, stressing the relevance of systematic reading and writing; the other one can be called the humanist style stressing the relevance of intense talk with the client. But where do these styles derive from? Is a style just a matter of personal choice? Does it conform to procedural affordances? The comparison of the instrumentalist and the humanist style evokes a more context-sensitive deliberation on the pros and cons of filing techniques.

I became aware of the different styles of file-work and its respective practical and ethical implications during my extended fieldwork in the

[1] An earlier version of this chapter was published in the International Journal of the Legal Profession (Scheffer 2007b).

law firm. While one criminal solicitor, Jane, preferred minimalist filing, her colleague, Jack, performed rather intense file-work as the *non plus ultra*. The latter (instrumentalist) style relates to the file as the primary means of casework, while the former (humanist) style relates to the file in terms of a compulsory exercise. In the solicitors' community of practice, the instrumentalist style counts as the elaborated, professional file-work, while the humanist style is often regarded as deficient and unprofessional.

But why do these differences exist in the first place? Why does one solicitor immerse in the papers, while the other tries to get rid off them? I seek explanation by relating the differences to the criminal cases filed (1), to gender differences in the legal profession (2), and to the professional habitus of either solicitor (3). In conclusion, I suggest an explanation involving the legal procedure served: there are good reasons for either style depending on the procedural demands for case-making. What is more, to stick habitually to one style while for reasons of competence moving on to another procedure may cause unwanted consequences.

Lawyers, generally, receive some reservation in public and academic reception. Lawyers, it is stated, live on others' troubles with the law. They advise the client 'what he should not do', 'what she should not say', or 'that one should give in'. Lawyers are criticized for being far from properly representing clients. They educate them. Lawyers represent the system, legitimate its authority, and convert everything mundane into juridical sense.[2] Lawyers are not, to remain within this critical picture, interested in the clients' real problems, emotions, fears, etc. They are far from a "client-centred practice," or from sharing the client's view.[3] One finds, of course, other, rather differentiating voices on the role of lawyers in law and society research. Some argue that a relevant minority of lawyers is, indeed, client-centred or receptive for the client's perspective.[4] Others argue that the academic maligning of

[2] Along these lines, lawyers are portrayed as "conceptive ideologist" (Cain 1983), as "translators of interests" or "symbol traders" (Cain/Harrington 1994), as "managers of conflicts" (Christie 2000), or as "managers of uncertainty" (Flood 1991).

[3] These widespread complaints are discussed by Emmelman in her "qualitative assessment of the Defenders' ethical defence behaviour" (1994:224) or in Hutchinson (1998).

[4] See Sarat and Felstiner (1995) and Eekelaar and MacLean (2000) on the client-lawyer relations in family law, here in divorce cases. See Rosenthal (1974) on the client-lawyer negotiations of their responsibilities in personal injury cases.

professional lawyers is unsophisticated and unbalanced (Moorhead et al. 2003b).

For the widespread critique, let it be justified or unjustified, the lawyer-file connection serves as a forceful symbol. The file, it is asserted, dissociates the expert from the client. Intense file-work, it is asserted, goes against client-centeredness. Instead of caring for the client, the lawyer *only* serves his or her papers. The file is consulted as a substitute for the one who should know better, the client (Moorhead et al. 2003a). The file embodies, for this widespread critique of the lawyers' conduct, a professional aberration: an inappropriate focus, meaning a wrong and untimely replacement of the client's perspective. Filing steps in between lawyer and client, shielding the former from the latter. The file, it is implied, interrupts the otherwise inter-subjective flow of emotions.[5] I will challenge this humanist critique in the light of some "specification of what lawyers do in handling cases" (Saks and Benedict 1977:374), or better, how papers, clients, and lawyers are systematically entangled in the ongoing everyday casework.

The humanist critique is echoed in the methodological scope of the respective studies on lawyers' work. Socio-legal studies on "what do lawyers do" (Griffiths 1986) focus on first meetings (Sherr 1986), on interviewing the client (Travers 1997), or on dispute management by the court (Yngvesson 1988). Generally, they pay attention to direct interaction and talk, both on the trial and on the pre-trial stage. They highlight the delivery of the case in court, in plea bargaining sessions, or in client-lawyer sessions, while often fading out the methodical and ongoing composition of cases.[6] According to most law-in-action studies (Travers and Manzo 1997), lawyers are occupied with talking to their clients, with their colleagues, or in open court. At times, files are mentioned as props or equipment. Only a few scholars, however, analyse filing[7] as a systematic feature of legal discourse formation and

[5] A similar critique is often formulated for the medical profession. Here, the patient record or the patient's file interrupts the 'human' flow of care and emotions (Luff et al 1993). See for the implications in medical treatment and the patient's involvement, Berg (1996) or with a focus on the electronic patient record, Svennigsen (2003).

[6] As one researcher put it already in the early fifties, "most lawyers today recognise that their most important work is done in the office, not in the courtroom; the elaborate masked ritual of the courtroom holds attraction only for the neophyte and the layman" (Riesman 1951-2:122).

[7] A systematic appreciation of defence lawyers' file-work can be found in Mann's ethnographic study on "defending white-collar crime" (1985). Mann presents a peculiar succession of occurrences. The defence lawyer starts his work already before the

case-making. Filing, in this view, is not separated from but strings together the various social situations of lawyering, including the lawyer-client interactions.

New studies in legal anthropology draw on this work. They situate the lawyers' practice within productive socio-material relations. Legal devices such as documents, files or archives co-exist in alliances that re-constitute agency and interactivity. The file, thus, does not just report and represent; it also involves and constitutes an extended nexus of those present and absent. What is more, the file does not compete with face-to-face interaction, but initiates, anchors and frames it. In this process, legal texts and legal talk are mutually transformed, thus producing a new situation that cannot be reduced to exchanges of either texts alone or talks without text.

In the following, I compare the file-work of (just) two solicitors: Jack and Jane. I use two cases in order to indicate a need for practical differentiation underneath the widespread concepts of legal profession, legal culture, or law. The ethnographic data indicates different styles of file-work that go together with certain understandings of legal care and professionalism. In a second part, I attempt some sociological explanations in order to make sense of the variant styles of file-work: Why do the lawyers treat their files – and their clients – so differently?

Styles of file-work in a criminal law firm

This chapter expresses the ethnographer's disturbing experience that, what was meant to be the same, can be done in vastly different ways. This experience demanded re-conceptualization because it contradicted the idea of a mono-cultural ethnographic field. How can I explain the diversity of something as (seemingly) formal, uniform, and bureaucratic as file-work?[8] Do the differences point towards alternative

---

prosecution puts its case against the client. She aims to prevent her client from being charged by extended paper-work. On the role of writing and inscriptions in institutional settings, see Smith (1985: 2000).

[8] Solicitors' workplaces seem like supplements of a legal bureaucracy, equipped with the standard habitat: desk, chair, filing cabinet, book shelf, etc. The orderliness invites inferences such as this one: "[…] files, more files, nothing but files, to which one should add cupboards, tables and chairs – which differ in price, depending on the rank of the employee – varying numbers of books, and, last but not least, a profusion of elastic bands, paper clips, folders, and rubber stamps. […] therefore, the nature of the

solutions for similar problems? Did I observe functional equivalents? And if so, can differences be evaluated in terms of procedural efficacy or even work ethics?

Recent comments on legal file-work relate to ethics in various respects. Critical studies emphasize the increasing relevance of mediated work. The medium is, despite its promises, far from being neutral. Rather, it over-standardizes and undermines the lawyer-client relationship. It disallows a grounded and truly informative connection. (Promising, holistic) human relations are distracted, misled, and occupied by the file's intrinsic and selective dynamic. The file-bias degrades the client to the file's appendix. This is the "standard indictment of the legal profession for its 'clinical' treatment of clients: the tendency of professionals to treat clients like hypothetical problems, like bits of memoranda or like fee notes" (Tuitt 2005:122). The medium takes over and presses the client into a template of fixed categories. The client with all his fears, worries, experiences, and expertise is reduced to an extension of the file (not the other way around). A different approach towards files, file-work, and its ethics is given by Patricia Tuitt (2005). Unlike Jürgen Habermas' inter-subjective universal pragmatics, for instance, she does not opt for the humanist celebration of direct life-world encounters, a celebration that goes along with the critique of technology.[9] Filing, Tuitt argues instead, is an appropriate mode of caring.

> The essence of the argument is that the legal file is (as much as the client) a proper object of care, and that the care of the file – its maintenance and management – is an appropriate objective for lawyers, and necessary for the development of a legal profession that is truly client-centred. (2005:113)

Caring for the file or caring for the client does not constitute a contradiction. Treating "clients like files is in a very real sense the only way to treat a client and to acknowledge that the legal file is already invested

Conseil does not depend on its equipment, but on the homogeneity of the world of files that are kept, ordered, archived, and processed, and upon the homogeneity of a staff that is renewed, maintained and disciplined" (Latour 2002:3f.).

[9] Tuitt seeks to "ensure that in the move towards a client-centred profession, the legal file is not, along with other legal technologies, 'overcome' as a dangerous, potentially dominant 'instrument'; rather, it should be welcomed as one of the multiple points of reference in any moral or ethical exploration of the practice of law" (2005:122).

with human properties, and is in a very real sense the only way to engage with the legal file" (Ibid.). Can Tuitt escape the limitations of instrumentalism by following Latour's idea of "distributed agency?" For her, the file is not just a (distracting) medium, but a constitutive participant in legal discourse.

The file, in this view, does not drive the lawyer away from the client. It rather gives a 'resonating' voice to the client and renders it available over time and for others in the legal discourse. It empowers what was said and meant by clients – and by doing so, it creates what one could call procedural agency (as the ability to act upon the case). I interrupt this line of thought here in order to display the styles of file-work that I encountered during my fieldwork. In order to do so, I consult my field notes, in particular the jottings on file-related activities. How do solicitors handle the files and how do they envision their role for case-work?[10]

The instrumentalist style: advocacy as paperwork

Jack spends the entire day in his office, at his desk, behind a stack of case-files. He reads the incoming papers, dictates notes, and delegates paperwork to his secretary.[11] Files seem to be his major inter-actants. Jack's file-work is remarkably systematic and methodical. His work – and one may add, office – days follow a routine course. First, Jack's secretary prints the due "diary notes" and places them on his desk. After receiving the day's work 'in total',[12] Jack orders the tasks according to their relevance. He decides what needs to be done first. What is urgent? Are there procedural deadlines to adhere to? The resulting order structures the entire work day. In order to start, Jack collects the respective files from the filing cabinet. This is also where his secretary places and locks them at the end of each workday.

What do the "diary notes" do in terms of casework? The notes arrange on what days Jack is going to consult the file (again) and on what issue. The case-file is the linchpin for incoming and outgoing

---

[10] For a similar perspective on social workers and their files, see Lau and Wolff (1981).

[11] See Suchman (2000) on the flows of paper in a small law firm.

[12] He would comment on the workload only exceptionally – and often ironically: "Oh Eva, are you sure you don't have more work for me today?" or "This will be a short lunch break!"

Fig. 9: The case files for the workday. © fotolia

messages. In one case Jack dictated the following "diary notes" to himself or any other future case-worker. Jack dictates the notes while flipping through the file: the left hand turns the pages, while the right hand operates the Dictaphone. By this method, he joins reading and writing activities. The active reading prolongs the file-record and adds new tasks to the ongoing file-work. In this manner he puts the following tasks to himself:

> 3.1^{+2} Check if CC [Crown Court] have responded regarding the application to extend the time and also need to fully instruct Counsel.

6.1[+2] Has the conference been arranged and does everybody know, are we to pursue the lines of enquiry regarding Mr & Mrs … and the family history of the aggrieved and has Mr M. telephoned and have the CPS responded with Kate's second statement?

22.1[+2] hand-written checklist [with crossed out tasks, TS]: letter from Committee, character reference, drafting witness statement, CPS-letter, plus enclosed evidence, dictating new statements

26.1[+2] Need to file defence statement on J. case by today at the latest.

26.1[+2] Need to file defence statement by today the latest, have CC responded regarding "Certif. of Attendance," file copy of PDH questionnaire

1.2[+2] To arrange conference on J. case

14.2[+2] handwritten checklist [with crossed out tasks]: letter from Committee, character reference, drafting witness statement, CPS-letter, plus enclosed evidence, dictating new statements

According to the diary notes, Jack has to check, to inquire, to file, to arrange conference, to draft, or to dictate. The tasks are specified in regard to relevant others: he has "to fully instruct counsel"; he has to check whether the "CPS responded"; he has to "arrange a conference" [with the defence team]". The tasks are, moreover, specified in regard to relevant objects and motions: an "application to extend the time"; the family history of the aggrieved; "Kate's second statement." Planned activities involve others and certain objects. And they involve various dates: definite dates (marking procedural deadlines or binding appointments), recurrent dates (following a personal control rhythm or conventions of resubmission), and approximate dates (applying certain rule of thumb for practicalities). These specifications on what, whom, and when ensure that Jack knows after weeks or sometimes months, what exactly he needs to be doing. This tasking by diary notes is complemented by a handwritten task-list. The list provides an overview on what remains to be done for the solicitor in charge. The list serves as the supplementary sheet outside the chronological order of messages and notes: a constant, self-made monitoring device.

The diary notes are characteristic for the instrumentalist style of file-work. As a tendency, they attenuate momentary social pressure, the need for intuition, or the art of recollection. Jack already delegated the decisions on what to do next to these notes, so that they find their way back onto his desk at a pre-defined date. The style builds on a technological device that creates continuity, reliability and regularity.

The workdays are set up to be fairly independent of the file-worker's changing moods or missing flashes of wit.[13]

The memory notes create a certain temporality of casework. They put the emphasis away from the 'exciting events'. They emphasize instead the many minute operations inside an emerging project. They partition the casework into productive steps that precede each other. The notes perform some routine even when the matter heats up and becomes stirring. One would not, in this respect, find Jack getting involved in lengthy reports on his cases, in heated debates on what should not have happened, or in sharp comments on colleagues.[14] He seems rather absorbed by the pulsation of file-work.

Jack picks one file after the other in accordance with the arranged diary notes. He attaches solutions or replies to his self-given tasks.[15] But there is more going on. Textuality matters here: the notes do not just extend the working memory; they also create new kinds of commitment. Here, it is not just the self that is demanding something. It is as well the filed inscription that creates expectations and, at times, exigencies. The diary notes confront Jack with the unwritten rule of instructions. They co-define what counts as good work. They require attendance. They employ the caseworker as much as he employs them. The case-worker delegates mastery and initiative to the records. The file fills up in sequences of lawyer-file encounters. Case-making follows a progressing cloze test that requires ongoing completion.

The memory notes are only one point of departure for the instrumentalist style. They are closely geared to other file acts and filed acts: file notes, statement drafts, incoming evidence, or business letters. For instance: Jack writes a letter to the prosecution asking for the full protocol of the police interview. He then briefly reports on his time-consuming – and cost-effective – work by means of a file note, for

[13] This brings us close to stereotypical contrasts, such as artists versus bureaucrats, or intellectuals versus engineers. I do not claim, however, that routine or method has no place in creative processes, or that routine work is not part of inventions. I simply claim that these oppositions are created around different problematizations that occur in tinkering processes: one around the question of how to assure stability, the other one around the question of how to deliver something novel. See for the notion of "tinkering" in Science & Technology Studies, Knorr-Cetina (1984:282 sqq.).

[14] There seems to be an affinity between this style and my own fieldwork. From the outset, I did exactly what my lawyer did. I read through files, made notes, and blackened and copied certain documents. We both sat at the desk, now and then complaining about the heat, the bulky files, or the telephone ringing.

[15] The diary notes matter since they can be read by others. They prove that the caseworker could have known better.

instance: "10 minutes dictating letter to CPS asking for Jane's full statement." He then creates continuity by dictating a memory note that will remind him later: "Check whether the CPS disclosed Jane's statement." Tasks are not simply done and over with: they trigger follow-ups.[16] Instrumentalist file-work, thus, takes place in a sequential and rhythmical order, in which diary notes are just one link in a chain.

After completing one task, Jack turns to the next in the same or another case: "There are so many details you can easily forget about." He worked on more than six cases at that time, which, by the way, pays in fees. In this way, Jack spends his days keeping file notes, writing letters, filing copies, and accounting for these artefacts as 'work units' for the legal aid office. I was fascinated by his ability to reduce complex matters to single tasks within larger projects. Jack, it seemed, did not get lost in the details of cases. He did see the wood for the trees.[17] At the same time, however, this seems the biggest danger of the instrumentalist style: that decomposition thwarts a holistic view on the legal matter.

Despite his discipline (and regular overtime), he would not be able to get all of his tasks done in one day all of the time.[18] I noted some of his complaints in this regard: "Sometimes there is just too much"; "The notes do not tell you what you better leave for tomorrow." Additionally, he would remain sceptical with regard to procedural contingencies: "You cannot plan everything." The first quote refers to 'busy days', when too much awaits completion. There is no systematic checking of the diary notes in this respect. (The secretary just prints them all, no matter whether the workload is actually manageable.) The second quote relates to the fact that not all casework done is actually planned or could have been planned in advance. Clients turn up without advance notification. Conferences last longer than expected. 'Urgent' telephone

[16] Jack's style of file-work invited the author to study careers, work processes and methods of mobilisation. The danger of this invitation is obvious: one is tempted to overemphasize progression and continuation, while underestimating the relevance of ruptures and events. Jack's method itself creates this tendency.

[17] For instance, he was not occupied with minor troubles enclosed in every file: the insufficiencies, mislaid papers, or missing updates. He would delegate these to his secretary.

[18] The office-based work allowed us to have coffee breaks at fixed hours. We would leave our desks and meet other (male) lawyers in the little kitchen downstairs. We would stand together, three or four of us, having a cigarette and some coffee. Here, Jack would not talk about his cases. He would rather start some "blokes' talk," meaning some chitchat on sports, cars, or our home countries.

calls break into the routine. And on top of all this: the tasks themselves often require unexpected effort; they are easier noted than done.

This does not mean that Jack experiences client-lawyer meetings, conferences with the barrister, or other contacts as 'annoying' distractions from the casework proper. It does not mean that the instrumentalist style renders orality less valuable. Encounters are, quite the opposite, framed by, built into and amplified by extended paper-trails that evolve before and after them. Speech events stipulate paperwork: announcements and protocols, invitations and warrants.[19] Read: he prepares these events by means of file-work and, by doing so, utilizes the events for the projected case under construction. The efficacy of the meetings cannot be separated from the apparatus of inscription. One engages the other.

The defence-case is developed on the basis of inscriptions, or more precisely, on the basis of past inscriptions serving as clues for Jack's present casework. Facing the file, he dictates letters, assesses evidence, and amends protocols. In this way, statements for/of the case surpass several pilot versions before they are fit for the procedural public. They are thickened, assessed, and sharpened.

The humanist style: Advocacy by dialogue

Jane and Jack seem opposite types. Jane talks to her clients (and to me) for hours. She takes her time. She listens carefully. She gets involved. She takes the client seriously as a person deeply concerned. The clients, she stresses, tell her things that they would normally keep to themselves. "I get them to talk, which gives me insights what all this is really about." The meetings take time. She goes through the issues again and again. She scribbles brief notes somewhere into her note pad. At times she is left disillusioned. Then she complains that she "cannot believe a single word," that "this is a nasty person," or that "truly it was him." None of this, I am confident, would be brought up by Jack.

Jane talks a lot about her cases. The information, it seems, comes to her mind while telling the case. Her ideas materialise, while discussing

[19] The same kind of reframing is mentioned by Luhmann (1995) in another context: love relations. With the invention of love letters, the performance of love affairs changed radically. The time before and after became more relevant (than the meeting itself).

case issues with her apprentices, some of whom she dislikes because of their "little engagement."[20] She rarely takes breaks. She is too busy doing her work, meaning writing letters and being on the phone. She talks on the phone often. During the rare breaks, she heads to town to get a bite to eat or she invites me for coffee, during which we discuss (again) the major case under work. She is always happy – even when stressed – to respond to my enquiries. She is a rich source of what this or that case is about, what it is that bothers her right now.

Jane's file notes resemble linear reports of contacts. They list the issues raised and the information delivered from a telephone conversation with the psychiatric expert, the talk with the CPS caseworker, or a meeting with a probable witness. The latter file-note, for instance, included an entire, yet not signed, statement:

> "I take down her statement from her and read it through to her for her signature. She is basically saying that she has known the family for well over 30 years having been married to her husband for 20 …" The file-note covers four pages, arraying paragraphs, each starting with "She spoke of …", "She referred to …", "She says that …" or "She goes on to say off the record, that …" The note ends as follows: "She signs the statement with all the information that she will put on the record and I explain to her that she will have it typed up and sent to her to remind her of what she has said. I remind her that she may be required by the barrister once he has had an opportunity to read through the statement to give evidence on Leo's behalf, if it comes to that." (17.3^{+3})

Her reports are exhaustive. They tend to include 'the details' without clearly establishing differences in relevance.[21] This, by the way, makes the barrister grumble about the quantity of undifferentiated information that he receives in her cases. She passes on too much of the same.[22]

It is hard to reconstruct from Jane's files how these information gathering occasions came about in the first place. Was it on her mental task list? Did some letter remind her? Did she happen to be surprised

[20] Such complaints take the following form: "He does not do more than absolutely necessary. He seems rather concerned with fees and cars."

[21] At times, thorough conversations - here with the barrister (6.3^{+3}) - enter the file notes, which then alternate between "I ask …", and "He says …" The file notes resemble a braindump.

[22] There are widespread complaints about solicitors that their briefs are packed with nearly everything. It requires extra work by the barrister to identify the core matters of the case and the relevant arguments. See Morison and Leith (1992) and Lex-Scripta (1999).

by an informant? Her filing appears rather reactive than active, rather reporting than initiating. Then, how does she know what to do next? She knows, it seems, from the multiple communicative circles she is involved in. These circles utilize her – and not the file – as their primary working memory. This involvement makes her do the casework 'naturally', meaning without much delay and without intermediaries which would organise her attendance over time. Here, casework takes a different rhythm and shape. It is erratic and clustered. 'One case at a time' is the preferred modus.

Nonetheless, her desk is covered with open and closed files 'under work'. Incoming letters enter the 'currently active' file loosely, meaning they are not yet 'sorted' into the series of dated sheets. A number of documents from currently resting files need to be tidied away, others are missing.[23] The head of the firm or Jack regularly has to remind Jane to complete her accounting for the legal aid office on schedule. "My office is a mess," she stresses not without some coquetry. However, sometimes she feels panicked when realising the outstanding file tasks. She simply does not keep up with the daily filing business – and loses the overview after some busy days in court.

Her file notes correspond with what one could call "oral text." Or better, her writing seems to be an extension of the realm of spoken language or – in parts – the dialogue's crutch or supplement. Her legal work performs a talk-bias: the dialogues equip and guide the filing. Her notes employ directness[24]. They display eagerness[25] and emotional involvement. She uses written letters to pass on the client's 'proper' intentions to her barrister[26] or to reassure the client's version vis-à-vis

[23] These missing links become objects of joint search involving not just the secretary, but at times the ethnographer as well. The secretary, in charge of typing and the filing cabinet, complains to colleagues (not to me) about the mess, and the unnecessary work caused by this.

[24] In a file note taken after a telephone conversation with the barrister, she emphasizes the urgency of the matter: "He is in the process of completing the PDH from which he knows it has to be served by tomorrow" (19.2^{+2}).

[25] Her dedicated style, thus, tends to some – perhaps quite useful – amplification. The barrister's request is reported as follows: "He says that there are a number of items which he would ask us to request now from the Crown;" she then formulates in a letter to the CPS: "We confirm that the Defence requires the following items as soon as ever possible" (7.2^{+2}).

[26] "As Counsel is aware, client is anxious for a bail application to be made on his behalf. When would counsel suggest this should be attended to?" (19.2^{+2}). She would even forward the client's letters to 'her barrister' to assure the client's voice reaches him.

the barrister.[27] In both respects, she is keen to keep alive or even reinvigorate emotions shared with the client in their meetings. This may explain why she normally presents her requests as urgent and the overall situation as dramatic. The inscriptions echo her talk.

Different from Tuitt's notion of "a mode of dying," the file serves as a means to perform and nurture "emotional energy" (Collins 2004:102 sqq.). Filing turns into an extension and "amplification" (Latour 1987) – rather than a technical replacement – of intimate talk. Only in this regard, filing is a legitimate practice in the humanist logic. This becomes clear in Jane's various critical comments on legal files: they occupy too much work-time; they become an end in itself; the file-management takes over; the legal aid office assesses her work performance according to the files, not according to the clients' satisfaction.[28] Jane performs minimalist filing in order to avoid these backdrops.

Good reasons for different styles of file-work

The following section builds on this introduction of the instrumentalist and humanist styles of file-work. I will discuss three model explanations for the differences in style. I will do so not just to reject or support them, but to introduce further insights into everyday file-work and the legal discourses that this work contributes to and unfolds. The explanatory lines relate to different – local, organisational, and societal – contexts: (1) the cases under work themselves, (2) the difference in gender between the solicitors, and (3) the adopted procedural requirements. Context, I aim to show, does not 'have a bearing' naturally, but requires translation into current affairs.[29]

---

[27] In the following line, she backs her client's story of a death certificate that he was allegedly given in the hospital: "It occurs to me that it may well be the case that client was given a document ..." (19.2^{+2}).

[28] Sommerlad (2002a) criticizes the formal requirements of legal aid – the endless lists on what you did, for how long and why – as being unrelated to doing a good job in the first place. Sommerlad studied solicitors' firms contracting with the Legal Services Commission. She interviewed solicitors about the impact of quality management reforms (Ibid.:365). Interviewees viewed the reforms and the changes to legal work as "'inextricably part of the new managerial culture'" (Ibid.:378). Besides the reforms' tangible benefits, the reforms were "viewed as having a moral and professional cost in that they were antithetical to what the political solicitors characterised as an holistic approach to legal service" (Ibid.). See as well Kronman (1993).

[29] See for the general argument, Schegloff (1987).

Case-specific advocacy

The sociological method of case-study would locate practical differences in the nature of the single case. Accordingly, cases are considered as requiring different practical solutions. I put this explanation to the test by presenting two cases that fit the sketched styles. I start with one case that Jane dealt with in her typical manner. It is a murder case.[30] The client is charged with having pushed his mother and by doing so having caused her subsequent death. The case involves expert statements on the client's mental condition and its implications for the occurrences in question.

The client is special indeed. He writes long letters to Jane every other day.[31] He seems rather incapable of fully grasping what is going on in legal terms. He is concerned and confronts Jane with all sorts of worries about what is going to happen. He calls her from prison whenever he gets the chance to. He wants to see her, involve her in his personal affairs, and make her look after things beyond the realm of advocacy.[32] Accordingly, she organises a new home for his dog, gets his washing from the local laundry, or contacts friends to visit him in prison. She becomes aware of her shifting role: from advocacy to a kind of mothering. She relates this role to his psychological illness.

The client, she says, is incapable of handling boundaries, of taking responsibilities, of being independent. He is barely capable of taking the role of the client, which is why her advocacy turns the usual order of delegation upside down: she instructs her client on the case after she finds out that his instructions are, to put it nicely, misleading. At the same time, he instructs her in rather private matters. He knows what he desires and dreads at the very moments of his life, for instance when

30 For an extended analysis of this matter and its moral implications, see the last case-study in this book.

31 She responds to each of them carefully and repetitively. At one point, for instance, the client is bothered by neighbours turning up at a Plea and Directions Hearing: "Even if the persons giving witness statements for the Prosecution attend Court on 9th May, they will not be attending Court to give evidence. The only time that any witness will give evidence in Court is if this matter goes to a full trial and those witnesses are called by the Prosecution to give such evidence. Please do not concern yourself any further with in respect of witnesses attending Court and giving evidence against you prior to the trial" (11.3^{+2}).

32 His long, uninterrupted, and tightly hand-written letters would contain obligatory cries for help such as the following: "I am not to (sic!) well at the moment my stomach aches are very bad cant (sic!) hardly walk/legs tightening up" (13.3^{+2}).

he is "alone" in prison or awaiting the next hearing. He is desperate for somebody to look after him, to care, and to sort out his daily concerns. Her care, in this sense, is highly case-related – an exception, so to speak.[33]

The case represented by Jack is different: here, the client is charged with having sexually assaulted a 25 years younger "friend of the family." It is a delicate matter.[34] The client has problems talking about it, which in turn causes problems already with the police during the first interview. "I cannot remember doing this," he repeatedly responded when he found himself confronted with the detailed allegations (themselves going back to the 'victim's version'). The case created these gaps – and allowed a range of imaginaries (of what really happened) to fill and dwell on them. All these – the unspeakable, the gaps, the lack of remembrance – were not articulated in the client-lawyer-talk. Jack would not criticize this, point at it, or even shed light on this. His routine writing worked over the silence and vagueness. The solicitor's summaries, letters, instructions, etc. overcame the client's silence, shame, and vagueness. He fabricated inscriptions that can enter the defence-case both for the inner relations and for the outer demonstrations.

File-work, in this regard, takes a case-specific function. It is not just routine and usual business, but it fits the case-related problems of articulation in the first place. The defence team, by means of the file, comes to terms with the matter; the client, by means of the file, is geared to a consistent position. There is, of course, more than just the juridical translation of silence into accounts, of the "I cannot remember" into a robust case. By dealing with it in a 'professional manner', Jack creates some kind of comfort. The instrumentalist style normalises the bizarre. No doubts are expressed, no accusations are implied, and no 'how could you!' is raised. Jack does his job, and by doing so, makes the client increasingly confident that an articulated and confident stance is feasible.

Another case-related difference may serve as an explanation: a more complex case requires a synchronic mode of communication, while a rather simple matter allows for the primacy of diachronic face-to-face interaction. Systematic paperwork, in this logic, provides the lawyer

---

[33] This reminds of "the lawyer as a kind of friend" as part in an "advantage-friendship" (O'Gorman 1963:9; as well Morris 2001-02).

[34] The extended case-study can be found in chapter VII.

with efficient means to manage complexity. In rather small matters, by contrast, the file seems less relevant as a means of ordering and processing information. The small cases – or better their details, facets, versions and side-stories – seem to fall relatively effortlessly into a schematic order. No elaborate orchestration and composition seems to delay and complicate their translation into a coherent position for the procedure at hand.

Does this point fit the two cases above? Jane's murder case is, by nature, a highly eminent, prestigious matter. It is far from being the straightforward case that translates easily into a presentable defence. The murder case was, by procedural rules, a complicated one. This is reflected in the casting mandatory for such an offence. Jane had to hire and instruct an additional in-court lawyer – next to the barrister, a Queen's Counsel – whom she had to provide with all the relevant case materials. The indecent assault case, on the other hand, represents a rather frequent charge that is far from unproblematic for the instructed in-court lawyer[35], but not particularly so for the case-making solicitor.

There is more to the relation of case and casework that is invested into its realization. A legal case is not a fixed, external measure. It is not by definition complex or simple, overwhelming or routine. The case itself is the upshot of casework. The resulting case is the upshot of background inquiries, the in-house assessment of evidence, the recruitment, and first-hand examination of witnesses, in short: of the various efforts that are organised and mediated by file-work. By virtue of this particular character of the case, the instrumentalist or humanist style of file-work feeds back into the case's complexity. There are good reasons to believe that the dominance of orality keeps things rather down-to-earth and simplistic. There are good reasons to believe, likewise, that systematic file-work allows a trial-and-error method, which sets in motion some rather complex case-making, including changing directions, tactics, and positions.

The two styles seem to fit the specific defences and this fit resembles a certain legal ethic: Adjust your style to the individual case! However, such an imperative does not hold once we look at the effects of the

[35] The barrister describes the cross-examination of alleged victims in rape or indecent assault cases as most difficult. Questions operate 'always' on the edge. They should not be "too aggressive and not too soft." Both extremes stage the witness as a 'victim' in front of the jury.

(routine) styles on the cases under review.[36] How does Jane's style co-produce certain features of the case? The same question applies to the indecent assault case. Jack's style resonates with the performed case. Case and (style of) file-work are entangled. The case is inseparable from its filing.

Gendered advocacy

Feminist scholars in socio-legal studies and criminology discuss legal ethics extensively. They take critical positions against a 'hegemonic' juridical discourse.[37] They denote the latter as male, technocratic, and distanced from clients as well as victims. The feminist position, in contrast, advocates those dominated by the hegemonic system. In this framework, female lawyers are probable bearers of an alternative advocacy and, at the same time, are themselves confronted with and sidelined by "the patriarchal nature of the legal profession."[38]

The two cases brought up here point to gender-related issues, in particular with respect to the client-lawyer combination. In other words, the two client-lawyer pairs seem to fit perfectly in terms of gender relations. The pairs seem complementary: here the male client desperately in need for help and attention, there the female lawyer who takes the role of 'care-giver'; here the embarrassed and speechless client, there the male lawyer who 'does not care'. Jane and Jack's styles seem to fit their respective legal matter: her 'trustful' mastery of listening and responsiveness; his 'relieving' mastery of precision and technicality.

---

[36] This invites some self-reflection. Does the same hold for the ethnographic principle that one should adjust the (mix of) methods to the specific field? How does ethnography as a research style shape the field it examines? See chapter II.

[37] Haney argues for an exchange of feminist approaches to jurisprudence, criminology, and welfare state theory: "Early feminist work on the state analyzed how women were subordinated by a centralized state. More recently, feminist scholars unearthed how states are differentiated entities, comprised of multiple gender arrangements. [...] Feminist legal theorists concentrated on multiple legal discourses, feminist criminologists on the diverse sites of case processing, and feminist welfare theorists on the varied dimensions of welfare stratification" (2000:641). See as well, Dixon et al. (1995).

[38] See the volume on "Women and the Criminal Justice System" (Van Wormer 2000:chapter 7). Likewise, feminist criminology covers all facets of the criminal process. An emphasis is, however, put on female victims, here especially of battery, sexual assault, and rape. The feminist critique points out how 'victims' are mistreated by a male-biased system. They become victims again, 'assaulted and raped for a second time' by the system that is generally meant to protect them. See for instance, Konradi (1997) or Wood (1994).

Let me, from the admittedly minimal number of two contrastive cases, generate some more hypotheses that point in the direction of 'gendered work'.

Can we explain the different styles of advocacy with "doing gender?" Do the specific cases support a gender-specific structure of supply and demand?[39] Do we encounter gendered differentiation within the legal profession? The styles of file-work seem to fit female and male stereotypes quite clearly. In this line of argument, the literature, on the one hand, refers to the legal profession as a "masculine cultural project" that qualifies the "professional practice around the notions of expertise, rationality, control, predictability and commitment" (Bolton and Muzio 2005:6). The masculine codes, on the other hand, "exclude values and behaviours associated with the feminine as weak and ineffectual" (Ibid.).

According to this male hegemony, the legal profession seems dominated by a technical, distant, and emotionally disengaged attitude. The sidelined female advocacy, in contrast, represents the human component, being client-centred and caring for the person 'behind the client'. In our example, only the male lawyer would embody the winning type of advocacy. Only he seems to (know how to) play the game of "commercialised professionalism" (Hanlon 1997), while she may fail in what is referred to as "cut-throat competition" (Sommerlad 2002b:214). Jane wastes her time with 'sentimentalities', while he complies with the economic implications of advocacy.

This common conception provides some strong explanatory force weighed against the two cases. Jane, indeed, supports the 'ill client' in ways that would not be expected from a male lawyer in the first place. Her mothering style resonates with expectations that address her as a *female* lawyer. The same gender relation applies to the assault case. Jack's client, I guess, was relieved to find a male lawyer in order to cope

[39] This may serve as an example for gender stereotypes in the area of advocacy: "Are women attorneys better? Some people look for women lawyers for a variety of reasons. They think women listen better, work harder, are more sympathetic, or are more likely to resolve matters without litigation. They may also think that a woman attorney might have a favourable impact on juries, particularly if the woman is defending a man accused of harming a woman in some way. Of course, all such thoughts are based on stereotypes and will not necessarily be true. Male attorneys can be just as hard working and sympathetic as female attorneys, and female attorneys can be just as aggressive and bull-headed as male attorneys. Your best course is to choose an attorney, male or female, with the qualifications and qualities that you think will best serve your needs." See on http://www.lawyers-uk.org.uk/guide_lawyers_advice.asp.

better with the embarrassment that goes along with the matter. In this line, the male lawyer's discreetness assists the 'suppressing' client in ways that cannot be expected from a female lawyer. His technical and distanced style responds to expectations that address him as a *male* lawyer. In this sense, gender roles come into play as social co-constructions. They become relevant in the interplay of expectations, requests and responses. The defence ensembles, as they were, rely on gender relations. They make use of gender as a 'cultural resource'.[40] The client-lawyer relations, it seems, would not have been feasible outside these constellations.

The two styles seem to fit the widespread understanding of female and male skills and ethics.[41] The male style is instrumentalist (focussed on the file), functionalist and distanced. He does not seem to care much. The female ethics appear to fit the second style: humanist, interested in the person, caring for more than just the case. But do we meet these different styles because they resonate with the ways lawyers are *doing female* or *male*? Are the styles resources for or rather effects of these doings?

Advocacy and professional habitué

The two explanations, presented so far, contain weak points. The first one (case-specificity) does not account for the regularities and routines in the styles of file-work. One cannot easily reduce practices of file-work and care for clients to single cases. It became clear that specificities of cases do not always support the idea of appropriateness and flexibility. What is more, cases are themselves upshots of case-making including file-work. One cannot easily explain one by the other. The second explanation (doing gender) seems strong in relation to the two lawyers. It provokes, however, the widespread critique against feminist

[40] This argument is used to explain the gendered sedimentation in the legal profession: "Both men and women actively do gender. In this case, women draw on the symbolic resource of feminine knowledge when they state that they practice certain areas of the law due to their 'people skills' and 'non-adversarial approach' just as men draw on the same symbolic resource … This leads to processes of occupational sedimentation, whereby women capitalise on the symbolic resource of femininity to colonise certain areas of legal practice" (Sanders 1987:11). See as well Sommerlad et al. (1998).

[41] Some authors evaluate these skills and ethics as misconceptions. See Bolton (2004).

reductionism. Gender, it is argued, appears next to other relational properties such as class, ethnicity, or profession. There is no natural hierarchy amongst these. What is more, styles of file-work are themselves valuable devices of doing gender. They are invested to serve the 'gendered' expectations by the client as customer.

Instead of engaging such reservations, I would like to suggest another explanation that remains closer to the ethnographic material and that – but only partially — involves case and gender attributes. It is, so to speak, less general. The argument is that lawyers learn styles of advocacy in the context of specific procedures or procedural regimes. The styles are responses to practical problems that appear on a day-to-day basis. While being engaged with a procedural regime lawyers adopt embodied capacities, basic assumptions, and multiple routines, altogether well captured as professional habitus[42]. Here, I refer to the systematic effects of an ongoing professional involvement. The idea is straightforward: the professional, by 'taking part (successfully)' or 'playing the game (appropriately)', undergoes a certain learning-by-doing.[43] The legal 'game' shapes those who are continuously engaged in it. Instead of employing a rather general field-participant relation, the ethnographer may wish to be pretty specific here: concrete work demands, as long as they dominate for a longer period of time, are able to shape a certain practical and ethical attitude towards, for instance, how to care for and handle a file.

---

[42] Habitus is generally, in various dictionaries, defined as "the physical and constitutional characteristics of an individual, especially as related to the tendency to develop a certain disease". Bourdieu uses the term sociologically in order to delineate a "system of acquired dispositions functioning on the practical level as categories of perception and assessment or as classificatory principles as well as being the organizing principles of action" (1990:53). He applied this concept to various fields including the "juridical field" and the "legal profession" mainly in the French context (Bourdieu 1987). I use the concept to stress the temporal dimension of professional dispositions. Habitus highlights the effect of a certain praxis for those who are involved in it over longer periods of time. Practice 'somehow' imbues the members' constitution with its demands. The single member learns how to play the game.

[43] For Bourdieu, there is no centre, no single educator, no conductor at work here: "…systems of durable, transposable dispositions, structured structures predisposed to function as structuring structures, that is, as principles of the generation and structuring of practices and representations which can be objectively 'regulated' and 'regular' without in any way being the product of obedience to rules, objectively adapted to their goals without presupposing a conscious aiming at ends or an express mastery of the operations necessary to attain them and, being all this, collectively orchestrated without being the product of the orchestrating action of a conductor" (1977:72).

How specific may I be when defining the field of legal practice and habitualisation? There are relevant practical layers relating to the everyday tactics of casework below the established categories of "legal culture" (Friedman 1985; Nelken 1995), or "professional culture" (Johnson 1978; Ariens 1992). These tactics are inseparable from the socio-logics of the court-related procedure, its demands, requirements, and selectivity. This means for our two cases: the specific procedural regime in which each lawyer is trained shapes the way he or she goes about casework – and file-work. Jane represented cases in the Magistrates' Court (MC). She was, until recently, in charge of all MC cases arriving at the firm or directly to her in court as a duty solicitor. Jack, before he changed to a bigger local firm, was in charge of Crown Court (CC) cases. How does this division of labour matter?

The MC procedure entails brief pre-trials and rapid trials. Often, the casework in these matters takes no longer than a day. The lawyer extracts relevant and helpful information from the client right before the hearing. As a result, there is a strong emphasis on the client-solicitor interview which lasts mostly no longer than half an hour or an hour. Here, the solicitor reports the accusations, asks the client "what happened," and designs a case strategy. The information gathered orally is the only argumentative ammunition for the solicitor's performance in court: both for purposes of bargaining and for trial purposes. The solicitor needs to manage the speed and shortness that is inbuilt in this regime.[44] Jane developed mastery in quick interviewing, memorising the client's account, and representing it vis-à-vis the Magistrates. In the MC context, Jane could not check the stories extracted or extend the defence-case by independent fact-finding. The solicitor, in the MC regime, relies on the client's account in order to deliver it in open court as the case for the defence or, more often, as just a list of mitigating factors. This immediate representation, what is more, demands some personal and emotional involvement,[45] analogous to the advocacy in other inquisitorial settings. In contrast, a copious witness examination is a rather rare event in the MC setting.

Jack, in contrast, is socialised in the Crown Court regime. This setting is characterized by the division of labour between a caseworker

[44] See Kozin (2008) for the detailed exploration of an attorney's file-work in 'quick' US-American State Court cases, here of drinking-driving.

[45] See Roach and Mack (2005) on "emotional labour" in Australian Magistrates' Courts.

Fig. 10: Witness Examination at Magistrates Court. Photograph from http://lcjb.cjsonline.gov.uk/Cambridgeshire/1354.html. © Crown

(solicitor) and an in-court lawyer (barrister). The solicitor stays outside court, while the barrister stages the case and negotiates[46] the matter with his counterpart. This procedural regime is characterized by an extended pre-trial during which both parties undertake independent investigations into the matter. The adversaries keep their own inquiry files, they interview witnesses, collect statements, and they put together the pieces to build a 'strong case'. The CC solicitor focuses on the mobilisation of these value objects. Accordingly, Jack emphasizes the following context of file-work:

> Yah, my function is to get the files, do what's needed in terms of getting together information, documents, etc., talking all that is needed.

[46] The plea bargaining practices vary drastically depending on the procedural regime. In the MC context, the bargaining option depends on the instant assessment of the (normal features of the) defence in light of the accusations. A guilty plea on reduced grounds appears as the naturally preferred option. See Sudnow (1965) for similar inbuilt preferences in a lower US-American court. In the CC context, bargaining appears as a recurrent weighing of two more or less co-emerging, fully developed cases. On the professional and procedural rationales to bargain, see Schumann (1977).

> And then my primary, prime function is to pass that on to barrister as I said before, the case is run between the solicitor and the barrister, but it's mainly the barrister. (Interview, 5.3+2)

The socio-legal settings, I argue, make different lawyers, different responsibilities, and different attitudes.[47] They educate different participants, equipping them with different ways of furnishing and performing 'good' lawyering. This is why the status of file-work and the actual practices of filing can vary drastically. The solicitor develops a style of work in response to the practical demands of the respective procedural regime. The style of file-work corresponds to one regime – and would 'miss the point' for another. Solicitors as a profession – unlike barristers – face different regimes and different tasks. Is this the decisive clue to explain the solicitors' divergent styles of file-work in a single law firm?

Conclusion: legal care in context

Our three-steps-exercise allows a number of conclusions. First, the explanatory contexts turn out to be either too broad or too intertwined with the phenomenon in question. The *gender categories* lack precision in relation to the practices of file-work. They are under-specified in so far as they do not translate directly into discourse practices. There are, moreover, a range of other categories – such as culture, class, or ethnicity – that are applicable on the same level of generality and coherence. The *case-specific context* falls short because it cannot account for the regularities and routines of styles. Why, one may wonder, do the two lawyers sustain their respective styles across a broad range of cases and clients? It is unsatisfying on a more basic level, because the styles co-produce the relevant features (simplicity, complexity) of the 'fitting' cases. The notion of habitus seems more promising if specified as

[47] Mather et al. ask "how lawyers think about and make the decisions that constitute their daily practices" (2001:175). They offer the following explanations: "One vision of these decisions finds their roots in the organized profession – its educational processes, formal organizations, and rules of conduct. Another explanation sees these decisions as shaped by the economic forces acting on lawyers, with firm profits or client pockets controlling the choices that attorneys make in their work. Yet another perspective underlines the role of lawyers' individual values and identities in making day-to-day decisions" (Ibid.). These three explanations are relevant, but miss out one immediate point: the actual demands of the procedural regime that is regularly served by the lawyer.

professional habitus. But even then, once connected to the becoming of lawyers in certain procedural regimes, one may wonder in how far the composed files (and offices) themselves contribute to the perpetuation of working styles. The co-productive role of procedural infrastructure[48] prohibits linear explanations. In this line, habitus turns into a set of dispositions supported by a local infrastructure of corresponding artefacts. Context is far from being the unmoved mover. Each of the three analytical options creates feedback instead of linearity. The feedback marks context and practice, to various degrees, as co-emerging features.

How can we make sense of the different styles of file-work and their discrepancies? How do they relate to the ethics of advocacy? To answer this, I specify the notion of 'professional habitus'. Lawyers, I claimed, adjust to the procedural regimes that they attend to on a day-to-day basis. The regime serves as the frame that tells apart good from bad practice, successful from failing strategies, available from unavailable communications, and useless from useful information. The regime teaches the practicalities necessary to 'do the job properly' and to 'play the game successfully'. The regime, however, is not identical with legal tradition, legal system, or legal culture; the procedural regime is more selective than these frames which scholars commonly use to explain or rationalize cases. The MC procedure and the CC procedure each translate into different discourse practices. They employ filing and file-work in different ways.

In the CC procedure, the solicitor's (instrumental) file-work is concerned with mobilising ideas and utterances into fully fledged case components. This includes developing ideas, tracing rumours, recruiting witnesses, recording their accounts, instructing the barrister, putting new ideas to a test, etc. These activities are carried out and enabled by means of precise time management, thorough synchronization, a focussed memorisation, and systematic accumulation. In terms of the "duality of mobilisation" (chapter I), file-work organizes the cross-correlation of versions of the same and of statements concerning similar issues. Ideas and utterances are mobilised as statements-in-becoming that merely exist inside the party's inquiry file – and not yet for the integrated legal discourse or for the procedural

[48] The reader will find more on the concept and the role of procedural infrastructure in chapter VI.

public. The CC-regime requires a broad range of filing activities and their meticulous coordination.

In the MC procedure, the solicitor's (minimalist) file-work is concerned with largely different tasks. Here, the solicitor prepares his or her own court-performance. This performance implicates quick responses to the prosecuting CPS-solicitor and a defence position for the Magistrates. The MC's preference for plea bargaining is attended by minimalist file-work. The case rarely ends in a confrontational trial. Rather the filing facilitates an inquisitorial process in which the accusation delivered by the authority is answered with excuse, explanation, and regret. Hence, file-work for the MC regime concerns the gathering and ordering of a few planned items – not of a speech manuscript — that the solicitor will (very soon) put to the relevant audience. This procedural regime cultivates instant filing of items to be ready at hand for the file-keeper's performance in court.

As a consequence, we derive at different styles of file-work not in terms of "rules versus relationships" (Conley and O'Barr 1990), "distance" versus "solidarity" (Bogoch 1994), "control" versus "wishes of the client" (Bogoch and Danet 1984), "client-centeredness" versus "self-interest" (Moorhead et al. 2003a), or in terms of a "moral division of labour in the legal profession."[49] In this chapter, I circumvented these oppositions by placing the relation of case-file and client-care within contextual lawyering. Legal ethics shift in light of the appropriateness of casework. Could it be, then, that – under given conditions – either style of file-work is not contrary but supportive to legal care? What if, for instance, the talk-bias of the humanist style is at times not supportive but disruptive to legal care? What about the ethical controversies between humanism vs. instrumentalism if the procedural regimes demand for different styles?

For Tuitt (2005), the file unfolds moral capacities by showing traces of humanity: emotions and passions. Just as if the client's spirit could be retained by ways of filing. 'But for whom and to what effect?' one may wish to ask. Such pragmatic query requires more awareness for

[49] Hughes explained this division as follows: "In fact, the division of labour among lawyers is as much one of respectability (hence of self concept and role) as of specialized knowledge and skills. One might even call it a moral division of labour, if one keeps in mind … that the very demand for highly scrupulous and respectable lawyers depends in various ways upon the availability of less scrupulous people to attend to the less respectable legal problems" (1971:306).

the formation of cases in procedure. For the moment, we can deduce two general points on solicitor's filing. (1) The file's major role is not to record the client's utterances, but to transform and fit them into the procedural course. The file is caring insofar as – and because – it is the *words* that the lawyer cares for in order to safeguard the client. (2) Files and filing contribute to specific procedural regimes and, thus, will and must vary profoundly. The filing style – as habitual and embodied capacity – may turn problematic when a file-worker moves from one regime to another. Then, the contextual fit of styles turns into a source of trouble.

The humanist style, in our example, seems to withstand the pragmatic adjustment to the CC regime. The persistence of Jane's style may relate to a common 'ethical' ascription (in terms of client-centeredness) and to her positive self-image (in light of past coups). The same inflexibility, however, may appear in Jack's case if he suddenly had to conduct cases in Magistrates' Court, which is, however, relatively unlikely for a male lawyer in his position. The procedure as practical demand and regularity teaches certain lessons on an everyday basis, while it apparently makes professionals unlearn certain methods that belong to another register. This applies in principle to both solicitors, but concerns mostly (female) lawyers in small and less prestigious law firms.

In the next chapter we will move closer to the legal work practices that have been developed and cultivated to serve certain procedural needs. Therewith, the ethnography of case-making moves back to the staging of cases in the Crown Court setting, something that the solicitor is no longer in charge of. The case-study explores the methods by which a barrister modulates a case of "wounding with intent" that has been given over to him by way of a "brief to counsel." I will study the barrister's 'pedantic' underlining, listing, noting, etc. as his compound technique to bridge texts and talk, various witnesses' statements and testimonies, the competing cases and the single defence.

V. A CASE OF WOUNDING WITH INTENT: THE BARRISTER'S DAY IN COURT

This case-study is about a dense process in event, a relatively short time-span not much longer than a working day. The study is focussed on the barrister's jottings, here in a case of "wounding with intent." The jottings provide insights into the barrister's modulation of case-material for all practical purposes. They show the formation of the facts down to the very details of, e.g., the body moves or the verbal exchanges before the ominous blow with a bottle (or a glass?).

What does a barrister do on the very day of the trial hearing? How does he put together his case-representation during this work day? The resulting case study[1] criss-crosses the realms of text and talk that are usually held apart. These final stages of case-making involve official material that was handed over shortly in advance. Also, they involve the lawyer's personal inscriptions, such as marks on the brief or the lists of points and sketched maps in his notebook. I integrate these diverse materials as participant observer by help of the trans-sequential method: the stepwise process of case-formation and the moments of writing and talking. Linking process and events sheds light on case-making right before and during the trial hearing – and on the complexity, contingency, and urgency of the barrister's craft.

According to the canon of qualitative methods, discourses are either made out of talk or text. Actors, members, or participants seem to either speak or write, listen or read.[2] Similarly, the legal sphere is understood as being driven by "two types of legal discourse: first the largely written discourse of judges, lawyers, and scholars about law and legal doctrine; and second, what the participants in legal institutions are saying" (Conley and O'Barr 1991:2). This implies that lawyers, in English criminal cases, keep files in the law firm or speak in court. In

---

[1] An earlier version of this case-study was published in *Research on Language and Social Interaction* (Scheffer 2006).

[2] Methodical branches are specialized along this line (see e.g. Silverman 2000). They are restricted to either documents or transcripts, regardless of the entanglements of text and talk in discourse praxis. Additionally, there is a general preference for talk as the genuine mode. "Voice becomes the metaphor of truth and authenticity, a source of self-present 'living' speech as opposed to the secondary lifeless emanations of writing." (Norris 1988:28) See also Derrida's (1977) critique of Saussure and especially his notion of "phonocentrism".

jury trials, this conceptual separation is echoed in a professional division of labour: the instructing solicitor keeps the case-file and gathers the material, while the instructed barrister or counsel articulates the scripted matter in open court. Solicitors and barristers collaborate along the text/talk and preparation/performance difference. In theory, the solicitor appears as the liable caseworker, while the barrister performs as the case's spokesperson.

This case study offers a different picture. It explores the interplay of paperwork and speech. This perspective goes back to Goffman's late studies of speech-production. Goffman distinguished "three main modes of animating spoken words: memorisation, aloud reading, and fresh talk" (1981:171 sq.). Most discourse studies, Goffman noted, treat speech on the whole as "fresh talk."[3] They rule out other (assorted) modes of speech-production. And they do so in "intertextual fields," in which, as Lynch and Bogen put it, "talk was but one discursive register" (1996:201). The following analysis accounts for various sources, modalities, and transformations involved in the barristers' speech-production.

For this empirical case I propose the analysis of sequences within production phases *and* between them. This trans-sequential analysis comprises diverse modes and materials of (the final stages of) case-making while (a) following a practical course, (b) sticking to the current state of the succession, (c) reconstructing the interim products that are (made) available to move on, and (d) accounting for the effects in terms of the case-in-becoming. Trans-sequential analysis employs basic discourse analytical concepts for its ethnographic case studies: discourse *formation* captures the diachronic and synchronic positioning by which value objects (or modules) reach certain states (and relevancies); each state represents a temporary *field of presence* in which value objects are directly related (and matter); the ethnographer accesses the (legal) discourse (or procedure) only partially (here: through the barrister's work of putting together the defence case).

[3] "In the case of fresh talk, the text is formulated by the animator from moment to moment, or at least from clause to clause. This conveys the impression that the formulation is responsive to the current situation in which the words are delivered, including the current content of the auditorium and of the speaker's head, and including but not merely, what could have been envisaged and anticipated" (Goffman 1981:171).

The data for this case study originate from the defence of "our client:" Steve Hit. Hit was indicted with a serious offence:

> WOUNDING WITH INTENT, contrary to Section 18 of the Offences Against the Person Act 1861.
>
> PARTICULARS OF OFFENSE: STEVE HIT on the 29th day of February 200X, unlawfully and maliciously wounded Tim Vic with intent to do him grievous bodily harm.

My case study refers to natural data and its emergence in time: the barrister's notes, the hearing's official transcript, the "brief to Counsel," and the ethnographer's field notes. The barrister's notes are central since they give orientation to 'the order in which he did what' in this case. The notes chronicle the details of the representational project and its completion in speech. All this took place within just two days in the courthouse, which is why I will not add dates to the materials analysed.

The trans-sequential analysis follows a series of discourse practices in their temporal occurrence. It sets off with the barrister's work before the hearing (1), continues with operations carried out during the witness-examinations (2), and arrives at the preparation of the closing speech (3). This tour reveals the in-court lawyer's work of case-representation.[4]

The barrister proceeds by preparing inconspicuous (minimalist, de-contextualized, multi-functional) modules, each of them appearing incidentally extracted, processed, and arranged in the course of case-making. The modules play a key role since they "can be swapped and changed as required. As a result they make possible a highly differentiated memory that can tolerate and indeed facilitate a rapid change of topic with the proviso of return to topics put aside at that

[4] About four months later, the barrister emailed his recollection: "I did things in the following order: 1. underlined important parts in the prosecution evidence (I normally do this the first time I read the brief), 2. noted the crucial points of evidence in my notebook (I normally do this, but not always), 3. met the client to take his instructions and confirm what he said in police interview (In this case he had in fact made a comment in interview which implied that he wanted to do serious harm – but I can't remember exactly what it was. However, in conference he maintained that he did not intend serious harm.) 4. advised him to plead not guilty to the section 18. [...] 5. I think that I probably drew a plan of the club with the client shortly before trial began."

moment" (Luhmann 2000:102). The barrister modulates written and oral, old and new, friendly and hostile statements. All these occurrences across and in-between text and talk mark out this reconstructive discourse analysis as an ethnographic endeavour. It is not restricted to the public exchange. It includes the routine creation of artefacts that in return nourish the barrister's case-representation in the jury trial.

Before trial

I met the barrister around nine o'clock in the court's entrance hall. Like all those mornings, I welcomed him in my dark-blue suit equipped with a notepad and pen. My informant brought a number of implements to carry out his craft: (a) the barrister's outfit including the obligatory grey wig (kept in a hat-box), black robe and white collar, (b) the classical manual "Blackstone's Criminal Practice" containing general and authorised rules, precedents, statutes and commentaries for all practical purposes, (c) his red notebook plus his fountain pen, (d) a briefcase with other briefs and manuals, and (e) the brief with the particulars of the offence and the written statements by all witnesses to be called by the prosecution. Some of these props are shown in the following photograph:

Fig. 11: Archbold, paperwork and wig. Photograph from http://lcjb.cjsonline.gov.uk/Lincolnshire/1030.html. © Crown.

The instructions to Counsel contain the following printed documents:

> The indictment with the statement of offence, an evidence list announcing 7 statements for the CPS[5], named, dated and page-numbered, a list of exhibits (proof photos of injuries, audio tape, record of police interview [with our client] and the "OUTLINE OF ALLEGATION AND ISSUES FOR JUDGE AND DEFENSE". Additionally it contained the following documents: the witness statements by Tim Vic (the complainant), by another club-guest, a doorman, the police officers at the scene, the police constable who conducted the interview with the defendant, the doctor who examined Tim Vic's wounds, and a long "RECORD OF TAPED INTERVIEW" with the suspect.

The defence barrister's case-representation is to be based on the grounds of the brief that he received from his "instructing solicitor." The brief is referred to as "instructions."[6] The brief is supposed to cover all relevant information. It should instruct in the case for the defence.[7] The instructed barrister is not left alone with the pre-compiled papers. He is, in fact, accompanied by another importer: a delegate from the instructing law firm who carries the entire defence-file. The comprehensive written instructions pose another question on the legal craft of courtroom lawyers: how is the amount of papers and information made available for the actual trial?

The brief was nothing unusual in terms of its complexity. The brief, however, was unusual in other respects that may qualify it as a natural crisis experiment. First, it reached the barrister on the very morning of the trial. It was handed over by a colleague from the Chambers[8]. My barrister had no opportunity to consult the instructing solicitor or,

---

[5] The Crown Prosecution Service decides whether to prosecute the case on the basis of the collected evidence. In case of a positive assessment, the CPS hires a barrister to represent the case in Crown Court. The barrister may advice the CPS not to carry on but needs the okay from the instructing solicitor. The same is true in the case of successful plea bargaining. Any result needs the approval of the CPS-solicitor who consults the alleged victim before any definite decision.

[6] The barrister's instructions are more complex than, for instance, the written instructions for standardised telephone interviews (Lynch 2002) in sociological surveys.

[7] It should not be confused with the judge's instructions given to the jury, or with the instructions formulated by the defendant right before or in the course of the trial hearing.

[8] Barristers are organised in Chambers to share the overheads for clerks, secretaries, library, etc. In this case, the Barrister's Chamber hosted around 30 barristers, all instructed at times by the defence, at times by the prosecution. Thus, it happened regularly that barristers from the same chamber faced each other in court on opposite sides.

what seems worse, the defendant himself. He came, one may think, ill-equipped. All necessary work had to be attained during the day in court. This situation, however, is not as unusual as it seems. Tague, for instance, reports that "in representing a criminal defendant, the barrister, in most cases, will not be briefed until very near the date of the trial" (1995:31). Second, the brief seemed quite incomplete:[9] there was no written statement taken from the client.[10] There were no accurate instructions either (only some scribbled notes by his barrister colleague). Even the pre-trial groundwork – usually already completed by the instructing solicitor – was left to the barrister.

Marking the brief

The first steps in the process of the barrister's case-making seem banal. The barrister browses through his brief from the beginning to the end. Although this reading seems quick and cursory, it leaves some traces on the documents. The barrister, while reading the brief, underlines sections and scribbles comments with his fountain pen. He starts with the indictment followed by the trial's outline, and the list of evidence. This way, he works through the several witness statements taken by the police. They altogether embody the Crown's case and the 'good reasons' to convict our client, Steve Hit.

In order to analyse the marks, I ask the following questions: What does the barrister do with the texts? How do his marks alter the texts? Let me provide some general answers first before I specify them in regard to the actual marks made on this particular brief. Marks modulate the text's surface. They transform the future reading of the copy. The marks break the text's rhythmical flow of signs, conventionally organised in intervals of lines, paragraphs, and pages. The text is interrupted and supplemented by marks as in the following excerpt of Tim Vic's statement:

---

[9] See Morris (1991) on what characterizes a "good brief" from the barrister's point of view.

[10] The barrister's client is, formally speaking, the law firm represented by the solicitor in charge. The solicitor instructs the barrister to represent the case in court. The solicitor, in turn, receives instructions by the defendant. In our case, the solicitor did not pass on *any* instructions by the defendant to the barrister. The usual excuse ("The client never turned up in the firm!") cannot satisfy here, because Steve Hit was available for legal visits during pre-trial. He sat in prison.

X	Inside the club I was stood at the bar with my friends having a drink when a male that I know came up to me and said " THAT LAD THERE HAS JUST BEEN GIVING ME SHIT," the male he was talking about was walking past us to go to the bar or toilet. On his way back the male tripped over my foot as I was leaning on the bar, when I turned round the male called me 'DICKHEAD'. At this point I walked over to this male and asked him what his problem was to which he shrugged me off so I put my hand on his shoulder to try and get his attention as he was walking away from me. At this point the male then turned round and swung at me with a glass bottle which hit me on the ear...	*X*

Fig. 12: Marked Interview Protocol

Generally speaking, the marks add a new dimension to the given text. They divide the text into regular and exceptional fragments, into foreground and background. When a few words are underscored, others are set into the background by the very same operation. The same is true for whole lines: a few are flagged as significant, while the rest is set back as ordinary. The discrimination of important and trivial provokes selective re-reading. The forecast of future reading includes another general effect: the marks make former reading activities observable (for the barrister and especially for the researcher who requested the notes afterwards). The traces, technically speaking, inscribe invested work and, in this way, enable a cumulative work process. We will see later how this memory by inscription is employed to deal with subsequent tasks.

What does it mean to mark this passage and not another, these words but not neighbouring ones? To analyse the specific marks that I found in the brief, I propose two integrated analytical manoeuvres. Firstly, I identify the functions of marks for the ongoing representational project. Secondly, I preview the complete marking of the brief. As a result, I display the barrister's markings as a net of foci thrown over the seven interview protocols (S1 - S7). The net creates an inter- and trans-textual perspective. On this basis I ask three questions: Which passages are chosen and which are left aside? Are there systematic clusters? How does the respective cluster facilitate further steps in the project?

The foci serve the barrister's search and ordering strategies: they present a game of trial-and-error; a method to collect versions of the same. I suggest that each single mark responds to one of the following queries: (1) Who else was involved? (2) When did all this take place? (3) Where did it take place? (4) What happened prior to the blow? (5) In what condition was Steve Hit at that point? (6) What injuries did he aim to inflict? These concerns, I argue, create intertextual units that can be described in Foucault's terms as one "field of presence:" a dynamic net of coexisting and interrelated statements, each of them deriving from certain formalised events, here a destined supplier to procedure (police interviews).

For a better orientation, I specify the source for the marks: S1 = statement of Tim Vic, the complainant; S2 = of the doorman; S3-S4 = of police officers; S5 = of the medical doctor; S6 = of Steve Hit, the defendant; S7 = [handwritten statement] of a club-guest. I comment on each group of marks by hypothesizing whether they become operative foci for the representational project. Additionally, I give details on the other types of inscriptions left by the barrister's active reading.

(1) Who else was involved?

Each mark in the following group can be read as an answer to the standard "*who* was involved"-question. The marked fragments derive from 6 of the 7 interview protocols. The barrister added some handwriting (here shown in *italics* in S1 and S3). The following passages were marked accordingly:

(S1) male that I know [*who?*];
(S2) one of the aggrieved friends; a friend of the aggrieved
(S3) 20 persons; 5 people standing around a male, who I know to be def.; the 5 people who had been stood around *~friends? ~*;
(S4) volatility was being displayed by several people;
(S6) guy with long blond hair.

However, other references to 'co-present persons' (e.g. the defendant, the victim or the bouncers) who are mentioned in other sections of the statements are not marked by the barrister. Only those fragments are highlighted that differ from what the main prosecution witness (S1) states. Apparently, the marking is partial (to the defence) and purposeful (showing discrepancies). I rephrase the focus accordingly. It is apparently not a standard query, but a specified and local concern: "Who *else* was involved?" This seems the implicit question answered by the barrister's marking.

(2) When did all this take place?
A further set of marks concerns the temporal structure of events. Both absolute and relative time specifications can be used to determine when something happened. We find such a mark right in the first interview protocol (S1). The barrister underlines the time (20.30), but he does so only with one temporal preposition which occurred right at the beginning of the brief. Other times given, such as the one at the end of the brief ("HIT says that he had been in a pub between 5.30pm and 10pm …") remain plain text. Why is the initial perspective not pursued any further? And why does this sole mark appear at all? The initial mark hints at the barrister's standard method for putting together a defence. Usually, the chronological order of events provides resources to destabilize the prosecution's case. In this case, however, this aspect looses significance; there are no other temporal indices that would allow the barrister to compare and to draw conclusions.

(3) Where did things take place in the club?
The next aspect of markings seems obligatory and standard as well. Asking 'where' – corresponding to questions of 'who' and 'when' – shall establish a first overview on the main data of the case. However, we find only one mark referring to this complex:

(S2) on the inside ~*X 3m away*~[11]; a male stood in front of him; left hand staircase.

The spatial focus does not produce any further marks in the other statements. It seems that the barrister's reading does not attend to the spatial specificities of the offence beyond the initial mention. Are they irrelevant? Such a conclusion, however, would be hasty. Later on, the barrister indeed develops a great interest in the spatial composition, even though it manifests differently: the barrister, instead of marking such sections, prepares himself a drawing on an extra page of his notepad. Here, the barrister maps the spatial positions of major protagonists in the club according to the witness statements (and later testimonies).

[11] These parts (~ …~) refer to comments that the barrister places on the page margin.

(4) What happened prior to the blow?

Marked passages on 'what happened prior' can be found in nearly all witness statements:

(S1) That lad there has just been giving me shit; tripped over my foot; I did nothing to provoke
(S2) a male stood just *~getting up~* on the inside of the door; his hand pulled back behind his body *~X~;* a male stood in front of him; to which the male then went to grab the aggrieved friend; (one friend said) "I've got him!" *~X~*;
(S4) "I was getting stamped on, the bouncers were grinning so I bottled him because they were coming after me again." This was recorded in my pocket notebook which he signed accordingly.
(S6) came up to me, punched me, I fell on the floor, and; "I was getting stamped on, the bouncers were grinning so I bottled him."; he ended up punching me; I turned round as I was getting up and just seen him and smacked him ~ *didn't realise* ~
(S7) I saw a young looking male run from my left to my right in front of me; lifting the bottle with his right hand before bringing it down on the right side of the man's head

The barrister frequently underscores passages on the sequence of events. Accordingly, we find marked passages in five of seven interview protocols. Most passages point at some sort of earlier quarrel and provocation. Nearly all statements contain, from the barrister's point of view, clues that 'more' did happen prior to the blow. Depth and distribution of the marks indicate a weighty focus. Quite early in the barrister's work, the marks seem to provide plenty of material to substantiate a line of inquiry.

(5) In what condition was the defendant at that point?

In this group, we find underlined fragments from three different interview protocols. In the police-interview with the defendant (S6), what is more, the barrister crossed out a whole related phrase (He agrees …). Scoring out is a different writing activity than underlining. While the latter extends the protocol's usability, scoring out restricts it.

(S2) had dried blood on his nose and a graze to the left side of his face ~//~; his words were slurred and his eyes glazed he was extremely drunk ~V~
(S4) in fact drunk; dried blood under his nose and graze to the left side of his left eye; [def.:] "Fuck off" ~*V*~ "C'mon you bastards" ~*V*~
(S6) drunk a small bottle of vodka and around 6 pints of lager; He agrees that he has a short temper.

Passages on the defendant's 'poor state' appear in nearly half of the interview protocols. Taken together, they indicate restricted accountability: Steve Hit was described as drunk, provoked, hurt, and outraged. Also of interest is the crossing out of the bracketed phrase inserted originally by the interviewing police officer. What is scored through is not information regarding the client's physical and/or emotional state at the time of the offence, but a statement on his general character. Such overall self-assessment – especially due to its production under inexplicit circumstances ("He agrees…") – can be easily invalidated as inadmissible in court. The prosecuting barrister will, later on, fully agree with this evaluation and the crossing out of the phrase.

(6) What injuries did he aim to inflict?

The allegation that Hit "unlawfully and maliciously wounded Tim Vic with intent to do him grievous bodily harm" imposes another focus on the barrister. He marks all the clues that are brought up by the prosecution that support their claim. He does so by using two more types of inscriptions. The barrister puts question marks next to the marked phrase. The question marks, I suggest, point to inconsistencies in the protocol ("[…] basically correct"). Another new type of inscription appears with the doubly crossed-out phrase. This mark, I propose, accentuates the restricted usability of the phrase: The (doubly) crossed out phrase must not be allowed to reach the jury.

(S1) 10 itches to the cuts;
(S3; S4) … you've hit him intensively on the side of the head, obviously it creates a wound. NO. I WASN'T FINISHED; [what more?] I DON'T KNOW ~*Not GBH*~; I have to say you seem almost quite proud of what you have done.; agrees that his statement is basically correct ~*??//*~.
(S5) He was hit on left side of face [*by a bottle*]

These markings refer to issues of intent in a broad sense. They highlight phrases that indicate the severity of the injuries caused, which in turn allow inferences as to the offence itself. A 'self-betraying' statement (apparently) made by the client subsequently to the interrogation at the police station is also marked. The passages, however, are already flanked by other restrictive markings: by an open question ("what more?"), by a legal evaluation ("not GBH" means 'not grievous bodily harm'), by signs of doubt ("??//"), and by repudiation in its strongest form: doubly crossing out. Crossing out implies the inadmissibility of a statement; it is marked as futile for the courtroom.

This last section was commented on by the prosecuting barrister who sat, during the reading session, opposite the defence barrister in the barristers' lounge[12]. The following exchange comes from my field notes:

> During the marking session, he demonstrated some amusement: "I like this bit *I wasn't finished*! Where was it again?" (No comment from my barrister. He does not even look up from his papers.) "Here it is: *Did you feel any remorse for what you'd done or anything?* And now listen: *No. I wasn't finished.* Isn't that grand? *Not finished!* [...] What were you about to do? Killing him?"

The address used by the prosecuting barrister is noteworthy. He creates some symbolic directness: "You" instead of "He," "yours" instead of "his." The shift implicates an advanced kind of role-play, the cultivation of intense representation. The barristers symbolically and playfully associate each other with his/her case – and by doing so, they simulate the matter as a debate 'outside court.' They interact "as if" the respective other was involved in a rivalry, as if 'my barrister' was identical with the one he represents. This frame modulation (Goffman 1974) allows the barristers to express provocation, triumph, or frustration without their underlying consequences. Just minutes later, once they step in front of judge and jury, these expressions will be banned from the repertoire at hand. What is more, the barristers' warming-up carries some ethical connotations. A counsel should identify with and advocate the matter of his or her entrusted layperson and he or she should do so wholeheartedly. Both barristers know, of course, that this is a professional idealisation.

Taking instructions from the client

So far, the marking renders a number of issues tangible. It generates initial doubts and concerns, strategies and hopes. However, one cannot yet infer from the marking how the case will be eventually presented in court. The latter requires further steps and modulations: First, the

[12] The barristers' lounge is an important site for representational projects. It is used to get ready for trial, to study the brief or the law books, to wait for hearings to start or continue, to negotiate with opponents, or to chat over a coffee or tea about this and that with colleagues. Here, agreements are discussed and drafted. The lounge is the place where the barristers can discuss their issues directly (meaning without being mediated by the judge and observed by the jurors).

barrister needed a 'representational' version authorised by his client. Immediately after the barrister worked through the brief, he rushed down to the cells to take instructions from "our client." How do these instructions relate to the bundle that the barrister received from the solicitor in charge? The instructions taken right before the trial not only establish how the client wishes to plea, but they also set what the definite defence-case is. It is this case with all its details that the barrister is asked to stage in open court. The barrister had little time to approach Steve Hit, because the hearing was scheduled to begin the same morning.[13]

The (marked) police interview played a central role during his meeting with the client. The barrister, at this point equipped with a general idea of the brief and some ideas of vital issues, led the client through the police interview and took notes on Steve Hit's responses. To take instructions from the client, the barrister did not pose open questions ("what happened?"), but simply asked him to confirm or correct the interview protocol. The questions, in this line, act upon the procedural history. Barrister and client, instead of creating new grounds, perform the first story that came out of the documented police interview as binding for the upcoming trial. The 'scripted' client-barrister session results in the following notes:

> … Guy bumped into me so I turned round + sd 'sorry'. He just punched me – I called him 'dickhead' There was no need of punching me 'cos I apologized.
>
> He came up and punched me. I fell on the floor + he + another started stamping on me.
>
> I had drink in my hand. When I got up it was empty. I got the chance to get up + I hit him with it. Smacked in his face (LHS[14] of head).
>
> Pint glass.

The instructed version is the confirmed version of the interview. The case sticks closely to the 'original' police protocol. The barrister can use this agreed-upon version to cross-examine the prosecution witnesses

[13] At the beginning of the hearing, the following interesting exchange took place: "Judge: Have you had sufficient time, Mr Doubt [Def. Barr], to discuss the case with the defendant? Mr Doubt: Yes, your Honour. Yes." Why this question? The judge reassures the proper conduct in order to proceed with the case on a firm basis. The confirmation 'absorbs' all kinds of local problems: that the brief was handed over the same morning or that there were no instructions by the defendant.

[14] Denotes 'left hand side of head'.

and to examine the only available defence witness (the defendant). The resulting notes correspond to these lines in the official protocol of the police interview. After the barrister's marking, his copy of the official interview protocol looked as follows:

PC What happened last night?
Hit WELL I WAS OUT WITH MY BROTHER AND HIS MATE IN A NIGHTCLUB. JUST COMING BACK FROM THE TOILET, THIS GUY *BUMPED INTO ME, SO I TURNED ROUND AND SAID "SORRY;" AND HE PUSHED ME… THEN I STARTED CALLING HIM… I DON'T KNOW EXACTLY WHAT I WAS CLALLING HIM, "DICKHEAT;" … "FAGGOT."*
PC He was calling you?
HIT NO, I WAS CALLING HIM THAT … COS I THOUGHT *THERE WAS NO NEED FOR PUSHING ME … COS I APOLOGISED … AND THEN HE CAME UP TO ME, PUNCHED ME, I FELL ON THE FLOOR, AND THEN HIM AND THIS OTHER LAD STARTED STAMPING ON ME. I HAD A DRINK IN ME HAND, SO WHEN I GOT UP IT WAS EMPTY, SO I JUST HIT HIM WITH IT. I GOT THE CHANCE TO GET UP AND THEN I JUST HIT HIM WITH IT.*
PC When you said "hit him with it," what do you mean by that?
HIT *WELL, I HAD IT IN ME HAND AND I JUST SMACKED IT IN HIS FACE.*
PC That's your right hand, is it?
HIT ME RIGHT HAND.
PC … What is it? A bottle? A glass?
HIT IT WAS A GLASS, IT WASN'T A BOTTLE.
PC What kind of glass?
HIT A *PINT GLASS.*
PC … So you've hit him on which side of his …
HIT HIS LEFT.
PC *Left hand side of his head*, or his face?
HIT IT'S HERE, I THINK.
PC His head …
HIT YEAH.

The noted instructions merge the relatively long police interview into one handy version. The noted instructions include most of the sections that the barrister underlined during his first reading of his client's police interview. They cover, furthermore, core foci that came up during the inter-textual marking. But the notes do not only repeat and condense what was already filed during the pre-trial. They accomplish several other transformations that could be phrased as a formula or recipe:

(a) Turn the dialogue into a monologue!
(b) Stick to the documented story-line!
(c) Emphasize potentials for the case!

The resulting text ascribes authorship just to the witness. It selects certain points *and* absorbs their production. It performs fully available, procedural contributions, and, at the same token, leaves their indexical character behind. The resulting points are such stuff that cases are made on. In the following, I refer to this re-framing of utterances as modulation and the resulting artefacts as modules. Modules are available and allow for a number of case-making operations.

The notes keep to the interview protocol as if it was an original version, even where topoi are repeated and information is doubled. The instruction notes are not primarily meant to collect information, but to assemble discursive facts. Reiteration, for instance, gains relevance, because it is a marker of credibility. The barrister's notes carry on accordingly:

> I bumped into him. Turned + sd sorry. He punched me. I sd "watch what you are doing – dickhead." Had sd sorry.
>
> His mate (shorter than me – long blonde hair) also there ended up punching me (cheek) – came up to me, kicked me + started stumping on my head.
>
> I turned round as I was getting up + just seen him + smacked him. Just getting up + I just turned round + smacked him. Twisted round – like a haymaker.
>
> I didn't intent to hit him on head I just flipped.
>
> I was angry.
>
> Once o/s felt effects of alcohol.... Don't remember what happened when police arrived.

The instructions noted in the barrister's red book clearly accentuate those aspects of Hit's official answers to the police (S6) that may be beneficial to his defence. The "haymaker-movement," for instance, implicates impulse, not intent; the prior occurrences implicate provocation, and so forth. The resulting instructions are partial and strategic. They are bound to the discursive facts that have been already in place (see Scheffer et al 2007). The notes' partial character becomes evident again when tracing rather damning passages of the police interview. The following episode, among others, is kept out. It bothered the barrister already during his marking (6/ what injuries ...?):

PC You've hit him intensively on the side of the head, obviously it creates a wound. When you did it, did you see the fact you'd cut him?
Hit YEH.
PC Did it start bleed straight away?
Hit YEH.
PC Did you feel any remorse for what you'd done or anything?
Hit NO, I WASN'T FINISHED.
PC What would you have done to him?
Hit I DON'T KNOW

The barrister removes the self-incriminating answers from the instruction-notes. Parts of the procedural history are rendered obsolete. It remains a list of modules that can guide the barrister's negotiations with the opposing barrister and, more so, his verbal contributions during the subsequent trial hearing. The 'positive' notes define the horizon for the representational project. They define what to claim and what to aim for in the adversarial contest. But is the defence really able to get rid of the damning parts, to cut back text *and* guilt? We will be able to answer this question once the barrister put his 'instructing' notes into work in open court.

Pinpointing the prosecution case

After the barrister has taken instructions from his client, he returns to the brief: to its appropriation and modulation for all practical purposes. This time, he does not read through and mark the written statements but takes notes on the grounds of the already marked sections. Specifically, he writes down short versions of the 'hostile' witness statements as they are disclosed in the brief. In the barrister's notes, the police interviews shrink, again, to handy lists of modules. The list follows, just like the noted instructions, the chronology of the 'original'. What are these lists of modules good for? How do they facilitate the representational project? The following list translates the police interview with Tim Vic (S1):

a male who I know (?) came up to me + said that lad there has just been giving me shit'

on his way to bar/toilet

By coincidence! "tripped over my foot" on way back

walked over to male?! to ask what problem was

He shrugged me off!

put hand on shoulder to get his attention as he was walking away from me.

At that point he turned round + swung at me with a glass bottle

Each module includes an act (including an object and a preposition) or acts in a row ("came up to me + said") and an actant ("a male"). The series of modules provides for chronological clues. Something was done or happened after/before something else. What is more, the sequence of modules provides for semantic context. It allows for ellipses. For instance, the subject is missing in the second ("he") module. A verb ("*was* on his way") is missing as well. The modules are cut short by leaving out articles throughout. This is how the barrister's compressing modulation proceeds.

The modules for Vic's statement (S1) imply some recurrent and dramatic confrontations between offender and victim. They intensify the impression that the final blow has a pre-history that casts doubts on the clear-cut division of moral roles manifested as 'victim' and 'offender'. What are the effects of transforming the witness statement from police protocol into barrister's notes? How does the barrister transform Vic's statement? First of all, the notes produce continuity with the markings; the selection here seems to serve a line of inquiry that I previously revealed as *the* focus for the marking: the "build-up before the blow" (4). The notes allow yet another insight. They permit a double approach for the subsequent critical analysis of the prosecution's case. How is this accomplished?

The modulations render two usages or connection points possible. They single out units ('this took place'); they line up these units ('then this, then that'). On the one hand the modules allow point-by-point comparisons across witness statements. The modules, on the other hand, might reveal incoherence within one account. Once modulated, the witness statements are evaluable in these two directions, as illustrated by the following table:

The following pages in the barrister's red book are filled with similar lists, again affording vertical and horizontal contrasts. The interview

	Witness 1	Witness 2	Witness 3	Witness 4
1.	a male who I know came up ...		?	
2.	he tripped over my foot ...	?		
3.	asked what the problem was ...			
4.	he shrugged me off			?
5.	I put hand on shoulder ...			
6.	swung at me with a glass bottle ...	?		

Fig. 13: Comparing Witness Statements

protocols are first cut into modules that are then lined up. Each module functions as a definite, transferable claim *and* as a moment in a story-line.

In order to grasp the productivity of the barrister's modulation, we need to look backwards and forwards in his extended case-making process. The following notes on the police interview with the doorman (S2) pick up on the two major foci of marks and they equip the barrister with ammunition for the later cross-examination of the doorman:

> walking from DJ Box to[wards] front door
>
> male (Def) stood just on inside of door with bottle in hand pulled back behind his body as though going to strike
>
> saw u/t prior to this- no build up (?)
>
> At this point struck male stood in front of him
>
> I grabbed him + escorted him off premises (alone?) To LH staircase (?)

The barrister notes the doorman's 'claims' on the spatial positions and movements of the protagonists (focus 3) and his 'claims' on the building-up (focus 4). The doorman's statement fully supports the allegation and accordingly the prosecution case: the doorman 'observed' intention ("as though going to strike") without provocation ("no build up"). But fortunately for the defence, he is not the only prosecuting witness. When applying exactly the same (focal) modulation to another witness statement – here the one by the club-guest (S7) -, the picture looks less clear:

> stood on dance floor (on L. as you enter) facing bar area.
>
> saw young looking male run from L to R in front of me (walked past quickly)
>
> holding bottle by neck in RH
>
> saw him approach RS of male stand next to entrance of doorway to club.
>
> lifted bottle above R. shoulder + brought it down on RHS of man's head.
>
> Then saw him run out of door of club (?)

Again, the modules apply the two core foci: spatial positions and the building-up. The barrister's persistent modulation pays out: instead of "stood just on inside of door," the defendant "stood on dance floor" and then "run from L to R ...;" instead of "bottle in hand pulled back behind his body", the bottle is now held "in RH" and "lifted [...] above R. shoulder". We will see in due course that this is the way, the barrister will confront all these 'claims': his modulation allows him to put them on top of each other and, by doing so, to detect the slightest irregularity und discrepancy.

This further usage is notified by the question marks next to certain modules. These extra marks do not signify questions to be solved. They highlight rather points that can be exploited to raise "reasonable doubts." They display first profits of the barrister's intertextual perspective. The modulation enables the barrister to identify weak points across all seven protocols. In this selective way, all the filed evidence is guided into *one* discursive field of presence.

A prospective mapping of the case

The analytical potentials of the modulations become apparent in another productive step. The barrister, after having marked and condensed all police interviews, draws a map of the positions and movements of those involved in the (build-up to the) assault. This is what the map looks like:

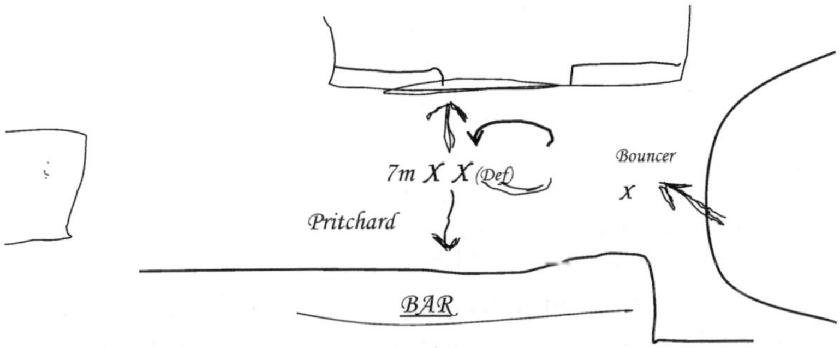

Fig. 14: Mapping the Case

The map creates a two-dimensional space filled with measures ("7m"), persons (Bouncer), lines (for areas), crosses (for positions), and arrows (for movements). The map is based on information from various interviews. It constructs – more plainly than the modules – one shared field that accommodates the various statements. It prolongs the intertextual orientation effected by the marks and modules. The map, moreover, co-enacts a single reality 'out there'. It implies that all former statements somehow refer to the same incident in time and space. It implies that they are all versions of *somehow the same matter*. Finally, the mapping assists in accessing and managing the intertextual field. With it, the barrister can evaluate the interrelations between the numerous modules: do they support or contradict each other?

The map, furthermore, marks the transition from pre-trial to trial activities. It connects the 'cold' text-analysis with the 'heated' in-court probing of evidence. Further entries derive not just from written protocols but also from testimonies. The map guides the barrister's perception of the oral examinations to follow. The procedural past plus the staging in court enter his map side by side. Pre-trial and trial now dwell within a single comparative framework. A longer passage from my barrister's cross-examination of the bouncer may demonstrate the potential of the barrister's sketched map:

> Q. So, if the layout is as I describe and the double doors are *here*? - A. Yes.
> Q. And if I am at the double – if I am the man with the bottle? - A. Right.
> Q. And I am close to the doors? - A. That is correct.
> Q. And so I am in roughly the right position? - A. Yes.
> Q. And would I therefore be facing *this* way? - A. Further round.
> Q. *That* way? - A. You'd basically have your back to me.
> Q. You would be coming from behind? - A. Yes.
> Q. From the deejay? - A. That is correct.
> Q. Right. And so his arm was out like *that*? - A. No, further back.
> Q. Well, further back. - A. Yes, that is correct.
> Q. And you could see from behind? - A. That is correct, yes.
> Q. All right. And the man that he struck, where was he? - A. Walking towards the dance floor.
> Q. So, was he coming from here? - A. That is correct.

The exchange in front of judge and jury is accompanied by pointing gestures and transfers. The barrister turns the courtroom and its furniture into a provisory mock-up model of the crime scene for demonstrative purposes. The interactive reconstruction of spatial positions and movements in the club turns into a complicate exercise that might easily have confused the jury. It leads the judge to repeatedly express his doubts as to the whole purpose of this exercise: "I think we have probably gone thought it a few times but, if there is to be any other enquiry, then maybe a plan, I don't know." The confusion is not accidental. Like in the other modularisations, the barrister produces 'more of the same'. The one case put forward by the prosecution is thus turned into multiple versions that cannot easily be reconciled with each other.

The map creates points of reference for both the critical assessment and the demonstration of contrastive facts. Statements from the police interview protocols as well as from the interrogations in court enter the drawing. As points, crosses, circles or letters they become part of *one* two-dimensional, albeit virtual, analytical space. The matter is inscribed into one field of presence, which now allows for additional operations of repetition and critique. Presence, here, does not mean that the 'real' crime scene is re-presented 'once again', but that statements from diverse social, spatial, and temporal sources congregate in a single scheme.

Final adjustments between the adversaries

It is this presence that encourages the barristers to make first prognoses on the strengths and weaknesses of the adversary cases, or rather of both representational projects before the trial hearing. Shortly before the trial would commence, the opposing barristers weigh up the relative score of their cases. However, their meeting is less one of competitors preying on each other, than one between colleagues: not for the first time, they are committing cases against each other in a jury trial; not for the first time, they arranged things with each other in advance. In a surprisingly relaxed manner, they sit together in the lounge and assess the situation over some hot drinks. Their evaluation of cases takes a rather joking tone (again) as if they tried to spur each other on: "You pulled off quite something!" The colleagues prepare themselves for a potential showdown in court.

Their chitchat does not develop into a proper negotiation such as plea bargaining. Too strong are the discrepancies and the insistence on one's own case. Minutes before they appear before the judge, prosecuting barrister (Pro) and defence barrister (Con) clarify their agreement on most elements of the case and on the one remaining area for negotiation:

Pro Is it a definite?
Con Yes, I guess so.
Pro The only issue between us then is the question of intent.
Con Yes, let's get it over with.

Their meeting does not end with this coordination. The barristers turn their attention to their briefs once more. The latter are adjusted in view of what has been erased (by crossing out text passages). What should be and what should not be part of the trial hearing? The two barristers agree on the debate that they are going to act out in front of the jury. Within this agreed upon agenda they will promote their cases for either acquittal or conviction.

The barrister's work during trial

So far, we could easily classify the barrister's work as preparation in expectation of a standard jury trial. The barrister prepared his court performance by way of marks and notes that would lead him to some kind of script. A clear-cut succession of noting (as preparation) and speech (as performance) cannot be upheld when looking at the barristers' actual casework. Preparation, in particular by taking notes, operates rather as a continual accumulation which does not cease with pre-trial activities. Once in court, the barrister keeps compiling lists of modules. He does so even while performing the witness-examination. Preparation and performance seems to some extent an alternation sequence that runs through the entire casework.

What the barrister does not note down whatsoever

There is much that does not enter the barrister's red book by way of selection and translation. There is much, moreover, that does not enter the barrister's red book by way of insignificance and taken-for-grantedness. Let us shortly consider the moments and impressions that the barrister would never note down.

> While waiting outside the courtroom, barrister and instructing solicitor communicate concerns like: "Will all witnesses turn up?" "How will they perform in the stand?" "Are they going to deliver?" 'Our prospects' turned pretty dim with the first impression we got from 'them'. All six prosecution witnesses turned up. On first sight, they all left a good impression, meaning here, they were wearing suits, neatly ironed shirts, and discreet ties. The prosecution-case seemed well casted. My barrister whispered to me half in jest: "Under normal conditions such a case can't be won: not with my client brought in from custody in jogging trousers …"[15]

---

[15] The legal arena favours and fosters a standard appearance. This is well explicated in a novel by Mortimer: " 'What are we doing to our clients?' Rumpole rhetorically asks his fellow barristers. 'Seeing they wear ties, and hats, keep their hands out of their pockets, keep their voices up, call the judge 'my lord'. Generally, behave like grocers at the funeral. Whoever they may be' " (1993:81).

These calculations do not enter the barrister's notes. The barrister, apparently, does not jot down everything that happens nor does he record everything of procedural relevance: He is eager not to miss out anything on the – hopefully unsophisticated – strategies of the opposite party. He wants to estimate whether and how prosecution witnesses will appear in court. He is interested in all this, but would never note down such impressions or guesswork. In all these aspects, his notes are far more focussed and selective – and thus far more practice-oriented – than those of his accompanying ethnographer, who pursues other, yet rather unspecified interests.

The specificity and selectiveness of the barrister's notes also become observable when turning our attention to the subsequent events in front of and in the court room. His notes – unlike the ethnographer's version – are not concerned with questions of atmosphere, tension, hope, and fears, or questions of hypotheses, strategies or change manoeuvres. There is no mention of what the adversary barrister utters. Nor does he take notes of what happens when the court trial commences: the selection of jurors, their orientation, administering the oaths. All the ritualized activities framing the introduction and orientation of the jury remain unlisted.

Precisely their ritualistic character might explain this omission: their orderliness and correctness can be assumed; in case of formal mistakes, one can immediately voice an objection or may order and consult the official transcript afterwards. It might also be explained by the division of labour at court. The clerk ticks off a meticulous checklist to ensure that nothing has been forgotten and everything has been carried out. This could explain why the judge's or the prosecuting barrister's introductory words are not jotted down, even though this omission does not mean that they go unnoticed. In fact, the barrister continues to complement his map while his colleagues go about their duties. Again, neither what will be at the centre of attention nor what this is all about enters his notes. The judge introduces the jury to their duties:

> So, Ladies and Gentlemen, there is one matter which is before you which is to be tried and, as will be explained in great detail, there is an alternative charge to which Mr Hit has just pleaded guilty before you. So, the issue is going to be a narrow issue as to the intent with regard to what happened.
>
> Now, the trial is going to take place and all of these matters will become clear to you. Very shortly, Mr Pro will tell you something about the allegations in this matter and thereafter you will hear from witnesses, they

> will be cross-examined by Mr Con on behalf of the Defence and in due course, of course, you will be the Jury deciding the case.

The prosecuting barrister specifies the decision criteria – and he does so along the usual formulas. He argues, the author notes with some amusement, like an anti-cognitivist Ethnomethodologist. The prosecuting barrister asks the jury to decide on "normative facts:"

> How do you judge somebody's intentions at the time they perform an act? Well, you can't cut open their head and read what is inside. In the evidence where you are deciding whether or not it proves what the Prosecution say the Defendant's intent was, you will judge his intent at the time by what he did in the same way that you judge the intentions of people in everyday life. You apply your ordinary, common, every day standards and common sense to the evidence that you hear. So, you judge his intentions by what he did and, indeed, by what he said about them.

Nothing of this enters the barrister's notes. Nothing seems contestable or worth mentioning to him. Actually, he seems to consent to his opposition's introductory statement in a way that reminds of accepting rules of the game. The latter are constitutive rules that cannot be openly disputed or reinterpreted.

The predictable and introductory speeches serve another practical role. They give the barrister additional time to arrange his first turns. His turn comes after the prosecuting barrister has completed his introduction and has finished his friendly examination of the first prosecution witness. Directly after, the barrister can cross-examine "their witness" – for the first time, he is expected to appear on stage in front of jury and audience in an active role. He should be prepared for this.

Excerpting modules from oral testimonies

In court, the barrister keeps up his analytical stance, listening with his fountain pen and notepad ready. He receives the witness testimonies in the same fashion like the written statements, by taking notes and creating modules. He performs a distanced and analytical *listener*. Inaccessible to the public eye, his notes are focused on "just words" that are instantly but carefully modulated for later utilization. The 'permanent' modulation harmonizes disparate materials and representations. They translate disclosed texts as well as staged testimonies. Different times and places are folded into one format. Stable and unstable materials become altogether available in one shared discursive field.

Does it matter whether modules refer back to texts or talk? Does the modulation echo the respective source? The short answer is no. One cannot deduce the source from the modules alone because the resulting modules take the same shape no matter their source. This, I argue, does not mark a lack of separating capability or over-standardization. The barrister's thin description is rather an accomplishment since it facilitates his intertextual diagnosis.

What notes do actually derive from the witness testimonies? The trial notes start with the friendly examination of the prosecution's "main witness," the alleged victim of intended bodily harm (t1):

Stood at bar

s/o walking past me – tipped over my head.

Turned & called me a "dickhead"

I was facing the bar. X

20 mins after arrival

Don't know how much to drink – merry – had had a bit.

Seen him before – didn't know him.

I approached him to ask problem. *<u>2 yrds.</u>*

I moved away from bar.

Facing me. I asked what problem was. he turned away. Don't know if he heard me. I was <u>a foot</u> away. Put my hand on sh. to get his attention. (RH on R. shoulder).

<u>He swung round +</u> hit a bottle in face – side of face.

No contact between us before this.

Fig. 15: The Barrister's Notes

Here we find patterns similar to the previous notes: again they single out acts and arrange them in an 'and then'-series. The diachronic order follows the co-narrated story-line. In addition to this all-purpose modulation, the barrister underlines phrases that detail spatial positions (2 yards, a foot) and the build-up to the blow (he swung round; no contact …). These modules extend some foci previously developed during the marking.

The friendly examination with the second prosecution witness (t2) prompts the barrister to leave more notes in his red book. He notes, for instance, this line - *Man who walked past first was struck. 2nd man carrying a bottle* – when listening to the following exchange between prosecuting barrister and 'his witness':

> Q. The man who walked past you first, was he the striker or the struck in this second incident? – A. He was the struck.
> Q. So, the man who walked past you second was he carrying anything? - A. Yes.
> Q. What was he carrying? - A. A bottle.

The notes are monotone. They amass more of the same. They operate a uniform translation program: a question/answer-pair is merged to short phrases; each phrase offers a new move in a story-line. In this constant form, the barrister takes up lines of inquiry (again) that were laid out already by him when underscoring the brief. The notes for the entire testimony (t2) demonstrate this thematic continuation:

> LHS close to dance floor. 5–6 ft from bar.
>
> Heard commotion over sh + saw ym. walk past me tow [towards] the bar
>
> I heard a glass smash + girl screamed. – then man walking to bar.
>
> over me rh – heading tow bar
>
> Walked (4m) ahead of
>
> Saw back of gentleman. Saw a gentleman strike ~ to side of head.
>
> Man who walked past first was struck. 2nd man carrying a bottle
>
> He hit gent. across side of head with it
>
> bottle shattered
>
> Distraction – another commotion – I went over + his face a lot of blood
>
> Didn't see a/t to provoke blow.
>
> No threat to man who hit him.
>
> Disturbances o/s several

The modules gather more details on the spatial positions in the club. They add more about the building up directly before the blow. The barrister, listening to all 'their' witnesses, finds and collects more versions of the same. He adds crosses in his map. Modules and crosses extend the intertextual grid, inviting repetition and difference. In this grid, the facts (and the witnesses) start contradicting each other. What sounded reasonable in one account, suddenly provokes doubts and confusion in the intertextual perspective. The former disadvantage of many witnesses against 'our' case turns into an advantage.

Modulating the cross-examination

The first time the defence barrister took the floor in court was to cross-examine the main prosecution witness, Tim Vic (t1). It is his turn due to the ritual order of the court hearing. It is generally expected that he asks 'unpleasant' questions at this point – and that he knows the case for the defence and how to represent it. The questions he is going to ask derive from the materials collected through marking, noting and mapping. The following questions contribute to an already instigated line of inquiry (No 3: the spatial positions). Here is the cross-examination as recorded and formatted in the official transcript:

Q. At that stage how far were you from the bar? – A. Probably about two yards.
Q. Right. It is relatively narrow the area in front of the bar, isn't it? – A. Very.
Q. And when I say that I think if you come into the main entrance I think there are double doors, is that right? – A. Yes.
Q. And you are facing the long bar, is that right? – A. Yes.
Q. And so at the time that this happened you say you might have been about a couple of yards away from the bar? – A. Yes
Q. Might it have been a little bit further to the middle of that area? – A. Well, it was …
Q. Perhaps three or four? – A. It was to the left as you walk in.
Q. Yes. But was it between the entrance – the doors – and the bar? Roughly between the two? – A. Yes.

After having involved Tim Vic in the 'confusing' mapping of the scenery, the barrister turns towards another line of inquiry: No. 4, the build-up to the incident. What did happen prior to the blow? The cross-examination turns to the pre-arranged modules[16] several times.

Q. Right. And so when this blow was inflicted he spun round to inflict that blow? – A. Yes.
Q. And did you see – I don't know if you were able to see, but was his arm swung round in a straight motion? – A. I didn't see.
Q. With his arm straight? – A. I didn't see.

[16] See the barrister's notes on S1: "Facing me. I asked what problem was. He turned away. Don't know if he heard me. I was *a foot* away. Put my hand on sth. to get his attention. (RH on R. shoulder)"

Q. You didn't see? – A. No.
Q. You had never spoken to him, but you had seen him? – A. I have seen him before, yes.

Another twenty questions later the barrister repudiates Tim Vic's version of events. The barrister contrasts the latter with the instructed defence version of 'what really happened'. The hostile questions do not demonstrate internal inconsistency, but confront the witness with the adversary version point by point. In the official transcript, this repetitive contrasting takes the form of 'suggestions':

Q. What did you hope to achieve by putting your hand on his shoulder? – A. I don't know. I was just trying to get his attention.
Q. To do what? – A. To ask him why he was being abusive.
Q. Well I suggest that you pushed him away and that he has then made comments to you such as "dickhead" and abusive comments to you, but you deny pushing him away? – Yes.
Q. And you then punched him? – A. I didn't punch him.
Q. Well, did you see any injury to his nose? – A. He was – he was bleeding beforehand, yes.
Q. Before? – A. Before.
Q. When did you notice him bleeding? – A. As soon as he – as soon as I saw him.

The barrister suggests a different truth – and by doing so, demonstrates that the 'clear-cut' evidence is not without alternative. But the 'suggestions'[17] do more: once put in a sequence, they recount the basic defence case. "I suggest that" provides for a suitable format to deliver the case while adhering to the obligatory adjacent pair of question/answer. In this way, the defence counsel – the same applies to his counterpart — smuggles in 'his' case various times. When doing so, the interrogator is not too interested in the answers or their content. The answers merely show that the interrogation-frame is still intact.

This, however, does not mean that the cross-examination is already 'in the book' and that the trial hearing is just the enactment of instructions or protocols. The 'suggested' confrontations perform their own effects and sometimes even surprises. The latter happens on occasion when the witness feels obliged or provoked to respond to the

[17] See as well an earlier suggestion: "Now, you say that he tripped over your foot. I am going to suggest that in fact it was shoulders that bumped, if I can put it that way, and that he perhaps bumped into your shoulder or you bumped into his shoulder and your shoulders nudged as he went past."

counter-version directly. One such response by Tim Vic may serve as a nice example: "He was – he was bleeding beforehand, yes." This was *not* in Vic's initial statement; it was not a weak link rendered available by the barrister by way of underscores or modulation. This new point opens up new inquiries: "When did you notice him bleeding?"

The following extract originates from the cross-examination of the third witness. Here, the barrister uses what Lynch and Bogen call "the documentary method of interrogation" (1996:201 sqq.). The barrister refers back to phrases from the police interview. He points at the same sections that he underscored already at the beginning of his casework and that he noted as a module in his red book. At this point, he picks up on these markers in order to generate replication and variation.

> Q. Now, I know you made a statement to the Police and I wonder if you could have a look at that? (*Handed*) - A. Thank you. Which part do you want me to look at?
> Q. Well I would like you to have a look at Page 2, if you would, but if you would just confirm that it is your statement? - A. It is my statement, yes.
> Q. Dated the 20th of May of this year? - A. Yes.
> Q. And it is I think signed by you on each page, is that correct? - A. That is correct, yes.
> Q. Now, on the second page I think you begin to describe what happened because up to then you are describing where you had been. You say you stood on the dance floor, to the left as you enter the club. You stood with your friend and his wife. You were facing the bar. Then you saw a young looking male run from your left to your right, in front of you, and this is the one who is holding the bottle is what you say in your statement? - A. Uh-huh, yes.
> Q. But you don't say there was another male who had passed you before that? - A. The male that passed me was the one that struck.
> Q. Well, we have heard evidence that two men walked past you in a hurry? - A. Yes, one that was struck. One walked past me that was struck followed by the man that struck him.
>
> Prosecuting Barrister: If it is suggested there is a difference between what the witness said today and what he said in his statement, your Honour, then perhaps the whole of that block ought to be read out so the Jury can confirm?

After a series of routine questions ("Now, I know you made a statement to the Police …") that establish the original statement as truly belonging to the witness, the barrister turns specific ("now on the second page"). He retells one of the many documented answers ("Then you saw a young looking male …") to render it available for an immediate confrontation with a related claim by another prosecution witness ("Well, we have heard evidence …"). As a consequence, the cross-examined witness can choose between two alternatives: he could stick to his original statement or he could change his mind and agree with the other witness. In both cases, the prosecution will be partially discredited and weakened.

Interestingly, the barrister uses indirect speech to refer to the protocol section. He does not quote directly from the document. The reasons might be twofold: the barrister employs his notes rather than the original version; the indirect speech allows for the selective construction and demonstration of 'loose' contradictions. The barrister can leave out disruptive or confusing fragments. This 'dirty' method is criticised by the prosecuting barrister. He demands proper quotes and aloud reading to the jury. In what follows, my barrister will neither present the "whole of that block," nor will he read out or hand over a copy to the jury. The textual basis remains with the counsel while he verbalises it in line with relevancies he has established before. The asymmetry between written source and oral demonstrations corresponds to the epistemic structure of jury trials. Officially, truth emerges from first-hand knowledge, orally presented vis-à-vis the 'judges of the facts'. The barristers' documentary method of interrogation works differently. It mobilises the procedural (archival) past – and its inherent authority — in order to discredit the spoken words.[18]

This strategic move of referring back to the past, performed by both contestants, has some unexpected consequences. The invited repetition, first of all, produces (even) more versions for cross-comparison. While amassing more versions of (assumingly) the same matter, the parties consolidate a mysterious third: a reality 'out there', close but unattained. It takes 'no more' than good questions and truthful answers

[18] The Auld Report diagnoses a similar tension between orality and textuality: "But it is common place for juries, having retired to consider their verdict, to return to court to ask the judge to be reminded of what a witness has said and, often, for a copy of his written statement. In most instances they know that there is such a statement because the advocates and the judge were plainly following their copies of it as he gave his evidence, the witness may have referred to it, or the advocates have cross-examined and re-examined him by reference to it. All the leading players in the courtroom have one, but not the jury." (2001:520) The report defends this rule: "[…] even with a proper warning and further reminder by the judge of the witness's oral evidence, they [the jurors] would be likely to give the statement more weight than their recollection of what he said." (Ibid.)

to find out what really happened. Something like this, *it* murmurs through all these examinations, did take place that day in the club. All these words in court, however imprecise, partial, and distorted, seem to echo one 'original' incident – the single truth.

Interim results

Equipped with the lists of modules, the barrister does not only jump back to early versions. Stimulated and guided by the notes, the counsel moves horizontally and vertically in 'his' intertextual field. In this sense, the barrister's questions derive from different times and places. The underlying contrasts cut through the intertextual field in various ways: while a first group of questions stays within a single testimony (t1-t1), the second group links 'original' statement and 'repeated' testimony (s1-t1). A third group crosses different testimonies (t1-t2): here, for instance, claims concerning the spatial positions and the build-up. The last excerpt is identical with a fourth group: a diagonal contrast of somebody's statement and a witness's testimony (s1-t2). One logical option remains unused in open court and refers to its preference for orality: written statements (s1-s2) are not contrasted in open court.

What does the barrister infer from collecting 'more of the same'? Let us take a look at his notes on the interrogation of Tim Vic (t1):

> put RH on RH sh [shoulder] to get att. [attention]
>
> he then swung round to hit with bottle in face. Happened too quickly to know sort of blow
>
> admits H turned to walk away
>
> about 7 pints
>
> to find out why being abusive?
>
> his nose was bleeding when he came in!
>
> with friend - long blond hair

Again, the notes ascribe exclusive authorship to the witness. Tim Vic states (1) that he put his right hand on the defendant's right hand shoulder, (2) that he does not know the "sort of blow", (4) that he himself was drunk, (5) that he approached Steve Hit himself, (6) that Hit was injured, (7) that a friend was with him. The choice of modules is more specific though. The seven points may not be simply factual. The witness, e.g., "*admits* H turned to walk away" (3). The admission implies a certain interactional context, for instance a confrontational question.[19] That the witness "admits" something implies, moreover, that this is a valuable point for the defence. In this way, all seven points can be rephrased as reproaches. Each point potentially weakens the prosecution case. These are the barrister's next interim-products: He disposes of points that allow him to raise reasonable doubt in open court and to serve as reasons for an acquittal.

Managing the friendly examination

The friendly examination of the defence witness(es) is the next opportunity for the defence to take the floor, which can easily turn into a burden. In this case, the barrister was uncertain about calling his client into the witness-box as the only defence witness. He was unsure about the impression this rather "shabby lad" would give the jury. And moreover: Would he stand the cross-examination? Would Steve Hit manage to stick to the instructed version? Or would he repeat those imprudent 'macho' threats that were reported by one police officer? Once in the witness-box, there would be no way to escape these risks.

In the friendly examination, the instructed version is performed in a play of question and answer. The notes obtain a vital role here. They guide the barrister to guide the defendant to present the case as instructed. Here, we face a demanding mode of speech-production. Words are not simply formed according to Goffman's "script" or "memory" but through imaginative and supportive questions following the modulated evidence and the prepared instructions.[20] The trans-sequential analysis of case-making unravels a chain of interim products and the members' methods to put them into use.

Barrister and defendant managed to stage the instructed version vis-à-vis judge, jury, and adversary. And they did it well. The barrister used his notes – the defendant the barrister's questions. In the hearing's transcript, the narration unfolds like this:

---

[19] On the use of contextual markers ("in an interview … talked," "under questioning," or "when asked") in newspaper reports on politicians' statements, see Clayman (1990).

[20] McConville et al. mention only half of this chain when quoting the barrister's advice to his client: "When I ask questions don't add to them unless I invite you to. I can't lead you, but I can ask questions to get the story out." The binding character is implicated right after: "You will have to tell a story, not a lie, a story. If you give a different answer, it's your own bloody fault" (1994:252). The 'different answer', I deduce, refers to a written statement that was already entered prior to this conference.

Q. And how long were you on the floor for, could you say? - A. About a minute.
Q. And who was involved in the stamping and kicking? - A. Jonathan Vic and his friend, the blonde one.
Q. What happened then? - A. Well then, after they had been stamping on me, I stood up and I had the glass in my hand and I spun round and just – just went for him.
Q. Right. Well, did you have any difficulty getting up? - A. Yes.
Q. Why did you have difficulty getting up? - A. Because they were still stamping on me. I just managed to get up somehow.
Q. And at what point did you start to swing the glass? - A. Well, as I got my feet on the floor I just spun round and lashed out as I was standing up - at the same time as I was just standing up. I was like crouched down.

The barrister provides the story-line and its moment-by-moment progression. His guidance reminds of prompting in a theatre, but with one crucial difference: it happens in the open, according to the court's ritual order of speech. The guidance is wrapped in the question-format. The typical guiding question works like a cloze: the interviewee is asked to complete it. This way, the defendant is assisted through the instructed version. The barrister's staccato of questions minimises the risk of losing track, of mixing up things, of coming up with novel (unchecked) details, or of showing unrestrained emotions. Owing to the guidance, the interviewee is left with hardly any room to go astray.

The "impression control" (Goffman 1986) via notes and questions allows the barrister certain motions. A crucial one is enacted at the end of the friendly examination and reflects the vulnerability of the defence. The barrister, instead of evading the case's Achilles' verse ("I wasn't finished"), refers to it openly. He tackles the damaging parts of the case not by exclusion, as one could infer from the 'cleansed' instructions, but by enunciation. This is how barrister and defendant undertook this risky move:

Q. And then you were asked, "Did you feel remorse for what you had done, or anything?", and you say, "No, I wasn't finished." What did you mean by that? - A. I don't know. I was still very angry. I just – I don't know.
Q. And, when you struck with the glass, what did you intend to do? - A. I don't know.
Q. Did you think about the fact that you had the glass in your hand? - A. No.
Q. Did you want to cause him really serious injury? - A. Not really serious injury, no.

Here, the barrister conducts the "documentary method of interrogation" by way of direct speech and quotation. First the defendant's responses seem little relieving. The defendant "did not know." Only later does the questioning invite a clear denial — right to the core criterion of "wounding with intent": "Not really serious injury, no." Does this 'friendly' confrontation pay out? The defendant gains an opportunity for repair in front of the jury. My barrister, what is more, could anticipate the adversary's cross-examination. (Undoubtedly, the prosecuting barrister would have used this weak link in order to provoke a revealing response by the defendant and to explain the true connotation of that 'self-incriminating' comment at the police station.) My barrister applied a forward defence, which seemed successful in the short run at least. The prosecuting barrister did not cross-examine 'our' defendant.

The closing speech

So far, our trans-sequential analysis of the representational project passed through divergent moments of marking, noting and mapping. On the one hand, the practices supply viable tokens for subsequent steps to move on. On the other hand, the tokens or traces neither fully actualize the former steps of the barrister's work nor do they fully anticipate what comes next. Another aspect shall be noted here: the preparation carried out in the barrister's book contributed already to the oral exchanges. The modules already left the protected sphere of his notebook to direct the public examination of witnesses.

The coupling of the written and the oral appears again on the final stage of the trial. The closing speech is laid out in the barrister's notes. The barrister's scripting deserves certain attention, because it is for the first time that the barrister will be able to deliver an uninterrupted speech in court. So far, the barrister's oral contributions were rather short. They were mainly restricted to the question-format. In this format he managed to convey doubts, scepticism, guidance, or alternative versions. Given this limitation, the closing speech signifies an exceptional moment. It is the culmination of the representational project. How does the barrister prepare for this event and how is the prepared script involved in the actual speech production?

Drafting the speech

The preparation of a script took time and demanded attention. So far the barrister could handle things simultaneously (and had to do so because of time pressure). He took notes while interviewing his client; he marked the brief while debating the matter with his counterpart; he collected contrastive points while listening to their witnesses. His 'private' notes accompany his 'public' activities. At this final stage, in contrast, the barrister was granted some extra time 'outside court' to do nothing but prepare his closing speech:

JUDGE REF:	… Mr Con, would you prefer to make your closing address tomorrow morning?
MR CON:	I would, your Honour. It won't be very long, but I would rather do it in the morning if that.…
JUDGE REF:	Well in that case, then, we will conclude now.
MR CON:	Thank you.
JUDGE REF (to the jury):	So, ladies and gentlemen, because we are moving into the next stage of the case, Mr Con is entitled to certainly be able to marshal his thoughts before he addresses you, and thereafter I have to sum the case up to you, and you will be retiring tomorrow morning. […]

What does the defence gain from this extra time? What can be done now that otherwise needed to be completed ad hoc in court?[21] The following notes reveal the benefits of having time to do proper scripting. The barrister used his preparation time – actually on his 'way to work' on the train – to scribble down arrangements of points such as the following:

1. persons contact/trouble/commot./coincidence
2. lead up to blow
   - position/direction
   - contact
   - steps
   -

[21] Usually, the closing speech is scripted during the trial. Defence barristers write last notes while the opponent is delivering his closing speech.

He continues the script with the witness testimonies in the order of their appearance. He noted:

3. Ev. of Mr. Vic
4. Ev. of Short[club-guest]
5. Ev. of Big [club-guest 2]

In the following, the barrister switches the argumentative frame. He now collects inconsistencies and open questions in the prosecution case. He does so in light of the defense case:

6. Bottle glass – not of great importance …
7. P's friend with blonde hair may be significant …
8. Explanation of injuries of Def …
9. Why was he so angry …
10. Given the 4 versions of events you have heart it wd be nonsense to me to suggest you that any one of the versions would be entirely correct
11. Ev. Big & Short is in direct conflict with Victim
    ⇒ There was some physical contact before
    ⇒ The def. was right next to him when blow…
    ⇒ The def. did spin round + no time to aim the blow or to stop or to consider what he was doing
    ⇒ Blow came imm. after some physical contact from Victim
12. Clearly, the def. has done wrong. Has admitted as much. Are you satisfied so sure that in split second before blow he had actually formed intention to do really serious harm?

The noted points are designed to direct the jury's attention towards certain issues – and away from others. In this regard, they stand for assorted moves: point 6 ("not of great importance") aims at removing one issue as 'irrelevant and distracting'. Points 7, 8 and 9 guide the court's attention to several 'obscurities' in the prosecution case. They raise 'reasonable doubts' against the alleged proofs. Point 10 appears as an interim result. The phrasing is more complicated than in the other points and may require aloud reading word by word. Point 11 reminds of essentials of the defence case. Point 12 concludes 'what the whole debate is about'. The barrister phrased this conclusion as a rhetorical question that suggests just one answer: "No – Not guilty!"

After he designed this line of argument, the barrister added a new intro. The barrister-author offers the following "initial remarks" to the barrister-animator:

1. *No part of my job to suggest that everything said by pros. witnesses is false to you must accept the ev. [evidence] of defendant. I represent def. + propose to make a no. of points*

2. *Certain essential facts are agreed: Def. just struck one blow, using bottle/glass, he was extremely drunk, has pleaded g. to unlawful wounding …*
3. *He pleaded to serious offence but Crown ask you to convict of a far more serious offence …*
4. *May think extremely difficult to determine what going on in his mind at any given time (let alone 19 yr old). Even more difficult in … of this case > mind was adhd by drink.*
5. *Whilst fact extremely drunk no defense – are entitled to +* must *consider how it may have affected his perception of events + appreciation of what he was about to do in the moment before this blow was struck…*

These remarks seek to set up the jury's point of view. They attempt to frame the jurors' reception of the overall demonstration. In other words, the remarks construe an audience. Interestingly, the notes do both in regard of the judgement: they assist the jury's decision-making and complicate it at the same time. They reduce the issues in debate and display the remaining ones as hard to resolve. In fact, this framing offers questions that are impossible to answer. The court, in this version, does not require a jury that 'chooses between two opposing versions of what happened', but a jury that 'reflects on all what remains necessarily unclear'. The jury's attention is directed to "reasonable doubts." This is at least the barrister's plan.

After the prologue, the script lists 'decisive criteria' and 'key controversies'. The defence, one may conclude, is narrowed down to conflicting accounts of what happened prior to the blow:

6. *Circs at time of (and leading up to blow) are of crucial importance: consider: (1) had a/t occurred prior to the blow being delivered? (2) Did he appear to stop + consider what he was doing or did it appear to be a r. quick response to some physical contact? (3) Was there more than one blow? (4) Did he take a no of steps or simply turn & strike in one move?*
7. *prosecution ev. is in conflict with these issues.*
8. *pros. ev. is inconsistent in other respects + may cause you to stop & consider reliability.*

We encountered this line of inquiry already – next to several others – in the barrister's marks on the brief. Now we know: this concern was sustained throughout the several work stages up to the closing speech. It turned out to be a fruitful focus of assessment.

Delivering the speech

How is this list of points put into use for the closing speech? How does the script contribute to the speech-production? One thing was evident to the participant observer: the notes were kept within reading distance during the speech. They were not simply memorized. While facing the jury, the barrister-animator kept the red book open, right in front of himself. The barrister turned pages with the uninterrupted progression of his speech. He did so in a body posture like this:

Fig. 16: Barrister and Judge. Photograph from http://lcjb.cjsonline.gov.uk/Lincolnshire/1029.html. © Crown

How did the barrister-animator attend to the notes? As a script, the notes seemed rather poor. They were neither written nor used for aloud reading. The notes rather equip the speaker with keywords or, to put it differently, with lighthouses that would guide him from point to point. Such assistance presupposes a competent speaker, capable of oscillating between two modes of speech-production: between scripted talk and fresh talk. The notes, as they are, were too thick to memorise, but too thin for aloud reading.

The following juxtaposition shows how the notes enter, guide, and put into motion the closing speech. The barrister addressed the jury as follows:

Notes	Speech
Circs at time of (and leading up to blow) are of crucial importance: *consider*: (1) had a/t occurred prior to the *blow* being *delivered* ? (2) Did he appear to stop + *consider what he was doing* or did it appear to be a r.*quick response* to some *physical* contact?	"You might want to consider the circumstances surrounding what happened, and in general terms, you might want to *consider* whether anything did happen before the *blow* was *delivered.* Was there any physical contact between Mr ... and the defendant? Is it a case in which he did appear to stop and *consider what he was doing*? Or was it a *quick response* to something which just happened – perhaps a touching on the shoulder or perhaps, as he suggests more *physical violence*?"

Fig. 17: From Notes to Speech

How do the notes stimulate the barrister's closing speech? The animator uses the notes as a supply of keywords, on the one hand, and as a chain of stimuli, on the other hand. The *italic* words in the transcript exemplify these echoes of the notes. Around these, the speech uses fresh and additional formulations. Keywords and formulations are embedded in a 'natural' flow of orality. From the animator's point of view, the script may be well understood in terms of risk-management. It serves as a safety net, not as a directive. It helps the barrister-animator not to miss out on crucial points or to confuse details. The script provides signposts in case of disorientation or blackout. The 'lost' animator would find his way back by consulting the notes. The notes, then, stabilize the barrister's case-representation for the decisive moments when addressing the jury directly and extensively.

The barrister's address adds much to the script, which does not mean that the script falls short. The speech is supposed to translate the stiff line of argument into a smooth oration. As a result, the barrister's speech progresses line by line without turning into aloud reading. The script enables the barrister to deliver fresh formulations without losing track. Speaker and script complement one another.

The script and its handling allow the barrister to foster the impression that the case is not the outcome of time-consuming, meticulous preparation but a consistent and self-evident *Gestalt*. This is how this (mode of) speech-production serves the official talk-bias of jury trials – and downplays the documentary basis of case-making. During the closing speech the barrister turns towards the jurors, while the red book remains, unobtrusively, on the desk. The speaker's eyes make only fleeting contact with the crucial lines. It seems as if the 'good reasons' emerged naturally, or better, as if they already took place in court. The 'praised' star during the closing speech is not the barrister but "the evidence."

Conclusion: the minutiae of case-representation

The careful reading of the barrister's brief and notebook provided us with some valuable insights into what it means to deliver a case in Crown Court. Both sources offered an unexpected variety of prediscursive objects: foci of inquiry, modules, lists, a map, etc. Not all of them are directly connected to what Goffman called speech-production. Not all count as means to speak out for the case in court. However, marking, note-taking, modulation, mapping and drafting contribute as a completed series of steps towards case-delivery.

Reading the barrister's red book put into the forefront certain achievements that one could easily disregard. The homogenisation of dispersed sources is one of them. Diffused texts are decomposed *and* interrelated. The 'folding' of process and event is another one. Procedural history is no longer just 'archived'.[22] What was stated before (often) returns as binding and (sometimes) as a resource for all procedural purposes. The modules play a key role in these underlying transformations. They make the filed evidence available for the current dealings. They convert 'everything' into one shared currency. They deconstruct statements and confront them in a unified field. The barrister's notes, hence, do not report on speech-production only. In fact, they teach us about the formation of legal discourses on the micro-level.

This formation is not a structure. It does not force the members' contributions into fixed value positions. It rather forces them into an ongoing competition, into oppositions and contrasts. The formation is operated by way of specific inscriptions 'before' the procedural public: modules. Modules represent statements and claims and the fact that something was stated and claimed by somebody. But modulation is not just memorisation. It provides, if anything, discursive 'ammunition' ready at hand. The resulting modules "never sleep." They stay in touch and resonate with all the others, whether past or present, until the procedure's very ending: the verdict.

One would, misunderstand the operation of legal discourse formation when conceiving it self-driven. The formation is not an actor. It is not an automatism. The barrister's notes show the contrary. Words do not just enter the legal discourse, but are methodically guided into it. They do not interact automatically, but are methodically confronted with one another. All this demands skill and know how. It is the barrister's craft. The relevance of witness statements and testimonies is, in this line, a methodical achievement just like the field of presence that they populate. Case-formation would not be feasible without the barristers' obsession with words, their nuances, and their potential meanings.

Case-making proceeds not by jumping from one modality to the other, meaning from text to talk, or from talk to text. Nor does case-making keep to just one modality, just talk or text. Case-making rather

---

[22] For a description of archives as dynamic and enacted in institutional settings, see Lynch (1999).

operates in-between, invents intermediaries, and bridges gaps. This explains the barrister's obsession with these minor and momentary entities in his red book. The jottings allow the in-court lawyer to represent *the* case in light of past and presence, of bound instructions and new occurrences. His jottings are, in this line, far more than just neutral links between text and talk. They place the case 'to be' in the midst of all that appears and counts as legal matter in this procedure.

In the following, I zoom out the minutiae of case-making in order to account for the resources that the procedure – not the barrister's professionalism — provides for. The Crown Court procedure, I suggest, can be characterised by these resources that together amount to a procedural infrastructure. The resources apply to the cases-in-the-making as well as to the cases-to-come.

VI. PROCEDURAL RESOURCES AND PROCEDURAL INFRASTRUCTURE

The member's methods of case-making rely on a number of resources provided by the procedure. In return, the resources promote certain modes of case-making identified with the procedure. From the point of view of the procedural event, resources are pre-established and co-producing. They gain significance in the course of the event, but do not derive from it. Once a trial hearing has started, resources can be referred to or interpreted in various ways, but not altered or erased. The resources' aversion to change imposes structuring restrictions to the members' situated case-making.[1]

So far, I presented case-making as a practical accomplishment by competing and collaborating case-makers. Legal meaning is carried out and achieved by interested actors, coordinated teams, and court authorities. Case-making resembles meticulous and momentous activities, which is why legal professionals are needed. In each chapter, however, we encountered various resources and equipments that facilitated case-making. Documents, notes, and files are the most pertinent examples of what is needed to actually make a case for all procedural purposes. In this chapter, I focus on case-making resources from the point of view of the court hearing. I argue that the procedure – as regime and discourse — provides means of case-making that are foundational and obligatory, enabling and restrictive.

Crown Court hearings are dense, complex, and weighty. They serve as needle-eyes for cases and biographies. How are the hearings, whether jury trials or sentencing hearings, feasible? One can answer this question by referring to their institutional conditions such as democratic rights, the rule of law, or the state's division of powers. One can answer this query by emphasising the court's embedding in a legal culture and its related beliefs, rationales, and customs. One can also answer this question by referring to the specific setting and the practical features that co-produce them. What are the features that

[1] An earlier version applied the notion of "materiality" from an interactionist point of view (Scheffer 2004). This view lacks, what one could call, the procedural point of view.

make the participants inter-act an orderly (evidentiary valid and binding) hearing 'into existence'? Goffman (1981), in his studies on "planned situations" and "talk production", raised awareness for the props and the media, for the front and the back regions, for the furniture and the ecology of settings as co-productive features. In the following, I account for the resources or materials that are of systematic relevance for the regular production of an orderly and valuable court hearing.

What are co-productive materials for the following sentencing hearing? What are the hearings resources? The following episode[2] took place at the start of the hearing. On the 26.03^{+2} the defendant, Mr Blue, pleaded guilty to the count of indecent assault:

Clerk:	Are you Tim Blue?
Def.:	I am.
Clerk:	Please sit down.
Mr Doubt:	Your honour, I defend Mr Blue.
Judge:	Yes, Mr Doubt.
Mr Doubt:	My learned friend Mr Hunt represents the prosecution. Your honour, this defendant pleaded not guilty to the single count of indecent assault. That plea was entered on the 19th July. Can I ask that he be re-arraigned, please?
Judge:	Yes, certainly.
Clerk:	Tim Blue, you are charged on this indictment with indecent assault. The particulars of the offence being that on the 3rd day of March 2000 you indecently assaulted Kim Baker, a female person. Do you plead guilty or not guilty?
Def.:	Guilty.
Clerk:	Guilty, thank you. Can you sit down?
Mr Hunt:	Yes, your honour, my learned friend's made it plain to me that that plea is entered on a basis of the defendant's interview, it's really page 5 of the interview.
Judge:	Yes, let me just have a look at that.
Mr Hunt:	At 24.08 just above that time where the defendant agrees that he cuddled up to the complainant and touched her breasts inside her clothing when she was saying "You better to." That encapsulates the conduct.
Judge:	The basis ---.
Mr Hunt:	--- the conduct.
Judge:	--- of the plea.
Mr Hunt:	Yes.

[2] Some of the occurrences in this case were already used in chapter II in order to exemplify and demonstrate event-process-relations.

In this sentencing hearing, the participants employ some components that are not produced in the interactional course only now. The components derive from earlier and elsewhere; they are procedural in a general and in a case-specific sense. The "particulars of the offence," for instance, were specified during a meeting of the two barristers shortly before the sentencing hearing. They provide a shared definition of what is at issue and what is not.

Other resources do not derive from the procedural history, but from past cases (such as precedence) or even from past epochs of legal culture (such as certain rituals or dress codes). The micro-sociological viewpoint on resources or materials does not include a definite origin. Resources are not defined by shape or essence.[3] Their identification only requires this: that the component is pre-produced and co-producing from the point of view of the talk-in-court. They are factual, stabilizing, and powerful in relation to something else, for example, a social situation. They function as materials in certain activity frames only. In this view, writing a text, compiling a file, or training a body brings about other 'things' in other 'rhythms' than does a court hearing (e.g., "oral testimonies") or the informal talk in the corridor (e.g., "rumours"). The usability and external character of something is closely related to its own mode and rhythm of production. Thus, the procedure can equip and besiege 'its' court hearings due to productive separations between, for instance, precedence, standards or files on the one hand, and talk-in-interaction on the other hand. To give an example, the participants cannot talk a file into existence; they cannot erase already disclosed versions; they cannot locally (re-)invent the witness-stand or other symbolic speech positions.

How can a micro-sociologist conceptualize events as being co-produced by different participants and materials? How can the ethnographer accept pre-established entities, while at the same time

[3] There are theoretical sources that support this viewpoint: (a) Emile Durkheim's definition of "faits sociale" possessing the "remarkable property of existing outside the consciousness of the individual" (Durkheim [1895]1982: 51) is modified accordingly: procedural resources are out of reach for the interaction course. (b) Parsons view on "symbols" (1967) implies that participants can refer to these externalised constants in order to stabilize a current social situation. These cultural resources appear as given or factual from the interactional point of view. (c) Gidden's idea of "allocative and authoritative resources" (1984:31 sqq. and 258 sqq.) is helpful because of its reference to power. Participants have to apply certain resources that are, at the same time, empowering and restrictive – and that make them re-produce the hegemonic structures, which in this case is procedure.

appreciating local contexts and contingencies?[4] In order to identify procedural resources, I combine two analytical motions that are commonly held apart. On the one hand, I account for materials of court hearings as *products* (how they emerged elsewhere/before); on the other hand, I account for the involvement of materials as *co-producing* resources (how they shape the case here/now).[5] The following definition combines production *and* consumption: (a) the entity is a constitutive element of the procedural event; (b) the entity is also productive outside this event; (c) it has been produced before the event. I explicate three resources – next to many others, such as legal rules or role models – for the above mentioned sentencing hearing: courtroom, files and story.

The court

> The hearing took place in the morning. It lasted no longer than ten minutes. Shortly before it commenced, two guards accompanied the defendant without hand-cuffs to the dock. The barristers arrived together after having enjoyed a quick instant coffee in the "counsel's lounge" (located just behind the public gallery). They climbed down the stairs, still absorbed by their previous chat. They took their seats at the two ends of the front bench and waited for the judge who just retired from another sentencing hearing. (There were six hearings this morning, plus several applications regarding bail and court orders.)
>
> Now, everybody was in place for the impending dealings: defendant, barristers, public, and clerk. Only the usher strolled around to ready the setting. "All rise in court," the usher suddenly growled. Everyone present got on their feet, including me. Everybody, from barrister down to court reporter, showed, as they say, "respect to judge and court." It was this

[4] Latour calls for answers that avoid the two "equally powerful dissatisfactions: when social scientists concentrate on what could be called the micro level, that is face to face interactions, local sites, they quickly realize that many of the elements necessary to make sense of the situation are already in place or are coming from far away [...] This is why so much work has been dedicated to notions such as society, norms, values [...] all terms that aim at designating what gives shape to micro interaction. But then, once this new level has been reached, a second type of dissatisfaction begins. Social scientists now feel that something is missing, that the abstraction of terms [...] seems too great, and that one needs to reconnect, through an opposite move, back to the flesh-and-blood local situations" (Latour 1999a:16 sq.).

[5] Keane's use of the term "trajectory" denotes a similar 'twofold': "By trajectory I mean to stress two dimensions of motion, that by which objects circulate through people's activities and that by which activities produce objects, relations, or events that can enter into new orders of activity" (Keane 1997:67).

> very moment of the judge entering the courtroom when the old assistant next to the clerk started the cassette-recorder. From now on, the hearing existed officially.
>
> After a brief exchange between clerk and defendant (about Mr Blue's personal data), the judge opened the hearing by addressing 'his' two barristers. The defence barrister got on his feet to kindly ask the judge whether the former plea could be altered. In order to address the judge, the barrister had to await permission, which was quickly granted by way of eye-contact. (There is a moment when the barrister is about to rise in order to demonstrate his wish to speak. At this very moment – neither fully on his feet nor on the bench – he can still be ignored and thus withdraw and fall back onto his seat. This happens frequently especially when the two barristers compete for the judge's attention.)
>
> The judge was happy to accept the barrister's suggestion to renew the plea. The clerk repeated the questions already asked weeks ago: "Do you plead guilty or not guilty?" Now it was on the defendant to rise from his seat. He was allowed to do so only after the clerk's signal. The defendant received the official question silently and responded without any further explanation: "Guilty." Now the floor was open for the presentation of aggravating and mitigating factors. The exchange took place in the ritual order: commenced by the prosecution, followed by the defence, and completed (right after) by the judge.

At the beginning of my fieldwork, I noted down this question: how, I wondered, is it possible that even I – as foreigner (German) and layperson (sociologist) – can somehow follow these hearings? The answer does not involve the ethnographer's intuition or pre-knowledge, but rests on the transparency of the hearing as such. My understanding was facilitated by the court's interaction order: the spatial positioning of the parties, the rhythm of verbal contributions, and the choreography of bodies. The interaction order guides the overall performance as well as its reception. It creates predictability to an extent that would be unusual in an inquisitorial, judge-centred setting. One does not need to know the judge in order to know, in general terms, what will happen in the hearing. In fact, the parties get to know the presiding judge only shortly before the hearing.

In order to appreciate this ordering effect we can reflect on what Crown Courts look like:

> During my fieldwork, I regularly visited two courthouses. One originated in the 14th century and had been serving as criminal and civil court for centuries. Architecture and furniture withstood the test of time. Local historians told me how trials were conducted in Victorian times, how the gallery was filled with "plebs," and the benches next to the judge with prosperous ladies. The jury was chosen from the honourable, credible,

> and male citizens.[6] Outside court, the penalty (mostly hanging) was executed as public spectacle, sometimes witnessed by thousands of people. The court building resembles a museum hosting a classical theatre.
>
> The other court looked entirely different. It is hosted in a functional building from the 1980s. The entrance area reminds of an airport. Scores of people pass quickly. Trials are announced on screens like flight arrivals/departures. Inside the court, the atmosphere is business-like. White walls, light furniture, no decoration – the rooms evoke efficacy rather than greatness. Plain carpets swallow most of the noise made by shoe heels and file trolleys. Moving through these courtrooms – entering, crossing, and leaving them – seems less distracting. The court resembles a machine emitting cases and judgements.

The old court reminded me of the extraordinary spectacles performed in the name of the Crown for all, nobles, gentlemen, and the people. The new court, in contrast, highlights the efficient treatment of the case-load.[7] Cases have numbers. Courtrooms are booked (mostly overbooked actually) on a daily basis.[8] The different atmospheres conveyed

Fig. 18: Old courtroom. http://www.istockphoto.com/stock-photo-6656352-inside-st-george-s-hall-in-liverpool.php. © iStockphoto

---

[6] See Shapin and Schaffer (1985) and Shapin (1994) for the shared Victorian roots of jury trials and public scientific experiments.

[7] This is, of course, just an impression. I came across reports on, for instance, the new Crown Court in Manchester that apparently did not fulfil its functions. The building, it was claimed by those working in it, "does not work." The staff criticized the slow security checks, the lack of conference rooms and storage space for files, the tiny library, and the uncomfortable barrister's lounge. See *The Guardian*, 30th June 2004.

[8] Crown Courts are often over-booked like airliners. The effect: cases together with their casts of characters wait in the corridors for a free courtroom. Good

by the courts are manifest: the old court, heavy and daunting, versus the modern court, light and efficient. Despite the huge differences in atmosphere, the two Crown Courts shared a lot of features. They positioned voices in time and space equally. Their interior arrangements, I argue, mark them out as Crown Courts and adhere to standards that can be legitimately expected. I illustrate the arrangement in a simplistic model:

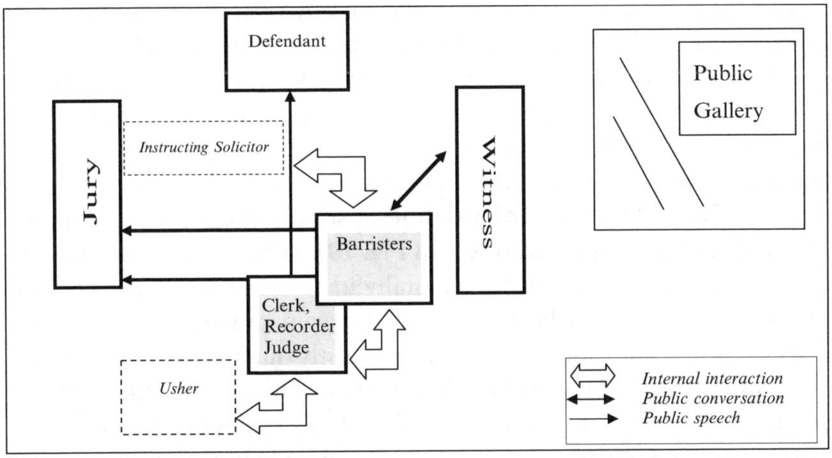

Fig. 19: Participation Framework of the Crown Court

The court setting embodies an order of complementary discourse-positions: in a trial hearing, the evidence-delivering witness is placed opposite the evidence-assessing jury; the presiding judge is, in any case, located opposite the defendant; defending and prosecuting barrister sit or stand right in front of the judge while facing both judge and jury[9]; the whole scenery is overlooked by a audience seated in the public gallery. The two barristers and the judge, uniformed with grey wigs and black robes – ritually covering individuality and, thus,

court-management is evaluated by statistical figures reporting the average waiting time especially for jurors on their days in court.

[9] "In the United States, it is accepted in most jurisdictions that the well of the courtroom is within the lawyers' control and lawyers are permitted to walk around that area rather freely. Sometimes they may go over to the jury box to make a point to them or sometimes to a spot distant from or close to a witness for dramatic effects" (Pizzi 1999:126). Such behaviour would not comply with English Crown Court rules.

'bias' – occupy the inner space, the centre of the setting, whereas the usher and the solicitors move in and out of the inner circle. The judge is assisted by the sound recordist and, more so, by the clerk, 'his left hand' placed right in front of him or her. Here, adversarialism translates into a spatial formation, "a pattern of relations" (Sørensen 2009:70). In this "coordinate system" (Ibid.:75) various interactional circles or regions are combined and are only virtually overlooked by the symbolically high position of the presiding judge.

The court is as a moral space governed by observable traffic rules. In this setting, the allocation of turns and the forms of talk are "prestructured" (Atkinson and Drew 1979). We find pedantic rituals, norms of performance, and conventional speech acts that are, in turn, interwoven with the minimum requirements for a generally accepted and legitimate procedure. The traffic rules concern orderly participation: (1) The interaction order defines a set of obligatory *participants* (displayed by thickly-lined boxes of Fig. 19). When anyone of this cast is missing (either physically or mentally in case of sleep or confusion), the trial hearing must be interrupted or even cancelled. The broken lines represent additional participants, mostly quiet suppliers of papers and information. (2) The *defendant* is placed away from his *barrister* and from the question-answer-rounds. From the defendant's bench, he or she must not address the court except when being asked directly by the clerk or by the judge via his or her barrister. (3) The *witnesses* enter the courtroom after having been called in. They are led to the witness stand and sworn in by the usher. From here, they do not address the jury directly. They answer the barristers' friendly or hostile questions and, by doing so, turn to judge and jury. (4) The *jurors* are supposed to focus quietly and exclusively on the staged dealings. They receive the cases solely from barrister-witness-interactions right in front. The barristers' closing speeches and the judge's summary only supplement this first-hand information. (5) The *barristers*, in order to speak, need to get up and stand by the bench. They are not allowed to walk around, e.g., over to the jury box or to the defendant. They are assisted by mobile participants, paralegals or the usher, who deliver documents, notes, or verbal massages in a whispering tone. (6) The *judge* speaks only from his or her lifted bench. He or she would ask questions to the barristers or to the witnesses. He or she would address the defendant only via the clerk ("the plea") or the barrister in charge ("instructions"). This does not apply to the final sentencing. (7) *Others* in the public gallery serve as the overhearing audience. The participants refer only exceptionally to them 'in general' (as the public) or 'directly' (as "family members" or "friends"). These others are meant to take a seat within the confines of the gallery space while listening to the dealings.

The spatial order including its traffic rules are not negotiable during trial. The order is taken for granted as the basic frame of this event as *procedural* event. By taking their spatial and symbolic positions, the members delegate some discursive ordering to the material setting. Thus, the courtroom is neither a passive discourse container nor simply the effect of the situated discourse-in-action. The courtroom is more adequately described as accommodating a bundle of co-producing forces from the point of view of the hearing:

- The spatial ordering co-constitutes and identifies significant others: the adversaries, the 'highest' authority, the decisive audience, the parties' witnesses, etc.
- The positioning of participants signifies the weight of their voices or contributions, such as being in the stand (witness), on the dock (defendant), or on the bench (judge). It amplifies the words spoken, identifies these with certain acts, and signifies their future usability.
- The individual hearing is freed of meta-discursive concerns regarding the appropriateness, the fairness, or the neutrality of the interaction order in the specific case. Only exceptionally can the judge arrange for special measures for "people described as vulnerable or intimidated witnesses."[10]

Standardization demonstrates distance and indifference. In view of the specific case or the specific trial, the clerk would not carry around tables, count the jurors' chairs, or build a balustrade to separate public gallery and legal arena. The court is set for the hearing to start and for the protagonists to take their predefined roles. The courtroom provides a stable frame that turns each case presented in front of it into a Crown Court case. This standardization does not exclude eventfulness, but specifies is: everything of importance must still happen; and only

[10] According to a leaflet by the CJS (the Criminal Justice agencies), the following exceptions are available: screens around the witness box, evidence via live link, video recorded evidence in chief, "removal of wigs and gowns so that the court feels less formal", evidence given in private, "use of communication aids for example an alphabet board", examination through an intermediary. See http://www.cjsonline.gov.uk (accessed in March 2010). According to the CJS, these measures have been available since 2002.

certain things are allowed to happen. This is why barristers wait with their plea bargaining until they know with certainty who will or will not turn up as witness. This is why the mobilised cases are no more than potentialities. They turn manifest and effective only when backed by talkative witnesses of flesh and blood.

Standardization carries vast implications for the concept of procedural justice. Standardization seems unproblematic when presented as equal treatment. It seems problematic when linked to discriminating effects. In this line, feminist critiques demand more sensitivity for 'exceptional' cases (Konradi 1997). Such sensitivity, however, creates new problems, because it requires judgements prior to the trial concerning the nature of the legal matter at hand. Any special treatment, for instance of 'the victim', involves presumptions that, ideally, have to remain open until the verdict. Standardization, in contrast, allows the court's detachment from the matter at hand. The cases are not pre-defined by the court but by the parties. By the same token, unspecialized courts seem incapable of living up to certain demands in relation to, for example, organised crime, the treatment of minorities, or drug-related offences. The frequent legal reforms – (rhetorically) aiming at (more) fairness, efficacy, and justice – face a field of controversy between standardization (criticized as disinterest) and specialization (criticized as discrimination). How, reformers ask, can courts be more case-sensitive without undermining the right to "equality before the law?"

Case-sensitivity arises by way of tactical usage of the ordered and standardized court space. The parties use the court as a coulisse to stage their cases; they strategically place certain characters in the designated positions. In the case of Tim Blue, the defence was keen to place his partner – well dressed and well behaved, of course – right in the public gallery. Her appearance should demonstrate forgiveness from within a long-standing, intimate relationship. This positioning should convey that he is indeed capable of having 'normal relationships with women', something that the probation officer later called into question. The defence can, moreover, utilize the courtroom by tactical avoidance. Whether the defendant should appear in the witness-box or should remain in the dock is a core decision often involving prolonged internal consultations. A mix of issues, such as appearance, reliance, self-discipline is considered in the decision process. The sentencing hearing involved other spatial motions: the defence tried to motivate a wide range of "character witnesses" to turn up and show solidarity.[11] The tactical use of the courtroom – as a communicative and case-making resource – can involve minor movements as well: for instance, standing up or remaining seated is not an option 'officially' offered to the defendants. However, as an exception, this choice turns into a powerful device to signify limited capabilities (see chapter VII). The Crown Court's strict order allows the parties to utilize deviance as a performative device.

The file

The standardized court is one procedural resource amongst others. Tim Blue's sentencing hearing in mind (see chapter II), we can collect more co-producing pre-products, meaning more materials at hand already before the hearing commences. There is one clear criterion for identifying these materials or resources: without them, the parties would not proceed.

In the sentencing hearing of Tim Blue, various participants kept case-files ready at hand. Some had entire files (folders keeping the full documented case history) at their disposal, while to others, the barristers, only certain parts were readily available, such as maps and scripts for the upcoming dealings. Each barrister carries his or her instructions as "our case." File and brief demonstrate the double character of adversarial procedure: a (confidential) file kept by and within each party and (shared) documents that have been put into circulation on both sides prior to the hearing.

The two barristers keep their briefs in reach throughout the day in court. The brief is held in form of a paper roll; it is unrolled in order to read through it; it is flattened to select and present pages. Prior to the hearing, the brief is carefully read and re-read, whereas in court, the barrister would treat the brief rather like a 'dead pledge': something that she or he can rely on if needed. In 'comprehensive cases', the barrister keeps an extra folder ordered by "evidence", "authorities", and "expertise." Additionally, the instructing law firm would keep the entire file ready on demand on a back bench in court.

---

[11] One remarkable case of the tactical use of the court space involved members of the British Army. Two soldiers received valid character statements by their superiors who turned up, of course, in their festive uniform attire including insignia of rank and power.

While the barrister works in proximity to his or her briefs, the solicitor works at close distance to his or her filing cabinet. The filing cabinet orders the files 'under construction' – before they are closed and archived. What is more, each file contains similar fractions, which provides orientation for its varying users, the secretary, the paralegal or the various solicitors in charge: (1) the prosecution-bundle containing the disclosed evidence against the defendant, mainly consisting of police protocols; (2) all correspondence in this case inside and outside the defence ensemble; (3) accountancy forms for the legal aid office that record everything that has been done in this case; (4) the defence-bundle with the drafted, corrected and sometimes signed statements of all successfully recruited defence witnesses. Each section is ordered chronologically and numbered throughout in order to identify missing pages.

The co-producing quality of the file and its satellite (the brief) becomes apparent in the course of the hearing. Participants, especially witnesses and examining counsels, turn to their papers either quickly glancing at them or, in exceptional cases, reading out certain phrases or paragraphs. The barristers would refer to certain shared documents in light of their instructions, such as to "page 5" of the police protocol in Tim Blue's case. Here, a piece of evidence is called into existence for the hearing that had been produced already five months prior to the hearing.

> The defence counsel referred to "page 5" in order to specify the (reduced) basis of the plea. He did so without reading out the relevant pages of the police interview. Judge and prosecuting barrister knew from their copies 'where the defence counsel was' and could check 'what he was talking about'. During pre-trial, the protocol became the focal object of negotiations and transformations. As an object it was transformed in various ways: sliced, measured, counted – and acknowledged as factual. The question of 'what really happened' and 'how far the defendant went' was measured in page-numbers: Is Tim Blue guilty up to page 4 or 5 or even 7? The barristers 'reported' their agreed-upon answer to this question in the sentencing hearing. (26.3[+2])

Referring to "page 5" is possible because defence-file and prosecution-file contain the similar police protocol. This shared piece of evidence enabled the two barristers to synchronize their case-making. Eventually, the barristers agreed on one version of guilt – and dismissed the possibility of a "not guilty" plea together with a full-blown jury trial. The shared grounds allow for recurrent calculations of the 'score', which is the strength of the prosecution-case compared to the defence-case. But how is the police protocol shared? The answer identifies the protocol as a procedural resource, a resource provided by procedural 'rules of the game'. The police protocol (PP) travelled all the way from the police interview via the Crown Prosecution Service (CPS) to the defence and, finally, to the sentencing hearing:

Defence	***Court***	**Prosecution / Police**
Def. barrister instructed by solicitor by means of PP PP used by barrister to interview defendant	*FINISH: Closing speech by judge* *Cross-examinations in light of PP* *Friendly examination by means of PP (26.3^{+2})*	Pros. barrister instructed by CPS PP used by barrister to interview victim
PP used by solicitor to instruct defence barrister PP used by solicitor to interview her client	*Judge receives PP as part of the disclosed bundle*	PP used by CPS-solicitor to instruct prosecuting barrister PP used by police officers to interview other witnesses
PP received as part of disclosed bundle		CPS-solicitor decides to disclose PP
Waiting for PP		CPS decides on evidential grounds (incl. PP) whether they have a case
		Account written down and signed in PP
Account noted by the solicitor	*[Account used to present the matter in the Magistrates' Court]*	START: Early account in the police interview (26.7^{+1})

Fig. 20: The Circulation of the Police Protocol

The circulation of the police protocol (PP) as a central piece of evidence is driven by rules of disclosure and multiple tactical considerations. As a result, we find stop-and-go traffic plus a procedural terrain comprising transparent and opaque regions. The PP circulated, first of all, within the police/prosecution side in the process of case-making. It circulated diagonally from the prosecution to the defence – with some delay and after persistent requests by the defence solicitor. Rather late, the PP became available to the court including the judge. By means of these circulations, the participants in court share a 'factual ground' on the legal matter. The circulations build a stock of shared documents for the adversaries, similar to the shared dossier in the inquisitorial procedure. Disclosure, thus, constitutes a procedural matter. The stock allows the parties to enter into negotiations and arguments.

The files do not just contain shared documents. They are not just public documents either. Each file resembles also an internal (work) memory of what the party did so far, what they refrained from doing, and what they wanted to do, or what they are still aiming for. In this way, the PP became part of different case-making operations: a map to search for inconsistencies; a stimulant to check for counter-versions; a source to try out demonstrations for the hearing. The file hosts a number of representational projects, themselves more or less developed and promising. See for instance the file notes on the 'indelicate inquires' on the "victim's family background:"

Case No. 5/ Topic No. 10: Family background

Statements	16.08^{+1}	25.08^{+1}	26.08^{+1}	23.10^{+1}	25.11^{+1}
Dubious family background	File note on meeting with client				
Check family history; ask his partner Lydia for more information		Diary note			
Lydia mentioned some irregularities in the ... More details?			Letter to client		
Changing partners of complainant's mother				File note on tel. talk with Lydia	
This information of not great help for trial					Instruct./ Counsel

Fig. 21: Data-sheet of a Failed Inquiry

Such inquiries are kept internal within the party for tactical and, perhaps, moral reasons.[12] Sometimes they are just isolated one-off speculations without any follow-up entry. Successful as well as unsuccessful inquiries shape and outline what the defence ensemble calls "our case" (for now). Here, the case remains something unfinished, unofficial, and preliminary. At the beginning, when I first read through the files,

[12] Speculations such as the following provide a good example: "Complainant was suffering from a sexually transmitted disease. Client says he would not have risked trying to have sex [...] Complainant was out clubbing between the date of the alleged incident and the date that our client was arrested which of course was about a four-week period. [...] He said that he believes she now has a new boyfriend. ." (5.9^{+1})

it struck me how often the version of "our case" changed and how quickly old versions were forgotten in due course. However, the defence had to arrive at internally binding agreements between client, solicitor and, later, barrister. The file contains reports of and comments on the "conferences" in which client and barrister reached such agreements:

19.3^{+2} Conference between counsel and client before trial: "Client admits to touching her breasts. Counsel then advises a guilty plea, but on a basis of plea that only the touching of breasts took place."

19.3^{+2} The solicitor adds a hand-written note: "Discussion with representative of the firm after Counsel has advised guilty plea is the right thing (on a certain basis) admission re: touch breast. Hope she (the complainant) does not turn up next week. If does, then offer plea ltd basis."

26.3^{+2} Notes by the solicitor about the last conference right before the court hearing: "[T]he client accepts, that in law he is guilty technically and obviously we want to get that on the best possible basis [...] Counsel has informed client that he will not go on the sex offenders register due to the victim's age and the fact that it was a relatively minor incident."

The file keeps track of the suggestions, negotiations, reformulations, and agreements on various issues simultaneously. It documents instructions that are meant to be utilized as binding resources for the public case-representations. Internally, the file resembles a creative and resourceful "scrapbook" (Kozin 2007). It is continuously filled with occurring bits and pieces: drafted stories, first ideas, memos on rumours, newspaper clips, photographs or sketches of the crime scene, to-do-lists, etc. The file hosts and stimulates inventive brainstorming as well as systematic legal service.

Similar to the courtroom's general interaction order and the case-specific cast of characters placed in this order, the file appears as a resource that is procedurally given, and that performs the case as something specific. Again, also, the hearing is freed of some configurations. Defence-file and prosecution-file – together with their satellites (the briefs) – assist in framing the hearing as a focussed multi-party encounter, restricted right from the start to a certain amount of (qualified) issues, problems, and solutions.

The file's potential as procedural resource rests on its availability *and* immutability from the point of view of the hearing. Participants can rewrite the defence statement before it is distributed; barristers can exclude parts of an interview protocol before it is delivered in court; the protagonists, however, cannot deny the written facts as such once the court hearing commenced. The file turns material through two basic processes: firstly, its availability and immutability derive from actual disclosure and the shared dossier that is fed by exchanges 'with the adversary'; secondly, the file becomes available and immutable for the court hearing due to the parties' representational projects and their manifestations in internal agreements. The adversarial case-file promotes a conservative, retrospective orientation of the court hearing – due to the procedure's rules of admissibility and due to the party's tactical considerations on how to stage the case here and now.

The story

The story of "what happened that night" seems inseparable from the file's inscriptions. Or more generally: the claims and statements seem bound to the materials delivering it. The story is turned into paper, filed, and circulated shortly after its first appearance. The documents make the story available, render it factual, and allow for its distribution. Despite this "materiality of communication" (Gumbrecht and Pfeiffer 1988), how can the story count as a procedural resource in its own right?

A first clue lies in the adversarial methods of fact-finding. The procedure shows a prevalence for the story-frame. The interviewers' questions are full with analogous framing devices: beginning and ending, characters, sequencing, a singular plot, indices as authenticity markers. They invite interviewees to narrate from one episode to the next. The barrister's notes (chapter V) display the epistemic role of stories: statements are perceived as autonomous entities *and* they are tied to and arrayed as a story line; the facts emerge in a sequence of actions, ascribed to certain actors, and placed in unique time and space. They are tested equally. Moreover, facts gain their relevance in contrast to other versions 'of the same'. This diagnostic reception can turn single facts ("he went out") into a matter of personal choice or biased view without neglecting the meta-narrative ("what really happened"). In the indecent assault case, police officers and lawyers confronted Tim Blue with a hegemonic account that *this* sequence of actions took place and that *his* actions amount to the sexual offence that he is therefore charged with.

The story-frame provides material for all procedural purposes. It grants investigators and lawyers additional questions on what happened, where, and when, and how exactly. The story-frame introduces not just facts and counter-facts, but imposes certain norms of what a competent eye witness should know about the events and in how far she or he should be able to report these events from his or her point of view at that time. It allows certain interpretations of agency and responsibility (meaning the ability to act upon certain situations that, according to the story, took place). The story-frame offers an excess of episodes, details, information, etc. and intrinsic cross-checks to assess the evidence as consistent and coherent.

A story turns material for situated activities in another, individual sense. Similar to the cast that populates the spatial grid of the courtroom, the story introduces case-specific relevancies from the point of view of the court hearing. Much is said, meant, and claimed before the first word is uttered in open court. Here, pre-production and immutability are linked to replication and iteration of a story's numerous appearances in the procedural course. The story turns into a resource for the court hearing because it has already been told and referred to in various procedural contexts prior to the hearing.[13]

The factuality of our story arose accordingly. It had been employed several times during pre-trial: in police-interviews, primary disclosure, the defence statement, the brief to counsel, the barrister's notes, etc. Every employment triggers re-appearance and modification. Because it is never fully and exactly repeated, one can observe some kind of idealization: the story's core features, its identity. The story was employed for a last time in the plea bargaining. The 'original' interview protocol (26.07^{+1}) became the shared case up to the following lines on "page 5:"

[13] My argument here resembles Foucault's view on the statements' discursive efficacy: "Instead of being something said once and for all – and lost in the past like the result of a battle, a geological catastrophe, or the death of a king – the statement, as it emerges in its materiality, appears with a status, enters various networks and various fields of use, is subjected to transferences of modifications, is integrated into operations and strategies in which its identity is maintained or effaced. Thus the statement circulates, is used, disappears, allows or prevents the realization of a desire, serves or resists various interests, participates in challenge and struggle, and becomes a theme of appropriation or rivalry" (Foucault 1972:118).

BLUE ... JUST SNOGGED WITH HER, JUST PLAYED WITH HER BREASTS, AS FAR AS I KNOW THAT'S ALL I DID, THEN I GOT UP AND SHE SAID YOU HAD BETTER GO AND I JUST APOLOGISED, I JUST SAID SORRY, I SAID YOU WON'T SAY A WORD TO JANE, WILL YOU?
DC So you'd started kissing with her, did she resist that?
BLUE SHE DID AT FIRST AND THEN SHE JUST RELAXED AFTERWARDS
DC Is that because you told her to relax?
BLUE NO I DIDN'T SAY, CAN'T REMEMBER SAYING THAT
DC Right, so you've been kissing with her and she's told you to go and you've carried on kissing with her, was that with consent or without?
BLUE WITHOUT I SHOULD THINK – ALL I CAN DO IS REMEMBER JUST CUDDLING UP TO HER AND JUST TOUCHING HER BREASTS
DC Is this outside her clothing or inside her pyjamas?
BLUE INSIDE I THINK
DC And what was she saying while you were doing this?
BLUE SHE JUST SAID YOU HAD BETTER GO

One can grasp the full significance of this announcement only in the light of the story's earlier versions. How much has been cut out here? How much remains unsaid? What is the price the parties pay for their bargaining of truth? Answering these queries requires a reference to the full story as a lasting, identical object that, at the same time, passes through a career which involves changes.

The story of what happened during that night appeared on the procedural screen for the first time at the police station. The complainant reported how Tim Blue entered the bedroom, how he started kissing and stroking her, how he went even further and made her "do things." Finally, she managed to get rid of him, of the one she trusted, of her good old father-like friend. The story unfolded dialogically in a question-answer play. Round by round the narration moved further into the territory of guilt and shame. As a result, the story thickens to a plot that resists changes at will, that is capable of incorporating vast details or of shrinking to its core, and that is anchored by a network of spatiotemporal tokens.

A variation of the story then reappears in the police interview with the accused (27.7^{+1}). The interviewers used the victim's story to confront the suspect with 'what really happened'. The questions led Tim Blue step by step through this account:

BLUE ... ALL I CAN DO IS REMEMBER JUST CUDDLING UP TO HER AND JUST TOUCHING HER BREASTS

DC	Is this outside her clothing or inside her pyjamas?
BLUE	INSIDE I THINK
DC	... She then says that you undid your trouser zip and your belt?
BLUE	NO – I CAN'T REMEMBER DOING THAT
DC	And that you then took hold of her left wrist and pulled her hand and put it down your trousers and inside your underpants and made her touch your erect penis?
BLUE	NO – I CAN'T REMEMBER DOING THAT
DC	And you then put your hand down her shorts and began to touch her vaginal area, do you remember that?
BLUE	NO, NO, BUT I CAN'T REMEMBER THAT BIT. I CAN REMEMBER GOING OUT THE DOOR BUT I CAN'T REMEMBER TAKING MY GLASS BACK.

The DC's questions start with a neutral request ("Is this ...?"). He displays just a need for factual advice. The next question conveys a reported allegation ("she then says ..."), which puts pressure on the interviewee. His answers apparently compete with another, already established version. The interview continues with a pertinent allegation ("And you then ..."). Here, the interviewer switches from forward looking questions ('what next') to backward-looking questions ('did you not'). The police officer seems to know the story's conclusion already. The source of this knowledge is no longer specified.

The police officer confronted Mr Blue with a preferred story-line that he borrowed from a story already in place. This method of interrogation succeeded in that the suspect and later defendant did not deny the invoked claims. He simply "can't remember."[14] Instead of offering a counter-narrative, Blue left gaps for imagination and 'common sense' to step in. As a result, the victim's story became the hegemonic account and a value object in procedural terms.

From this point onwards, the victim's story – together with the defendant's quasi-admissions – bore the prosecution-case. The defence's task was simple and complicated at the same time: the solicitor could now focus on delimiting the far-reaching inferences from the hegemonic account: 'He did not go that far! He stopped earlier...!'[15]

---

[14] 'My' defence lawyer complained about such weak (first) defences. Just like Mr Blue, many suspects would create such problematic starting points for professional case-making; the suspects themselves establish facts that are hard to cure later on.

[15] See the following letter that the solicitor wrote to the barrister [referred to as Counsel]: "Our client's interview with the police does contain some admissions of kissing and touching. Our client does state that there was a point when complainant resisted his advances and yet those advances continued. He, of course, denies all other allegations made by the complainant. [...] If the Crown insist that any guilty plea has

The solicitor prepared a defence statement that could be read as a minimal version of the hegemonic story – and as its denial:

> The Defendant put his arm around the Complainant and began to kiss her. The Defendant admits that there was contact between the Complainant and himself at this time and the Complainant was not resisting the Defendant's advances at this time. The Complainant was clearly giving her implied consent to this. When the Complainant indicated that she no longer consented to this, the Defendant stopped immediately and he left the Complainant's bedroom…. (26.01[+2])

The official "defence statement" replaced Blue's "I can't remember" by something more 'expedient' for case-making purposes: a counter-version. In a jury trial, by help of this counter-version, the prosecution would have led the 'victim' through the plot ensuring that the 'ideal story' reached the jury. During the cross-examination, the defence would have tried to undermine the victim's credibility thus adding to the story's appearances. But then, the defendant's earlier admissions from the police interview would have been still in place, after all. Such calculation provided the backdrop to the plea bargaining for the defence: there was a strong, even partially self-confirmed story in place that demanded concessions by Mr Blue. What, then, made the prosecution enter into plea bargaining? This way, I suggest, the complainant could avoid an unpleasant appearance in open court and the hostile questions by the skilled defence barrister. She did not wish to reveal "these things" in public. The defence feared the unsaid and what it could possibly do to the jurors' imagination; the prosecution feared the articulation of intimate details and how it could affect the victim's image.

What happened after the two barristers negotiated the scope of the story in their plea bargaining session? What happened after the prosecuting barrister announced the reduced basis of the guilty plea to the judge? The story 'of what happened' was cut down to "page 5." Later parts of the story were thus rendered irrelevant. Despite the agreement on what happened, the full story remained intact and effective. Tim Blue, very soon after the hearing, was confronted with the story's persistence, here with its overall moral implications.

---

to be on the basis of their evidence as it is at the moment then we do not think our client can plead guilty, as he does not accept all of the allegations that have been made."

> The story re-appeared in the local newspaper and caused extra-judicial punishment by his employer and neighbours. "Tim Blue, 52, who had worked for the past 23 years at [...] 'misread the signals' from a 26-year-old woman. One night at the [...] after the woman had gone to bed, Blue appeared at her bedside, carrying drinks, said prosecutor Mr Hunt. Blue began talking to her and then touched her breasts over the clothing and inside, Mr Hunt added. 'He kissed her, telling her to relax and enjoy it. Afterwards, he said he was sorry.' Blue told the police he had been 'totally stupid'". (27.3^{+2})

How can this series of appearances demonstrate the story's status as a procedural resource? Is the story really another pre-established co-producer of the hearing? The story's career went through several sites and included a series of utilizations plus some moments of disengagement. Its multi-sited existence and the different roles it played on the way to court illustrate striking similarities to court and file: the story was put together prior to the hearing; it grounded and informed the hearing; it survived the hearing; it spans time and space.

Two more specifications may help to understand the story as a procedural resource. Firstly, the story is well understood as decentred and multiple; it is 'more than one and less than many'.[16] The story continues to exist not just by narration, but by all references to it: quotes ("She then said 'you ...'"), confirmation ("This is right."), assessments ("So what you are implying then is that she was lying ..."), comments ("I don't know this!"), denials ("I never said this."), or invocation ("Her story ..."). As a decentred object the story extends by each reference to its imagined identity. The story remains *the* story even though 'its' enunciations include and exclude details (e.g. how long they knew each other; why at all he walked up to her room; what she wore; what they drank and how much; what they were talking about, etc.). This extensive mode of existence forces as well as allows its users to omit, thicken, or modify the story and, by doing so, to decentre it even further.

For some material-semiotic analysts, such stories come into view as distributed and spread – on a "pin-board" (Law 2002:2). The metaphor

---

[16] An "object such as an aircraft – an 'individual' and 'specific' aircraft – comes in different versions. It has no single centre. It is multiple. And yet these various versions also interfere with one another and shuffle themselves together to make a single aircraft. They make what I will call singularities, or singular objects out of their multiplicity. In short, they make objects that cohere" (Law 2002:2).

of a pin-board leads to intriguing mappings of appearances and their relations. The metaphor, however, is inaccurate when it comes to the story's being-in-time, its unfolding and procedural career. Firstly, the many versions and cross-references do not come into being all at once. Versions and references precede and follow each other. Secondly, not all reappearances and cross-references turn into relevant versions. Some leave their marks and add to the story, while others remain ephemeral. Both aspects – sequentiality and selection – can further an understanding of the story's relevance. The story, both as a general format and as a singular formation, serves our understanding of it as a procedural resource.

Fact-finding draws on the decentred story that has been used and re-used during pre-trial. Stories only exceptionally and surprisingly enter the court without such a pre-history. There is always already a prior version laying out 'what one should say' and 'what better remains unsaid'. Replication and re-narration, in this line, offer some means of testing a story. Its numerous enunciations enforce extra criteria to question and challenge the account(s) of "what happened." This way, the story becomes a rule for its successors and a source for its critiques.

Towards procedural infrastructure

At this point, I would like to return to the starting-point of this chapter: the conceptualization of procedural resources. How can courtrooms, files, and stories serve as co-productive materials? All three, I propose, extend, facilitate, and orientate the hearing as procedural event: the court as a standardised stage inhabiting a specific cast, the scriptural economy of files and documents with its case-specific formulations, the story as methodical truth-finding engine with its hegemonic and competing versions. All three materials are pre-produced and co-producers of the court. All three are procedural resources in the double meaning of procedure advocated in this book: general and case-related.

How do the three resources differ in temporal regards? They vary in the way they can be observed already before the hearing. They, furthermore, vary in terms of their becoming. The following synopsis provides an overview and some grounds for conclusive reflections.

	Observable as	Procedure is	Duration analogue to	Mode of production	Rhythm
Court	stable	standardized	Institution	Rituals	day-to-day
File	accumulative	directed	Case-work	Inscriptions	accelerated
Story	spread	grounded	Social career	Reference	unsteady

Fig. 22: Comparing Procedural Resources

The three resources are pre-established from the point of view of the hearing: the courtroom with its standardized speech-positions, the file as the site of creative and systematic investments or the story with its intertwined versions. All three seem immutable in the light of the hearing. From another perspective, for instance, of an historian investigating the rise and fall of jury-trials, the seemingly solid composition of the court turns into a dynamic becoming. The same is true for file or story. What reaches the court as a fixed bundle derives from contingent production processes. The three resources are in fact relative becomings, each with its duration and flexibility. Each corresponds to a unique time zone that shapes their emergence and disappearance.[17] Immutability is a relative state that is appreciable here from the point of view of the eventual court hearing.

The material quality can be observed in light of the care necessary to maintain it. The hearing, for instance, needs to be attended by co-present participants according to the grammar of participation. With core members absent, the hearing does not take place. The story, in contrast, is rather nomadic. It survives thanks to no more than sporadic references. To gain procedural impact, however, the story needs support and circulation at the right procedural junctures. The Crown Court, as another contrast, is formed in a comparably *longue durée* often referred to as legal tradition or culture. It is enacted in – but not immediately dependent on – the everyday of 'sitting courts'. Frequently, a single standard turns into the subject matter of

[17] Adam recommends a set of biological concepts to inform Social Sciences: "Biologists show us a world of orchestrated rhythms of varying speed and intensity, of temporally constituted uniqueness, a realm of organisms with the capacity for memory and foresight and of beings that time their actions and reckon time" (1994:72).

a legal reform. And the file? It is gathered over months of intervallic file-solicitor-interaction. The attendance rate accelerates as the 'day in court' approaches. The three equipments reveal, as Deleuze puts it, "other durations that beat to other rhythms" (Deleuze 1991:78). They reside in separate time zones.

What does the co-existence of the procedural resources mean for legal practice? Court, file, and story – together with other materials – facilitate the hearing. The hearing as it is (cumulative, anticipated, and condensed) is not feasible by means of direct interaction only. The resources add a sense of stability, historicity, and predictability. They fix past events, specify possible futures and steady expectations. They introduce a temporal division of labour that disburdens the current dealings and involves periods of preparation, or to go further back, of cultural formation. In short, they turn the gathering into a procedural event.

Court, file, and story do not simply serve the production of court hearings. They are not just functional components, supplementing the otherwise limited direct interaction. The co-producers, as well, disrupt, distract, and trouble the hearing. The story's versions jeopardise testimony given in court; the file holds an overload of information; the court does not stage the 'full story'; background knowledge exceeds the record. The procedural infrastructure, even though indispensable, turns out to be imprecise, lacking and fuzzy when it comes to the situated utilization. The resources trigger secondary problems for the participants and may explain the ensembles' practical – not just formal – dependency on experienced in-court lawyers.

The infrastructure does not quite fit the court hearing. It comprises wanted and unwanted qualities, helpful and troublesome aspects. There is, as Keane put it for signs, "in practice […] no way entirely to eliminate that factor of co-presence or what we might call 'bundling'" (2003:414). The materials are devices *and* challenges, props *and* troublemakers. That means: one cannot consume a thing without taking in its unwelcome properties that are attached to it. In this case, the (procedural) resource dependency drives the participants and parties into tricky situations. They have recourse only to imperfect resources: for instance, a story, knowing that it cannot be narrated; a file, knowing that some inquiries are inadmissible; or the court's interaction order although it might show *this* witness in an unfavourable way.

This ethnography reveals several tactics (e.g. waiting until the very end) and intermediaries (e.g. the barrister's notes) that address the problems of resource dependency. The practitioners employ additional intermediaries in order to streamline urgent local needs and given resources: the barrister as experienced in-court performer shall harmonize discourse automaton and instructed case; the brief as summary shall harmonize complex file and concise hearing; the defence statement as line of argument shall harmonize the spread story and 'his version'. These imperfect harmonisations indicate, like the members' adeptness, resistance that occur when case-making employs incongruent materials.

And finally: how are the three resources procedural? They are in two basic ways. Firstly, all three perform procedural regularities or standards. The story is procedural inasmuch as it fits singular matter into a set of definitions and conventions on how to deliver evidence properly as direct experience; the court is procedural inasmuch as it positions a unique cast of characters according to a standardized, legitimizing arrangement; the file is procedural inasmuch as it feeds into and is fed by the official paper trails according to the formal order of filing. Furthermore, court, file, and story are procedural in another respect: they are and remain effective throughout the procedure as *the* infrastructure of meaning-production. The resources exert a structuring force on the singularities of the case. In this way, they contribute to case-making and to "doing procedure."

The next chapter is concerned with the moral articulations of blame and regret in a murder case. Moralising is, in the Crown Court procedure, no singular moment of confrontation. Rather, it resembles a series of invitations that are hard to reject. Adversarial case-making pulls the defendant towards repetitive and intensifying self-moralising on the procedural backstages. This modality of (indirect) moralising differs from inquisitorial counterparts.

problems of resource dependence: the practitioner employs [illegible] and financial [illegible] in order to [illegible] local needs [illegible] [illegible]

And finally, how [illegible] the three [illegible] procedural. They [illegible] [illegible] sets of definitions and conventions [illegible] [illegible] by the formal [illegible] according to the formal [illegible] [illegible] court [illegible] and they are procedural in [illegible] [illegible] structure of [illegible] production [illegible] structure [illegible]

The [illegible] and [illegible] Nonetheless [illegible]

VII. A CASE OF MURDER: NO REGRET!

The procedure is demanding in other respects: it confronts defendants with the issues of guilt and remorse. In a case of murder, after first admissions, the focus of casework shifted towards the moral implications of the deed. Mr Grease, unusually so, showed no signs of regret, which intensified the efforts to elicit moral responses. The case-study examines how moralising is exercised in the Crown Court procedure and to what effects. It is exercised, I conclude, in an indirect, non-inquisitorial manner.

Case-making does not stop at the battle of facts and the integration of diverse knowledges. Case-making involves the evaluation of good and bad, of guilt and responsibility. It involves morals, especially relating to the character of the person who committed an offence or, like here, who pleaded guilty to the allegations. It demands moral work and moral responses by the one who fell out of favour with the moral community. In the following, I discuss the Crown Court's procedure by which guilt is attributed to the defendant and, moreover, how the defendant is expected to respond to this attribution.[1] We will see that the Crown Court handles this facet of case-making in an anti-inquisitorial manner. The defendant's self and his or her moral guilt and moral responsibility are issues that are not tackled in public. They are rather points for backstage deliberations and staged reports, altogether referred to as indirect moralising.

A growing number of socio-legal scholars are concerned with the expressive side of sentencing. They study what judges ought to say or do say when punishing the offender. Should they choose a rather retrospective or forward-looking orientation, a retributive or restorative stance, a monological or dialogical mode? Socio-legal scholars favour certain moralising messages and styles based on assumptions on how offenders react to them. For instance, von Hirsch (1993) wants judges to express censure and disapproval of the deed in order to justify the sanction and to remind the offender of moral standards. Duff (1986) asks judges to confront offenders with their wrongdoing in order to stimulate apologetic reparation or remorse. Weijers (2004) suggests

[1] An earlier version of the case-study was published in *Journal for the Theory of Social Behavior* (Scheffer 2010a).

that judges engage in a moral dialogue with the wrongdoer in order to raise awareness of the negative consequences of her or his acts. This dialogue could be stimulated by critical, confrontational questions about the harm, the injuries or the damage the offender caused. Depending on their normative standpoint in the "punishment as language"-debate[2], scholars criticize or praise the harsh, paternalistic, degrading or understanding tone of the judge's sentencing speech.

In the following, I choose a different take on moral communication and criminal law. Instead of restricting the analysis of moral communication to what judges say or should say in the sentencing hearing, I ask where, when, and how the Crown Court procedure invites and permits moral communication. The question then is more specific: when, how and to whom are defendants asked to express their moral feelings about the offence? How is a moral voice granted to or imposed on the defendant? The questions shift the focus from moral messages towards pre-defined speech positions and moralising sites. We will encounter a specific procedural style which I call "indirect moralising;" this style selects specific moments, settings, and audiences for self-moralising explanations to take place and to matter.

I will present indirect moralising as a procedural modality. As such, it is more than just missing directness. It does more than just avoid moral confrontation. The Crown Court operates a moralising apparatus which involves more than a single spectacle in open court. I intend to show that indirect moralising nests in a division of moralising sites, each with its own methods, foci and demands. A few characteristics pinpoint the procedural modality of indirect moralising. (1) The division of moralising allows a process-oriented view. The defendant can develop from one stage to the next, which is monitored and reported. (2) The structure of opportunities is manifold in relation to the diverse sites and formats. This includes therapeutic interviews and partisan discussions. (3) The defendant can articulate his moral feelings and reflections in face-to-face encounters with some seemingly indifferent recipients: an expert, his lawyer, a state official. The reception of indirect moralising is diversified. Indirect moralising, thus, constitutes a structure of possibility that the participants – moralising as well as moralised – adhere to.

---

[2] See Morris (1981), Hampton (1984), Duff (1986), von Hirsch (1993), or Primoratz (1989). For a critical review of core assumptions, see Davis (1991).

Direct and indirect moralising

What differentiates direct and indirect moralising? To start with, moralising, as I use it here, denotes the initiation of moral responses on the part of the addressee, here, the offender. People make somebody do something: here making moral explanations on some of his or her own acts. Self-moralising refers to a reflection on the biographical past in terms of admission, justification, or apology. Secondly, this distinction reminds of what Thomas Luckmann called communicative styles of moralising. Moralising, according to Luckmann, "may be either *direct*, in the form of straightforward praise or complaint, injunction, accusation, indignation, etc., or it may be *indirect* in the form of litotes, questions, if/then formulations, certain kinds of teasing, etc." (2002:20). However, there are a number of differences: Luckmann refers to somebody moralising about something; he identifies styles of moralising by their linguistic forms only; he refers to all moral communication, whether positive or negative, about whatever. In the following, I use moralising more narrowly. Moralising refers to communicative acts that ask somebody for a moral explanation or response. Somebody is moralized by making him or her take a moral position. Moralising, in other words, demands the addressee to take and express his/her moral standpoint; he or she has been moralised. Often, but not necessarily, this demand includes the expectation that the moralised person is going to articulate his or her moral standpoint vis-à-vis the moralising party (e.g., the judge or the prosecutor) and the morally affected party (e.g. the victim, his or her family, the community).

This narrowed view on moralising somebody (here: the defendant) carries vast implications for our observation of regularities of moral communication. Whereas Luckmann asks for the individual calculations to risk or to avoid direct moral comments (e.g., to whom do I speak like this and to what effects), my exploration leads towards procedural calculations of providing and avoiding certain 'moralising' constellations. In this sense, a procedure may favour or prevent face-to-face confrontations between the one moralised and the ones morally involved. Indirect moralising, then, can be systematized by procedure insofar as, for instance, 'moralising the defendant' may be bound to certain mediating objects or participants. The exchange of moral communication turns rather complex compared to Luckmann's encounters of moral agents. It involves a moralising agent (e.g. the barrister), a moralised party (e.g. the defendant), and a morally involved audience (e.g. the victim).

In the legal setting, direct moralising typically involves the copresence of offender and victim (plus solidary family or sympathetic friends or concerned others) in sometimes heated and emotional events. One rationale of this confrontation: the request for a moral response in public may unsettle the strategic façade of the accused and, ultimately, instigate moral learning for the time after. Another rationale: the community may experience symbolic amends for the immoral deed through meaningful signs of remorse. The following Sentencing Hearing in the South Dakota State Court[3] displays a typical moment of direct moralising; a moment that one would not find in the English Crown Court:

Judge Do you have anything to say?
Def. I apologize. I am ashamed. I have no excuse. I have to deal with my sin. It is MY sin. I know that. I am truly and honestly sorry for my crime.
Judge Okay, you may sit down now. The court will take your apology into consideration. So, dismissal of evidence is sustained. Objections to other paragraphs are overruled. The court may consider any information without any limitation as to the character of the defendant unless prohibited by law.

The defendant takes the judge's open question (rightly) as an invitation to engage with the moral implication of the offence. He serves the court's convention by delivering what is asked for: some self-moralising gesture. The judge affirms the moral status of the defendant's moral response ("I apologize. I am ashamed."). The brief and personal phrases are received by "the court" as fulfilling the criteria of an apology ("your apology"). The moralised defendant takes responsibility and accepts his moral debts ("MY sin," "my crime") and relates them partially ("I have to deal with my sin.") to the community's moral credit ("I apologize."). Socio-legal and criminological scholars would criticize the judge's message for its tendency to expose and to degrade the offender. The conventions leave no opportunity for excuse, self-defence, or relativism. Other scholars of criminal justice would praise the judge's "reintegrative shaming" (Braithwaite 1989). The offender

[3] In spring 2002, Alexander Kozin recorded the following exchange in his ethnographic fieldnotes. His fieldwork took place in South Dakota.

gets the opportunity to distance himself from and condemn the offence. The judge's moralising opens his or her way back into the community.

Another instance of direct moralising is reported by Szmania and Mangis (2005:346) from a jury trial in Texas. The defence lawyer imparts a moral voice to the defendant, again in open court at the very end of the hearing:

> *Q* Is there anything at this time that you would, and I mean very briefly, that you feel like you should say to the people in this courtroom, the families involved here and of course the jury?
>
> *A* Yes, there is. I would like to say that I'm sorry to the people …

Here again, the court allows the exchange of moralising and moral response or self-moralising to take place in public. A restorative justice approach, however, would consider the dialogue as highly restricted and limited. It would not be accepted as a full confrontation of moral responsibility and moral concernment since the exchange is not given its required space. For instance, it does not provide the victim with a designated speech- and recipient-position. Moreover, the offender's moral account is overshadowed by legal incentives and ritualistic conventions. Authentic or not, it will be received with some reservation.

In both instances, the wrongdoer is offered only limited opportunity to morally account for his deed in open court. Both offenders respond by offering an apology[4] right away. How does the procedure allow for this? In the first case, there is, directly after the guilty plea, a moment reserved for the "last word." The opportunity to say "anything" puts pressure on the offender to live up to the expected quantum of regret. In the second case, a moralising moment is created by the defence team. The interview is used to address the moral feelings of "the people" and "the family." In both cases, the moral responses, here the apologies, seem to fit the court's mission: the offender realises that he did wrong; the offender addresses the moral feelings of the community.

---

[4] Goffman describes the apology as a "remedial ritual": it includes an "expression of embarrassment and chagrin; clarification that one knows what conduct had been expected and sympathizes with the application of negative sanction; verbal rejection, and disavowal of the wrong way of behaving along with vilification of the self that so behaved; espousal of the right way and an avowal henceforth to pursue that course; performance of penance and volunteering of restitution" (1971:113).

The confrontational style is closely linked to inquisitorial jurisdictions.[5] In the German criminal procedure, the offender is granted "last words." She or he is given a last opportunity for self-moralising in open court. In the Dutch context, Komter (1998) observed that and how judges mingle forensic and moral aspects when putting questions to the defendant. Other cases of direct moralising can be found in restorative justice programs, post-civil war tribunals (see Kastner 2009), or educational settings (see Holly 1981). Here, the direct exchange of apology and pardon is seen as vital to pave the way for a new start in the moral community. Such inquisitorial processes remind of Durkheim's classical distinction between mechanical and organic solidarity and, here, to a rather mechanical treatment and response to delinquency. The offender faces the victim's agony and injury; in return, the community including the victim finds the offender in a state of distress and shame. There is a 'mechanical' element of public revenge – and an emotionally felt urge for such revenge – attached to this "ordeal of expressing remorse and apologizing" (Bibas and Bierschbach 2004:143) that "even if done initially for the wrong reasons, may in time promote genuine repentance" (Ibid.). From this perspective, the give and take of moral expressions should not be hampered by legal, procedural or organisational constraints. According to restorative justice scholars, traditional procedural regimes distort moral exchange and healing with their overload of technicalities, profit-oriented professionals, and their sophisticated strategies. The 'cold' procedural atmosphere leaves no room for immediate and authentic expressions of pain, remorse and forgiveness.[6]

English Crown Court hearings do not allow the offender to say "last words" in the dock or speak about his moral feelings in open court. He or she is not given the chance to morally account for her or his

---

[5] Weijers (2004) argues that the adversarial system in the common law tradition favours moral monologues by judge or advocates, while the inquisitorial tradition activates moral dialogues between judge and offender.

[6] The restorative justice critique focuses on the second step in this ideal healing process: "Legalistic settings do not support this high degree of self-disclosure because of the highly structured communicative environment" (Szmania and Mangis 2005:341); "When remorse and apology do appear, they do so in spite of the criminal process, not because of it" (Bibas and Bierschbach 2004:96). As Komter concludes, legal incentives make "it difficult for the court to distinguish between authentic and false expressions of morality and for the suspects to convince the court of the authenticity of their feelings" (1998:97).

wrongdoing; likewise, the victim, his or her family, or a resentful community can neither express moral feelings nor receive expressions of true remorse. At closer inspection, however, the Crown Court procedure does not lack instances of moralising, but shows another pattern: indirect moralising. The offender is given various opportunities to make a self-moralising statement outside the courtroom, shielded from the community. Does indirect moralising convey disinterest in morality? Does it manifest a technical, rather organic (as opposed to mechanic) legal order? Does indirect moralising signify the law's cynical, strategic, and superficial treatment of the community's moral feelings? In the following, I examine a single criminal case in order to discuss major properties, dynamics and limitations of indirect moralising.

Towards a procedural style of moralising

Luckmann's emphasis on moral communication is part of a bigger sociological argument. By tracing the different articulations of morality, Luckmann aims to weaken the functionalist argument that post-traditional societies are no longer integrated by morals. Luckmann insists on "the continued presence of morality" (2002:22). Moralising remains an ongoing business and force in everyday life. Moral communication mobilises the cultural inventory inbuilt in our language and in our communication styles. In social interactions, members utilize and develop these cultural repertoires of "a coherent view of the good life" (Ibid.). Morality remains a societal force, although it remains unclear to what extent. It can be found in various forms and styles, sometimes rather hidden in cloudy and ambiguous wording and phrasing.

Luckmann suggests "that in modern society the dominant style of moral communication shows a preference for indirect moralising" (2002:22). He explains this indirectness with the "pluralistic modern life" (Ibid.). Here "interactional, oral and moralising uncertainty is high outside an individual's own home group or milieu. In societies with an obligatory and uniform moral order, moral homogeneity between individuals could be assumed unless concrete evidence to the contrary was produced in interaction. One may say that in modern societies the reverse is the case" (Ibid.:28). Where uncertainty is high, indirect moralising "will be preferred in all communication outside the home milieus of the individuals" (Ibid.).

Luckmann's study of moral communication provides a good starting point for our argument. Firstly, it raises awareness for the details and actual formulations of moral communication. The formulations may hint at different addressees and recipients of moralising. Secondly, Luckmann raises awareness for the roles that moralising can play in modern society. Luckmann suggests systematic differences between encounters amongst strangers and encounters amongst acquaintances. Amongst strangers, participants tend to obscure or cover their own moral stance. Thirdly, Luckmann links the styles of moralising to risks of exposure and conflict. This might be the closest link to our question on how moralising is procedurally organised. Here, voices and ears are granted for purposes of moral self-explanation. Here, moralising is set up vis-à-vis selected publics or specialists only. The following case-study links various moralising sites, episodes and participants in order to understand the use and the rationale of indirect moralising in the Crown Court procedure.

An extreme case-study

The case method or "casing" (Ragin 1992b:217sqq.), despite its limitations in representational terms, allows the researcher to place data in the practical context of its occurrence. Various sources and instances can be integrated and add up to a meaningful sequence and nexus of events. The selected pieces of data, here moments of self-moralising, are not interpreted and weighed in isolation; they are accumulated by bits and pieces of the case-making process, especially of the defence lawyers' casework. Other cases are only mentioned in passing and merely to accentuate certain particularities of Mr. Grease's case. Overall, the case-study suggests three main sites of indirect moralising: the sentencing hearing, the psychiatric assessment, and the client-lawyer relationship.

The notion of case coincides with four usages. The case is, firstly, the *criminal matter* of Mr. Grease. At first, Mr. Grease was charged with murder. Later on, this charge was altered to manslaughter. Mr. Grease immediately entered a plea of guilty to this count, following his barrister's advice. The case seems, secondly, *exceptional* from the practitioners' point of view. The practitioners consider this combination exceptional (but still manageable): a guilty plea to such an offence on the one hand and the complete absence of signs of remorse on the other hand. The case is, thirdly, "a case of" (Ragin 1992a; Stake 2000) a certain institutional modality called indirect moralising. In light of this, fourthly, the case is an extreme case. It pushes the institutional modality to its limits. It does so, because Mr. Grease failed to comply with the normal expectations that 'such a defendant' would show remorse at some point. As a reaction, the moralising regime tries even harder to obtain his self-moralising by involving experts, extra meetings, harsher questioning, etc. Thus, this case seems ideal to explore indirect moralising, its practicalities, and limitations.

Why this combination of exceptionality and normality? The case exhibits a certain structure of opportunity in clear profile because of its exceptional feature: Mr. Grease's willingness to plead guilty together with his refusal to show any signs of regret. From the practitioners' point of view, 'not to regret' frustrates a routine feature of mitigation. A lack of remorse can impede mitigation efforts as Wagatsuma and Rosett emphasized: the criminal law "can be extremely harsh on those who persistently deny responsibility" (1986:470) due to the fact that the "codes and rules permit apologetic behaviour to be considered in mitigation of punishment" (Ibid.:479).[7] In addition, the Criminal Justice System is "dominated by official discretion that diverts a high percentage of offenders to relatively mild treatment and reserves the rigors of full prosecution for a few, including those who 'fail the attitude test' by not showing appropriate contrition and apology" (Ibid.:482). When considering these legal 'costs and benefits', the combination of 'pleading guilty' and 'not showing remorse' seems rather exceptional. A client would be *generally* ill-advised to follow this route. The defending Queen's Counsel[8] explicated this rare combination right at the beginning of his mitigating speech. Here is what the ethnographer noted that day in court:

> The Counsel, a greying gentleman in his sixties, rises and turns to face the judge. Following an initial survey of the case – how did Mr. Grease come to push her into the wall, and how did Mrs Grease, his mother,

[7] See also Archbold on the mitigating factors defined by the Criminal Justice and Public Order Act 1994: "In deciding whether to impose a custodial sentence in borderline cases the sentencing court would ordinarily take account of matters relating to the offender, such as an admission of responsibility for the offence, particularly if reflected in a plea of guilty tendered at the earliest opportunity and accompanied by hard evidence of genuine remorse as shown (for example) by an expression of regret to the victim and an offer of compensation" (2000:5–130).

[8] We are dealing here with a murder case, which necessitated the instruction of a Queen's Counsel (QC) next to the usual prosecuting barrister.

> succumb to her internal injuries – he starts talking about who this Mr. Grease is. Now something extraordinary happens. Instead of the ritualized claim of representing a repentant and regretful client, he sends ahead a seemingly disadvantageous bottom line: "He shows no remorse for the death of his mother and the fact that he caused it. Of course, there is a significant difficulty with this defendant." (7.8^{+3})

Does the "difficulty with this defendant" refer to a moral or rather a technical difficulty? Does his refusal to regret conflict with adversarial tactics or does it conflict with some kind of moral mission of the overall procedure? The Queen's Counsel seems uneasy about the fact that he acts on behalf of this 'questionable character'. He seems compelled to visibly dissociate himself from his client. What is more, such dissociation occurred many times in the course of casework as well. It became a regular practice in the assigned law firm. Secretaries and solicitors alike expressed their antipathy and disgust for "this client" on a daily basis. They wondered how one could do this "to his own mother." Just like everyone else, the lawyers seemed willing to believe that he did much more to her: constant harassment, frequent violence, even rape. "Now they've found out that…", or "this freak did not just kill his mother, he …" became an everyday opener in the coffee break chat. For the time being, Mr. Grease was *the* object of gossip and lurid tales amongst his own lawyers.

The moralising sites in a Crown Court case

The Queen's Counsel marks the exceptionality of the case by pointing to the fact that the defendant shows no remorse. The barrister obviously has not been instructed to represent the defendant as a moral self under these circumstances, meaning as the perpetrator of a very serious crime who truly regrets what he has done. Without such instruction, usually, the defence barrister would improvise: "My client is very sorry about what happened."; "He cannot cope with the guilt."; "He is ashamed." Instead, this barrister indicates a "significant difficulty with this client." When, during the case, did Mr. Grease prove as significantly difficult? When, in the procedural course, did he frustrate normal expectations and moral norms?

I undertake an ethnographic journey to the sites at which the offender is asked to and expected to address the deed in moral terms. At these sites, the offender is given a moral voice; he is put under pressure to express himself. The police had removed Mr. Grease from the community.[9] He had been discredited by multiple accusations of repeatedly abusing and maltreating his mother.[10] None of these will enter the official indictment,[11] but they serve as a moral subtext for the sentencing. It is not subjected to procedural technicalities such as admissibility or burden of proof. It is not put to test in open court. The prosecution introduces it as background information:

> Indeed, this account [...] was borne out by an examination of the victim's medical records. In due course, the examination of those records revealed and identified some sixteen documented injuries and some thirty separate incidents. It was concluded that the number of patterns of injuries indicated that she had been subjected to years of abuse. (7.8[+3])

The indications gathered by the police imply massive guilt on the part of the defendant. The moral atmosphere turns heavily against the defendant. One consequence: the law firm's informant, instructed to collect some information on the defendant's mother's "falling in front of a shop" or "being attacked by youngsters some months ago," returned from his visits disillusioned. Nobody would consider engaging with 'his lawyer', not to mention with Mr. Grease. He became an outcast. Much calls for a moralising showdown in open court: the victim's long tragedy, the perpetrator's massive guilt, the community's outrage.

The procedural set-up, however, offers some kind of avoidance strategy: a cautious, screened, and mediated form of moral communication. In the following, I present the three major sites of indirect moralising. The communicative arrangements in the sentencing hearing are flanked by recurring moralising activities on the backstage: in the law firm, involving instructed lawyers and client; and in the prison, involving psychiatric experts and inmate.

---

[9] Prior to this sentencing hearing, the Magistrates (in the lower Magistrates' Court) refused bail on the basis that "he was at risk from the public having regard to the nature and seriousness and the probable method of dealing with this offence in due course and also, in respect of the strength of the evidence against him" (Instructions to barrister, 1.5[+3]).

[10] Mr. Grease's guilt increases in the light of how his victim protected him: "Indeed, after Mrs Neighbour had contacted the police, she disclosed to them that she had known that Mrs Grease had been subjected to years of physical abuse by her son, and that this had been hidden from the authorities by Mrs Grease throughout the years in an endeavour to protect her son, even to the extent that in 2001 it would appear that she had fabricated a story about being mugged in order to explain some injuries." (7.8[+3])

[11] This is due to the 'rules of evidence'. None of the further accusations can be evidenced by eye witnesses. The police report lists "hearsay" (cf. Tapper 1999:529) which is not admissible in a jury trial.

Minimalist moralising: silencing the defendant in the sentencing hearing

The procedural modality of indirect moralising becomes visible, first of all, on the front stage of the sentencing hearing. Here, any direct moral confrontation is avoided. How is this done?

Judge	He knows the correct form to enter the plea, does he?
QC	He does, but my learned junior will stand by him to help him if help is required.
Clerk	Will you please stand, Mr. Grease? Michael Charles Grease, you are charged on indictment M45720099 with murder. The particulars being that on the 22nd day of November 2002 you murdered Christine Grease. Do you plead guilty or not guilty?
Grease	I plead guilty to … not guilty to murder but guilty to manslaughter. (7.8[+3])

In this poignant but short moment, the defendant takes centre stage in the trial at court. The Junior Barrister positions himself at Mr. Grease's side as if his client required assistance and standby. By displaying a need for help, the defence introduces the defendant as distinctive, as anomalous. This will not be the defence's last attempt to emphasize *his* pitiful weakness. The defendant's mental limitation is later considered in mitigation – and in the judge's peculiar address:

> It is not necessary for the *defendant* to stand. Mrs. Christine Grease, as she was known to her friends, was, at the time of her death, an old lady of 86 years. She did not enjoy good health. She was frail. She ate little. She was, of course, therefore, highly vulnerable. The defendant, Michael Charles Grease, is her son aged now 57. Ever since *he* was a young child, he has presented behavioural problems. Many arise from *his* very low intelligence.

There is another indication that this defendant is treated as exceptional, that he receives special treatment. He does not need to stand; he remains seated. Something else is peculiar here. Differently from other sentencing hearings, the judge would not address the defendant directly. The judge refers to him only in the third-person ("the defendant," "he," "his") and not, like judges would do in regular sentencing hearings, in the second-person ("Can you stand up please" or "Well, John Twist, you have pleaded guilty…" or "I give you full credit…"). The judge keeps talking *about* the defendant, not to him. This distancing is not accidental: it can be observed throughout and across all parties and roles. There is a further interpretation of this introduction that relates to the above mentioned "punishment as language"-debate. The judge's address displays this defendant as manifestly incapable of receiving the court's moral judgement. The judge cuts off the relation between him and Mr. Grease as fellow citizens. Put generally, the moralising figure denies the moralised other a "moral standing" (see Duff 2003). This asymmetry shows what is usually implicated by acts of moralising: the moralised other is assigned equal morality; she or he is approached as a member of the moral community.[12]

How does the sentencing hearing invite a moral response by the defendant? In fact, it does not invite any response whatsoever, except in the opening plea. Mr. Grease is offered no opportunity to give a personal explanation. He is turned into a "bystander in his own trial" (Szmania and Mangis 2005:347); he is "silenced" (Langbein 2003); he is – by ways of distancing – even turned into an untouchable, a non-person. This might be counterintuitive, since the sentencing hearing should focus on the defendant's personality, his character, and his moral sentience such as remorse or sorrow.[13]

The silencing, however, does not mean that the court excludes Mr. Grease as a moral self. But the court seems happy to hear about this self from others, to gather information about it. The court deals with a range of indications of the defendant's morality. Firstly, the court considers when and how Mr. Grease admitted and confessed the crime. Prosecuting barrister (1), judge (2) and defending barrister (3) mention the fact that the defendant did confess early – all again in third-person speech:

(1) So it was on the 10th of January that the defendant was arrested and interviewed by police officers. During the course of the first interview, the defendant *admitted* that he argued with his mother about money, and it was money that he needed for cigarettes and alcohol.

---

[12] Duff invites us to a thought experiment: "What we have to ask ourselves [...] is not merely whether the evidence we have heard suffices to prove his guilt, but whether we, as the jurors who are supposed to judge this defendant as our fellow citizen, have the right or moral standing to do so; and the answer to that question depends partly on whether we, as members of the polity of which we and he are supposedly fellow citizens, have treated him as a citizen." (2003:259)

[13] The purposes of sentencing are defined in the Criminal Justice Act 2003: "Any court dealing with an offender in respect of his offence must have regard to the following purposes of sentencing: a) the punishment of offenders; b) the reduction of crime (including its reduction by deterrence); c) reformation and rehabilitation of offenders; d) protection; e) the making of reparation by offenders to persons affected by their offences." (Sec. 142)

He *admitted* that in relation to the injuries that resulted in her admission in hospital he had lost his temper with her and pushed her ... (7.8^{+3})

(2) So he is entitled to credit not only for the plea that he has entered but for the admissions that he made to the police. (7.8^{+3})

(3) We would invite your lordship to give him full credit for that plea of guilty. It was not entered at the first opportunity, but he has never changed the account that he gave to the police in interview, and that is essential in the account upon which his plea is now based. (7.8^{+3})

Confession and early guilty plea are mentioned with three different connotations. The prosecuting barrister (1) mentions the early confession, not without reminding of cruel details of the offence. The judge (2) explicitly accepts the early admission as one of several factors affecting the sentence. The defending barrister's use (3) of the early admission goes even further. He highlights the early confession, not without hinting at some secondary value of the defendant such as forthrightness. The court distinguishes the admission of guilt from proper self-moralising. Ideally, the admission is about truth, while showing regret is about morals. In this sense, a mere admission does not satisfy the moral ear.[14] Accordingly, the barristers' speeches are awash with references to offence and remorse. The defence barrister introduces the theme by quoting from the files. This provokes some clarification by the judge:

Con My Lord, remorse is touched on in a number of places in the reports that your Lordship has. It is touched upon by Mr Blank. It is touched upon, particularly, by Miss Ear in her pre-sentence report – the suggestion that he shows no remorse for the death of his mother and the fact that he caused it.

Judge Well, his dissocial personality disorder makes it very difficult for him to understand these concepts [here: remorse].

Con Yes, it does, and I think Dr Blank – for your Lordship's note it is paragraph 11(8) at page 14.

Judge Yes.

Con Where, and I will take it from the sixth line down, "The defendant has demonstrated a limited capacity to feel guilt or remorse

[14] According to Komter's conversation analysis of Dutch criminal trials, the represented offence calls for corresponding signs of "moral awareness" (1998:96). Accordingly, a severe offence calls for some intense self-moralising vis-à-vis the judge. In our case, a similar correspondence is demanded 'indirectly', meaning as assurances by others.

> and has a poor sense of responsibility. There appears to be little evidence to suggest he learns from previous mistakes." (7.08^{+3})

The defence barrister uses the psychiatric reports to moderately introduce and explain his client's lack of remorse. His introduction can be described as careful or cautious. He invites the judge to reach a stronger interpretation, just as if he tried not to sound too excusing and forgiving. He makes the judge introduce the psychiatric diagnosis. Only afterwards, the defending barrister himself elaborates the "limited capacity to feel guilt". Is he able to heal the lack of remorse by introducing another diagnostic frame: mental impairment? Both the hesitation and the use of citations allow the barrister to keep his client's 'disinterest' or 'immorality' or 'incapability' at bay. All this talk *about* the defendant takes place while the defendant is awaiting the verdict quietly in the dock vis-à-vis the judge's desk and separated from his counsel. At this moment during the sentencing hearing, Mr. Grease is not just spatially, but also morally separated from his legal representative.

What is the role of the moral self in this lawyer-centred hearing? By avoiding immediate moral confrontation, the Crown Court procedure seems to protect the defendant from public shaming. The defendant's ability to show authentic remorse is not tested in open court. The defendant's inability to show remorse is not exposed to the public. The Court is protected from misleading, strategic performances. Instead, others talk on behalf of the defendant's inner feelings: interpreting his behaviour; carefully excusing the lack of remorse; explaining in technical terms what seems intolerable from a moral point of view. The court replaces direct moralising by means of delegation. It outsources moralising.

Moralising outsourced: talking about guilt with psychological experts

The procedure turns to external experts to have the defendant observed as a moral subject capable of speaking and explaining himself. By doing so, the procedure locates moralising in the run-up to the hearing. At first, it rests with the prosecution to introduce a written expert report on the offender's personality and personal history. The defence must and does respond to this psychiatric expertise by hiring and instructing its own expert. A second diagnostic session takes place, again in an interview room in prison. Again, the deed is forced on

Mr. Grease as a moral theme, a question of personal guilt. The two expert reports are filed prior to the sentencing hearing.[15] This might be the procedural calculus: via the experts, the court attains extra knowledge that would otherwise remain unavailable to the court. What kind of extra knowledge is this?

(1) The experts supply *additional temporal layers*. The psychiatrists ascribe a biography, a personal pattern, and an inner nature to Mr. Grease. They do so based on a number of historiographies such as "background history", "education and employment history", "relationship history", "drug and alcohol history", "previous psychiatric history & review of psychiatric/GP records". The historiographies are assembled from problem-centred and semi-structured interviews, medical and psychiatric records, the criminal record, and from the legal case files.

(2) The experts supply *other professional methods*. The Court does not organise a kind of substitute hearing of Mr. Grease to gain a 'truly genuine' impression. The defendant is exposed in other ways that are not discernable to the court. He is exposed to concealed face-to-face consultation, in which the psychiatric experts extract not just all kinds of biographical information but also signs of moral engagement. In the two clinical interviews, such is the procedural assumption of indirect moralising; the moral self can be dismantled on the basis of a controlled and scientific formula.

(3) The experts supply *far-reaching conclusions*. What conclusions do the expert reports arrive at with regard to the defendant's morality? The "Psychiatric Report" identifies a pattern of not showing remorse. It does so by confronting Mr. Grease with the criminal record and the forensic history:

> I noted that until I had access to a formal list of previous convictions Mr. Grease denied being convicted of any offence. He told me that he could (when I challenged him) recall the offence of indecent assault which he confirmed occurred in 1977. Mr. Grease did not wish to disclose further information in relation to this in spite of the formal record of the conviction stating by way of explanation 'he must have been gay' (referring to the boy). Mr. Grease received a two year probation order

[15] The judge received the defence material one day prior to the hearing. The judge had time to study the report and to form his opinion in camera. This may explain the judge's behaviour during the mitigating speech: he pays only partial attention; he leafs through files; he takes notes and whispers (presumably) orders to the clerk. He seems to know already how to treat the 'remorseless' offender.

> with a condition to receive psychiatric treatment. There was no sense of remorse, responsibility or of sophistication in his responses which were curt and verging on hostile. (5.7^{+3})

The expertise creates a personal and moral continuity. It contributes to the defendant's degradation, which marks, as Garfinkel put it, his "former identity as accidental; the new identity is the 'basic reality'. What he is now is what, 'after all,' he was all along" (1956:422). The conclusion on Mr. Grease's ability to regret reads as follows:

> He has demonstrated a limited capacity to feel guilt or remorse and has a poor sense of responsibility. There appears to be little evidence to suggest that he learns from previous mistakes. (5.7^{+3})

(4) The expert reports supply *contrastive perspectives*. The second report arrives at a similar conclusion. The defendant "is not fully capable of showing remorse." This psychological report has much in common with the first psychiatric report: it keeps to its questions and criteria (see chapter III); it focuses on questions of guilt and remorse; it speculates to what extent the defendant will be morally impressed or educated by the procedure. The following evaluations are taken from the "clinical interview" section:

> I noted that Mr. Grease was highly egocentric and found it difficult to reflect upon anything other than his own current circumstances and feelings. (20.7^{+3})
>
> Mr. Grease demonstrates no ability to empathize with his mother as a victim of violence and reports that she was a possessive parent. (20.7^{+3})
>
> Mr. Grease reports that he 'pushed her into the wall and she cracked her ribs'. Mr. Grease reports that there was no 'intention or malice' in his actions, it was 'something that just happened'. Mr. Grease demonstrates no emotion when discussing these events or their consequences. (20.7^{+3})

The second report seems to extend the scope of the first by adding more details, here recent emotional and moral responses by Mr. Grease. This way, the court accumulates different perspectives and opinions on the defendant.

(5) The experts supply *extra legitimization*. This extension is relevant because some of the court's decisions carry extra-legal implications concerning, for instance, minimal cognitive and social requirements for participation. Both expert reports raise the problem of legal capacity: is the defendant capable of attending and following the legal

dealings at all? The psychological report denies the defendant's fitness for trial, and retrospectively demands a legal guardian:

> Mr. Grease's deficits are such that he should have had an Appropriate Adult present throughout the course of these interviews in accordance with the Police and Criminal Evidence Act 1984 and the Codes of Practice. (20.7^{+3})

The first report concludes on the question of legal capacity:

> In spite of his apparent learning difficulties, he does appear to have sufficient intellectual capacity to instruct his defence and appears to have an ability to understand evidence which may be put before him. I believe he would have an ability to 'challenge' a juror and he has an ability to know the difference between right and wrong and guilty and not guilty. I believe he has the capacity to manage with the general proceedings in court [...] (5.7^{+3})

The one supporting report suffices to justify the court's decision not to introduce a delegate or trustee.

(6) Expertises supply *practical advice*. There is a third report under way, this time ordered by the judge in order to envision the range of sentencing measures. The probation officer, in her report, considers a range of practical options and discusses them in light of his one-hour interview with the defendant. In her report, the probation officer detects (first) signs of remorse. The respective passage reads:

> At the start of our interview, he showed little remorse and spoke only as to how this has affected him. However, at the conclusion of our meeting, the defendant did speak with what appeared to be genuine compassion and stated he 'missed his mother a lot and that she will always be in his thoughts'. He also expressed sorrow for his actions and contended that, although not previously a religious man, he now attends the prison chapel every Wednesday and finds solace in these visits. (6.8^{+3})

Apparently, the prison environment ("the prison chapel") allows the defendant to change and to develop morally. The probation officer seems encouraged to approve of a custodial sentence on professional grounds. What is more, she suggests certain therapies and accommodation after the prison sentence is served.

The expert reports offer some detached, detailed, and professional moralising on a broader basis and of different epistemic nature compared to legal evidence. In order to stimulate self-moralising, the experts utilize 'facts' that are available to the court as 'background' only. The expert reports supply the court with a range of extra-legal insights, second-hand information, authoritative definitions, diagnostic deductions, practical suggestions, and extra-legal legitimization.

The observation of the moral self is delegated to experts and their diagnostic procedures. Diagnostic events are created outside the procedural course in order to import condensed insights. Extra-procedural opportunities are created to bring the moral self back in. This way, a novel offender-person enters the arena, "a psychologico-ethical double of the offence" (Foucault 2003:16). The "doctor-judges" integrate forensics and morality. In the case of Mr. Grease, the experts make vast use of the indictment's subtext. They include the reported 'wounds' and 'injuries' that the police found in the victim's medical record.[16] The experts take these incidents as leading up to the final act of murder. After all, the final tragedy was just the last act, another manifestation of a behavioural pattern. The defendant's lack of morality is interpreted as a systematic feature of this pattern. In this sense, the experts simultaneously dramatize and explain Mr. Grease's deficiency of remorse. They add guilt and they excuse his inability to act upon it.

In-house moralising: the lawyer-client relationship

Can the defendant's moral self be discerned in the slowly-developing, protected and fostered relationship between lawyers and client? Do the former receive messages that court or experts will not? Does the moral self manifest itself here where no immediate consequences are to be feared? Can the lawyer, by virtue of his partisanship, get the client morally involved? Does moralising succeed when the defendant is addressed within a trustful relationship?[17] Is this lawyer-client relationship the hidden, morally driving, educational site of the procedure? In order to find out, one should try to trace the moralising moments between lawyer and client in the sequence of their occurrence, for instance, in their conferences, their correspondence, or their telephone conversations. In the following, I recapitulate the relationship of Mr. Grease and

[16] Thus the pre-sentence report: "[...] all the aspects of domestic violence, including humiliation, control, power, and no doubt psychological harm, feature heavily in his attitude towards the late Mrs Grease" (6.8[+3]).

[17] Motives, intentions, and moral reflections are expressed in the protected space of the lawyer-client relationship (Sarat and Felstiner 1988). Trust provides a basic ground in the lawyer-client relationship (see Blumberg 1967).

his lawyers. These confidential contacts underwent phases of partly confrontational and partly incidental moralising:

(1) In the early phase of the process, Mr. Grease, like so many clients before, displays incredulity. He emphasizes his inability to take the issue seriously: "I am supposed to have killed my mother? My mother, is she really dead?" After all, when he last saw her, she promised to be back in two or three days. Thus, the solicitor Jane (see chapter IV) notes in her early instructions to the barrister: "The defendant denies the murder of his mother, although he has accepted that he has used violence against her in the past." Here, denial still remains entirely in the context of questions of truth rather than of morality. The major questions are about what really happened. Mr. Grease's responses give hope to the solicitor. Jane encourages her client to remember and to list as many details as possible. Details are supposed to feed into the defence-case. The moral self remains unchallenged, protected still by the assumption of innocence.

(2) Jane animates the client to position himself in relation to the accusations. In his first internal comments, Mr. Grease will reject every single allegation – possibly, this is my impression at this stage, in order to preserve his moral integrity vis-à-vis the solicitor. His written statement contains the following assertions, complementary to the prosecution-case. At this point (15.4^{+3}) the prosecution speculated about rape, frequent domestic violence, anti-social behaviour, etc.:

> I never had sex with my mum. She brought me to a prostitute.
>
> I did not go to the pub every day.
>
> Mum never paid 12 Pounds.
>
> I have no debts.
>
> I did not forget about the funeral. In fact, I dealt with it on my own.

By denying all this, the defendant does (still) fit the lawyers' expectations of a normal client. He engages with the accusations. He gives reasons as to why they are false: "She is known to have fallen quite often. Maybe she got dizzy again." He gets bogged down in details, which the defence promises to follow up: the fraudulent death certificate, the hold-up at the petrol station, her dizzy spells at the shop. The solicitor hopes for further useful clues:

> To Barrister: "Received a very detailed account by him. Worth to be documented." (8.3^{+3})

> A file note: "Jane dictating transcript of the handwritten notes provided by client for forwarding to client for approval and to barrister." (15.3+3)

The defence initiates its own investigations following the hints and clues that the client delivers. However, none of it yields any results because named witnesses have not seen or do not remember "her falling in front of the corner shop" or her being "mugged by some youngsters by the supermarket". Some refuse any kind of support for 'this monster'.[18] They do not want to get in touch, not even with his lawyer.

(3) An exact point in time for a client's drifting off towards a deviant career is difficult to determine. Unnoticed by the preoccupied solicitor, Mr. Grease seems to get lost in the procedure. He does not care any longer. He loses interest. Instead, he worries about *self-evident* things. He asks the solicitor to take care of his dog, laundry and keys. This is a time of daily letters full of trifles and inconstant ideas. Later, the solicitor will say about Mr. Grease in interview that he somehow started treating her the way he used to treat 'his mother before'. He involves her in everything; he disregards professional or even personal boundaries; he fades out his own responsibilities. But all too obvious to her, Mr. Grease needs (her) help. Additionally, she seeks to gain his trust. She reminds him of the murder charge – and motivates him to cooperate with the experts. So he does. He provides them with some personal background and enjoys the attention and the distraction, according to the psychologist's feedback.

On the procedural backstage, in the protected space of the client-lawyer relationship, Mr. Grease shows this different face. He expresses himself 'privately' and 'confidentially' to the solicitor. In doing so, their relationship develops a certain pattern that oddly detaches itself from the facts of the case. The pattern emerges in the sequence and regularity of the letters and messages the client sends to his lawyer. I give the

[18] Foucault points out the relationship of the "human monster" and legal norms: "The monster is the limit, both the point at which law is overturned and the exception that is found only in extreme cases. The monster combines the impossible and the forbidden." (2003, 56) The monster is placed outside the community. At the end of a perfect moral career, one may locate Tavuchis' idea of apology as 'becoming member again': it "expresses itself as the exigency of a painful remembering, literally being mindful again, of what we were and had as members and, at the same time, what we have jeopardized or lost by virtue of our offensive speech or action" (1991:122).

dates and the dominant themes in his letters. The themes and quotes were referred to in the solicitor's answers:

Dates	Themes that dominated his letters
28.3^{+3}	"I need to see you urgently."
5.4^{+3}	Bandit (his dog); promises a plan of the Bungalow;"some facts of my mother's death"
10.4^{+3}	Asking for his radio
20.4^{+3}	"I am upset that you and Frazer never visited me." "I have come up with some new evidence ... I read you this list when I see you both."
1.5^{+3}	"I need to see you urgently."
20.5^{+3}	A note by the solicitor: He signed authority to Tuckers (big competing law firm).
20.5^{+3}	Another note by the solicitor: He remains with his current solicitor.
21.5^{+3}	"Please let me know when you will visit me as soon as possible. Please with my belongings."

Fig. 23: Client's Letters to Solicitor

Mr. Grease calls the solicitor – and later also the barrister – to the detention facility with 'lame excuses'. What is interpreted as worries about the case in the early stages will soon evoke the impression of pronounced disinterest. His letters speak of boredom, unease, concern, helplessness – and solitude. At times, however, there is also euphoria about an achieved status in prison, about ideas and sudden inspiration, about hope. Whether discouraging or encouraging, the letters insistently convey one message: 'Come see me, as soon as possible!' The solicitor soon proves to be annoyed by this constant siege. "He called *again*!"; "Oh no, not *another* letter from him!" Receiving his 'urgent' messages turns to routine, then to nuisance. More and more often, she cancels meetings[19] or ignores his requests. She points out professional limits.[20] She attempts to confine correspondence to essentials, with little success. His approaches are too frequent, and the professional convention to reply to every request weighs too heavily.

In the framework of the lawyer-client relationship, the lack of moral self-positioning constitutes an unsettling element. The client strangely relates to the accusations as if unconcerned and uninvolved, as if he

[19] 21.5^{+3}: "No other person that could come."
[20] 22.5^{+3}: "Limited by our duties and our compliance to the legal aid office."

was talking about far-away third persons. As if the 'regrettable' offence had happened in his absence. Self-consumed and without any moral resonance, he expresses fears in the face of the looming punishment, complains about the unbearable conditions of custody, and the loss of his familiar surroundings. In the context of casework, Mr. Grease's moral career of 'becoming a client and a defendant' proceeds erratically, if at all: personal fears appear next to phases of mere adaptation and vast forgetting. Mr. Grease helps in the library of the prison, starts reading, and attends the church on a regular basis. At times, he seems far away from being a client and defendant.

The meetings with Mr. Grease provide ever new opportunities to disappoint, puzzle, unsettle or even upset the lawyers. Consider this file note on a conference between Queen's Counsel, Junior Barrister and Mr. Grease:

> A discussion then went round to the offence itself and it is pointed out to client that in interview he admitted to pushing his mother 3 times. Client then says that he has changed that to once. He then says that he did push her 3 times but only once into the wall with the shelf. He says he saw red when she came back from the shop and said she had no cigarettes. When asked about that he says that he actually saw red in his eyes and that's the first time that that has happened. He is asked what time she came back from the shop and he said that he cannot recall now but it is ... He then goes on to say that his mother was as bad as him. (5.6^{+3})

The lawyers learn that their client does not undergo the usual learning process. There is not much of a progression towards a client-position or -identity. What is more, earlier achievements are easily forgotten, agreed upon points are reversed, instructions remain merely tentative. On top of these 'disruptions' of their casework, the lawyers register the absence of remorse. Inquiries on the offence provoke succinct answers that hardly show any moral involvement: "He was asked how hard he pushed his mother and he said 'medium, can't remember'." (5.6^{+3}) His reactions are received as cold, strangely technical and indifferent, as if he feels at liberty not to remember. Some file notes, however, testify the lawyers' attempts to raise the client's interest in his own case, to involve and challenge him:

> He was then referred to the witness statements. Counsel advises him that *inevitably* the Judge will ask him questions about those statements and what client accepts in those statements. The witness statements advise that client repeatedly hit his mother causing bruising to her or

> she was always going around bruised. The witness statements are saying that it was common knowledge that he caused that injury. Client's response to that is that it is poppycock. He admits to slapping her across the face and pushing her into furniture but denies causing her any serious harm. (5.6^{+3})

These attempts to involve him, be it by means of vague threat, mediated ascription of guilt, or unmasked confrontation, all miss their target. The lawyers are unable to produce 'presentable' replies, meaning replies that would allow the barrister to deliver his client's regrets in open court. Even worse, they garner morally questionable, even discrediting statements from Mr. Grease (e.g. "medium, can't remember," or "he denies causing her any serious harm"). Not to condemn the client becomes a difficult task for his legal representatives. The lawyers will try to reframe his 'improper' responds: they should be received not as signs of immorality, but as signs of an impairment that exceeds the court's sense of moralising on the one hand, while calming the public concern of re-offending on the other hand. A fine line indeed.

Beyond the mere failure in producing useful responses and instructions, the lawyers' attempts refer to their specific role. The legal counsel appears as a moralising stimulant, a kind of preliminary correctional facility. The lawyers opened up opportunities to morally position the client vis-à-vis the law. They taught him to admit guilt, to apologize or to demonstrate regret. In other words, the lawyers tried to win the client not just for the sake of the defence-case, but also for moral sentiments. The means of their invitation were confidentiality and partisanship.

The retrospect shows that solicitor and barrister were fishing for the client's moral response throughout. In turn, Mr. Grease's lack of remorse had a slackening effect on the lawyers' work. This highlights another function of this moralising site. The lawyers attempted to interest the client in 'his case', to get him enmeshed in the legal matter. Or in Bourdieu's words: "[…] to drive him to invest in his trial, the lawyer endeavours to soothe him with vague hopes and torment him with vague fears" (2000:238). On the one hand, the lawyers represent the system. On the other hand, they would not disclose Mr. Grease's morally discrediting responses. They remained inside the (confidential) lawyer-client relationship. The defence barrister reported the 'absence of remorse'; he did not convey the discrediting details of the defendant's refusal.

Discussion: characteristics and rationale of indirect moralising

The procedural design of indirect moralising implies a certain rationale that comes out in greater clarity when being contrasted with other forms. Ideally, direct moralising would affect the defendant instantly and enduringly. Ideally, it would resemble a shock therapy by which the personality would be shaken and transformed. As an effect, moral norms would remain like an imprint on the person's self. Students of moral communication doubt this efficacy in conventional court hearings: their rituals and routines of self-exposure, their legal incentives for showing remorse, their silencing of victims.

Indirect moralising, in contrast, adheres to a different rationale. Ideally, it would move the defendant from one stage of reflection to the next. It would entangle him or her in a web of moralising encounters. It would collect moral reactions of various forms. It would integrate reactions into a moral learning progression. The offender would not pass just one turning point, one moment of conversion; he would rather pass a sequence of moralising events that shall feed, ultimately, into a single educational process. Ideally, this process would move the defendant to permanently reshape his or her self-conception. Indirect moralising, this is the idea, would stimulate further "self-examination" and "self-judgements" (Hepworth and Turner 1979:232).[21]

In the case of Mr. Grease, indirect moralising is pushed towards its extremes due to the 'unexpected' and 'puzzling' absence of signs of regret. Throughout the pre-trial, Mr. Grease did not live up to the legal, the strategic, or the moral implications of 'his case'. This may be a worst case scenario of indirect moralising: the defendant seems to exit the case altogether. Mr. Grease displayed disinterest. He seemed preoccupied with other matters. He showed concern for the legal matter only every now and then. He remained unaffected when it came to the far-reaching moral connotations of his wrongdoing. At closer inspection, the moralising infrastructure of the procedure, its division of moralising failed altogether. The entire personnel, legal and extra-legal

[21] This reminds of Goffman's general concept of the character work of stigmatized persons: "Persons who have a particular stigma tend to have similar learning experiences regarding their plight, and similar changes in conception of self – a similar, moral career' that is both, cause and effect of commitment to a similar sequence of personal adjustments" (Goffman 1963:45).

establishment fell short of instigating visible and reportable signs of personal engagement and moral learning corresponding to the deed. Mr. Grease turned out to be unreformable and incorrigible. His participation changed in the procedural course, but it did not change in one direction, not to speak of progression and development. Mr. Grease's actions or reactions remained erratic as if coming out of nowhere. The case file reports a series of disappointments and frustrations on the side of his legal representatives.

Mr. Grease's exceptional case did not generate a successful moral career. The various moralising efforts did not even feed into a single developmental direction, neither positive nor negative: the biographical and problem-centred interviews by psychological experts, the relationship development by the lawyers, or the lawyer-centred approach by the criminal court. This pluralism, on the one hand, could protect the procedure against the defendant's refusal and ignorance; its fragmentation, on the other hand, may upset the communal audience and its urge for public reparation. It could protect the procedure from total failure, because it re-defined the amorality of Mr. Grease as a psychological deviance, an expert diagnosis that even worked in his favour. His inability to show remorse became a core property of his case.

Mr. Grease's case remains an irritation, a bone of contention. It is nonetheless completed within the conventional limits: a custodial sentence in line with the broad sentencing guidelines[22]. According to the barrister (in conference with Mr. Grease) the judge's option for a custodial sentence ranged from 15 years down to 3 years. His options for a non-custodial sentence included the placement in a mental hospital. Here is the judge's sentence:

> I must balance, as best I can, a number of conflicting considerations: the sentence must reflect the condemnation of society that the defendant has unlawfully killed his own mother who was elderly, frail and vulnerable; who has never showed him anything but love and indulgence; that the violence he used towards her was limited to pushes of moderate force, causing her to break three ribs which had these entirely unintended consequences.

[22] According to the "Sentencing Guidelines for manslaughter by reason of provocation" (2003), the sentence for cases with a "high degree of provocation" can be "up to four years if custody is necessary." For cases with a "low degree of provocation" the sentence ranges from "ten years to life." There are no definite guidelines for manslaughter or murder in general. The guidelines are published by the Sentencing Guidelines Council, http://www.sentencing-guidelines.gov.uk/.

> The mitigation arising from his personal circumstances I have already considered. Those conducting his defence have, very properly, investigated the possibility of a placement at Mulder Stones Hospital, but he does not have such learning difficulties as to amount to mental illness so a hospital order is not appropriate. He is, I agree, not a risk to anyone else. Prison no doubt, will bear hard upon him. The sentence of imprisonment, in my judgment, is inevitable. The sentence will be 3 ½ years. (7.8[+3])

From the final sentence, we can return to the unusual distancing moves by the judge ("It is not necessary for the defendant to stand.") and by the defending Queen's Counsel ("Of course, there is a significant difficulty with this defendant!"). Judge and counsel use expressions of indirectness on top of the pattern of indirect moralising; just as if they wanted to stay out of touch, to avoid contamination. Does this distancing reflect some moral disappointment? As if, being the actual operators of the criminal procedure, they provided invaluable moral care to the community? This is, in light of the case, a rather idealistic reading of the lawyers' verbal openers. A rather pragmatic version would take local requirements into account: the Queen's Counsel, for instance, had to reconcile Mr. Grease's refusal to regret with the defence. The Queen's Counsel had to face the fact that not to re-interpret the deviant ethos of his client would harm the case. Or even more: while his unusual comment degrades Mr. Grease as a person, it reaps beneficial effects in legal terms. Taken as an indication of a learning difficulty, the refusal to regret could become a point of mitigation.

This might be a disturbing lesson. Only the rare interplay of a still intact framework of indirect moralising – the defendant was kept within the normal procedural course despite his 'learning difficulty' – together with the defendant's persistent non-engagement – he frustrated the normal expectations of self-moralising – saved Mr. Grease from a more severe punishment. Either alternative, treating him as 'mentally ill' or as 'immoral', would have resulted in a presumably much longer detention (either in a psychiatric ward or in prison). The judge circumnavigated these two versions in his sentencing speech in order to derive at a relatively mild punishment. However, his "3 ½ years" stood out against his moral distancing, starting from his third-person address and followed by the judge's suspension of the defendant as fellow citizen. The judge's distancing shows, once again, the difficult moral terrain in this case. It allowed the judge to demonstrate that his sympathetic judgment does not imply sympathy with this character and what he caused. It allowed the judge to shield his own moral self. This seems another crucial dimension of indirect moralising.

What then may count as the rationale of indirect moralising? In light of this single case-study, I suggest the following rationales: (a) The court avoids public shaming and lasting degradation by exposing the defendant to moral interrogation only on the procedural backstages. (b) Indirect moralising prevents social conflicts or at least their diffusion by keeping the parties at distance. (c) The adversary lawyers are employed to demonstrate both, the judicial as well as the moral equivalence of guilt and punishment. (d) The court aims for a more comprehensive picture of the offender's moral self. The offender's morality is presented as a balancing act of limited biographical explanation and relative guilt. (e) Indirect moralising involves a whole series of moralising encounters. This expansion facilitates a soft but enduring force of moral education. It facilitates as well, and this seems to parallel a motive in Luckmann's communicative exploration of indirect moralising, protection against confrontational reception. With the defendant's self-explanations being placed on the procedural backstage, indirect moralising can hardly fail as a performance. Even problematic characters such as the remorseless Mr. Grease are integrated in a generally appropriate presentation of the matter and its judgement.

After the verdict, only one case remains. The former contradictions, disruptions, and tensions seem to vanish. The inclination that has stimulated adversarial case-making and that has been stimulated by it looses its grip. The factual and moral mismatches of the two competing cases and their related identity positions – just consider the inconsistency to call somebody the victim before the verdict – finally turn into powerful certainties. What remains after the procedure is done with is a single case that integrates matter, rule, and decision. Adversarial case-making comes to a halt for now, while the single case starts feeding into other case-making projects. In the following chapter, we will learn about the case as this integrated unity and how it relates to the various signifying processes in the case-system.

VIII. THE CASE IN THE CASE-SYSTEM

When it's all over for the client and the lawyers, what remains? This final chapter examines the (semiotic) life of the case in the legal system of cases. How and in what ways does the case relate to other cases? As a complex sign, a decided and reported case can enter various signifying processes. The case-sign offers itself to future case-making as a complex of matter, rule, and decision.

Once I returned home from my fieldwork I kept a number of connections to the field in Northern England. Some were interpersonal via electronic communication. Others were rather archival by ways of rereading all the copied documents and files. Others were academic – and pursued the research project as well. I consulted law books, legal articles, case reports, and press clips. I studied evaluation reports such as the one by Sir Auld and the Home Office's responses to it. These were the continuing links back to the common law system, which accentuated legal implications of my ethnography. I was frequently referred to the sources that, as I knew from my fieldwork, my lawyers, especially the barristers, would consult in their every day casework as well. I started studying the various case reports together with a colleague[1] and wondered how they relate to the cases-in-the-making that I previously followed as a participant observer over a period of more than two years.

Examining the case(s) in the case-system introduces a new focus. The focus is perhaps, at least in the established disciplinary and methodical understanding, rather discourse analytical than ethnographic, rather macroscopic than microscopic, rather distant than proximate. Such oppositions, however, mislead the overall ethnographic venture, because of various reasons. Firstly, they bracket out the members' orientation on (all the) cases. The case-makers rely on and attend to the case-system's continuation – and they do so by way of quoting or referring to cases and, at times, by contributing a relevant case themselves. The oppositions are misleading, secondly, because they bracket out the object under study: the case. The study of cases in

[1] My colleague Hyo-Eun Shin, herself a legal scholar, co-authored this chapter.

the case-system - although still performative - requires other 'matching' research strategies. The case-system is packed with cases in manifold versions; it is differently dimensioned; it operates by different means; it relates cases with cases. In order to understand what cases are/do in/for the case-system, we propose a semiotic perspective. In this perspective, the case is not a unit in the making, but a sign in meaning-producing interrelations.

"The case continues ..." it says at the end of newspaper articles on ongoing criminal trials. Here, the phrase has a different meaning. It does not apply to the prospect of more 'revealing' days in court, but to the fact that after the judgement, the completed case 'lives a life on its own'. The case does so in a new environment. It does so not any longer in the procedural course, but in an extended and enduring system of cases. A case might become precedence, example, or a re-specification for other cases. A case might be forgotten or it might be used for future case-making. The case continues insofar signifying processes relate to it. In the following, we analyse the case's fundamental availability for the signifying, relevance-generating processes. How does the case as sign afford this relational signification? The starting point for this semiotic exercise is the broad diversity of case-representations, which often confuses legal students. We argue that within the integrated system of remembrance and signification, cases are made relevant as similar/different exemplars (amongst many other ones) in regard to certain rules applied, matter heard, or decisions taken.

The case as tripartite sign

The case-system remembers, compares, and progresses through and with cases. Legal scholars, lawyers, and/or case-makers search for, report, summarize, cite, read, count, etc. other cases. Once it entered the case-system, the case is performed as a single immutable unit. These units appear in law books, journals, the press, in curricula. They leave traces in statistics, reform, and policy papers. In order to capture this manifold *case-remaking*, we draw attention to the multiple ways by which the case-system operates through cases. Let us take a look at a usual case from a casebook[2] and how it offers itself to and performs

[2] We randomly chose a short case from Templeman and Molan's Criminal Law Casebook (1998:235–36). Casebooks are usually intended as companions to

processes of signification. Similar versions of case can be found in digests, supplements and updates such as the "Case Alerter," or the usual law reports.

R* v *Lipman [1970] 1 QB 152 Court of Appeal (Criminal Division) (Widgery and Fenton Atkinson LJJ, and James J)

Intoxication as a defence to basic intent crimes

Facts
The defendant, having voluntarily consumed a quantity of an hallucenogenic drug, killed a woman whilst under the delusion that he was fighting snakes in the centre of the earth. His defence of intoxication was rejected at his trial. He was convicted of manslaughter, and appealed.

Held
The appeal would be dismissed.

Widgery LJ:

> 'As to manslaughter, the jury were directed that it would suffice for the Crown to prove that "he must have realised before he got himself into the condition he did by taking the drugs that acts such as those he subsequently performed and which resulted in the death were dangerous." In this court Mr Eastham contends that this was a misdirection, and that the jury should have been directed further that it was necessary for the Crown to prove that the defendant intended to do acts likely to result in harm, or foresaw that harm would result from what he was doing.
>
> For the purposes of criminal responsibility we see no reason to distinguish between the effect of drugs voluntarily taken and drunkenness voluntarily induced. As to the latter there is a great deal of authority.'

After referring, inter alia, to *DPP* v *Beard* [1920] AC 479, *Bratty* v *Attorney-General for Northern Ireland*, above, and *Attorney-General for Northern Ireland* v *Gallagher*, above, his Lordship continued:

> We can dispose of the present application by reiterating that when the killing results from an unlawful act of the prisoner no specific intent has to be proved to convict of manslaughter, and self-induced intoxication is accordingly no defence. Since in the present case the acts complained of were obviously likely to cause harm to the victim (and did, in fact, kill her) no acquittal was possible and the verdict of manslaughter, at the least, was inevitable.
>
> If and so far as this matter raises a point of law on which the defendant was entitled to appeal without leave, such appeal is dismissed.'

Fig. 24: Case from Templeman and Molan's Criminal Law Casebook (1998:235–36)

This representation starts with a code and the names of the judges who decided the case. The code leaves traces of the case in legal fields and maps the latter through routes, detours, short cuts, connections, bridges between cases. More than that, the code states the case as something factual, not imagined. The code identifies a defendant ("Lipman"), a year of trial ("1970"), a court ("Court of Appeal"), and judges ("Widgery and Fenton Atkinson LJJ, and James J"). The code

---

textbooks or as reference tools. They specifically address students of law. "Using a case book has two advantages for the learner. First, the case book saves him some of the trouble… of making his own notebook of cases. Secondly, it does something to eliminate immaterial facts, thus helping in the search … for the facts that are legally material. It should be added that the use of case books by no means dispenses with the need for reading the original reports" (Williams 1982:52–53).

refers to a case *of somebody* that has been decided *by somebody*. The personal link is moderate: the general reader does not obtain full names, exact dates, or exact venues. After the code, the representation provides a theme similar to keywords for an academic journal article. The theme can make the case's content accessible in a database, here as one of "Intoxication as a defence to basic crimes." The case is linked up to this legal theme and not, for example, to a sociological ("gender relations") or a medical theme ("effects of hallucinogenic drugs").[3]

Next, the representation offers "Facts" that evoke the *matter* of concern, the problem that awaits a decision. The matter is reduced to three phrases on (a) the offence, (b) the defence, and (c) a procedural (decision) history. There are no further details given on where, when and what exactly happened. Here, matter is geared towards decision and ruling. It summarizes the legal cause which brought a case back to court. It provides legal information relevant to the court's reasoning: voluntarily + consumed hallucinogenic drug + killed + woman + while under delusion + defence of intoxication + rejected at trial + convicted + of manslaughter + appealed.[4] The facts are served in terms belonging to both legal and everyday language. The categories provide passages between facts and norms, between matters of concern and legal matters.

Under "Held," the representation offers the decision reached plus the core reasoning of the appeal court. The reasoning confronts matter and rule. It mentions previous cases, "inter alia" one 'old' precedence (from 1920), by giving its name and providing its code. In the last part, the relation of the case at hand to the earlier case is specified. The textbook introduces the Court of Appeal's reasoning by directly quoting from the judgment. The decision ("appeal dismissed") appears as the

[3] The legal theme can also be supplied as a list of catchwords, e.g. in The Law Reports: "Crime – Sexual offences - Indecent assault - Man of 26 engaging in sexual activity with I4-year-old girl - Activity alleged to be consensual - Belief that girl over 16 - Whether amounting to defence - Whether prosecution required to prove absence of genuine belief-Sexual Offences Act 1956 (4 ~ 5 Eliz 2, c 69), s I4." (AC 2002:462) Here, the keywords comprise legal aspects under which the case may become relevant in the future. They embrace areas of legal rules ("Indecent assault"), matter in light of allegation vs. defence ("Man of 26 …" or "Belief that …"), decisions evoked by these matters ("Whether prosecution …") and rules ("absence of genuine belief …").

[4] This is a relative and floating transformation; one could, e.g. think of altering and reducing the matter even further (defendant + killed + person + defence of intoxication + rejected at trial + convicted + of manslaughter + appealed) or extend it slightly (defendant+ killed + person + defence of intoxication + rejected at trial + convicted + of manslaughter + appeal + about misdirection to jury).

result of applying a rule already in place. It is 'just' the application of an established rule or principle 'archived' in previous cases ("reiterating that when ..."). The overall representation gives the impression of a clear-cut and unavoidable decision, of clear-cut and ready-at-hand rules, and of clear-cut and easily summarized matter. All these components are right there and adapt to each other. They are put into circulation as a tripartite montage under the code, the case ID. By help of the code, the case can enter citations, reference lists, and keyword sources. The code safeguards the 'trinity' of case while allowing multiple vantage points.

This version of case provides first insights into the components of the case. There are three of them: matter, rule, and decision. The three components re-specify each other within, what we want to call, the case and in relation to signifying processes, that is to comparable matter, to similar rules, and to equivalently reasoned decisions.[5] The case-sign adapts to these three contexts of signification:

- It signifies decision. The case relates to certain other decisions in the case-system, meaning it is presented as bound to past decisions, while it sets an example to future decisions.
- It signifies rule and presents itself to certain other rules. The case relates to already introduced rules, while providing re-specification of these rules – new rules – for future cases.
- It signifies matter. The case relates to a template of matter in terms of categories and criteria, and by doing so introduces a comparable variant for future cases.

The three signifying relations order the different representations of case in the common law system. Our semiotic perspective provides clues for questions such as the following: How does the case-system allow for relations to past, present and future cases? How do cases obtain meaning? How can lawyers or legal scholars relate to or link up cases? Some cases remain relevant over centuries, while others circulate across national borders. This vast availability and the multiple re-appearances are achieved by the matter-rule-decision trinity under a certain address or code.

[5] With just one of these components, one could only state *that* something happened (not to what effect) or *that* there was a certain rule applied (not how) or *that* a decision was taken (not why). A single component does not make a case. We will come to these isolated representations at the end of this chapter.

The inner complexity of the case and its multi-directional signification shows in the many ways cases appear in directories, citation lists, digests, reports, indexes, encyclopaedia, newspaper archives, textbooks, casebooks, electronic databases, etc. A case can be searched and found by name of parties, name of judges, court, year of decision, subject-orientated keywords, etc. Even subsequent judicial case-operations (whether a case was "overruled," "doubted," "considered," "applied," "distinguished," "followed," "affirmed," "explained"[6] in relation to other cases) are available to archival operations (Thomas and Knowles 2006; Hanson 1999). In the following, we depict how cases, as expansions and contractions, are made available to the three relations or contexts.

Case, fact-sensitive

When looking at cases circulating in the case-system one finds matter – as indicated above – signified in a particular way. What previously needed to be established, what may have been subject of hard-fought battles between the adversarial parties, is now finalised as 'facts'. Facts are a vital part of case. Sometimes, they are afforded ample space as in the following extract from a case representation:[7]

> MR JUSTICE NELSON: On 23rd August 2005 at the Crown Court at Lewes, the appellant was convicted of eight offences of obtaining property or money transfer by deception. When he was sentenced the same day he asked for five offences of a similar nature of obtaining property or money transfer by deception to be taken into consideration and those were by the judge. On the same day, 23rd August 2005, he was sentenced to seven years' imprisonment on each of the eight counts concurrent, making a total of seven years' imprisonment. He appeals against that sentence by leave of the single judge. … The facts are that from the beginning of 2000 to the end of 2003 the appellant dishonestly obtained money from two elderly individuals, Mr Heal and Mrs Taylor, both of them at the time in their late seventies. The appellant's method was to pretend that their homes needed some roofing work, that he would carry out the work and that the monies paid to him, often in advance, were a fair price for the work. In fact such work as he carried out was of poor quality and

[6] See, e.g., the 'red indexes': The Consolidated Index to leading law reports (1991–2000).

[7] Extracts from the judgment Regina v Sam Mitchell (2006) EWCA Crim 244, provided as a transcript on http://www.bailii.org.

> he knew the value of it was far less than the amounts he obtained... The overall sum the appellant obtained from Mr Heal was nearly £94,000. This caused Mr Heal considerable financial hardship. ... Most of the payments were made to the appellant in cash. ... The offences came to light when Mr Heal's daughter visited her father in late November 2003 and on hearing her father's account of what was going on alerted the authorities. An independent surveyor was requested to look at Mr Heal's property. He did and found that the majority of the alleged work carried out was poor and that the overall amount of work carried out was actually worth in the region of £2,000. As a result of their enquiries, police officers found that the appellant had targeted Mrs Tylor, an 83-year-old woman, in 2002. She had hired him to do some work on her roof and had paid him £7,500 in total to do so. An independent surveyor considered the charges for that work to be extortionate, unnecessary and most of it was indeed worthless. ... He was arrested on 15th May 2004. In his first interview he said that he had done building work for Mr Heal for nothing since they were friends, that the money given to him by Heal was a gift and that no cash had changed hands.... The appellant is a man who was born on 25th January 1954. He has various convictions, none for which he received a custodial sentence and none in the recent past. When the judge sentenced him he said that on the clearest of evidence, which of course the judge had heard, the appellant had been convicted and his dishonesty as described by the account that he gave of what had happened was blatant. He was an unprincipled man without any idea of honesty or decency and had tried to talk his way out of the allegations and showed no remorse or regret. ... He preyed on the elderly and had done here...

This version of case starts off with a previous sentencing decision and the appeal motion. Subsequently, "the facts" are provided similar to a story-line. In chronological order, we are told of the trouble Mr. Mitchell caused, we get to know his and the victims' names and ages, we learn about his "method" of deception, get an idea what kind of person the defendant (here appellant) is, and even what he "knew" contrary to his claims. This resembles a moral story where it involves a moral evaluation (the story of an "unprincipled man" who "preyed on the elderly" and "showed no remorse or regret"). Nevertheless, it is not primarily seeking to entertain or teach, it does not stop at the morale but, in the subsequent passages, the case informs the reader about the sentencing in the court of first instance and the arguments brought forward to the Court of Appeal by the defendant's counsel to strengthen his claim that the sentence was too long. Then this case version offers some judicial consideration with references to other cases ending with the decision ("... the sentence of seven years was too long. In our view a sentence of six years would meet the justice of the case. Accordingly, the sentence of seven years... is quashed and a sentence of six years... is substituted for it, making a total of six years. To this extent the appeal is allowed.").

Here, we come across a case with an emphasis on matter. The original matter dominates this representation. However, rule and decision are not omitted but an integral part of the case. Facts are introduced with specific reference to the latter; here, rule and decision highly depend on the intricate details of matter. Where sentencing is in question, cases seem to have a strong proclivity to real-life matter, since the personality of defendant and victim(s), the 'how' all become part of the 'what'; they are vital to evaluate the severity of the deed ("In our view a sentence of six years would meet the justice of the case").

We find other cases with an emphasis on matter. In the following example taken from the Archbold (2000), case orientates itself towards real-life matter, even when provided as a statement of legal rules or judicial reasoning, rendering the former decidable:

In *R. v. M.* [1995] Crim.L.R. 344, Lord Taylor C.J. said that in a case of rape committed by a man on his wife where the parties were cohabiting normally at the time and the husband insisted on intercourse against the wife's wishes but without threats or violence, the previous relationship would be an important factor in reducing the length of the sentence. There was a distinction between the husband who was estranged from his wife and who returned to the house as an intruder either by forcing his way in or worming his way in through some device before raping her, and a husband who was still living in the same house and with consent occupying the same bed as his wife. This class of case was not so grave as the former class of case, but nonetheless required a custodial sentence; it must be clearly understood by husbands that they do not have an absolute right to use their wives for sexual purposes whatever the relationship between them and whether or not there was consent. The court substituted a sentence of 18 months' imprisonment.

Fig. 25: Case-representation I in Archbold (2000)

Here, we find a case representation that provides judicial reasoning as a guideline for future sentencing decisions. The case does not explicitly introduce 'facts' or 'matter'; the original real-life matter is, at first sight, not included in the case: We do not get to know (any)more in detail when, where and how something exactly happened; we do not learn what kind of persons the 'defendant' and the 'victim' are nor how they made their case in court, etc. However, in this version of case, one can see how real-life matter permeates and saturates rule. We find some remains of a once more detailed story: a man, living together with and sharing the same bed as his wife, did somehow (without threatening or using violence) force the latter to have sexual intercourse against her wishes. What may appear as bits and pieces of a story, equips the legal practitioner with a set of criteria that help determine the gravity of the deed and thus influence the length of sentence in similar cases. The criteria are abstracted from matter, they are translations or traces of the variability of social life under a certain legal theme ("case of rape committed by a man on his wife"). Their combinations build up into legal variations, into "classes of case": for instance, cases of men "estranged from their wives," cases of men "worming" their way into the house before committing the rape, cases of men living together with their wives and "having sexual intercourse regularly over a period of nearly two years." Even though or exactly because "[l]aw is about life and life rarely replicates itself" (Hanson 1999:62), variations in facts feed into distinguishable legal categories that operate as potential replica. Case may then also call for an absorption of more matter: "...the previous relationship would be an important factor in reducing the length of the sentence."

This version of case presents cases as highly fact-sensitive: 'matter matters' for both decision and rule. This is highly visible for the rule which extensively borrows from the individual case; the underlying matter is transformed into a general rule securing its applicability to other cases, thus limiting judges' discretion and guiding counsels' submissions. Matter as rule creates decidability. Additionally, the decision ("sentence of 18 months imprisonment") appears as a direct consequence of the matter at hand: Several variations are weighed up against each other, they can aggravate/mitigate, diversify/specify each others' legal consequences, rendering cases more or "not so grave." Cases as fact-sensitive account for the intricacy of human relationships as well as for developments of the law.

Case, ruled and ruling

In encyclopaedia, law books, and more specifically textbooks, principles and rules are illustrated or better explored by means of cases. References place a rule back into their past enactment, meaning right into the original triad. This reference leads back to the rule's legal application, to its role for deciding a legal matter. Rules and principles are extracted from an array of related cases such as these in the following example from Archbold (2000:1747):

> To constitute a defence under this proviso, where it applies, the defendant must have reasonable cause to believe, and, in fact, must have believed that the girl was over the age of 16 years: *R. v. Banks* [1916] 2 K.B. 621, 12 Cr.App.R. 74, CCA; *R. v. Harrison*, 26 Cr.App.R. 166, CCA. The question of the existence of reasonable cause to believe is one for the jury: *R. v. Forde* [1923] 2 K.B. 400, 17 Cr.App.R. 99, CCA. This proviso is not applicable to the offence of indecent assault. As to this incongruity, see *R. v. Forde, ante*; *R. v. Keech*, 21 Cr.App.R. 125, CCA; *R. v. Maughan*, 24 Cr.App.R. 130, CCA.
>
> The defence is available not only where intercourse has taken place, but also where it has been merely attempted: *R. v. Collier* [1960] Crim.L.R. 204, Assizes (Streatfeild J.).

Fig. 26: Case-representation II in Archbold (2000)

In the exploration of rules regarding a certain defence of consent on part of the victim, cases are introduced as containers and sources of rules: rules are stated one after the other and are given further weight and authority by reconnecting them to comparable cases as codes. This version of case shows a strong affinity to rule. However, even with such strong focus on rules and ruling, the case representations still refer to the two other components: matter and decision. The rules do not appear without the 'facts', even though they are not detailed anymore; what is left of the 'facts' is what was considered legally relevant when reaching the decision, and what, thus, can be used to typify the case. This can be said even in 'extreme' rule-centred versions of a case, for instance, in the above example, "The defence is available not only where intercourse has taken place, but also where it has been merely attempted," because they still safeguard the tripartite composition in two ways: firstly, such a statement would not stand without the ID of the case which the statement was deduced from, referring it back to the composition. No matter how specific, the reference to case is complete only with the full case citation. This way, cases are kept in play in relation to a certain rule or a class of rules. Secondly, case as ruled and ruling offer principles and rules as abstracted, purified real-life matter, aligned towards the decision.

The above text constructs the contribution of single cases to a retraceable rule-tradition or rule-history. From case to case, the case system provides a better understanding of what the rule is (after all), how the rule was applied, and how, thereafter, the rule became what it is now. Rules are presented as deriving from cases, while determining certain legal problems of cases. Shifting focus towards the rule dimension, cases do not appear as individuals, but as instances of long processes (in the example starting with a case from 1916) that continue until today. Cases, in this perspective, serve as re-specification of a more general rule. Cases in light of their application or their invention of rules may shape juridical oppositions, controversies, opinions, etc.:

> In *DPP v Majewski*, the House of Lords confirmed the rule, obscurely stated in *Beard*, that evidence of self-induced intoxication negativing *mens rea* is a defence to a charge of a crime requiring a specific intent but not to a charge of any other crime. ... [Majewski] claimed that his self induced intoxication prevented him forming the *mens rea*, and that the evidence of the intoxication ought to be admissible to support that plea... He was convicted and this was upheld by the House of Lords. He was charged with a crime of basic intent and it has long been recognized that voluntary intoxication was no defence to such a charge even if it did cause D [defendant] to lack *mens rea*. ... On one interpretation, the case imposes a rule of substantive law that, where D relies on voluntary intoxication as a defence to a charge of a crime not requiring 'specific intent', the prosecution need not prove any intention or foresight, whatever the definition of the crime may say, nor indeed any voluntary act. ... An alternative view is that *Majewski* does not create a rule of substantive law, but one of evidence. On this view, once D has been shown to be voluntarily intoxicated in a basic intent crime the evidence of intoxication is irrelevant to the question whether D held the *mens rea*, but the prosecution is still obliged to prove that D had the relevant *mens rea*. ... This interpretation of *Majewski* as a rule of evidence also poses problems. Take *Lipman*, where D strangled V [victim] after taking LSD and believing that he was fighting off a serpent at the centre of the earth. How can a judge seriously tell a jury to decide whether D did intent to do an unlawful and dangerous act to V – ignoring the undisputed evidence that he was unconscious at the time? (Ormerod 2008:298–300)

Here, cases are named by the defendant's name ("Majewski," "Lipman") and footnoted as code ("Lipman [1970] 1 QB 152").[8] They are assembled from the point of view of a rule and its application. There is, e.g., some controversy about the 'right' application and interpretation of a rule deriving from a case ("In *DPP v Majewski*, the House of Lords

[8] Right at the end of this extract, we find an alternative representation of the case example taken from Templeman and Molan before. This illustrates how versatile cases and its representations can be in the case-system: here, in comparison, initial matter is slightly more pinpointed ("strangled," "LSD") while ruling appears as a problematisation of this specific interpretation vis-à-vis competing readings of a previously decided case.

confirmed the rule, obscurely stated in *Beard*..."). The representation of this case shows again a minimal version of case as a tripartite montage: despite the strong emphasis on rule, matter and decision are given within the unit case. The extract, furthermore, presents a good illustration of cases as ruled and ruling. They are open to interpretation and application in other cases. Rules are achieved, remembered, and kept 'alive' through cases; a specific case may then appear as a deviation, an aberration (Lipman) from another case (Majewski).

In terms of rules, the case-system organises itself not merely in symmetrical but in hierarchical order. Law books describe processes of ruling in terms of conventions and canons. This general settlement does not relate to a play of rational choice or democratic measures, but of relevance, hierarchy, and authority. Decisions on individual matter are granted weight according to the courts and judges that enacted the rule (of more general rules and for future cases). Accordingly, there are cases that matter, landmark cases, precedence, cases of persuasive authority, or test cases[9]. This does not exclude several acceptable opinions on similar matters existing side by side. The case-system is integrated precisely through these collections and chains of relevant cases under a certain rule, embracing the cases' orderliness and decidability, plus its potential impact on future cases in these respects.[10]

However, the role of constructing rule traditions and formation of authorities is not a pure technical matter.[11] The cases cited so far are

[9] One subgroup are test cases: its outcome is promised to serve as precedent for future cases and especially for pending cases involving similar or related issues or circumstances and often some of the same parties; a test case is selected from a number of cases in order to avoid a flood of litigation. All parties to the cases must agree to accept the outcome of the test case as binding.

[10] Reworking the tradition of rules is specifically important in legal education. Case collections originated in this practical context; they go back to Harvard Law School professor Christopher Columbus Langdell who introduced what came to be known as the 'case method' in 1870. For Langdell, cases were the 'raw-material' of legal science (Moskovitz 1992), or in the words of Pound: "The cases being to him what the specimen is to the geologist." (1888 quoted in Redlich 1914:16) In this line, Langdell issued a collection of cases to his students to be analysed in class under the guidance of the instructor (Lind 2004:95sq.; Redlich 1914). The "Socratic method" (Redlich 1914:12) was meant to teach the "habit of legal thought" and to do what practitioners (are going to) do: "It is through applying oneself to cases that one gets to understand how legal problems present themselves and how legal argument is conducted." (Williams 1982:48).

[11] This task constitutes a creative and archaeological science: "Law, considered as a science, consists of certain principles or doctrines. To have such a mastery of these as to be able to apply them with constant facility and certainty to the ever-tangled skin

'digested' by detached authors or editors of the law reports, who were not involved in the case itself. Their summaries do not address the participants at court (see also the use of past tense differently from judgments delivered in present tense), but a "generalized other." Rule-oriented case-representations are less occupied with details, but more with enabling the 'user' to quickly grasp 'what this case was about'. Some legal scholars utter reservations about the supposed neutral perspective of the reporters. They remind of the unavoidability of interpretation and of the original quality of the reported judgement. The latter remains authoritative (Thomas and Knowles 2006; Slapper and Kelly 2001), or as Hanson puts it: "Only the judgment can be trusted" (1999:74). This is, of course, not how the case-system works. It gains its efficacy and integrative force exactly by its complex reference system that bypasses the original case. The latter is kept in play because of, not despite of all the shortcuts. And it is kept in play because of the ability to keep the triad of rule, matter, and decision intact.

Case, decision-oriented

Another triadic appearance of case is provided by judgments themselves which can be found as the main text of cases in law reports or in the numerous databases offering transcripts of judgments. The following exemplar, documented in a law report[12] and referred to in various law books by its code, provides such a decision-oriented case representation. An identification number of the case, given in the page header, anchors the representation within the Law Report: "R v K (HL(E)) [2002] 1 AC 462." Like for every individual, this number allows to backtrack more particulars from any point in the case-system. Again, we find elements of the code as discussed above: abbreviation for the two

of human affairs is what constitutes a true lawyer; and hence to acquire that mastery should be the business of every earnest student of law. Each of these doctrines has arrived at its present state by slow degrees; in other words, it is a growth, extending in many cases through centuries. This growth is to be traced in the main through a series of cases… If these doctrines could be so classified and arranged that each should be found in its proper place, and nowhere else, they would cease to be formidable from their number. It seemed to me, therefore, to be possible to take such a branch of the law … and… to select, classify, and arrange all the cases which had contributed in any important degree to the growth, development, or establishment of any of its essential doctrines…" (Langdell 1871, quoted in Redlich 1914:11).

[12] The Law Reports, Appeal Cases, 2002, Volume I.

parties, the court instance, the year, as well as the case's address. However, this representation offers additional details in the title to the case:

> House of Lords
>
> Regina v K
>
> [2001] UKHL 41
>
> 2001 July II; 25
>
> Lord Bingham of Cornhill, Lord Nicholls of Birkenhead, Lord Steyn, Lord Hobhouse of Woodborough and Lord Millet

Here, identification is further organised around the decision. We find an alternative case code: "Regina v K [2001] UKHL 41," a so called 'neutral citation' which identifies the court of decision (UK House of Lords), not the publication. Furthermore, the day in court, and the actual decision-takers (with their full titular) identify the case as decided. The decision provides a distinct and individual point in time and space: the place and date and personnel of the case's closure.

The judgment presents the case in the genre of public speech, Lord Bingham of Cornhill addressing 'his fellow Lords':

> 25. July. LORD BINGHAM OF CORNHILL
>
> 1 My Lords, the appellant K was indicted on a single count of indecent assault committed against a girl C who at the time was aged 14, contrary to section 14 (I) of the Sexual Offences Act 1956. His defence was to be that the sexual activity between him and C was consensual, that she had told him she was 16 and that he had had no reason to disbelieve her. He is a man of good character, aged 26 at the date of the offence charged against him. Before the trial a preliminary issues was raised on behalf of K: whether, to establish K's guilt under the section, the prosecution had to prove that at the time of the incident K did not honestly believe that C was 16 or over. Argument on this issue was heard by Judge Thorpe at Chichester Crown Court. He ruled, in favour of K, that the prosecution did have to prove an absence of genuine belief on the part of the accused that the victim was aged 16 or over. In so ruling the judge relied on the recent decision of the House of Lords in *B (A Minor) v Director of Public Prosecutions [2002]* 2 AC 428. The prosecution appealed against that ruling under section 35 of the Criminal procedure and Investigations Act 1996. The Court of Appeal (Criminal Division) (Roch LJ, Rougier and Gray JJ) [2001] I Cr App R 493 allowed the appeal and held that such absence of genuine belief did not have to be proved. The Court certified the following point of law of general public importance:
>
> "(a) Is a defendant entitled to be acquitted of the offence of indecent assault on a complainant under the age of 16 years, contrary to section 14 (I) of the Sexual offences Act 1956, if he may hold an honest belief that

> the complainant in question was aged 16 years or over? (b) If yes, must the belief be held on reasonable grounds?
>
> Leave to appeal was refused by the Court of Appeal but granted by the House.

The judgment starts off with an introduction of the matter, again comprising story plus history of the case so far. By relying on arguments contended in court, the presentation of matter already defines the perspective and scope of what will be reasoned subsequently. It states the problem explicitly in the form of two questions (a) and (b). What follows[13] is an inquiry by the 'speaker' Lord Bingham; he states the relevant Section 14 Sexual Offences Act 1956, takes up points made by counsel, and, to develop his own take on the question, inquires into the historical context of this particular law and the will of legislature when passing the Sexual Offences Act. In this part, the judgment draws onto various sources of law (statutes, cases) and other legal material (policy and reform papers, encyclopaedia) which are introduced in a narration of sequential, partly cross-cutting development in light of the intentions, the enactments, and arguments surrounding Section 14, e.g.:

> 9 Since the 1956 Act was a consolidation Act, with corrections and improvements to the expression but not to the substance of existing provisions (see generally *Halsbury's Laws of England*, 4th ed reissue, vol 44 (I) (1995), para 1247), it is not surprising that the terms of section 14 reflected their miscellaneous origins. But that section cannot properly be considered in isolation. Section 50 of the 1861 Act made unlawful carnal knowledge of a girl under the age of ten a felony punishable by penal servitude for life. Section 51 made unlawful carnal knowledge of a girl aged 10 or 11 a misdemeanour punishable by up to three years' penal servitude. It was these sections to which Blackburn J, with the concurrence of nine other judges, referred in the course of ruling in *R v Prince* (1875) LR 2 CCR 154, 171–172 that for purposes of section 55 of the 1861 Act it was no defence for a defendant charged with taking an unmarried girl under the age of 16 out of the possession of her father to establish a reasonable belief that she was over 16...But the law did not rest there.

These pieces of information operate as hints and arguments pro or contra the requirement for the prosecution to "prove absence of genuine belief on the part of the defendant that the girl was 16" with regard

[13] For matters of space the original judgment (15 pages) has been largely paraphrased. The full-text judgment as well as an alternative summary of the case given by the law report editor can be found under the given 'address' in the Law Reports.

to section 14 Sexual Offences Act 1956. They are weighed against each other with view to causing or not causing absurdities or anomalies in terms of justice. They inform further reasoning, and eventually lead to a decision:

> 20 Neither in section 14 nor elsewhere in the 1956 Act is there any expressed exclusion of the need to prove an absence of genuine belief on the part of a defendant as to the age of an under-age victim. Had it been intended to exclude the element of mens rea it could very conveniently have been so provided in or following subsection (2). …
>
> 22 I consider that Judge Thorpe reached the right conclusion. The Court of Appeal gave more weight to the re-enactment of the relevant provisions in 1956 than was appropriate for a consolidation Act….
>
> 26 For these reasons, and also those given by my noble and learned friends Lord Steyn and Lord Hobhouse of Woodborough, I would allow this appeal.

This opinion of Lord Bingham is followed by those of the other four lords involved in the case; one by one they express their agreement with Lord Bingham with the effect of reaching the same decision, or they add further or alternative observations from other cases, provide further insight into the statute's history or voice their misgivings about certain issues:

> LORD MILLET
>
> 40 My Lords, I have had the advantage of reading in draft the speech of my noble and learned friend Lord Bingham of Cornhill, with which I agree. For the reasons he gives I would allow the appeal and answer the certified questions as he proposes.
>
> 41 I do so without reluctance but with some misgiving, for I have little doubt that we shall be failing to give effect to the intention of Parliament and will reduce section 14 of the Sexual Offences Act 1956 to incoherence…
>
> 44 But the age of consent has long ceased to reflect ordinary life, and in this respect Parliament has signally failed to discharge its responsibility for keeping the criminal law in touch with the needs of society. I am persuaded that the piecemeal introduction of the various elements of section 14, coupled with the persistent failure of Parliament to rationalize this branch of the law even to the extent of removing absurdities which the courts have identified, means that we ought not to strain after internal coherence even in a single offence. Injustice is too high a price to pay for consistency.
>
> Appeal allowed.
>
> Solicitors: Marsh Ferriman & Cheale, Worthing; Crown Prosecution Service, Headquarters

The case is represented here as a case as decided. From the point of view of the judgment, the case-system seems tailored towards the establishment/application of a rule or principle that is vital in reaching a decision on *such a* matter; 'irrelevant' aspects of the case (whatever is considered 'immaterial' for the decision-making) are omitted. The judgment documents that the decision is reasoned; that it has been reached on legal grounds only.

The judgment illustrates how a decision history involves rule and matter. It illustrates how the legal decision in the common law tradition is concerned with fixing the relation of rule and real-life matter. Both, it is argued, are not separated or additive components. They become relevant only when referred to each other in the legally binding decision (see, e.g. Thomas and Knowles 2006; Slapper and Kelly 2001 Manchester et al. 2000, or Hanson 1999). The decision performs a certain meaning of rule in light of the matter and vice versa. Research is then focussed on the logical space and the systematic relations between rule and matter as facets of legal ordering.

The decision-centred case enters a complex and hierarchical system of reports: material and intellectual reference points for the stare decisis. At first sight, the legal case-system seems to prefer decision as the starting-point or foundation. Only with the decision, the case turns into a completed unit; only now can the system refer to components of *one* case. This might explain why the legal literature focuses on courts' decisions interchangeably called 'case', 'judicial decisions', 'judicial opinions', or 'judgments'.

Once a case is decided, the judgment occupies *the case* in all its facets. The decision-oriented case gives all the names as if holding all participants accountable for closing the triad. The case is definite, closed, and ready to circulate as a – more or less authoritative – measure for the cases to come. The triad of matter, rule, and decision is set for once – until an appeal will stir it up once again in order to introduce another balance. The case, here, is represented as pure retrospection; it is re-narration from the ending.[14] It is a demonstration that the matter had to be decided this way. Contingency re-enters later.

[14] A version of criminal case that is similar in this respect can be found in the press and in humorous literature. Here, cases are not puzzles to be solved, but often resemble a 'freak show' of human nature, exemplifying the strange endeavours of human beings. Or in anecdotal caricatures, short stories tailored to get some laughs, or stir up emotions. See the introduction to such case representations in *The Times Online*:

Saying that a case is fixed and closed does not mean that its relevance is set once and for all. In the future, one and the same case will play different roles, will be objected to different usages, and will reach various relevancies. Interestingly, 'what has been decided' will show in coming pasts, let us say in ten or twenty years after the verdict. The question of 'what has been decided' points towards the circulation, efficacy and interpretation of the case. In a general sense, the scope of 'decision' can reach towards conformity with past precedents; in a narrower sense, the decision can reach towards 'just' the case. A way to expand or to narrow the decision is by ways of representing the "ratio decidendi".[15] The "ratio decidendi" is a rule of the single case that decides whether and how one case is capable of limiting the ambit of judicial discretion (see McDonnell 1998–99:fn. 10) in a number of similar other cases. This decision is orientated and geared towards "what has been decided previously" (Cross and Harris 1991:3).[16]

The *ratio decidendi* can be understood as the "statement of the law applied in deciding the legal problem raised by the concrete facts of the case" (Slapper and Kelly 2001:75). The ratio consists of the "general reasons given for the decision or the general grounds upon which it is

---

"The world's weirdest cases. From the man who sued God to the man who sued TV for making his wife fat, people turn to lawyers for the strangest things. A meticulous collector of amusing and curious anecdotes from the world of law, Professor Gary Slapper's Case Notes column has long been a staple of The Times' Law section. His collection of legal oddities is on display in a new column, Weird Cases. As a taster, we asked him to select 20 of his favourite bizarre disputes, prosecutions and lawsuits from the archive." http://business.timesonline.co.uk/tol/business/law/article2741049.ece.

[15] The binding precedent is set by the proposition or rule of law on which the decision is founded. A decision on questions of fact does not constitute a proposition of law and may not be cited as precedent, even though or exactly because the vast bulk of cases are argued and decided on their facts rather than on principles of law (even though it can be difficult to differentiate facts from law; generally, an issue is one of fact where it refers to the admissibility of evidence): "The ratio decidendi of a case is any rule of law expressly or impliedly treated by the judge as a necessary step in reaching his conclusion, having regard to the line of reasoning adopted by him, or a necessary part of his direction to the jury" (Cross and Harris 1991:3). This is taken from *the* leading English monograph on precedent. The definition was endorsed by the court of Appeal and may itself resemble a ratio decidendi. See R. (Kadhim) v. Brent London Borough Council Housing Benefit Review Board [2001] 2 W.L.R. 674.

[16] The notion and practice of relying on precedents developed over a longue durée (see Alien 1964:187–235). Only in the nineteenth and twentieth centuries the modern rule emerged whereby precedents decided by higher courts can be binding even if 'unreasonable and inconvenient'. This development was furthered by the regularisation and improvements in law reporting subsequent to the establishment of the Incorporated Council of Law Reporting and the reorganisation of the courts with a clear hierarchical structure in 1873.

based, detached or abstracted from the specific peculiarities of the particular case which gives rise to the decision" (Halsbury's Laws of England 2000:573). Any statement of law that is not an essential part of the ratio decidendi is called *obiter dictum*. This might be a proposition which concerns a matter which has not been raised in the case or which is more general/wider than necessary for the facts of the case at hand. Obiter dicta do not form part of the binding precedent. However, they can be taken into consideration in later cases as persuasive authority if the judge considers it appropriate to do so; likewise, precedents that are not technically binding can be cited as persuasive or well reasoned.

The archive of the case-system

The multi-faceted and distributed case-archive is operated through lists or indexes typically appearing on the first pages of legal publications. See for instance the "Table of Cases" included in the Archbold (2000), the 'bible' for criminal law practitioners:

Table of Cases

Allen (1866) 10 Cox 406	2–74
—— (1872) L.R. 1 C.C.R. 367	31–8
—— [1965] 2 Q.B. 295; [1964] 3 W.L.R. 1173; [1964] 3 All E.R. 401; 48 Cr.App.R. 314	4–404q
—— [1985] A.C. 1029; [1985] 3 W.L.R. 107; [1985] 2 All E.R. 641; 81 Cr.App.R. 200; [1985] Crim.L.R. 739, HL; affirming [1985] 1 W.L.R. 50	21–352
——, 9 Cr.App.R.(S.) 169, CA	5–194, 5–198
—— [1992] Crim.L.R. 297, CA	15–441
—— [1995] Crim.L.R. 643, CA	15–15
—— (K.) [1988] Crim.L.R. 698, CA	17–104
—— v. Chief Constable of Cheshire Constabulary, *The Times*, July 16, 1988, CA (Civ Div)	15–130
—— v. Westley (1629) Hetley 97	28–162
Allgood, ex p., *The Times*, November 25, 1994, DC	1–71, 21–159
Allison (1806) R. & R. 109	31–8, 31–11
——, unreported, January 31, 1977	5–549
Almon (1765) Wilm. 243; 97 E.R. 94	28–108
—— (1770) 20 St. Tr. 803; 5 Burr. 2686	25–267, 28–40
Alowi [1999] 5 *Archbold News* 2, CA (97 08493 W3)	4–262, 4–433, 4–447, 4–450

Fig. 27: Extract from Table of Cases in Archbold (2000)

Such A-Z lists deserve closer examination. Here, cases have a name, a year and some characters and numbers to it, altogether constituting a code. The characters after the year in brackets signify the source, i.e., the law report publishing a case, such as The Law Reports, Appeals Cases ("A.C.") or the All England Law Reports ("All E.R."), specialist series and journals ("Crim. L.R." = Criminal Law Review), less often other law books or their supplements ("Archbold News"), and newspapers ("The Times"). Rarely, a case is listed as "unreported" ("Allison January 31, 1977"). The same case can appear in several law reports, e.g. the Allen case, according to this index, was reported in different law reports: in "[1965] 2 Q.B. 295; [1964] 3 W.L.R. 1173; [1964] 3 All E.R. 401; 48 Cr.App.R. 314." At the same time, the attached page numbers show where exactly cases are mentioned in the Archbold, e.g. "Alowi in chapter 4, paragraphs 262, 433, 447 and 450."

The "Table of Cases" can be read similarly to a telephone book: the code derives from the name of the defendant (while "R v" remains the general reference to the official counterpart: the prosecution representing the Crown, and is thus omitted in the Archbold's list of cases). These names are sorted alphabetically and by years. The addresses allow caseworker, law student, or lawyer to visit the more or less comprehensive versions of the case. At the same time, a case can be immediately called up(on) in the Archbold under given page numbers and paragraphs. Here, one would find one case mentioned in various contexts, for instance, the Alowi case is related to questions such as the "effect of discharge," "majority verdicts," "receiving the verdict," etc. The overall "Table of Cases" combined with the various text passages in the law book reveal a network of references and cross-references. The (use of) references resemble academic citations: they demonstrate that one is knowledgeable of authorities and that one can apply them to the matter at hand.

The integration of the case-system and the relevance of a case in terms of ruling and precedence depend on an elaborated report system. Any legal system based on judicial precedent requires an effective archive by which authoritative cases are reported and indexed. It seems somewhat paradoxical that there are no official series of law reports in England. The publication of cases is traditionally in the hands of private publishers. The reports enjoy different grades of authority: in England and Wales, "The Law Reports" are most authoritative. They have been published since 1865 by the Incorporated Council of Law Reporting for England and Wales. Its reporters are barristers or solicitors who are in court for the hearing and for the handing down of judgment. Their reports are then sent to the judges and counsel concerned for approval prior to publication. "The Weekly Law Reports" as well as the "All England Law Reports" obtain less authority. Specialist series, journals, and newspaper reports are at the low end of this hierarchy.

The reports offer a continual and concise overview of criminal cases to a wider audience: to legal practitioners and students of law, to legal academics and the judicial administration, to law enforcement agencies and to more or less critical lobby groups. The reported case together with its extensions in keyword lists and subject collections constitutes the most saturated version of the legal case once it has been decided. It is not the courts but the law report editors who select and revise cases for publication. The diverse reports involve differing coverage and presentation of cases. The overall format, however, remains similar. The reports include:

> Names of parties, address, court in which case was decided; name of judge/s; date/s of hearing; keywords; headnote (case summary) by the editor; lists of cases discussed and cited; previous history of the litigation incl. summary of claims made and result of proceedings in lower courts; facts, names of counsel; sometimes arguments of counsel; the judgment/s in full-text or summary; order of court (and indication whether leave to appeal is granted or refused); names of solicitors; name of reporter.

The parts are interconnected to each other and allow multiple access points to cases. One case is searchable and available in multiple ways. Interestingly enough, the law report editors would limit the number of cases reportable in their law reports. Williams provides some indication for the criteria of this selection: "Law reports are reports of the more important cases decided by the superior courts. Not all cases are reported: only those of legal interest" (1982:34). The Law Reporting Committee (HMSO 1940) phrases it more poetically: "What remains [unreported judgments] is less likely to be a treasure house than a rubbish heap in which a jewel will rarely, if ever, be discovered." Selection seems unavoidable in order to render cases relevant. Criteria for selection are provided by the ICLR:

1. All cases which introduce, or appear to introduce, a new principle or a new rule.
2. All cases which materially modify an existing principle or rule.
3. All cases which settle, or materially tend to settle, a question upon which the law is doubtful.
4. All cases which for any reason are peculiarly instructive.[17]

[17] These points go back to a Paper on Legal Reports by Nathaniel Lindley QC prior to establishment of ICLR, see http://www.lawreports.co.uk/Publications/siforward.htm#I.

Not included should be cases, which are passed without discussion, which are valueless as precedents, which are substantially repetitions of what has been reported before. And furthermore, reports should be accurate, contain everything material and useful; particularly, they should name the parties, the nature of the pleadings, the essential facts, the points contended for by counsel, the grounds on which the judgment was based, and the judgment as actually pronounced.

The selection and formatting of cases hint towards the practical implications of law reports.[18] For legal practitioners, the abundance of previously decided cases is reduced and, moreover, made available through several mechanisms: for instance, cases are located in an existing body of law; cases are placed in chains of traditions; cases are placed vis-à-vis analogous cases, meaning in relation to similar/distinguishable or typical/atypical ones; or cases are placed in a court hierarchy, meaning in a tableau of relevancy. In retrospection, cases are promoted by the archival and categorical work. This way, the reporting produces, for example, "landmark cases" marking "a significant turning point on a particular issue" (Webster's Law Dictionary 1996) or "settl[ing] some important point and [being] frequently cited as a precedent" (Oxford English Dictionary 2009). Cases gain or lose weight and significance over time. New cases together with the archive ready at hand invite the practitioners to re-trace and reconstruct legal tradition. Being reported grants a case a good chance to have wider implications beyond its own life time, to stretch out into new and future cases.

In theory, a case may be cited as a precedent even it if has not been reported.[19] In practice, though, comparatively few cases are referred to in textbooks or cited in court unless they have been reported in one of the series of law reports. However, 'direct' references are becoming more common, given the newest developments of information and communication technology; online databases providing full-text judgments are growing now. Free online databases such as BAILII or

---

[18] There are, of course, academic dimensions as well: law reports provide the material and intellectual resources to observe historic developments of the overall case-system. Ibbetson and Wijffels (1997) provide an account of early judicial records and law reports in continental Europe, England, and America in light of their significance for the development of case-law.

[19] Unreported judgments can – if not included in online databases – be found differently, e.g., transcripts of judgments of the Court of Appeal (Criminal Division) from 1960 onwards are archived in the Criminal Appeals' Office in the Royal Courts of Justice; copies of unreported House of Lords decisions are kept in the House of Lords Records Office.

commercial, subscription-based online databases such as LexisNexis (Smith et al. 2002, Hanson 1999) extend the archive and therefore the sources that enter the construction of rule-traditions. The controversies and rivalry between private publishers of reports and the 'Free the Law'-movement remind of extra-functions of case-archives (cf. Brooke LJ 2003; Freedman and Ury 2008). The open archives warrant fairness, equality, justice for those working in the field of law and for those exposed to it.[20] The archives keep the judicial system transparent – and bound to legal tradition. Recent developments led to the adoption of minimal standards in both public and private case reports, to new regulations concerning "copyrights on case transcripts", the inclusion of paragraph numbers, and the introduction of a "neutral citation" (Brooke LJ 2003) for ease of reference.[21]

So far, we analysed cases that were different to the cases dealt with in the previous 'case-making'-chapters. The alibi-case, the sleepwalking-case, the 'I was not finished' case, the murder-case – none of these exceptional specimens were reported and circulated in the case-system. They appeared, however, somewhere: in regional and federal statistics, in judicial evaluations, in executive figures, etc. These appearances are 'off the case', because they no longer communicate the tripartite case-sign. They are reductionist because they isolate components and count or process just case-fragments.

---

[20] Brooke LJ considers the pros and cons of free access to cases online as follows: "The good side of all this is that we are creating a level playing field, and those of us who are interpreting the law in the higher courts are being supplied with up to date copies of unreported judgments relevant to the points we are deciding. ... The law would be in chaos if our early decisions were being made in ignorance of what another court had been saying on the same point... This does not only mean that people immediately know what the law is. It also means that press comment is more likely to be accurate, because we are treating the Press like adults...The bad side is that we often suffer from information overload. Cases are cited to us which decide no new point of law, and which merely illustrate the application of familiar law to a new set of facts. We published a practice direction last year to try and bring things under some sort of control, but very often lawyers can't recognize a principle of law when they see one. We are getting steadily more and more overloaded with citations of cases which frequently don't help us in the task we have got to do, but which just add to the paper we have to read" (2003).

[21] See for England and Wales: Practice Statement on Judgments (22nd April 1998), Further Practice Statement on Judgments (25th November 1998), Practice Direction on the Form of Judgments, Paragraph Marking, and Neutral Citation (11th January 2001), Practice Direction on Citation of Authorities (10th April 2001), and Practice Direction on Neutral Citations (14th January 2002).

Off the case: components in isolation

Reports allow for retracing the single case back to the actual court proceedings. However, not all representations of case keep the case-sources available. Some do not offer a balanced or focussed composition of matter, rule, and decision. They isolate components for administrative, managerial, educative, or regulative purposes. This is the case with the presentation of real-life matter in teaching examples. At law schools, 'cases' are presented as problems without any rule or decision to it. Such as this exercise from "OCR," the Oxford, Cambridge, and RSA Examinations:

> While shopping Susan places some items of food in the wire basket which is provided. She also hides a bottle of perfume in her coat pocket. She then takes a label off an expensive CD, switches it with the label from a reduced price CD and places the expensive one in the basket. She goes to the checkout and only pays for the items in the basket. Outside the shop Susan sees a bike which was there when she went in and which she remembers seeing there for several days. She rides home on it alongside a caravan park. She notices a personal CD player on a table inside one of the caravans. She goes inside and takes the CD player. She leaves the bike at the end of her road and goes home. (GCE Law Mark Scheme for the Units June 2008:34–35).

Here, the tripartite composition of case is pried open; the facts are all there is. What reminds, at first sight, of a unit in an English language course for speakers of foreign languages, will be complemented by an exam question such as: "Discuss Susan's potential criminal liability for the above incidents" (OCR 2008:35). This is a hypothetical case, a narration of 'someone doing something' which resembles 'reality out there' just closely enough to apply given rules to it. The case is exemplary, an arrangement of acts and objects. There is no natural person to deal with, no further context to consider, no other version of the story to win against. It resembles the dream of legal doctrine. (Similar cases serve as basic material for moot courts inviting students to enact and perform a trial.) What is expected of students here is to spot the relevant legal issues and develop 'right' legal solutions for the given problem combination (Kerr 2007). The marking scheme for examiners defines the following standard solutions:

> Assessment Objective 1 (25 marks); Define theft, Theft Act 1968; Refer to appropriation S.3 and *McPherson; Morris; Gomez; Hinks;* etc as regards the items in the shop and show knowledge and understanding of the

> assumption of rights of the owner; Refer to S.2 (1) (c) Theft Act with regard to dishonesty and *Small;* Explain S.6 (1) Theft Act with regard to 'borrowing' of the bike; Define burglary S.9 (1) (a) Theft Act 1969; Explain the term 'inhabited vessel' by reference to the S.9 (4) Theft Act 1968; Credit reference to a potential reasoned argument for a S.9 (1)(a)/(b) burglary for the incidents in the shop...; Discuss whether a caravan, which can be an 'inhabited vehicle' S.9 (4), is capable of being a 'building' within S.9 and reasoning that she 'enters' it with the intention to steal.

It becomes clear from the earlier elaboration of the case as systemic token that such arrangements of pure matter would not enter the case-system. However, it still refers to the case-system, insofar as it supports the general idea that matter, rule and decision operate in a succession – and not in feedback loops or in interrelation.

Another single-edged construction of cases can be found in terms of rule. Here, the legal system offers representations of how cases are dealt with in general and where a case should be and is expected to be according to the program or regulations. Let us consider the following depiction of the Crown Court procedure for Not Guilty plea cases according to the Office for Criminal Justice Reform (2008). The plan shows how "The Adult Criminal Case Management Framework" works in chronological and synchronic order[22]:

Here, the case is not an individual case, but a standard "adult criminal case." There is no real-life matter attached to it. There is only the promise of a decision to be reached at one procedural stage. The depiction comes down to a route map that is both, the outcome and the object of political regulations and judicial evaluation and controlling. By such route maps, cases are controlled, streamlined, and evaluated.

Case categories are no longer attached to categorized matter, but to a managerial and technical terminology. We find summary cases, either-way cases, indictable only cases, guilty plea cases, not guilty plea cases, etc. The categories relate to templates or standards of 'to do'-lists, to input-output models, to forms to be filled out, and statistics to be reported. The case is only an abstracted, disaggregated, one-directional 'task' with minimal, obligatory components to it: participants, activities, choices, duties, deadlines, etc. The program level is far from just normative or just ideal-typical. It causes practical problems and solutions en masse. It channels the practices of case-making. It organises money flows and legal aid schemes. It makes lawyers hurry or relax.

---

[22] For details see http://ccmf.cjsonline.gov.uk/adult/crown/index.html.

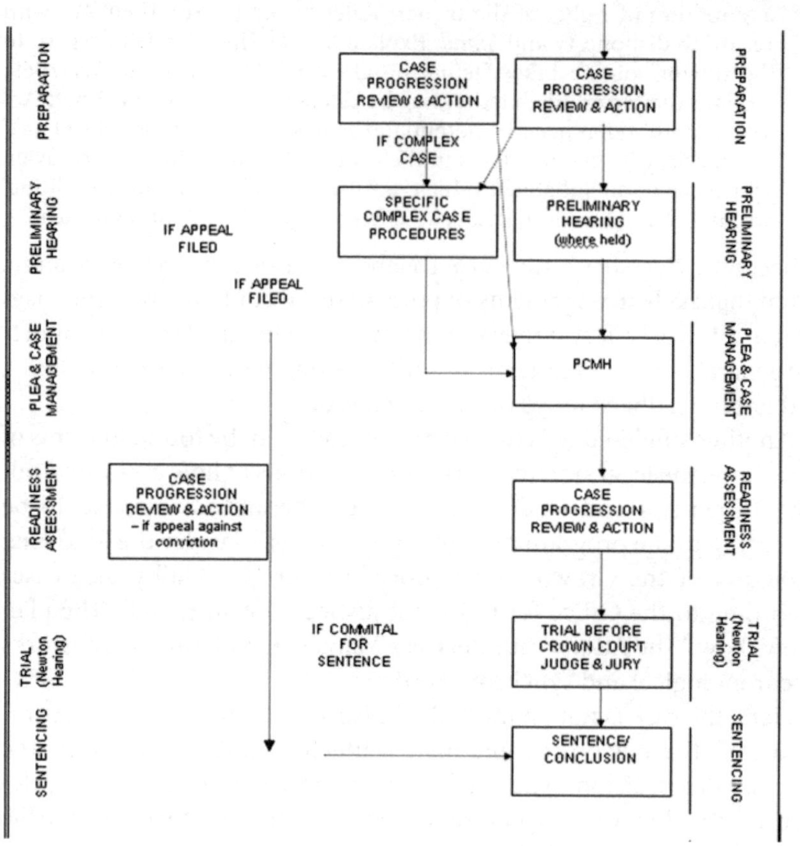

Fig. 28: "The Adult Criminal Case Management Framework" (Office for Criminal Justice Reform 2008)

Cases are disaggregated in another form as well. We find cases reduced to pure decision. The latter are counted and compared over space and in time, which means from district to district and from period to period. The Department for Constitutional Affairs,[23] for instance, published the following "Judicial Statistics Annual Report" for the year 2002 isolating specific forms of finalisation of Crown Court cases:[24]

[23] Now the Ministry of Justice is responsible for this kind of information (http://www.justice.gov.uk).

[24] See http://www.dca.gov.uk/publications/annual_reports/2002/judstat02_ch06.pdf.

Table 6.7
Cracked trials: By reason for crack, 2002

	Defendant pleads guilty		Prosecution accepts plea		No evidence offered		Bind over		Unfit to plead/ deceased		Total
	number	%	number	%	number	%	number	%	number	%	number
Circuit											
Midland	2,381	59.1	743	18.4	772	19.2	131	3.2	4	0.1	4,031
North Eastern	2,274	68.4	540	16.2	444	13.4	66	2.0	1	-	3,325
Northern	3,026	68.3	589	13.3	696	15.7	115	2.6	3	0.1	4,429
South Eastern:											
London	1,887	55.9	341	10.1	1,046	31.0	94	2.8	7	0.2	3,375
Provinces	1,414	65.8	294	13.7	393	18.3	46	2.1	3	0.1	2,150
Wales & Chester	676	65.3	242	23.4	99	9.6	19	1.8	-	-	1,036
Western	786	60.9	234	18.1	225	17.4	42	3.3	3	0.2	1,290
England & Wales	**12,444**	**63.4**	**2,983**	**15.2**	**3,675**	**18.7**	**513**	**2.6**	**21**	**0.1**	**19,636**

Fig. 29: Judicial Statistics Annual Report for 2002

Cases are re-specified as "cracked trials," meaning cases which were listed at Crown Court for a trial by jury but were disposed of in some other way on the day of trial. The table accounts for surprises and variations in procedural course: case files are being closed by decisions 'off track', e.g. when "defendants plead guilty," "prosecution accepts plea" of guilty to an alternative charge, "no evidence [is] offered" by the prosecution, or when defendants are bound over in a sum of money to keep the peace. Unfitness to plead or death on the part of the defendant also turns 'intact' cases into 'cracked' trials. Here, we encounter a snapshot of case at the point of finalisation. However, obviously, the reader of these statistics is not asked to study the individual cases. Nameless and faceless figures are differentiated according to Crown Court Circuits for 2002, raising or minimising, in result, the total number of 19,636 in England and Wales. Whether this figure is alarming or pleasing is a different story that can be told only with recourse to similar statistics for previous and coming years.

In this example, representation moves as far as separating cases from their trinity of matter, rule and decision. The "Judicial Statistics: Annual Reports" provide dozens of tables which use and relate various components and elements of the case: tables reporting cases as received, disposed, and outstanding, committed for trial, for sentence, cases classified by type of judge, by verdict, by waiting times, etc., as well as cases as trials or defendants.[25] The once tripartite case is amassed and accumulated and is turned into a provisional indicator of workload and 'trends' in judicial handling of criminal cases.[26] From here, the pure figures, there is no way back to the triply signifying case, not to speak about the events and processes of case-making that went into it.

In a similar fashion, the Crown Court documents and monitors its own work over time through cases even though they may not be immediately 'visible' anymore as exemplified in the following table, extracted from the "Crown Court Annual Report 2002/03" – Table of Courts.[27]

Code	Names	KPI 5	Average Waiting Time (weeks)	% committals outstanding over 16 weeks	Disposal Rate	Courtroom Usage (hours)	Cracked Trial Rate	Ineffective Trial Rate	Days jurors sit as a % of attendance and non attendance
446	Plymouth	78.9%	13.21	41.9%	0.82	3.82	15.2%	26.9%	51.7%
447	Portsmouth	84.2%	12.98	22.4%	0.67	3.73	16.1%	17.6%	61.5%
448	Preston	67.0%	20.42	37.8%	0.93	4.43	32.3%	27.6%	60.7%
449	Reading	74.5%	15.13	45.1%	0.62	4.44	18.7%	30.4%	68.0%

Fig. 30: *Table of Courts in Crown Court Annual Report 2002/03*

[25] Statistical information on criminal cases and the courts varies with respect to differences in the data collation and the counting and validation rules used which reflect "the different underlying drivers of the analyses being performed. By way of broad illustration, CS [Criminal Statistics] counts numbers of defendants and is focused on the final outcomes of criminal court proceedings, while JCS [Judicial and Court Statistics] counts numbers of cases and is focused on flows through the court system" (Criminal Statistics: England and Wales 2007:147).

[26] Case representations within the "CPS Management Information System" seem different from these rather 'neutral' case extractions in the Judicial Statistics: in monthly reports on the Crown Prosecution Service's overall performance, prosecution-cases are distinguished as "convictions" and "unsuccessful" (depicted in graphics as gentle blue and distressing red respectively). Not cases serve as problems to be solved, but "defendants" and "number of defendants" that were unsuccessfully prosecuted. The statistics imply that the defendants are in fact 'criminals' that 'in principal' deserve punishment, but 'too often' go free. Breaking down case outcomes into the two categories of conviction and unsuccessful outcomes insinuates that the CPS performs well when all cases handled by them are finalised by conviction; there is a strong normative component in this representation of caseload as an indicator of performance. As performance management information, cases as figures are used in order to document and monitor the institutional output (case as a working unit of the CPS). They are reduced to certain elements which are deemed 'expressive' to maintain, lubricate, record, evaluate, and control the workings of the criminal justice system. The CPS' performance, one may infer, is not a function of justice (it does not seem to depend on the question whether each conviction was safe or just). For details, see http://www.cps.gov.uk/publications/performance/case_outcomes/.

[27] http://www.hmcourts-service.gov.uk/docs/crown_court_stats02-03.pdf

These Court tables are produced annually by the Court Service collating information provided by all Crown and County Court Centres. Here, the performance of alphabetically listed Crown Court centres is evaluated on the basis of eight key performance measures which ask no more for matter, rule or decision, but for speed ("Disposal Rate"), for capacity utilization ("Courtroom usage"), or other measures of efficiency or malpractice. Administrative, managerial and reform-orientated questions are guiding these (non-)case representations. Cases are not more than mathematical parts of statistical measures: factors, multipliers, divisors.[28] They are units of the judicial business and count according to the simple distinction: done or not done with.

On this policy and reform-orientated level, the case has vanished in the course of absolute and relative calculations. These 'empty skins' of cases can then be compared for each area over time, and be referred to, e.g. by Court Managers as well as resident judges as reasons for shame (poor performance) or pride (good performance):

> I am pleased to report that this year's statistics show a most significant improvement in performance in a number of key areas. The number of receipts was more or less constant but the disposals were up 14%, the disposal rate was up 8%, the number of stale cases fell significantly and the outstanding trials were reduced by 28% (as against a national average reduction of just 3%). In fact in recent months the KPI 5 (78% of all cases being met within target) has been met. Even with the disruption to be caused by the structural works resulting from the Courts and Tribunals Modernisation Programme, I confidently look forward to even better figures next year. This is a considerable achievement reflecting credit on the court managers and staff and indeed on the judges working in partnership and co-operation. (Resident Judge of Preston Crown Court, Crown Court Annual report 2002–2003:67–68)

This is not about justice, it seems, it is about "better figures." One does not need to be overly sarcastic, though. Striving for justice in (individual) criminal cases just seems to be delegated to other levels and domains with their own text corpus, e.g. reform papers.[29]

---

[28] Consider, e.g. the definition of key performance indicator (KPI) 5: "Calculated using the number of committed trials commencing within 16 weeks plus the number of cases sent for trial commencing within 26 weeks plus the number of sentences dealt with in 10 weeks plus the number of appeals dealt with all divided by the total number of trials, sentences and appeals disposed of. The Court Service target is 78%. This year's performance figure across England and Wales is 79.5% compared to 76% in 2000/2001 and 77.6% in 2001/2002."

[29] For example, see the CJS White paper "Justice for All" (2002) which uses (administrative) cases in form of statistical data. Again, cases are purified: "During 2001–02

We stop our grand tour of the various representations of case in the adversarial case-system at this point. Our aim was to demonstrate the various signifying relation of the case in the case-system. The case – as a multi-faceted unit – functions when it links up to and when it creates relevance in relation to matter, rule and decision in other cases. The case keeps the case-system integrated and going. It memorises and actualizes legal knowledge in various, standardized respects. One case, therefore, can re-appear and act upon a number of different legal issues.

The fieldwork in the law firm, the chambers and the Crown Court revealed that and how case-makers are busy in keeping deadlines, serving formal requirements, and pleasing their camp. Case-making contributes to the case-system by ultimately delivering cases. Case-making prolongs some rulings and standards by means of re-specification; it enacts some authoritative decisions by breaking them down; it places a slightly new matter in the scope of illegality and criminality. However, it would be largely misleading to conclude that the case-makers contributed to the case-system directly and deliberately. They are, first of all, occupied with the case-at-hand, and when working on burning issues, cannot help but apply rules, taking decisions, and specifying matter. The reconstruction of case-making, on the one hand, retrieves excesses of details, norms and selections, while on the other hand, it sheds light on methods that render these excesses momentary. Case-making forgets most of its transitional stages: its attempts, tests, and troubles. What remains for all legal purposes, instead, is *the* case.

In the ensuing conclusion, I argue for a complex understanding of adversarial case-making. The complexity derives not only from the many case-making agents, methods, practices, resources, and sites, but as well from the diverse courses of meaning-production. There are various mechanisms at work that turn fleeting utterances into lasting

---

recorded crime totalled 5.5 million. The police only successfully detected 23% of these offences that is 1.20 million…. Of these detected cases there were the following outcomes: 12% of those bailed to appear at court fail to do so; nearly a quarter of defendants commit at least one offence whilst on bail – rising to 38% of offenders under 18…" In this governmental policy paper, which aims at focusing "the CJS on its purpose – fighting and reducing crime and delivering justice on behalf of victims, defendants and the community" (13), cases are used both as quality markers of the current state of the criminal justice system and as indicators of justice gaps. Extrapolations from cases (excess of decisions) attest to certain shortcomings in the criminal justice system; these 'faults' shall be eradicated by re-programming the case procedure.

statements: we find 'procedural relevance' by ways of staging, mobilisation, and replication. These mechanisms give rise to fully-fledged cases only when being methodically combined. The trans-sequentiality of case-making carries further implications in terms of law-in-action, in terms of participation and procedure, and in terms of a basic distinction in comparative law: adversarial vs. inquisitorial.

CONCLUSION: THE MICRO-FOUNDATIONS OF ADVERSARIALISM

This legal ethnography was a journey to the heartland of adversarialism: to the land of, in Kagan's categories, "formal legal contestation," "litigant activism," and "substantive uncertainty" (1994:3 sq.), where a "weak centre" and "two competing and fact-finding parties" provide the grounds for the "democratic deliberation of the decision" (Kagan 2003:3). However, the destination was not what legal or political scholars would expect it to be. The journey did *not* lead the socio-legal ethnographer to all "policy arenas and administrative systems" of a country and its legal culture. I did not travel every area of decision-making, covering "policy-making, policy implementation, and dispute resolution by means of lawyer-dominated litigation" (Ibid.).

I approached the heartland of adversarialism by staying in North-western England. I visited one region, one law firm, one Barrister's Chamber, and two Crown Court centres. How could I then elaborate on adversarialism? Different to Kagan and his followers and critiques, I approached the very details of law-in-action, of casework and its procedure. This movement to the micro-foundation resembles a methodological manoeuvre that produces peculiar objects of study. Instead of quoting from 'major' statutes or programs, the author analysed 'minor' cases, file notes, protocol excerpts, jottings, and field observations. By turning to the micro-level, to case-making and its materials, I circumvented certain presumptions: for instance, that one pattern is at work throughout all aspects of legal culture, no matter whether criminal or civil law, legislation or administration, low court or high court.[1] By turning to the micro-level, I encountered a confusing nexus of moments, techniques, and tactics – all dedicated to case-making at its procedural stage (not to law or legal norms as such). From within, something like *the* English legal system or *the* adversarial culture looks like being differentiated in procedural regimes, each procedure

[1] The big picture forces Kagan to elide differences within the 'more or less' homogenous legal culture: "Adversarial legalism is not uniformly distributed throughout the American legal order. Some policy arenas and administrative systems are rather free of litigation and the threat of it. Some communities, subcultures, and industries disparage and eschew legal contestation" (1994:5).

demanding different moves. In this view, what appeared as a demarcated legal culture or system seems no longer separated from other 'patchworks', meaning from other cultures or systems.[2]

This ethnography is small in scope. I restricted my interrogation of adversarial case-making to one procedural regime: the English Crown Court. I reconstructed procedural (discourse) practices from one position: here, putting together a case for the defence (see chapter III for the only exception). These specifications did not, as one might expect, lead to a clear-cut picture of the workings of adversarialism, its rationale, its efficacy. The opposite is true: the narrowed view allowed the local 'jumble' back in. The narrow focus allowed for a 'thick description' of what is going on where and when in the procedural course and certain cases.

I allowed myself another twist that may take aback socio-legal scholars for whom law-in-action is synonymous with evaluation or interpretation. I did not examine whether the law is applied precisely; I did not restrict the status of law to a situated interpretative task. The study of case-making diverts from these paradigmatic versions of law-in-action in that it focuses on the activities, methods and resources that are necessary to contribute to and participate in *this* procedure. This 'tight' context allowed my research to move closer to the actual circumstances and to grasp nuances, such as the defendant's hesitation to contribute, the emotional work of the solicitor, or early ideas and their failing. This book demonstrates how case-making involves events and processes, how its interim results turn into circumstances for subsequent events, and how this historicity creates awkward speech positions, especially, but not exclusively, in court.

The empirical cases – the alibi-case (chapter I), the "I was not ready yet"-case (chapter V), the sleep-walking-case (chapter III), the unregretful murderer-case (chapter VII) – together with the conceptual sites – event/process relations (chapter II), file-work (chapter IV), resources (chapter VI), case-signs (chapter VIII) – revealed, I conclude, different mechanisms of case-making. The participants serve, operate, and utilize the mechanisms to their best knowledge(s). Knowing how to control the mechanisms and knowing where and when control is infeasible, distinguishes lawyers from laypeople, experienced from inexperienced participants.

---

[2] The legal comparativist, David Nelken, criticized "Kagan's insistence on putting U.S. law into a class of its own" (2001:813) and his denial of any differences in degree.

The mechanisms of case-making translate momentary expressions into lasting statements. The mechanisms convey legal relevance – and they do so in profoundly different ways. Adversarial case-making employs three mechanisms and by doing so unfolds three event/process relations: mobilisation, replication, and staging. *Mobilisation* renders statements relevant by way of manipulations on the procedural backstage; *replication* invokes statements as official versions of the same and accentuates similarities and differences; *staging* allows for the direct utilisation of utterances as statements by way of symbolic speech-positions in open court.

The three mechanisms do not generate one determinate discourse machinery. However, they gear case-making to a certain level of saturation and qualification. They allow several choices, while disallowing certain 'late', 'displaced' and 'inappropriate' contributions. Hence, what seems determinate and automatic from a discourse analytical distance turns contingent under the ethnographic microscope. Professional and lay case-makers try their best in operating the mechanisms, in calculating their effects, in deploying them 'successfully', in avoiding mistakes. This general panorama includes insights like the following: The mechanisms of case-making are, firstly, not invented by the actors, but juggled with enormous skill. Secondly, the procedural infrastructure, the professional ethics, and the cultural techniques and methods are closely entwined with and enforced by the case-making mechanisms. The mechanisms are, thirdly, not integrated to one homogeneous force or apparatus, but are rather heterogeneous and disruptive. They involve contingency, rather than overcoming or controlling it.

Mechanisms of case-making

How is something qualified as legally relevant in the Crown Court procedure? The answer cannot be deduced from the case as end-product. Case-making frequently updates statements-in-formation, whereas case-signs update the overall case-system. Case-signs extend an identified path of rule, decision, and matter, whereas case-making invites and, later on, interrupts an excess of rule, decision and matter[3].

[3] There is an excess of ruling by rituals, architecture, discursive formats, professional methods, etc. There is an excess of decision-making in the procedural course involving not just the judge, but decisions by witnesses, experts and lawyers as the

The mechanisms of case-making cut through the mix of 'potentials' and 'candidates', establishing different points of no return and different qualifications. Case-making only eventually, once the cases are fully delegated to the judges of the facts and the judge of the law, obtain one compatible triad: *the* case. Adversarial case-making, thus, does not contribute to the case-system in a straight and linear fashion. It deals with other components and operates first and foremost within another field. The tri-partite case-sign emerges as a by-product; it is not the primary aspiration of case-making in the Crown Court procedure.[4]

There are three mechanisms of case-making, meaning three different ways to guide local utterances to procedurally relevant contributions:

	Staging	**Replication**	**Mobilisation**
What is the paradigmatic situation?	Testimony under oath	Repeated question	Drafting a statement
Site of transformation?	Public arena / front region	Series of procedural events	Internal public / back region
From utterance to statement?	A jump / identical	More of the same	Composition / improvement
Resource?	Courtroom / speaker's body	File as archive / protocols	File as scrapbook / drafts
Resulting case representation?	Fresh talk	Archival speech	Scripted speech
Main temporal orientation	Procedural present	Procedural past	Procedural future

Fig. 31: Mechanisms of Case-making

As the table suggests, adversarial case-making takes place at different sites, in different rhythms, and supported by different resources. Depending on the mechanism of case-making, 'contributing' and 'participating' mean different things. How do the mechanisms work?

ones who invest into statements. There is an excess of matter due to the two parallel projects of case-making, due to the clients' ever changing versions, and due to the communal gossip and speculation.

[4] This is different in constitutional courts or in, so called, test cases. The law's status varies depending on the procedure of its application.

Mobilisation favours process over event. It emphasises the solicitors' resourceful filing, the professional design process, and socially assigned career stages. Statements gain relevance by meticulous mobilising activities: brainstorming, drafting sessions, witness-recruitment, etc. (chapter I). The same applies to other features, such as the client's morality (chapter VII) or the expert's image (chapter III). Mobilisation takes place on the backstages of procedure, flanked by rules of discretion and professional ethics of confidentiality. The plans and aspirations, the assessments and adjustments, the interim results and their weak links are kept within the party. Mobilisation proceeds by more or less promising projects that internally configure the case as a dependent optimum. In its course, mobilisation leaves behind previous projects and tends towards tasks, to-do-lists, and the attainable future. Mobilisation gives the impression that in *this* case there is always already something to develop further or to refine. Definitions of adversarialism emphasize the independent role of the parties when it comes to fact-finding – and they contrast this with the centred truth-finding of the inquisitorial bureaucracy. In this line, mobilisation is an adversarial mechanism par excellence.

Replication balances events and process. It couples the "documentary method of interrogation" and archival practices to collect 'more of the same'. Replication echoes the bureaucratic character of procedure. It employs authoritative techniques and resources of memorising (e.g., disclosed protocols reminding of a "shared dossier") that are identified with inquisitorial systems such as Germany or France. In this line, prosecution *and* defence overlook 'originals' to be tested in open court. Replication is feasible due to the police inquiry and due to a programmed series of hearings. Here, a version becomes relevant not because it has been deliberately designed on the backstage, but because it is re-used at various procedural sites. Relevance derives from repetition and difference. In light of former versions, relevance (as, e.g., incoherence) shows often at points that are substantially marginal. Trained case-makers produce replica by repeating questions, themes, or concerns – and by placing dispersed responses right next to each other (see chapter V). Replication gives the impression that a statement has always already existed as such. It performs 'one original version' that binds all subsequent representations. Replication provides decision-makers with reasoning powers by way of its text-bias.

Staging enjoys most popularity in the media as well as in socio-legal research. It favours event over process, embodied speech over intertextuality. Staging is flanked by the rules of evidence[5] and an interaction order, altogether enforcing an experimental setting, promising judge and jury direct access to the facts. Staging serves as a rupture; it opens up contingency in relation to mobilisation and replication. Staging renders something relevant because and insofar it emerges right here and right now. Something gains relevance as evidence because and only if it is supplied from the witness-stand in the order of speech (acts). Due to staging, the trial hearing appears as the decisive procedural moment: Does she remember? Will he give evidence? Can she respond to this attack? Does his body language reveal guilt? Stage and staging allow for far-reaching reception: something is of weight by the very second of it being spoken. The pressure is on the witness, who needs to stand the interrogation, the critical gazes, the publicity, etc. Adversarial case-making often falls short, because people are not willing to appear as witnesses on the court-stage. Staging infuses the procedure with openness, surprise, and tension. Context, within this mechanism, is a matter of adjacent turn-pairs (mainly: question/answer) and their symbolic/procedural amplification.

It is clear now, why the case-signs' re-specifications are of quite a different nature than the mechanisms of case-making. The re-specifications operate 'on top of', not in concert with staging, replication, and mobilisation. They take place after the case is completed and take over once case-making has come to a halt. Re-specifications do not add new components, only new relations and accentuation. They operate with the rules, matter, and decision that have been identified and laid down with the case. The case as a sign, however, does not carry a definite meaning. It sets off for an additional career without its case-makers. In what follows, the ruled, defined, and decided case will relate to other cases concerning their application of rules, selection of matter, and reasoning of decisions.

Complexities of case-making

Adversarial case-making cannot be reduced to talk or text, to trial or pre-trial, to lawyer or client, to event or process. It cannot hinge on just one mechanism or the other. We do not find, moreover, a neat sequence

[5] Certain 'indirect' demonstrations are generally devalued, such as reading out written statements or delivering 'just' hearsay.

of mechanisms: one after the other. This is why this book does not offer one chapter on staging, one on replication, and one on mobilization. Instead, there were various instances, projects, sites, and protagonists of case-making. Case-studies and cross-case studies showed case-making as a complex achievement. Mechanisms of case-making always only emerged in combination. The alibi's changing relevance (chapter I), for instance, was a result not only of mobilisation, but also of replicated statements; the same applies to the relevance of the "single blow" (chapter V), the "sleep-walking defence" (chapter III), or the "inability to regret" (chapter VII) all deriving from a combination of mechanisms. The same applies to the cross-case studies: the solicitors' file-work turns out being applicable when it supports mobilisation, replication, and staging alike (chapter IV); the procedural infrastructure (chapter VI) engages resources with a tendency towards mobilisation (file and file-notes), staging (court as interaction order) or replication (the story across various mediations). In these ways, the ethnography does not provide simple answers to the question of how criminal cases come about in the Crown Court procedure. Adversarial case-making is distributed not just in terms of the various members, sites, and materials contributing to it, but also in terms of the three mechanisms imparting basic relevance.

A sequential analysis of just staging, just mobilisation, or just replication, however sophisticated and detailed, would not capture the formation of statements and case. The procedure and its various event and process relations are multi-sequential and transformative. Due to the concerted mechanisms, adversarial case-making turns out to be well documented but fuzzy, planned but unpredictable, programmed but indeterminable – even for the professionals. There is, as a consequence, no position from which the analyst can fully look over the procedural course and the case-formation. Too much happens simultaneously; too much exceeds the embodied gaze; too much remains off-the-record and outside the procedure. Lawyering as well as law-in-action is trained guesswork, after all.

How are the mechanisms combined? How are they put into work together? With a focus on participation, the case-studies showed that and how, e.g., witnesses are invited to testify in court about "what really happened," while at the same time their evidence is assessed in light of their previous written statements. We accompanied the defence during case preparation, while the members anticipated the staging of their work results in the probable jury trial. We encountered series of replicated accounts that in return provided orientation to the mobilisation of a defence and, hence, forced a binding past even on the internal case-composition. The barrister worked across materials and mechanisms. The instrumental file-work did so as well. The professional protagonists, it seems, manage the complexity of case-making; they are at least aware of it.

From a procedural point of view, the concert of case-making mechanisms creates a mix of pull- and push-factors, a mix of invitation and obligation, of promise and threat, of invention and adaptation. The complexity creates uncertainty and, as an effect, involvement and engagement. In this line, the procedural interplay of orality and inscriptions, of proximity and history, of various rhythms and modes of case-making is highly prolific. It makes participants speak out now even when they do not know exactly to what effect. It makes participants contribute in a definite way even when they do not know exactly what they are contributing to. The interplay of the relevance-making mechanisms creates a constant deficit that makes the parties try more and even harder. As a result, the procedure fills the files, meetings and hearings with an overload of discursive facts of first order ("Then I went to ...!") and second order ("You said that 'then I went ...!"). Procedure amasses claims, contrasts and clues that eventually turn something that seems *not* decidable into something that everybody – not just the judge or the legal expert – feels *is* actually decidable: *the* case about the world out there.

Taking together the foci on participation and procedure, we may derive at a diagnosis of the procedure's discursive force. Is this the way in which systems theorists like Niklas Luhmann imagined the legal procedure to be so forceful?[6] Is this the power strategy that made Michel Foucault's "I" hesitate before entering the "risky world of [not just legal, TS] discourse?"[7] The complexity of concerted mechanisms

[6] According to Luhmann "(I)n legal procedure every communication, even the unintended presentation that contributes to the proceeding, counts as information that opens, thickens and excludes opportunities that define the acting persons and their relevant history, and reduces their options to decide. Every contribution enters the procedural history and can be reinterpreted but not neglected" ([1969]1989:44 [my translation]). Luhmann names a number of preconditions for this forceful mechanism to work: the contributor can decide freely amongst several options (no torture!); he/she is accountable for the decisions taken (no insanity!); the outcome of the contest remains open until the end (no premature closure!).

[7] "Inclination speaks out: 'I don't want to have to enter this risky world of discourse; I want nothing to do with it insofar as it is decisive and final [...]' Institutions reply:

seems capable of trapping participants in their own choices, while they cannot help making choices in the first place. Legal discourse formation or procedural system, both twist around utterances and aim them at 'their authors'. As a result, lay participants who enter the legal contest full of hope and aspiration are quite likely to leave it confused and disappointed. But is the Crown Court procedure well grasped as a trickster in this sense? Is it well described as a double play that invites and exploits 'naïve' contributions? Both, Luhmann and Foucault, identified forces and constraints that go along with systemic, disciplinary discourse. While these theorists seem to be plain about the immense power effects of legal procedure, they seem to disregard the legal regulations that protect participants (as authors) from their own words. In the course of this book, we encountered various protections that work against one straight procedural force. Suspects are warned, allowed to remain silent. Witnesses can reject misleading questions. Defendants are protected from gossip, false burden, or undue standards of truth. The defendant is provided with legal advice and legal representation. He or she is guaranteed a standardised jury trial, whereas the jury should not know his or her previous convictions.

These protections, one may criticize from the point of view of procedural sway, are not sufficient to counter the procedural hegemony. They may not be sufficient to reinforce the shattered "impression management" (Goffman 1959:208–212) of those held accountable. The protections, furthermore, bear problems themselves, such as self-interested lawyers, misleading information, over-standardized hearings, etc. Because of the protections, participants may be bound even tighter to the legally advised, thought-through, and agreed-upon version. Within the concept of procedural supremacy, protections can easily be turned into 'slippery' ingredients whose only function is to create free *and* binding accounts. Are the protections nothing but resources that add to a procedural hegemony? Is it just a powerful device, an assertive strategy?

In light of the mechanisms of case-making and in light of the procedural ruptures, I hesitate to ascribe one single rationale to the procedural

'But you have nothing to fear from launching out; we're here to show your discourse is within the established order of things, that we've waited a long time for its arrival [...]'" (Foucault 1972:7).

regime. Perhaps the regime's power is as little centred as the related case-formation itself. The regime presented here does not follow one mono-logical order. It cannot be reduced to a single *raison d'être*. This does not exclude but rather promotes procedural unity. The three concerted mechanisms feed facts and statements into two cases, plus they assure that these cases are placed into juxtaposition. This is the proper adversarial situation, or better, its crucial moment: two cases are fully developed in their own terms and present themselves as alternatives of the one truth which is in urgent need for and ready to receive a final judgment. The judgment brings case-making to a halt. From then onwards, there is just a single case that is reported, re-read and re-specified for cases-to-come.

For the ethnography of adversarial case-making the Crown Court procedure served as the perfect environment. The fabrication of two competing cases and the validation or falsification of the primary one (the prosecution case) in light of the secondary (the defence case) may be considered as *the* adversarial principle; a principle often criticized due to its costs and losses. Exploring two cases (and not just one) is an accomplishment under attack by (compromising) plea bargaining, (managerial) legal reforms, and (populist) judicial centralism. It is under attack wherever guilt and not innocence serves as the operational presumption.

'Below' such idealisation of adversarialism-in-action, the view on the mechanisms of case-making rather led to relativism when applied to the established distinction of adversarial *versus* inquisitorial procedure. The latter are no longer a property of *the* legal system or *the* legal culture. They cannot even be safely attributed to all Crown Court cases – in contrast to Magistrates' Court cases – as has been proposed at the beginning of this book. On the case level, we can encounter more or less adversarial or inquisitorial case-making. *This* particular case-making may be dominated by mobilisation/staging (without early counter versions and admissions) or it may be dominated by staging/replication (with a strong counter-case), or it may proceed merely on the basis of replication/mobilisation (in early plea bargaining orientation). Depending on the mix of mechanisms, a case can result from a rather adversarial case-making or a somewhat inquisitorial one. Only the biased infrastructure, the practitioners' presumptions, and the regular pull towards mobilization and staging allowed me to refer to the Crown Court procedure as being still adversarial. At the end and across all these empirical traits, it is the enduring orientation of the case-making (and case-makers) towards the jury trial that assures this attribute.

Epilogue

This ethnography is and is not about law. This ethnography is about this or that law (in-action) insofar it is put into work and reinvented in cases, during case-making, by strategies, by certain motions and moves, for a procedural design. It is *not about* law, in a universal sense. Instead of ascribing general properties to the law, I decided to remain close to the law-in-action, to its material resources, and to the discourse practices that generate cases systematically. I am somehow hopeful though that this turn towards case-making teaches something about law, nonetheless. The major meaning-producing frame of law-in-action, this book suggests, is not talk or interaction, nor tradition or culture, nor system or doctrine, but the procedure as discourse. Procedure demands for given facts, binding norms, and powerful decisions which are commonly reified as legal or lawful. Adversarial case-making and its cases implicate to doing procedure in this double sense: parties act upon their (still open) procedure as it is available to them right now; parties perform the (standard) procedure as a fixed and legitimate frame that everyone can rely on.

The case continues.

REFERENCES

Abbott, Andrew. 1983. Sequences of social events: Concepts and methods for the analysis of order in social processes. *Historical Methods* 16: 129–147.

Abu-Lughod, Lila. 2000. Locating ethnography. *Ethnography* 1(2): 261–267.

Adam, Barbara. 1994. *Time and social theory*. Cambridge: Polity Press.

Akera, Atsushi. 2007. Constructing a representation for an ecology of knowledge: Methodological advances in the integration of knowledge and its various contexts. *Social Studies of Science* 37(3): 413–441.

Albrow, Martin and Elizabeth King. 1981. *Globalization, Knowledge and Society*. London: Sage Publications.

Amit, Vered. 1999. *Constructing the field*. London: Routledge.

Anderson, Bob. 1997. Work, ethnography, and system design. In *The Encyclopaedia of microcomputers*, Vol. 20, ed. Allen Kent and James G. Williams, 159–183. New York: Dekker.

Archbold. 2000. *Criminal Pleading, evidence and practice*, ed. Richardson, P. James. London: Sweet & Maxwell.

Ariens, Michael. 1992. Modern legal times: Making a professional legal culture. *The Journal of American Culture* 15(1): 25–35.

Asimow, Michael R. 2007. Popular culture and the adversarial system. *Loyola of Los Angeles Law Review* 40: 653–85.

Athens, Lonnie. 2009. The roots of "Radical Interactionism." *Journal for the Theory of Social Behavior* 39(4): 387–414.

Atkinson, John M. and Paul Drew. 1979. *Order in Court: The Organisation of Verbal Interaction in Judicial Settings*. London: Macmillan Press.

Augé, Marc. 1995. Non-places: Introduction to an anthropology of supermodernity. London: Verso.

Auld Report. 2001. *Review of the Criminal Courts of England and Wales*, by The Right Honourable Lord Justice Auld, September (http://www.criminal-courts-review.org.uk/).

Bash, Harry H. 2000. A sense of time: Temporality and historicity in sociological inquiry. *Time & Society* 9(2/3): 187–204.

Behar, Ruth. 2003. Ethnography and the book that was lost. *Ethnography* 4(1): 15–39.

Berg, Marc. 1996. Practices of reading and writing: The constitutive role of the patient record in medical work. *Sociology of Health & Illness* 18(4): 499–524.

Bergmann, Jörg. 1993. *Discrete indiscretions: The social organization of gossip*. New York: Aldine De Gruyter.

Bibas, Stephanos and Richard A. Bierschbach. 2004. Integrating Remorse and Apology into Criminal Procedure. The Yale Law Journal 114: 85–148.

Blok, Anders. 2007. Experts on public trial: On democratizing expertise through a Danish consensus conference. *Public Understanding of Science* 16(2): 163–182.

Blumberg, Abraham. 1967. The practice of law as a confidence game: Organizational cooptation of the profession. *Law and Society Review* 1: 15–39.

Bogoch, Bryna. 1994. Power, distance and solidarity: Models of professional-client interaction in an Israeli legal aid setting. *Discourse and Society* 5(1): 65–88.

Bogoch, Bryna and Brenda Danet. 1984. Challenge and control in lawyer-client interaction: A case study in an Israeli legal aid office. *Text* 4(1–3): 249–275.

Bolton, Sharon and Daniel Muzio. 2005. *Can't live with 'em; Can't live without 'em: Gendered segmentation in the legal profession*. Lancaster: Lancaster University Management School Working paper.

Bolton, Sharon. 2004. Conceptual confusions: Emotion work as skilled work. In *The skills that matter*, ed. Christopher Warhust, Ewart Keep and Irena Grugulis, 19–34. London: Unwin Hyman.

Bonkalo, Alex. 1974. Impulsive acts and confusional states during incomplete arousal from sleep: Criminological and forensic implications. *Psychiatric Quarterly* 48: 400–409.

Boon, Andy and John Flood. 1999. Trials of strength: The reconfiguration of litigation as a contested terrain. *Law and Society Review* 33(3): 595–636.

Bourdieu, Pierre. 1977. *Outline of a Theory of Practice*. Cambridge: Cambridge University Press.

Bourdieu, Pierre. 1987. The force of law: Toward a sociology of the juridical field. *The Hastings Law Journal* 38: 805–853.

Bourdieu, Pierre. 1990. *In Other Words: Essays Towards a Reflexive Sociology*. Stanford, CA: Stanford University Press.

Bourdieu, Pierre. 2000. *Pascalian Meditations*. Cambridge: Polity Press.

Bourdieu, Pierre. 2003. Participant objectivation. *The Journal of the Royal Anthropological Institute* 9(2): 281–94.

Bourdieu, Pierre and Lo?c Wacquant. 1992. *An invitation to reflexive sociology*. Cambridge: Polity Press.

Braithwaite, John. 1989. *Crime, Shame and Reintegration*. Cambridge: Cambridge University Press.

Braudel, Ferdinand. 1969. Pour une économie historique. In *Écrits sur l'histoire*, 123–33. Paris: Flammarion.

Brooke Lord Justice. 2003. *Publishing the courts: Judgments and public information on the internet. An address at the commonwealth law conference*. Melbourne. 15th April 2003.

Burgess, Ernest W. 1961. Social problems and social processes. In *Human behavior and social processes: An interactionist approach*, ed. Arnold M. Rose, 381–401. London: Routledge and Kegan Paul.

Cain, Maureen. 1983. The general practice. Lawyer and client: Toward a radical reconception. In *The Sociology of the Profession*, ed. Robert Dingwall. London, The Macmillan Press.

Cain, Maureen and Harrington, Christine B. 1994. *Lawyers in a postmodern world. Translation and transgression*. Buckingham: Open University Press.

Callon, Michel. 1986. Some elements of a sociology of translation: Domestication of the scallops and the fishermen of Saint Brieuc Bay. In: *Power, action and belief: A new sociology of knowledge? Sociological Review Monograph* 32, ed. John Law. 196–223.

Cambrosio, Alberto, Camille Limoges and Denyse Pronovost. 1990. Representing biotechnology: An ethnography of Quebec science policy. *Social Studies of Science* 20: 195–227.

Carter, Jonathan A. 2003. Telling Times: History, Emplotment, and Truth. *History and Theory*, 42(1): 1–27.

Chaudhury, N.K. Syam and Das, M.M. 1973. *The Lalung society: A theme for analytical ethnography*. Calcutta: Anthropological Survey of India.

Christie, George C. 2000. *The Notion of an Ideal Audience in Legal Argument*. Dordrecht: Kluwer.

Cicourel, Aaron. 1968. *The Social Organisation of Juvenile Justice*. New York: John Wiley & Sons, Inc.

Clayman, Steven E. 1990. From talk to text: newspaper accounts of reporter-source interactions. *Media, Culture & Society*, 12, 79–103.

Clifford, James. 1993. Über ethnographische Autorität. In *Kultur, soziale Praxis, Text. Die Krise der ethnographischen Repräsentation*, ed. Eberhard Berg and Martin Fuchs, 109–157. Frankfurt a.M.: Suhrkamp.

Cole, Simon A. 2006. Witnessing Creation. *Social Studies of Science* 36(6): 855–860.

Coles, E.M. and H.O.F. Veiel. 2001. Expert testimony and pseudoscience: How mental health professionals are taking over the courtroom. *International Journal of Law and Psychiatry* 24(6): 607–625.

Collier, Jane F. 1975. Legal Processes. *Annual Reviews* 4: 121–144.

Collins, Harry M. and Robert Evans. 2002. The third wave of science studies: Studies of expertise and experience. *Social Studies of Science* 32(2): 235–296.

Collins, Hugh. 1999. *Regulating Contracts*. Oxford: Oxford University Press.

Collins, Randall. 2004. *Interaction ritual chains*. Princeton: Princeton University Press.

Comaroff, John and Jean Comaroff. 1992. *Ethnography and the historical imagination*. Boulder, CO: Westview Press.

Conley, John M. and William M. O'Barr. 1998. *Just words. Law, language and power*. Chicago and London: The University of Chicago Press

Conley, John M. and William M. O'Barr. 1990. *Rules versus relationships. The ethnography of legal discourse*. Chicago and London: The University of Chicago Press.

Cotterell, Roger. 2006. Law, culture and society. Legal ideas in the mirror of social theory. Aldshot: Ashgate.

Cramer Bornemann, Mike A., Mark W. Mohawald, and Carlos H. Schenck. 2006. Parasomnias: Clinical features and forensic implications. *Chest. The Cardiopulmonary and Critical Care Journal*, December 14, 605–610.

Cross, Rupert Sir and J.W. Harris. 1991. *Precedent in English Law*. Oxford: Oxford University Press.

Crown Prosecution Service. 2008. *CPS case outcomes by principal offence*. http://www.cps.gov.uk/Publications/performance/case_outcomes/.

Damaska, Mirjan R. 1986. *Faces of justice and state authority*. New Haven, CT: Yale University Press.

Darrough, William D. 1978. When versions collide: Police and the dialectics of accountability. *Urban Life* 7(3): 379–403.

Davis, Michael. 1991. Punishment as language: Misleading analogy for desert theorists. *Law and Philosophy* 10: 311–322.

De Certeau, Michel. 1984. *The practice of everyday life*. Berkeley: University of California Press.

Deleuze, Gilles. 1991. *Bergsonism*. New York: Zone Books.

Denzin, Norman K. and Charles M. Keller. 1981. Review: Frame Analysis Reconsidered. *Contemporary Sociology* 10(1): 52–60.

Denzin, Norman K. and Yvonna S. Lincoln. 2005. *The Sage handbook of qualitative research*. London: Sage Publications.

Department for Constitutional Affairs. 2002. *Judicial Statistics 2002*. http://www.dca.gov.uk/publications/annual_reports/judstat2002.htm.

Derrida, Jacques. 1977. *Of Grammatology*. Baltimore, Md.: John Hopkins University Press.

Derrida, Jacques. 1988. *Writing and difference*. Chicago: University of Chicago Press.

Dixon, Jo and Carroll Seron. 1995. Stratification in the legal profession: Sex, sector, and salary. *Law and Society Review* 29: 381–412.

Doering, Hilke and Stefan Hirschauer. 1997. Die Biographie der Dinge. Eine Ethnographie musealer Repräsentation. In *Die Befremdung der eigenen Kultur. Zur ethnographischen Herausforderung soziologischer Empirie*, ed. Klaus Amann and Stefan Hirschauer, 267–297. Frankfurt a.M.: Suhrkamp.

Drew, Paul. 1992. Contested evidence in courtroom cross-examination: the case of a trial for rape. In *Talk at work: Interaction in institutional settings*, ed. Paul Drew and John Heritage, 470–521. Cambridge: Cambridge University Press.

Dreyfus, Hubert L. and Paul Rabinow. 1987. *Michel Foucault. Jenseits von Strukturalismus und Hermeneutik*. Frankfurt a.M.: Athenäum.

Duff, Anthony. 1986. *Trials and Punishment*. Cambridge: Cambridge University Press.

Duff, Anthony. 2003. I might be guilty, but you can't try me. Estoppel and other bars to trial. *Ohio State Journal of Criminal Law* 1: 244–259.

Durkheim, Emile. [1895]1982. *The rules of sociological method. And selected texts on sociology and its method*. (Edited with an Introduction by Steven Lukes; Translated by W.D. Halls). London and Basingstoke: The Macmillan Press Ltd.

Eekelaar, John, Mavis Maclean and Sarah Beinart. 2000. *Family Lawyers: The divorce work of solicitors*. Oxford: Hart Publishing Ltd.

Elias, Norbert and John L. Scotson. 1993. *Etablierte und Außenseiter. Zur Theorie von Etablierten-Außenseiter-Beziehungen*. Frankfurt a.M.: Suhrkamp.

Emmelman, Debra S. 1994. The effect of social class on the adjudication of criminal cases: Class-linked behavior tendencies, common sense, and the interpretive procedures of court-appointed defense attorneys. *Symbolic Interaction* 17(1): 1–20.

Engeström, Yrjö. 1995. Objects, contradictions and collaboration in medical cognition: An activity-theoretical perspective. *Artificial Intelligence in Medicine* 7: 395–412.

Epp, Charles R. 2003. The judge over your shoulder: is adversarial legalism exceptionally American? *Law and Social Inquiry* 28: 743–770.

Eriksen, Thomas H. 2001. Small places, large issues: An introduction to social and cultural anthropology. London: Pluto Press.

Ewick, Patricia and Susan S. Silbey. 1998. *The Common place of law. Stories from everyday life*. Chicago, London: University of Chicago Press.

Flaherty, Michael G. and Gary A. Fine. 2001. Present, past, and future: Conjugating George Herbert Mead's perspective on time. *Time and Society* 10(2/3): 147–161.

Flick, Uwe, Kardorff, Ernst von und Ines Steinke, ed. 2004. *A companion to qualitative research*. London: Sage.

Flood, John A. 1983. *Barristers' clerks: The Law's Middlemen*. Manchester: Manchester University Press.

Flood, John A. 1991. Doing business: The management of uncertainty in lawyers' work. *Law and Society Review* 25(1): 41–71.

Fog Olwig, Karen and Kirsten Hastrup, ed. 1997. *Siting culture: The shifting anthropological object*. London: Routledge.

Foucault, Michel. 1972. *The archaeology of knowledge and the discourse of language*. London: Tavistock.

Foucault, Michel. 1977. Nietzsche, genealogy, history. In *Language, counter-memory, practice: Selected essays and interviews*, ed. Donald F. Bouchard, 139–164. Ithaca: Cornell University Press.

Foucault, Michel. 2003. *Die Wahrheit und die juristischen Formen*. Frankfurt am Main: Suhrkamp.

Foucault, Michel. 2004. *Abnormal. Lectures at the College de France*. Transl. Graham Bruchell. New York: Picador.

Fraser, Mariam. 2006. Event. *Theory, Culture & Society*. 23(2–3): 129–132.

Frederick, Jeffrey T. 1987. *The psychology of the American jury*. Charlottesville, Virginia: Lexis Law Publishing

Freedman, Clive and Joe Ury. 2008. BAILII's continuing expansion. *Computers & Law* 19(3). http://www.scl.org/editorial.asp?i=1883&r=3%A31920.

Friedman, Lawrence M. 1985. Transformations in American Legal Culture 1800–1985. *Zeitschrift für Rechtssoziologie* 6: 191–205.

Fuller, Steve. 2001. A critical guide to knowledge society newspeak: or, how not to take the great leap backward. *Current Sociology* 49(4): 177–201.

Garfinkel, Harold. 1956. Conditions of Successful Degradation Ceremonies. *American Journal of Sociology* 61(5): 420–424.

Garfinkel, Harold. 1967. *Good reasons for bad clinic records. Studies in Ethnomethodology*. Englewood Cliffs, N.J.: Prentice Hall.

Garfinkel, Harold. 1972. Common sense knowledge of social structures: The documentary method of interpretation. In *Symbolic interaction: A reader in social psychology*, ed. Manis, Jerome G. and Bernard N. Meltzer (2nd ed), Boston: Allyn and Bacon, Inc.

Garfinkel, Harold. 2006. *Seeing sociologically. The routine grounds of social action.* Boulder/CO: Paradigm Publishers.

Geertz, Clifford. 1973. *The interpretation of cultures*. New York: Basic Books.

Geertz, Clifford. 1983. Fact and law in comparative perspective. In *Local knowledge. Further essays in interpretive anthropology*, ed. by Clifford Geertz, 167–234. New York: Basic Books.

Genn, Hazel. 1988. *Hard bargaining: out of court settlement in personal injury actions.* Oxford: Oxford Univ. Press.

Gerth, Hans H. and C. Wright Mills. 1957. Introduction: The man and his work. In *Max Weber. Essays in sociology*, 3–76. London: Routledge & Kegan Paul.

Giddens, Anthony. 1984. Time, space and regionalization. In *The constitution of society. Outline of the Theory of Structuration*. Cambridge: Polity Press.

Goffman, Erving. 1959. *The presentation of self in every-day life*. New York, Doubleday.

Goffman, Erving. 1961. *Asylums: Essays on the social situation of mental patients and other inmates*. New York: Doubleday.

Goffman, Erving. 1963. *Stigma: Notes on the management of spoiled identity*. Englewood Cliffs, New Jersey: Prentice Hall Inc.

Goffman, Erving. 1967. *Interaction Ritual: Essays on Face-to-Face Behavior*, Doubleday: Anchor Books.

Goffman, Erving. 1971. *Relations in public: microstudies of the public order*. New York: Harper & Row.

Goffman, Erving. 1974. *Frame analysis: An essay on the organization of experience*. Boston: Northeastern University Press.

Goffman, Erving. 1981. *Forms of Talk*. Oxford: Blackwell.

Goffman, Erving. 1983. The interaction order. *American Sociological Review* 48: 1–17.

Goffman, Erving. 1989. On fieldwork. *Journal of Contemporary Ethnography* 18(2), 123–132.

Goldstone, Jack A. 1998. Initial conditions, general laws, path dependence, and explanation in historical sociology. *American Journal of Sociology* 104: 829–845.

Gonos, George. 1977. "Situation" versus "Frame": The "Interactionist" and the "Structuralist" Analyses of Everyday Life. *American Sociological Review* 42: 854-867.

Goodwin, Charles. 2003. Embedded context. *Research on Language and Social Interaction*, 36(4): 323-350.

Goodwin, Marjorie Harness. 1990. *He-said-she-said: talk as social organisation among Black children*. Bloomington and Indianapolis: Indiana University Press.

Greenwood, Royston, Suddaby, Roy and C.R. Hinings. 2002. Theorizing change: The role of professional associations in the transformation of institutionalized fields. *Academy of Management Journal* 45(1): 58–80.

Griffiths, John. 1986. What do Dutch lawyers actually do in divorce cases? *Law and Society Review*. 20(1): 135–175.

Gumbrecht, Hans Ulrich and K. Ludwig Pfeiffer, ed. 1988. *Materialität der Kommunikation*. Frankfurt am Main: Suhrkamp.

Gupta, Akhil and James Ferguson. 1997. *Anthropological locations: boundaries and grounds of a field science*. Berkeley: University of California Press.

Habermas, Jürgen. 1992. *Faktizität und Geltung*: Beiträge zur Diskurstheorie des Rechts und des demokratischen Rechtsstaates. Frankfurt am Main: Suhrkamp.
Hägerstrand, Torsten. 1985. Time and culture. In *Time preferences: An interdisciplinary theoretical and empirical approach*, ed. Guy Kirsch, Peter Nijkamp and Klaus Zimmermann, 1–15. Berlin: Wissenschaftszentrum.
Hailsham of St Marylebone Lord, ed. 2000. *Halsbury's Laws of England: Fourth Edition: Cumulative Supplement 2000*, vol 26. London: Butterworths.
Hammersley, Martyn. 1990. What's wrong with ethnography? The myth of theoretical description. *Sociology* 24(4): 597–615.
Hampton, Jean. 1984. The moral education theory of punishment. *Philosophy and Public Affairs* 13: 208–238.
Haney, Lynne A. 2000. Feminist state theory: applications to jurisprudence, criminology, and the welfare state. *Annual Review of Sociology* 26: 641–666.
Hanlon, Gerard. 1997. A profession in transition? Lawyers, the market and significant others. *Sociology* 32(1): 43–63.
Hannken-Illjes, Kati. 2006. In the field: the development of reasons in criminal proceedings. *Argumentation* 20: 309–325.
Hanson, Sharon. 1999. *Legal Method*. London: Cavendish Publishing.
Harris, Sandra. 2001. Fragmented narratives and multiple tellers: witness and defendant accounts in trials. *Discourse studies* 3(1): 53–74.
Haraway, Donna. 1997. Modest witness@second millennium. FemaleMan meets oncomouse: Feminism and technoscience. New York: Routledge.
Hassard, John. 1990. Introduction: The sociological study of time. In *The sociology of time*, ed. John Hassard, 1–18. New York: St Martins Press.
Heath, Robert L. and Jennings Bryant. 2000. *Human communication: theory and research*. Mahwah, NJ; London: Erlbaum.
Heffer, Chris N. 2007. The language of conviction and the convictions of certainty: is 'sure' an impossible standard of proof? *International Commentary on Evidence* 5(1): 1–32.
Hepworth, Mike and Bryan S. Turner. 1979. Confession, guilt, and responsibility. *Law & Society Review* 6: 219–234.
Her Majesty's Court Service. 2003. *Crown Court Annual Report 2002/03*. http://www.hmcourts-service.gov.uk/publications/annual_reports/crown/index.htm.
Heritage, John and David Greatbatch. 1991. On the institutional character of institutional talk. In *Talk and social structure. Studies in ethnomethodology and conversation analysis*, ed. Deirdre Boden and Don H. Zimmerman, 93–137. Berkeley: University of California Press.
Hester, Stephen and Peter Eglin. 1992. *A sociology of crime*. London and New York: Routledge.
Hirschauer, Stefan. 1991. The manufacture of bodies in surgery. *Social Studies of Science* 21: 279–319.
Hirschauer, Stefan. 1994. Towards a methodology of investigations into strangeness of one's own culture: a response to Collins. *Social Studies of Science* 24: 335–346.
Hirschauer, Stefan und Klaus Amann. 1997. Die Befremdung der eigenen Kultur: Ein Programm. In *Die Befremdung der eigenen Kultur - Zur ethnographischen Herausforderung soziologischer Empirie*, ed. Stefan Hirschauer, 7–53. Frankfurt am Main: Suhrkamp.
Hirschauer, Stefan. 2005. Publizierte Fachurteile. Lektüre und Bewertungspraxis im Peer Review. *Soziale Systeme*, 11(1), 52–82.
Holly, Werner. 1981. Der doppelte Boden in Verhören. Sprachliche Strategien von Verhörenden. In *Pragmatik. Theorie und Praxis*, ed. Wolfgang Frier, 275–319. Amsterdam: Rodopi.
House of Commons. 2005. *Forensic science on trial. Seventh report of session 2004–05. HC 96–I*, published on 29 March 2005 by authority of the House of Commons, London: The Stationary Office Limited.

Hubert, Henri. 1999. Essay on time. A brief study of the representation of time in religion and magic. Oxford: Durkheim Press.

Hughes, Everett C. 1971. *The sociological eye*. Chicago: Aldine de Gruyter.

Hutchinson, Allan C. 1998. Legal ethics for a fragmented society: between professional and personal. *International Journal of the Legal Profession* 5(2/3): 175–192.

Ibbetson, David and Alan Wijffels. 1997. Case law in the making: the techniques and methods of judicial records and law reports. In *Case law in the making. Volume 1: Essays*, ed. Alan Wijffels, 13–35. Berlin: Duncker & Humblot.

Isaac, Larry W., Street, Debra A. and Stan J. Knapp. 1994. Analysing historical contingency with formal methods: the case of the "relief explosion" and 1968. *Sociological Methods and Research* 23: 114–141.

Jasanoff, Sheila. 1995. *Science at the bar*. Cambridge, MA: Harvard University Press.

Jasanoff, Sheila. 2005. Law's knowledge: science for justice in legal settings. *American Journal of Public Health* 95(1): 49–58.

Johnson, William R. 1978. *Schooled lawyers: a study in the clash of professional cultures*. New York: New York University Press.

Kagan, Robert A. 1994. Do lawyers cause adversarial legalism? A preliminary inquiry. *Law and Social Inquiry* 19: 1–62.

Kagan, Robert A. 2001. *Adversarial legalism: The American way of law*. Cambridge, MA: Harvard University Press.

Kagan, Robert A. 2006. American and European ways of law: six entrenched differences. *Institute of European Studies. Paper 060407*. University of California, Berkeley.

Kastner, Fatima. 2009. Trojanische Pferde: Universalistische Normen und globaler Wahrheits- und Versöhnungsdiskurs. Zur Evolution der Weltgesellschaft. In. Demokratie in der Weltgesellschaft. Ed. by Hauke Brunkhorst, 259–276. Baden-Baden: Nomos.

Katz, Jack. 2002. Start here: social ontology and research strategy. *Theoretical Criminology* 6(3): 255–278.

Katz, Jack. 2004. On the rhetoric and politics of ethnographic methodology. *The ANNALS of the American Academy of Political and Social Science* 595: 280–308.

Keane, Webb. 1997. *Signs of recognition. Powers and hazards of representation in an Indonesian society*. Berkeley, Los Angeles, London: University of California Press.

Keane, Webb. 2003. Semiotics and the social analysis of material things. *Language & Communication* 23: 409–425.

Keppler, Angela. 1994. *Tischgespräche. Über Formen kommunikativer Vergemeinschaftung am Beispiel der Konversation in Familien*. Frankfurt a. M.: Suhrkamp.

Kelemen, R. Daniel 2006: Suing for Europe: Adversarial Legalism and European Governance. *Comparative political studies*, 39(1): 101–127.

Kerr, Orin S. 2007. How to read a legal opinion. A guide for new law students. *The Green Bag. An Entertaining Journal of Law* 11(1): 51–63.

Knoblauch, Hubert and Christian Heath. 1999. Technologie, Interaktion und Organisation: Die workplace studies. *Schweizerische Zeitschrift für Soziologie* 25: 163–181.

Knoblauch, Hubert. 2001. Fokussierte Ethnographie. *Sozialer Sinn* 1: 123–141.

Knorr-Cetina, Karin. 1984. *Die Fabrikation von Erkenntnis*. Frankfurt am Main: Suhrkamp.

Knorr, Karin. 2003. *Epistemic cultures: how the sciences make knowledge*. Cambridge, MA; London: Harvard University Press.

Knorr-Cetina, Karin and Urs Bruegger. 2002. Global microstructures: the virtual societies of financial markets. *American Journal of Sociology* 107: 905–950.

Komter, Martha L. 1998. *Dilemmas in the courtroom: a study of trials of violent crime in the Netherlands*. Mahwah, N.J.; London: Lawrence Erlbaum.

Konradi, Amanda. 1997. Too little too late: prosecutors' pre-court preparation of rape survivors. *Law and Social Inquiry* 22(1): 1–54.

Koptytoff, Igor. 1986. The cultural biography of things: commodification as process. In *The social life of things: commodities in cultural perspective,* ed. Arjun Appadurai, 64–91. Cambridge: Cambridge University.
Kozin, Alexander. 2007. Standing for the client: on the Interactional Becoming of the Defence Attorney. *International Journal of Legal Profession,* 14(2), 173–193.
Kozin, Alexander. 2008. Scrapbooking the Criminal Defense File. *Crime, Media, Culture,* 4(1), 31–52.
Kronman, Anthony T. 1993. *The lost lawyer: falling ideals of the legal profession.* Cambridge, Mass; London, the Belknap Press of Harvard University Press.
Langbein, John H. 2003. *The origins of adversary criminal trial.* Oxford, N.J.: Oxford University Press.
Lanzara, Giovan Francesco and Gerrardo Patriotta. 2001. Technology and the courtroom: an inquiry into knowledge making in organizations. *Journal of Management Studies* 38: 944–971.
Lassiter, Luke E. 2005. *The Chicago guide to collaborative ethnography.* Chicago: University of Chicago Press.
Latour, Bruno and Steve Woolgar. 1979. *Laboratory life: social construction of scientific facts.* New York: Sage Publications.
Latour, Bruno. 1987. *Science in action. How to follow scientists and engineers through society.* Cambridge MA, London: Harvard University Press.
Latour, Bruno. 1999a. *Pandora's hope. Essay on the reality of science studies.* Cambridge MA, London: Harvard University Press.
Latour, Bruno. 1999b. On recalling ANT. In *Actor Network Theory and after,* ed. John Law and John Hassard, 15–25. Oxford: Blackwell Publishers.
Latour, Bruno. 2005. Reassembling the social: an introduction to actor-network-theory. Oxford: Clarendon.
Latour, Bruno. 2010. The Making of Law. An Ethnography of the Conseil D'État. Cambridge: Polity Press.
Lau, Thomas und Stephan Wolff. 1981. Bündnis wider Willen - Sozialarbeiter und ihre Akten. *Neue Praxis* 11: 199–214.
Law, John. 2002. *Aircraft stories. Decentring the object in technoscience.* Durham and London: Duke University Press.
Lex-Scripta. 1999. *Briefing barristers: Ten ways to make the experience a happier one.* http://www.lexscripta.com/pdf/briefing.pdf
Lind, Douglas W. 2004. An economic analysis of early casebook publishing. *In Law Library Journal* 96(1): 95–126.
Lloyd-Bostock, Sally and Cheryl Thomas. 1999. Decline of the 'little parliament': juries and jury reform in England and Wales. *Law and Contemporary Problems* 62(2), 7–40.
Lofland, John and Lynn H. Lofland. 1984. *Analyzing social settings. A Guide to Qualitative Observation and Analysis.* Belmont, CA: Wadsworth.
Lord Templeman and Molan, Michael T., ed. 1998. *Casebook criminal law.* London: Old Bailey Press.
Luckmann, Thomas. 2002. Moral communications in modern societies. *Human Studies* 25: 19–32.
Luff, Paul, Christian Heath and David Greatbatch. 1992. Tasks-in-interaction: paper and screen based documentation in collaborative activity. *Proceedings of CSCW'92*: 163–70.
Luhmann, Niklas. 1987. Gesellschaft und Interaktion. In *Soziale Systeme,* 551–592. Frankfurt a.M.: Suhrkamp.
Luhmann, Niklas. [1969]1989. *Legitimation durch Verfahren.* Frankfurt a.M.: Suhrkamp.
Luhmann, Niklas. 1995. Die Funktion des Rechts. In *Das Recht der Gesellschaft,* 124–165. Frankfurt a.M.: Suhrkamp.

Luhmann, Niklas. 1998. Temporalisierungen. In *Die Gesellschaft der Gesellschaft*, 997–1016. Frankfurt a.M.: Suhrkamp.
Luhmann, Niklas. 2000. *The reality of the mass media*. Cambridge: Polity Press.
Lynch, Michael. 1993. Scientific practice and ordinary action: ethnomethodology and social studies of science. New York: Cambridge University Press.
Lynch, Michael and David Bogen. 1996. *The spectacle of history. Speech, text, and memory at the Iran-contra hearings*. Durham and London: Duke University Press.
Lynch, Michael. 1999. Archives in formation: privileged spaces, popular archives and paper trails. In *History of the Human Sciences* 12(2): 65–87.
Lynch, Michael. 2002. The Living Text: Written Instructions and Situated Actions in Telephone Surveys. In *Standardization and Tacit Knowledge: Interaction and Practice in the Survey Interview*, ed. Douglas W. Maynard, Hanneke Houtkoop-Steenstra, Nora C. Schaeffer and Johannes van der Zouwen, 125–147. New York: John Wiley & Sons.
Lynch, Michael and Ruth McNally. 2003. "Science," "common sense," and DNA evidence: a legal controversy about the public understanding of science. *Public Understanding of Science* 12(1): 83–103.
Lynch, Michael and Simon Cole. 2005. Science and technology studies on trial: Dilemmas of Expertise. *Social Studies of Science* 35(2): 269–311.
Lynch, Michael. 2006. From Ruse to Farce. *Social Studies of Science* 36(6): 819–826.
Magnus, P.D. 2007. Distributed cognition and the task of science. *Social Studies of Science* 37(2): 297–310.
Mahoney, James. 2000. Path dependence in historical sociology. *Theory and Society* 29: 507–548.
Mahowald, Mark W. 2003. Parasomnias: sleepwalking and the law. *Sleep Medicine Reviews* 4(4): 321–339.
Manchester, Colin, David Salter and Peter Moodie. 2000. *Exploring the law: The dynamics of precedent and statutory interpretation*. London: Sweet & Maxwell.
Mann, Kenneth. 1985. *Defending white-collar crime. A portrait of attorneys at work*. New Haven: Yale University Press.
Manning, Peter K. 1970. Talking and becoming: A view of organizational socialization. In *Understanding Everyday Life*, ed. Jack D. Douglas, 239–256. Chicago: Aldine Publishing Company.
Marcus, George E. 1995. Ethnography in/of the world system: The emergence of multi-sited ethnography. In *Annual Reviews of Anthropology* 24, 95–117.
Marcus, George E. 1998. *Ethnography through thick and thin*. Princeton: Princeton University Press.
Marx, Karl. [1852]1963. *The eighteenth Brumaire of Louis Bonaparte*. New York: International Pub.
Mather, Lynn, Craig A. McEwen and Richard J. Maiman. 2001. *Divorce lawyers at work. Varieties of professionalism in practice*. Oxford: Oxford University Press.
Matoesian, Gregory M. 1993. *Reproducing rape: Domination through talk in the courtroom*. Chicago: University of Chicago Press.
Matoesian, Gregory M. 1997. 'You were interested in him as a person?': Rhythms of domination in the Kennedy Smith rape trial. *Law & Social Inquiry* 22(1): 55–93.
Maughan, Caroline and Julian Webb. 1995. *Lawyering skills and the legal process*. London: Butterworths.
McBarnet, Doreen. 1977. Pre-trial procedures and the construction of conviction. In *The Sociology of Law*, ed. Pat Carlen. Keele: Wood Mitchell.
Micaville, Mike, Jacqueline Hodgson, Lee Bridges and Anita Pavlovic. 1994. *Standing accused. The organisation and practices of criminal defense lawyers in Britain*. Oxford: Clarendon Press.

McDonnell, Thomas Michael. 1998. Playing beyond the rules: A realist and rhetoric-based approach to researching the law and solving legal problems. *UMKC Law Review* 67: 285–342.

McLaren, Sally. 2006. Transcripts of judicial proceedings in England and Wales. A guide to sources. Inner Temple Library, available on: http://www.innertemplelibrary.org.uk/Guides/Transcripts%20Guide.pdf

McSherry, Bernadette. 2000. R v Stone [1999] 2 SCR 290: Case commentary. *Psychiatry, Psychology and Law* 7: 279–283.

Mead, George H. 1932. *The philosophy of the present*. Chicago: University of Chicago Press.

Meehan, Albert. 1993. Internal police records and the control of juveniles: Politics and policing in a suburban town. *British Journal of Criminology* 33(4): 504–524.

Meehan, Albert. 2000. The organizational career of gang statistics: The politics of policing gangs. *Sociological Quarterly* 41(3): 337–370.

Merriam-Webster's Dictionary of law. 1996.

Michon, Pascal. 2002. Strata, blocks, pieces, spirals, elastics and verticals: Six figures of time in Michel Foucault. In *Time & Society* 11(2/3): 163–192.

Mol, Annemarie. 2002. *The body multiple: Ontology in medical practice*. Durham, NC: Duke University Press.

Mooney, Jayne. 2000. *Gender, violence and the social order*. Basingstoke: Macmillan Press.

Moore, Sally Falk. 1987. Explaining the present: Theoretical dilemmas in processual ethnography. *American Ethnologist* 14: 727–736.

Moorhead, Richard, Avrom Sherr and Alan Paterson. 2003a. What clients know: Client perspectives and legal competence. *International Journal of the Legal Profession* 10 (1): 5–35.

Moorhead Richard, Avrom Sherr and Alan Paterson. 2003b. Contesting professionalism: Legal aid and non lawyers in England and Wales. In *Law and Society Review* 37 (4): 765–808.

Morison, John and Philip Leith. 1992. *The barrister's world: And the nature of law*. London: McGraw-Hill.

Morris, Anthony. 1991. Briefing barristers: Ten ways to make the experience a happier one. *Queensland Law Society Journal,* 21 (3).

Morris, Herbert. 1981. A paternalistic theory of punishment. *American Philosophical Review* 18: 263–271.

Morris, Stephen R. 2001–2002. The lawyer as friend: An Aristotelian inquiry. *Journal of the Legal Profession* 26: 55–66.

Mortimer, John. 1993. *The Best of Rumpole,* London: Penguin Books.

Moskovitz, Myron. 1992. Beyond the case method: It's time to teach with problems. *Journal of Legal Education* 42: 241–270.

Mulkay, Michael. 1986. Conversations and Texts. *Human Studies* 9: 303–321.

Munir, Kamal A. 2005. The social construction of events: A study of institutional change in the photographic field. In *Organization Studies* 26(1): 93–112.

Nelken, David. 1995. Understanding/Invoking legal culture. In *Special issue on legal culture, diversity and globalization*, ed. David Nelken, 435–452.

Nelken, David. 2003. Beyond compare? Criticizing "The American way of law". *Law and Social Inquiry* 28: 799–831.

Nelken, David. 2006. Law and knowledge/Law as knowledge. *Social Legal Studies* 15: 570–573.

Norris, Christopher. 1988. *Deconstruction: Theory and practice*. London and New York: Methuen.

Oevermann, Ulrich. 1979. Die Methodologie einer "Objektiven Hermeneutik" und ihre allgemeine forschungslogische Bedeutung in den Sozialwissenschaften. In *Interpretative Verfahren in den Sozial- und Textwissenschaften,* ed. Hans-Georg Soeffner, 352–434. Stuttgart: Metzler.

Office for Criminal Justice Reform. 2002. *Justice for All*. CJS White Paper. http://www.cjsonline.gov.uk/downloads/application/pdf/CJS%20White%20Paper%20–%20Justice%20For%20All.pdf.

Office for Criminal Justice Reform. 2004. *Cutting crime, delivering justice: A strategic plan for criminal justice 2004–2008*. http://www.cjsonline.gov.uk, retrieved February 2007.

Office for Criminal Justice Reform. 2007. *Criminal Statistics: England and Wales 2007*. http://www.justice.gov.uk/publications/docs/crim-stats-2007–tag.pdf.

Office for Criminal Justice Reform. 2008. *The adult criminal case management framework*. Part 2. http://www.cjsonline.gov.uk.

O'Gorman, Hubert J. 1963. *Lawyers and matrimonial cases - A study of informal pressures in private professional practice*. London: Glencoe Collier Macmillan.

Olesen, Finn and Randi Markussen. 2001. *How to place material things from essentialism to material-semiotic analysis of sociotechnical practice*. Paper presented on the conference 'Doing Things with Things' at Copenhagen University in September.

Ormerod, David. 2008. *Smith and Hogan Criminal Law*. Oxford: Oxford University Press.

Oxford English Dictionary. 2009.

Patton, Michael Q. 2002. *Qualitative research & evaluation methods* (3rd ed.). Thousand Oaks, CA: Sage Publications.

Pickering, Andrew. 1995. *The mangle of practice. Time, agency, and science*. Chicago and London: The University of Chicago Press.

Pizzi, William T. 1999. *Trials Without Truth. Why Our System of Criminal Trials Has Become an Expensive Failure and What We Need to Do to Rebuild It*. New York, London: New York University Press.

Pierson, Paul. 2000a. Increasing returns, path dependence, and the study of politics. *American Political Science Review* 94: 251–267.

Pierson, Paul. 2000b. Not just what, but when: Timing and sequence in political processes. *Studies in American Political Development* 14: 73–93.

Ploscowe, Morris. 1935. The expert witness in criminal cases in France, Germany, and Italy. *Law and Contemporary Problems* 2(4): 504–509.

Potter, Jonathan. 1996. *Representing reality. Discourse, rhetoric and social construction*. London, Thousand Oaks, New Delhi: Sage Publications.

Pound, Roscoe. 1910. Law in the books and law in action. *American Law Review*, XLIV(44).

Primoratz, Igor. 1989. Punishment as language. *Philosophy* 64: 187–205.

Rabinow, Paul. 1977. *Reflections on fieldwork in Morocco*. Berkeley: University of California Press.

Ragin, Charles C. 1992a. Cases of "What is a case?" In *What is a case? Exploring the foundations of social inquiry*, ed. Charles C. Ragin and Howard S. Becker, 1–18. Cambridge: Cambridge University Press.

Ragin, Charles C. 1992b. "Casing" and the process of social inquiry. In *What is a case? Exploring the foundations of social inquiry*, ed. Charles C. Ragin and Howard S. Becker, 217–226. Cambridge: Cambridge University Press.

Raymond, Geoffrey. 2003. Grammar and Social Organization: Yes/No Interrogatives and the Structure of Responding. *American Sociological Review* 68: 939–967.

Redlich, Josef. 1914. *The Common law and the case method in American university law schools*. A report to the Carnegie Foundation for the advancement of teaching. New York: Carnegie Foundation.

Riesman, David. 1951–2. Toward an anthropological science of law and the legal profession. *American Journal of Sociology* 57(2): 121 ff.

Roach Anleu, Sharyn and Kathy Mack. 2005. Magistrates' everyday work and emotional labour. *Journal of Law and Society* 32(4): 590–614.

Rock, Paul. 1993. *The social world of an English Crown Court*. Witnesses and professionals in the Crown Court Centre at Wood Green. Oxford: Clarendon Press.

Rosa, Hartmut. 2005. Beschleunigung: Die Veränderung der Zeitstrukturen in der Moderne. Frankfurt a.M.: Suhrkamp.

Rosenfeld, David Saul and Antoine Jean Elhajjar. 1998. Sleepsex: A variant of sleepwalking. *Archives of Sexual Behavior* 27(3): 269–278.

Rosenthal, Douglas. 1974. *Lawyer and client: Who's in charge?* New Brunswick: Transaction Books.

Royal Commission on Criminal Justice. 1995. *Runciman report*, Cm 2263. London: HMSO.

Sacks, Harvey. 1978. Some technical considerations of a dirty joke. Studies in the organization of conversational interaction. In *Studies in the organization of conversational interaction*, ed. Jim Schenkein, 249–269. New York: Academic.

Sacks, Harvey, Emanuel A. Schegloff and Gail Jefferson 1974. A simplest systematics for the organization of turn-taking for conversation. *Language* 50: 696–735.

Saks, Michael J. and Alice R. Benedict. 1977. Evaluation and quality assurance of legal services. Concepts and research. In *Law and Human Behavior* 1(4): 373 384.

Saks, Michael J. 1990. Expert witnesses, nonexpert witnesses, and nonwitness experts. In *Law and Human Behavior* 14(4): 291–313.

Sanders, Andrew. 1987. Constructing the case for the prosecution. In *Journal of Law and Society* 14: 229.

Sarat, Austin and William L. Felstiner. 1986. Law and strategy in the divorce lawyer's office. In *Law & Society Review* 20: 93–134.

Sarat, Austin and William L. Felstiner. 1988. Law and social relations: Vocabularies of motive in lawyer/client interaction. In *Law & Society Review* 22(4): 737–770.

Sarat, Austin and William L. Felstiner. 1995. *Divorce lawyers and their clients. Power and meaning in the legal process*. New York: Oxford U.P.

Scheffer, Thomas. 1998a. Jenseits der Konversation: Zur Konzeptualisierung von Asylanhörungen anhand der ethnographischen Analyse ihrer Eröffnung. In *Schweizerische Zeitschrift für Soziologie* 24: 291–326.

Scheffer, Thomas. 1998b. Übergänge von Wort und Schrift: Zur Genese und Gestaltung von Anhörungsprotokollen im Asylverfahren. In *Zeitschrift für Rechtssoziologie* 20(2): 230–265.

Scheffer, Thomas. 2001. *Asylgewährung: Eine ethnographische Analyse des deutschen Asylverfahrens*. Stuttgart: Lucius & Lucius.

Scheffer, Thomas. 2002. Das Beobachten als sozialwissenschaftliche Methode: Von den Grenzen der Beobachtbarkeit und ihrer methodischen Bearbeitung. In *Qualitative Forschung in den Gesundheits- und Pflegewissenschaften*, ed. Doris Schaeffer und Gabriele Müller-Mundt, 351–374. Bern: Huber-Verlag.

Scheffer, Thomas. 2003. The duality of mobilisation. Following the rise and fall of an alibi-story on its way to court. In *Journal for the Theory of Social Behaviour* 33(3): 313–347.

Scheffer, Thomas. 2004. Materialities of legal proceedings. In *International Journal for Semiotics of Law* 17(4): 356–389.

Scheffer, Thomas. 2005. Courses of mobilisation: Writing systematic micro-histories on legal discourse. In *Theory and method in socio-legal research*, ed. Max Travers and Reza Banakar, 75–89. Oxford: Hart Publishing.

Scheffer, Thomas. 2006. The micro-formation of criminal defense. On the barrister's notes, speech-production, and a field of presence. *Research on Language and Social Interaction* 39(3): 303–342.

Scheffer, Thomas. 2007a. On procecdural discoursivation - Or how local utterances are turned into binding Facts. *Language & Communication* 27: 1–27.

Scheffer, Thomas. 2007b. The duplicity of testimonial interviews: Unfolding and utilising multiple temporalization in compound procedures and projects. *Forum Qualitative Social Research* 8(1), Art. 15. Retrieved June 28, 2007 Available: http://www.qualitative-research.net/fqs-texte/1-07/07-1-15-e.htm.

Scheffer, Thomas. 2007c. Relating event and process: An exercise in analytical ethnography. *Human Studies* 30(1): 167–197.

Scheffer, Thomas. 2007d. File work, legal care, and professional habitus – An ethnographic reflection on different styles of advocacy. *International Journal of the Legal Profession* 14(1): 57–81.

Scheffer, Thomas. 2009. Knowing how to sleep walk. Placing Psychological Expert Evidence in an English Jury Trial. *OnlineFirst* in *Science, Technology and Human Values (ST&HV)*.

Scheffer, Thomas. 2010a. Indirect Moralising. An Ethnographic Exploration of a Procedural Modality. *FirstView* in *Journal for the Theory of Social Behavior (JTSB)*.

Scheffer, Thomas. 2010b. Learning being guilty: on the procedural attribution of deficit. In: Christopher N. Candlin and Jonathan Crichton (Eds.) *Discourses of Deficit*. New York: Palgrave.

Scheffer, Thomas, Kati Hannken-Illjes and Alexander Kozin. 2007. Bound to one's own words? Early Defenses and their binding effects in different criminal cases. *Law & Social Inquiry* 32(1): 5–39.

Scheffer, Thomas, Kati Hannken-Illjes, and Alexander Kozin. 2009. How Courts know. Comparing English Crown Court, U.S.-American State Court, and German District Court. *Space and Culture* 12: 183–204.

Scheffer, Thomas amd Jörg Niewöhner. 2010. *Thick Comparison. Reviving the Ethnographic Aspiration*. Leiden: Brill.

Schegloff, Emanuel A. 1987. Between macro and micro: Contexts and other connections. In *The micro-macro link*, ed. Jeffrey C. Alexander, Bernhard Giesen, Richard Münch and Neil J. Smelser, 207–237. Berkeley: University of California Press.

Schumann, Karl F. 1977. *Der Handel mit Gerechtigkeit*. Funktionsprobleme der Strafjustiz und ihre Lösungen - am Beispiel des amerikanischen plea bargaining. Frankfurt a.M.: Suhrkamp.

Schütz, Alfred. 1981. *Theorie der Lebensformen*. (Frühe Manuskripte aus der Bergson-Periode) Hrsg. und eingeleitet von Ilja Srubar, Frankfurt a.M.: Suhrkamp.

Seibert, Thomas-Michael. 2004. *Gerichtsrede. Wirklichkeit und Möglichkeit im forensischen Diskurs*. Berlin: Duncker & Humblot.

Sennett, Richard. 1992. *The fall of public man*. New York: W.W. Norton & Company.

Sewell Jr., William H. 1996a. Historical events as transformations of structures: Inventing revolution at the Bastille. *Theory and Society* 25: 841–881.

Sewell Jr., William H. 1996b. Three temporalities: Toward an eventful sociology. In *The historic turn in the human sciences*, ed. Terrence J. McDonald, 245–80. Ann Arbor: University of Michigan Press.

Shapin, Steven and Simon Schaffer. 1985. *Leviathan and the Air-Pump. Hobbes, Boyle, and the Experimental Life*. Princeton: Princeton University Press.

Shapin, Steven. 1995. *A social history of truth. Civility and science in seventeenth-century England*. Chicago: The University of Chicago Press.

Shapiro, Colin M., Nikola N. Trajanovic, and J. Paul Fedoroff. 2003. Sexsomnia: A new parasomnia? *Canadian Journal of Psychiatry* 48: 311–317.

Sherr, Avrom. 1986. Lawyers and clients: The first meeting. *The Modern Law Review* 49(3): 323–357.

Sherr, Avrom, Richard Moorhead, and Alan Paterson. 1994. Assessing the quality of legal work: Measuring process. *International Journal of the Legal Profession* 1(2): 135–158.

Shuy, Roger W. 1993. *Language crimes: The use and abuse of language evidence in the courtroom*. Oxford: Blackwell.

Shuy, Roger W. 2000. Breaking into language and law. The trials of the insider-linguist. *Georgetown University Round Table on Languages and Linguistics*: 67–80.

Simmel, Georg. 1989. *Philosophie des Geldes*. Eds. by David P. Frisby and Klaus C. Köhnke. Frankfurt a.M.: Suhrkamp.

Silverman, David. 2000. Analysing talk and text. In *Handbook of Qualitative Research,* ed. Norman K. Denzin and Yvonna S. Lincoln, 2nd Edition, 821–835. Thousand Oaks, London, New Delhi: Sage Publications

Slapper, Gary and David Kelly. 2001. *The English legal system.* London: Cavendish Publishing Limited.

Slovenko, Ralph. 1999. Responsibility of the Psychopath. *Philosophy, Psychiatry, & Psychology* 6(1): 53–55.

Smith, Dorothy E. 1985. Textually mediated social organisation. *International Social Science Journal* 99: 59–76.

Smith, Dorothy E. 2000. Writing the social: Critique, theory and investigations. *Revue Canadienne de Sociologie et d'Anthropologie* 37(3): 368–370.

Snow, David A., Calvin Morrill, and Leon Anderson. 2003. Elaborating analytic ethnography: Linking fieldwork and theory. *Ethnography* 4(2): 181–200.

Sørensen, Estrid. 2009. The Materiality of Learning. Technology and Knowledge in Educational Practice. Cambridge: Cambridge University Press.

Sommerlad, Hilary and Peter Sanderson. 1998. *Gender, choice, and commitment: Women solicitors in England and Wales and the struggle for equal status.* Alder-shot, Hampshire: Ashgate Publishing.

Sommerlad, Hilary. 2002a. Women solicitors in a fractured profession: Intersections of gender and professionalism in England and Wales. *International Journal of the Legal Profession* 9(3): 213–234.

Sommerlad, Hilary. 2002b. Costs & benefits of quality assurance mechanisms in the delivery of public funded legal services: Some qualitative views. *Paper at Legal Services Research Centre International Conference* 2002. Jesus College, Oxford, March.

Spradley, James P. 1980. *Participant observation.* New York: Holt, Rinehart and Winston.

Spurk, Jan. 2004. Simultaneity within non-simultaneity? Continuity, rupture, emergence: On the temporal dynamic of social formation. *Time & Society: An International Interdisciplinary Journal* 13(1): 41–49.

Stake, Robert E. 2000. Case Studies. In *Handbook of Qualitative Research,* ed. Norman K. Denzin and Yvonne S. Lincoln, 435–455. Thousand Oaks, London, New Delhi: Sage Publications.

Star, Susan L. and James R. Griesemer. 1989. Institutional Ecology, 'Translations' and Boundary Objects: Amateurs and Professionals in Berkeley's Museum of Vertebrate Zoology, 1907–39. *Social Studies of Science* 19: 387–420.

Star, Susan Leigh and Anselm Strauss. 1999. Layers of silence, arenas of voice: The ecology of visible and invisible work. *Computer Supported Cooperative Work* 8: 9–30.

Stegmaier, Peter. 2008. *Wissen, was Recht ist. Richterliche Rechtspraxis aus wissenssoziologisch-ethnografischer Sicht.* Wiesbaden: *VS Verlag für Sozialwissenschaften.*

Stehr, Nico. 1994. *Knowledge Societies.* London: Sage Publications.

Stichweh, Rudolf. 2004. Wissensgesellschaft und Wissenschaftssystem. *Schweizerische Zeitschrift für Soziologie* 30:147–165.

Stygall, Gail. 2001. A different class of witnesses: Experts in the courtroom. *Discourse Studies* 3(3): 327–351.

Suchman, Lucy. 1987. *Plans and situated actions. The problem of human-machine-communication.* Cambridge, New York, Melbourne: Cambridge University Press.

Suchman, Lucy. 2000. Making a case: 'Knowledge' and 'routine' work in document production. *Work, Interaction and Technology,* ed. Hindmarsh, Jon, Christian Heath and Paul Luff. Cambridge, UK: Cambridge University Press.

Sudnow, David. 1965. Normal Crimes: Sociological Features of the Penal Code in a Public Defender's Office. *Social Problems* 12(3): 255–76.

Svennigsen, Signe. 2003. *Electronic patient records and medical practice - reorganization of roles, responsibilities and risks.* Copenhagen Business School, Samfundslitteratur PhD-Series.
Szmania, Susan J. and Daniel E. Mangis. 2005. Finding the Right Time and Place: A Case Study Comparison of the Expression of Offender Remorse in Traditional Justice and Restorative Justice Contexts. *Marquette Law Review* 89: 335–358.
Tague, Peter W. 1996. Effective advocacy for the criminal defendant: the barrister vs. the lawyer. New York: William S. Hein & Co., Inc.
Tapper, Colin. 1999. *Cross and tapper on evidence.* London, Edinburgh and Dublin: Butterworths.
Taslitz, Andrew E. 2006. Temporal adversarialism, criminal justice, and Rehnquist Court: The sluggish life of political factfinding. *The Georgetown Law Journal* 94: 1589–1626.
Tavuchis, Nicholas. 1991. *Mea culpa: A sociology of apology and reconciliation.* Stanford, CA: Stanford University Press.
Temkin, Jennifer. 2000. Prosecuting and defending rape: Perspectives from the bar. *Journal of Law and Society* 27(2): 219–48.
The Incorporated Council of Law Reporting for England and Wales. 2002. *The Law Reports. Appeal Cases,* Volume I. London: ICLR.
Thomas, Philip A. and John Knowles. 2006. *Effective Legal Research.* London: Thomson Sweet & Maxwell.
Thomas, Thomas N. 1997. Sleepwalking disorder and mens rea: A review and case report. *Journal of Forensic Science* 42(1): 17–24.
Tomlins, Christopher L. 2000. Framing the field of law's disciplinary encounters: A historical narrative. *Law & Society Review* 34: 911.
Travers, Max. 1997. *The reality of law: Work and talk in a firm of criminal lawyers.* Dartmouth: Dartmouth Publishing Company.
Travers, Max and John E. Manzo. 1997. *Law in action: ethnomethodological and conversation analytical approaches to law.* Aldershot: Ashgate.
Travers, Max and Reza Banakar, ed. 2005. *Theory and method in socio-legal research.* Oxford and Portland Oregon: Hart Publishing.
Tuitt, Patricia. 2005. Legal practice and modes of dying: Bruno Latour, technology and the critical legal instance. *Law and Critique* 16(16): 113–129.
Turner, Victor. 1985. *On The Edge Of The Bush. Anthropology as Experience.* Tuscon Arizona: The University of Arizona Press.
Valverde, Mariana. 2003. *Law's dream of common knowledge.* Princeton: Princeton University Press.
Van Koppen, Peter J. and Steven D. Penrod, ed. 2003. *Adversarial versus inquisitorial justice: Psychological perspectives on criminal justice systems.* Berlin: Springer.
Van Maanen, John. 1998. *Tales of the field: On writing ethnography.* Chicago: University of Chicago Press.
Van Wormer, Katherine Stuart et al. 2000. *Women and the criminal justice system.* Boston: Allyn and Bacon.
Vayda, Andrew P., Bonnie J. McCay and Cristina Eghenter. 1991. Concepts of process in social science explanations. *Philosophy of the Social Sciences* 21(3): 318–331.
Von Hirsch, Andrew. 1993. *Past or future crimes.* New Brunswick, NJ: Rutgers University Press.
Wagatsuma, Hiroshi and Arthur Rosett. 1986. The implications of apology: Law and culture in Japan and the United States. *Law & Society Review* 20: 461–498.
Walby Sylvia an Jonathan Allen. 2004. Domestic violence, sexual assault and stalking: Findings from the British Crime Survey. *Home Office Research Study* 276: 73–88.
Weber, Max. 1980. Soziologie der Herrschaft. In *Wirtschaft und Gesellschaft*, 541–868. Tübingen: Mohr.

Weick, Karl E. 1985. *Der Prozess des Organisierens*. Frankfurt am Main: Suhrkamp.
Weihofen, Henry. 1935. An alternative to the battle of experts: Hospital examination of criminal defendants before trial. *Law and Contemporary Problems* 2(4): 419–435.
Weihofen, Henry. 1950. Eliminating the battle of experts in criminal insanity cases. *Michigan Law Review* 48(7): 961–982.
Weijers, Ido. 2004. Requirements for communication in the courtroom: a comparative perspective on the youth court in England/Wales and the Netherlands. *Youth Justice* 4(1): 22–31.
Wells, Helene and Paul Wilson. 2004. The role of expert witnesses in psychological blow automatism cases. *Humanities & Social Sciences Papers*. Electronically published by the Faculty of Humanities and Social Sciences, Bond University. [http://epublication.bond.edu.au/hss_pubs/35]
Wexler, David B. 2005. Therapeutic jurisprudence and the rehabilitation role of the criminal defense lawyer. *St. Thomas Law Review* 17: 743–774.
White, Hayden. 1978. *Tropics of discourse*. Baltimore, MD: John Hopkins University Press.
White, Stuart and Timothy J. Baldwin. 2004. *Legal and ethical aspects of anaesthesia, critical care and preoperative medicine*. Cambridge: Cambridge University Press.
Williams, C.R. 2000. Development and change in insanity and related defences. *Melbourne University Law Review* 28: 711.
Williams, Glanville. 1982. *Learning the Law*. London: Stevens and Sons.
Wood, Linda A. and Heather Rennie. 1994. Formulating rape: The discursive construction of victims and villains. *Discourse and Society* 5(1): 125–148.
Yngvesson, Barbara. 1988. Making law at the doorway: The clerk, the court, and the construction of community in a New England Town. *Law and Society Review* 22: 409–448.
Zerubavel, Eviatar. 1979. *Patterns of time in hospital life: A sociological perspective*. Chicago: The University of Chicago Press.

INDEX